LAUREL and HARDY

The Magic Behind the Movies

by Randy Skretvedt

Foreword by Steve Allen

Editor/Research Associate
Jordan R. Young

MOONSTONE PRESS

To the memory of the gentle genius
who made the music box play —
T. Marvin Hatley

LAUREL AND HARDY
The Magic Behind the Movies

FIRST EDITION

Published by Moonstone Press, P.O. Box 142, Beverly Hills CA 90213

Copyright © 1987 by Randy Skretvedt

Printed in the United States of America

Cover design by Theodore von Schwarzenhoffen

Typeset by Suzette Mahr, Words & Deeds, Los Angeles, California

The foreword is excerpted from *More Funny People*, copyright © 1982 by Steve Allen, and is reprinted by permission.

Library of Congress Cataloging in Publication Data
Skretvedt, Randy
  Laurel and Hardy.

  Bibliography: p.
  Includes index.
1. Laurel, Stan. 2. Hardy, Oliver, 1892-1957. 3. Comedy films — United States — History and criticism. I. Young, Jordan R. II. Title.
PN2287.L285S53 1987   791.43′028′0922   87-1520
ISBN 0-940410-78-8 (alk. paper)
ISBN 0-940410-77-X (pbk. : alk. paper)

10 9 8 7 6 5 4 3 2 1

Contents

Foreword

For whatever the point is worth — and I say this as a Chaplin fan — from early childhood I have considered Laurel and Hardy *funnier* than Chaplin. Perhaps the point will be clarified if I refer to the modern comedy of Lily Tomlin. Lily is unquestionably one of our *greatest* comediennes. She is, however, by no means always the *funniest*.

Part of the explanation for the great superiority of Laurel and Hardy over other comedy teams — the Marx Brothers, for example — is that you cared about them as human beings. Jokes, as such, were of little importance to Stan and Oliver. Stan and Oliver simply *were* funny, just by showing up.

In the successful Laurel and Hardy formula Ollie was the aggressor. But the relationship is much different from that which prevailed betwen Abbott and Costello. Bud Abbott was always sharp, demanding, strongly manipulative. It was never thus with Oliver Hardy. He dominated in a gentle, if-you-will-permit-me way. From time to time Stanley's ineptitude would drive him to moments of fury. But the dominant element in his character was his strange, silly courtliness, his niceness and decency. Oliver Hardy played straight to Stan Laurel but was brilliantly, richly funny in his own right. As my wife, Jayne, has pointed out, in many filmed sequences Hardy is actually doing funnier things than Laurel, but is more subtle. His tie-twiddling, drumming of his fingers on air, and his ways of conveying exasperation are among these.

Garson Kanin in his *Together Again!*, a study of great Hollywood teams, makes the insightful observation that although on screen Oliver Hardy was dominant, the pattern was completely reversed in reality. Stanley was the writer, the creator, the director. Ollie, for the most part, did as he was instructed. To his credit, he repeatedly conceded that Laurel was the more creative member of the team and deferred to Stanley on practically every question where judgment was required.

In 1959 some of my writers and I visited Stan. All of us reminisced about particular favorite films, scenes, and comedy routines we remembered seeing Laurel do, and were thunderstruck when it became apparent that he was more interested in talking to us about our shows and sketches than recalling his old films. He was a gentle, soft-spoken man and could not have been more charming.

Because Stan in person seemed like his screen image — though much more intelligent — I was surprised when a painter who did some work at my home early in 1982 told me that when he had worked as part of the crew on a Laurel and Hardy film many years earlier, he had liked Oliver but not Stan.

"What was wrong with Stan Laurel, in your opinion?" I asked.

"Oh," replied the painter, "he just seemed stuck-up. He was too much of a perfectionist. He always wanted everything to be just right and if it wasn't, he could be kind of a son-of-a-bitch about it."

The same might be said, I suppose, of every talented perfectionist who ever lived.

Steve Allen

About the Author

Randy Skretvedt, a Laurel and Hardy buff since the age of five, is host of the popular radio program, *Forward Into the Past* (KSPC, Los Angeles) and co-author of *Steve Martin: The Unauthorized Biography*. He has done exhaustive research into the history of motion picture comedy.

Preface

Stan Laurel and Oliver Hardy made their finest films in the 1920s and '30s, yet their popularity continues to grow. International conventions are regularly held in their honor; plays have been written about them; they adorn a commemorative stamp issued by the United States Postal Service. Many of their films have recently resurfaced in new 35mm prints at revival theaters; others are available for the home market on video cassettes and laser discs. The Hal Roach Studios (an organization with which Hal Roach himself no longer has any connection) has a weekly Laurel and Hardy television series in syndication, and has "colorized" some of the films.

Ever since Laurel and Hardy became a team, they've been the subject of countless articles and books; Stan and Ollie have been profiled, analyzed and criticized by hundreds of writers over the years. As a lifelong devotee, I read anything I could find about the team, and yet I never felt completely satisfied; I wanted to know more about the unorthodox way in which they made their films, what it was like to work with them, and why their career took such a drastic decline in the 1940s.

When, as a teenager, I began attending meetings of the Sons of the Desert — the international Laurel and Hardy appreciation society — I listened to the comments of people who had worked with Stan and Babe. They provided a perspective and an immediacy which I hadn't found in any printed works. These people were *there*; they knew Laurel and Hardy as collaborators and as friends. I was captivated by them, and I was determined to preserve their first-hand accounts.

Eventually, I came across other material which brought new light to the story. I stumbled (almost literally) upon a collection of original scripts which yielded a number of surprises, not the least of which were dozens of scenes which had never been filmed. Photographs in the private collections of the people whom I interviewed also provided more information about the way Laurel and Hardy created their films. After casually amassing a great deal of material, I decided in 1979 to write a book that would chronicle the story of how Laurel and Hardy actually made their films — told largely in the words of the people who helped make them.

Virtually everyone I met between 1979 and 1986 helped, in some way, to get this book completed. Particular thanks are due to Douglas Hart of Backlot Books in Hollywood and John McLaughlin of The Book Sail in Orange, California. They allowed me access to their massive collections of scripts and other studio files, and without their remarkable generosity I would *still* be trying to fill the gaps.

The staff of the Cinema division of the Doheny Library of the University of Southern California helped greatly, particularly Ned Comstock, whose enthusiasm and knowledge made my work there much easier. Thanks also to Sam Gill, Carol Cullen and the staff of the Margaret Herrick Library at the Academy of Motion Picture Arts and Sciences, who didn't mind at all when I spent two summers dictating articles from old trade papers into my trusty tape recorder.

Carl Macek and the folks at the Special Collections department of the California State University, Fullerton library provided access to the papers of the late Fred Guiol; and Thomas Lutgen guided me through the archives of the *Los Angeles Times*.

Bob Satterfield and Lori Jones of the Los Angeles Way Out West Tent of Sons of the Desert not only introduced me to many of the interview subjects, but located them in the first place. Rick and Linda Greene of the San Diego Saps at Sea Tent loaned me rare films and other material.

Special thanks to my parents, Spencer and Zelda Skretvedt, who offered support far beyond the call of duty; to Richard W. Bann, who realigned my thinking while somehow resisting the temptation to realign my skull; and to Jordan R. Young, without whose ruthless yet sensitive editing this book would be twice as long and half as interesting. Jordan also had the good sense to interview Iris Adrian, George Marshall, Jess Robbins, Frank Saputo, Rolfe Sedan and Edward Sutherland, among others, before I'd even thought about writing a book.

I'm grateful to Larry Ward, Robert Wicks, Chris Christian and Doug Phelps for instruction and inspiration; to Don and John Cannon at Aladdin Books in Fullerton, California, for their friendship and encouragement; to Greg Lenburg and Jeff Lenburg for constant loyalty and support; and to Rob Ray, whose friendship has made the writing of this book, and life in general, a lot more fun.

Since this book has a behind the scenes emphasis, so do the photos. The result: illustrations which are primarily candid shots, stills of deleted scenes, snapshots and personal photos. Many of them were generously loaned by interview subjects, and also by private collectors, all of whom safeguarded these photographs for so many years. Alphabetically, credit is due to the Academy of Motion Picture Arts and Sciences, Alan Aperlo, Backlot Books, Richard W. Bann, Blackhawk Films, Eddie Brandt's Saturday Matinee, Cinema Collectors, Richard Currier, Larry Edmunds Cinema Bookshop, Film Favorites, Clarence "Stax" Graves of Hal Roach Studios, Rick Greene, Marvin Hatley, Irv Hyatt, Art Kendall, Marshall Korby, Greg Lenburg, Venice Lloyd, Raul Moreno, Lucille Hardy Price, Quality First, R & R Enterprises, Joe Rinaudo, Joe Rock, Bill Schutte, Roy Seawright, Anita Garvin Stanley, Jeff Stern, Bob Stowell, the University of Southern California, Marc Wanamaker of Bison Archives and Jordan R. Young.

Other fine people who gave help included Jefry N. Abraham, Steve Allen, Jim Baum, Judy Baum, Bill Bax, Bob Borgen, Leo M. Brooks, Larry Byrd, Hector Caballero, Chris Carmen, Charles Christ, Scott Comerford, Rich D'Albert, Gene Davidson, Matt Davis, Anna Denbow, Andy Edmonds, Vince Giordano, John Gloske, Sylvia Griffith, Chuck Gustafson, Tom Hatten, Michael Hawks, David Hayes, Tom Heath, Alice Jackson, Jeff Jensen, Hank Jones, Mike Kieffer, David Koenig, Paul and Chris Krank, Earl Kress, Lovera LaCroix, Mike Lefebvre, Lori Leo, Richard Madsen, Leonard Maltin, Wilma Maurer, Dennis

McLellan, Marcia Opal, Bill Patterson, Robert R. Pierce, Casey Piotrowski, Vance Piper, John Quinn, Bill Rabe, Steve Randisi, Jack Roth, Rima Snyder, Esther Spaits, John and Margaret Stern, John and Susie Tefteller, Tracy Tolzmann, Brent Walker, Doris Walker, Alan Warner and Derek Wood.

A tip of the derby to those who helped from afar: Glenn Mitchell, Rob Lewis, Malcolm Stuart Fellows, Jack Stevenson and Paul van Someren in England; Peter Mikkelsen in Denmark; and Bram Reijnhoudt and Piet Schreuders in the Netherlands.

Finally, my greatest thanks go to the people who were part of the Laurel and Hardy story, and who generously gave of their time to me:

Christine Baker, Charlie and Julie Barton, Ham Bennett, Vivian Blaine, Billy and Arline Bletcher, Henry Brandon, Lou Breslow, Ruth Burch, Bob Chatterton, Clyde Cook, Richard Currier, Jay Dare, Muriel Evans, Ray Golden, Darla Hood Granson, Marvin and Josephine Hatley, Tony and Lois Laurel Hawes, Katherine Hewett, Dorothy Granger Hilder, William Janney, Florence Jepperson, Bert Jordan, Walter Woolf King, Virginia Kinsey, Felix Knight, Fred Knoth, Frederick Kohner, Charles Lamont, Richard Lane, Mabel Langdon, Della Lind, Venice Lloyd, Glen MacWilliams, Rosina Lawrence Marchisio, George Marshall, John McCabe, Lisa Mitchell, Joe Mole, Lois Owens, Ben and Lucille Hardy Price, Art Quenzer, Eddie Quillan, Trudy Marshall Raffin, Hal Roach, Lucille Roach, Thomas Benton Roberts, Joe Rock, Betty Goulding Saunders, Roy and Bunny Seawright, Rolfe Sedan, Rodney Sprigg, Anita Garvin Stanley, Bob Stowell, Connie Thompson, Lawrence Tibbett Jr. and Harvey Wasden.

I have been privileged to call many of these people my friends; I wish that more of them had lived to see this book.

Although I never met them, I have to thank the two men who have united all of us in the bonds of friendship and laughter. To Stan Laurel and Babe Hardy, my deepest gratitude.

Randy Skretvedt
Los Angeles
1987

NOTE: The entries about individual films appear in the order of production — unlike all previous Laurel and Hardy filmographies — which is not necessarily the order in which they were released. The italicized synopses describe the finished films; scenes which were deleted are described in the body of each entry.

Prologue

Why Laurel and Hardy?

The question is inevitable: Why have Laurel and Hardy remained so popular for so long?

Many of their contemporaries were more highly regarded by the film industry and by critics. But once-popular teams like Wheeler and Woolsey and Clark and McCullough have been forgotten, while Laurel and Hardy continue to win new fans more than 50 years after their best films were made. Why? What keeps Stan and Ollie in the hearts of the public long after their comic contemporaries have been forgotten?

Stan Laurel always believed that to dissect comedy was to kill it. "Never, for God's sake, ask me what makes people laugh," he said. "I just don't know." What makes Laurel and Hardy funny may be too subjective to define, but one thing is undeniable: they have a special appeal which goes beyond mere laughter.

It isn't just their comedy that makes them so captivating. Most L&H fans have seen each of the films dozens of times. They *know* all of the gags. Yet they will eagerly sit through the pictures dozens of times more. The special magic of Laurel and Hardy isn't in their gags, but simply in *them*.

Lisa Mitchell, who visited Stan often in her teens and grew up to become an eloquent writer about film, articulates their appeal. "My way of laughing at Laurel and Hardy was never explosive," she says. "It was just an incredible savoring. It was not just clutching the sides and falling over and laughing, as much as it was being struck to the heart with the love, the tenderness and the intelligence which was mixed up with the absurdity in those timeless gags.

"The thing that will still make me weep, literally, for the effectual tenderness, is when you see something like the dance in *Way Out West*. That interaction of love between those two fellows is as important as any gag. And they take themselves so seriously that their absurdity makes us realize how we take ourselves too seriously. It releases us from our own pomposity."

Laurel and Hardy are the most inviting of comedians. When Ollie looks at us in despair or disgust, he takes us in as his confidantes; he shares his thoughts with us. L&H don't have the superhuman agility which distances us from Chaplin; nor do they possess Keaton's melancholy, Fields' malevolence, the subversiveness of the Marx Brothers or the reserve of Harold Lloyd. They are closer to real people than the other great clowns, and they are truly nice people, without ever being cloying.

They want to fit into the world, but they are too innocent and the world too cynical. Their grandiose dreams — and even their modest ones — are smashed time and again, but they're never bitter about it; they just get up and start over. Their friendship is constant, even though it's often a strain for both of them. Ollie can't figure out why Stan is unable to perform even the simplest tasks, and Stan can't figure out why Ollie gets so angry at him. But under the surface, and not very far under it, is a tremendous concern and caring for each other.

Stan takes a mountainous load of abuse from Ollie, yet he never fails to help him when called. And despite Ollie's almost continual exasperation with Stan, whenever his diminutive partner is threatened, Ollie comes to the rescue. It is obvious even to them that their love for each other will always endure. They are kindred spirits in alien surroundings, two innocents trapped in a nightmare world populated by ill-tempered people who want only to exploit them.

They are us as we were, before we were corrupted. We all start out as trusting, guileless, optimistic people — but somehow Laurel and Hardy held on to those qualities while the rest of us turned bitter and deceitful. Maybe we seek communion with them because they, in their innocence, stayed on a higher level of humanity which we're trying to recapture.

In Laurel and Hardy movies, as in life, the nice guys don't often win — but they endure. And Stan and Ollie may not be smart, but without even knowing it, they are wise.

Stan

Stan Laurel was one of those lucky individuals who knew, almost from birth, what his life's work would be. He lived almost solely to create laughter. Stan was the opposite of the stereotypical comedian who is lovable and funny on stage and a miserable wretch off stage. If anything, he was even funnier when he wasn't performing. He possessed a quick, sharp wit which was the total opposite of his screen character's dimwittedness, and he was able to find humor in just about anything.

When Stan had a paralyzing stroke in the mid-1950s and his ability to work again was in doubt, he said, "Tell them I'm available — but I can only play statues." He often said that people needed laughter just as much as they needed food; his philosophy that a sense of humor would see one through conflicts saw him through a lifetime that provided plenty of them.

That lifetime began when Arthur Stanley Jefferson was born on June 16, 1890, in Ulverston, Lancashire, England. As a child, Stan eagerly watched the comedians who paraded through his father's theaters; he spent much of his time jotting down their jokes and aping their mannerisms when no one was looking. By the time he was seven or eight, he had already developed an impressive arsenal of jokes. As a result, he spent many evenings at boarding school entertaining his teachers in their private quarters, instead of studying.

His father recalled that young Stan always asked for toys that had something to do with the world of entertainment: miniature theaters, puppets, magic lanterns. For a time, Stan had his own theater — built in the basement of his parents' home. He put together a play which was suspiciously similar to several of the bloodthirsty melodramas which his father had written and produced. Stan also directed and cast himself as the hero, but his early career was cur-

Arthur Stanley Jefferson, 1897.

The young comic, circa 1910.

Right: Emulating his former
roommate in American vaudeville,
circa 1915.

With Mae Laurel in a 1924 Roach one-reeler, *Near Dublin*.

tailed when, during an on-stage battle, Stan and another young would-be actor knocked over an oil lamp and set the curtains ablaze.

This preoccupation with all things theatrical meant that Stan was not a very good student. His scholastic career was extremely checkered; he was sent to some of the best schools in the north of England, but the only subject Stan really studied was comedy. In later life, he regretted his lack of education — because he felt more schooling might have made him a better comedian.

He made his debut at 16 (billed as "Stan Jefferson — He of the Funny Ways") at a tiny museum-cum-theater called the Panopticon, then played a "Golliwog" — a large stuffed doll — in a touring production of *Sleeping Beauty*. In 1910 he sailed to the United States for the first time in a troupe of Fred Karno's London Comedians. Karno, a legend of British show business, was not only Stan's mentor but Chaplin's — whom Stan understudied in a number of zany sketches.

Unable to get a much-needed raise from Karno, Stan and another comic returned to England and played (as "The Barto Brothers") in a sketch called *The Rum 'uns From Rome*. After a number of odd engagements — including a disastrous tour of Belgium — he was back with Karno, on a second tour of the States. Chaplin, now firmly the star of the troupe, was a sensation; when Charlie quit in November 1913 to join the Keystone Film Company, the Karno troupe faltered and finally disbanded.

From 1914 to 1922, Stan toured in American vaudeville in a variety of sketches with a number of partners. Mae Charlotte Dahlberg Cuthbert, an Australian dancer, became his partner offstage as well as on, in a stormy common-law marriage which lasted until 1925. Although Mae did not legally adopt Stan's surname, she gave *him* a new one when she found an illustration of a Roman general wearing a wreath of laurel. While maintaining a hectic touring schedule, the newly-renamed Stan Laurel began acting in films, beginning in 1917 with *Nuts in May*.

For someone who always knew what he wanted to do, Stan spent an awful lot of time figuring out just how to do it. During his entire solo career, Stan was a frustrated comedian in search of a personality. In the 60-odd films he made alone, he played by turns a brash go-getter and a stupid simpleton — he usually shows traits of both types in any given film. Laurel had another trait which wasn't particularly enduring.

As George Stevens once put it, "Some time before beginning at Roach, I had seen Stan work, and I thought he was one of the unfunniest comedians around... He needed and wanted laughs so much that he made a habit of laughing at himself as a player, which is extremely poor comic technique. How he changed!"

He atoned for his sins by eventually creating one of the most endearing characters in films. He struggled for almost 20 years to find his own unique, recognizable comic personality, but once he found it he imbued his creation with more depth and subtlety than virtually any other comic figure.

As a performer, Stan never really lost his stage technique. While his partner scaled everything down for the more intimate medium of motion pictures, Stan was more inclined to use broad gestures. He could often employ great subtlety in his performances, but one senses that he'd been trained to play everything for the back row of the house.

To those who know Stan Laurel only as an actor it may be surprising to

Anita Garvin admires the hero of *The Snow Hawk,* a 1925 Joe Rock two-reeler.

learn that he considered himself primarily a gag writer. To Stan, his performances were merely the conduit for his comedy ideas. He'd written his own sketches when he appeared in vaudeville, and he similarly took an active part in the writing of his solo films. "Stan was in everything — he'd come in early, work with the writers, look at the rushes; he always wanted to be involved," said Joe Rock, producer of 12 Laurel two-reelers.

Stan's mind was always working on gags; his daughter Lois recalled that the Laurel home was always littered with pads of yellow paper, which Stan kept handy for the moments when inspiration struck. He wrote gags at home and at the studio, and between takes on the set — for other comics at the Hal Roach Studios as well.

Comedy was Laurel's hobby as well as his job. His only other true recreation was fishing. Occasionally he dabbled in other interests: he raised ducks on his ranch in the San Fernando Valley, and indulged a fondness for gardening by cross-breeding a potato and an onion. (He couldn't get anyone to eat it, however.)

He had a genuine respect for his fans. He felt that anyone who really wanted to talk to him was entitled to do so; in his years of retirement, he kept his name in the phone book. He felt obligated to answer his fan mail, which continued to arrive by the sackful. And he gladly entertained total strangers who simply wanted to meet him.

There had never been any sense of class distinction in Stan. His close friends during his moneyed days were old vaudeville cronies and crew people from the studio; he socialized very little with the "important" people in the film industry. During the war years, he often gave lavish dinner parties for visiting soldiers and sailors. He could never understand racial prejudice.

Laurel was never much of a businessman. Most of his earnings went for alimony and taxes, and to the end of his life he supported a battery of down- and-out friends. His kindness caused him to suffer financially: all through their career, Laurel and Hardy had only one representative, Ben Shipman — a shy, retiring, stooped little man with a great shock of white hair and a soft whisper of a voice. He was no more an aggressive deal-maker than Stan — but Laurel kept him on out of loyalty.

Stan was not a religious man, although he did believe in reincarnation. He found humor in his beliefs, devising a gag for *The Flying Deuces* in which Ollie dies and comes back as a horse. Stan never felt that a political or social message should be injected into comedy films, however — he thought Chaplin's *The Great Dictator* was "lousy in the serious parts." Stan had little patience with highfalutin critics who blathered about the sociopolitical commentary in Laurel and Hardy movies. "They think deep down we all put some kind of bloody message in our films," he complained. "Well, they're wrong. We were just trying to make people laugh."

He could be a severe critic of his own work. He liked individual bits of each film, but didn't think any of them were perfect. When his old pictures started running on television, he wanted to re-edit them to eliminate the long pauses that had been designed to accommodate a large audience's reaction to the gags. "On TV, the films seem so slow," he lamented. "Sometimes you think they'll never end."

Laurel could be a severe critic of other performers, too. He loved talent and was dismayed when untalented people such as game show hosts and bad stand-up comics were hyped as "stars." He loved Jackie Gleason, Art Carney, Jack Benny, Sid Caesar, Lucille Ball and Red Skelton when he wasn't breaking up at his own jokes. Stan always preferred quiet, low-key comedians; he didn't care for brash comics like the Marx Brothers, with their "rough type of nut humor." Jerry Lewis perplexed him; he liked Lewis as a friend but thought his work was undisciplined and rather pointless.

He retained a special affection for old British music-hall artists and had a sizable collection of their old recordings. He loved to sing hoary old music-hall tunes when in the company of friends, and played the piano a bit. The bouncy songs he'd heard as a youngster influenced his timing; when he and Babe appeared on stage, Stan always started his entrance on a particular beat of their theme song.

The graciousness which marked his screen character was deeply ingrained in the real man. He could be ebullient in his younger days, which occasionally miffed his associates, but Stan mellowed with age. He could still be a practical joker late in life, however: One day, Stan was visiting a stationery store and the clerk seemed to recognize him. "Say," the clerk stammered, "aren't you — " and Stan replied, "Oliver Hardy." "Right," exclaimed he clerk. "Say, whatever happened to Laurel?" Stan sadly responded, "He went balmy."

At times he could display a quick temper, but his anger quickly subsided. Only three things really irritated him: the cutting of his films by insensitive television editors; memories of the shameful treatment he'd received from 20th Century-Fox in the '40s; and sensational newspaper articles about his supposed poverty and his many marriages. Many reporters tried to portray Stan as a womanizer, but this was far from the truth — even though he married four women and had a fifth sue to be declared his common-law wife.

Murray Rock serves lunch during the filming of *Half a Man* (1925).

With Stan's dad, A.J. Jefferson, and stepmother Venitia on the *Bohemian Girl* set.

As one of Laurel's close friends noted, he didn't treat marriage casually; on the contrary, his troubles came about because he fell in love too deeply, too fast. The often-reprinted quote attributed to Stan — "You know my hobby — and I married them all" — was actually dreamt up by columnist James Bacon, and Stan was not happy when he read it.

Stan was never a facetious man; he never strained to make humor, nor was he the type of comedian who was always performing in real life. He just naturally found something funny about most aspects of day-to-day living. But that's what happens when you're born to create laughter.

Babe

Stan Laurel and Babe Hardy were remarkably alike in one aspect: both men were unfailingly courteous, but aside from that they were almost the complete opposites of their screen characters. Stan may have been meek and slow-witted on screen, but in real life he was the dominant member of the team. Likewise, Babe Hardy possessed few of his screen character's traits. "Ollie" could do hardly anything well, and masked his inadequacy with an air of superiority. Babe was a man of many talents, yet he was hampered all of his life by a feeling of inferiority.

When he was asked about the team's plans for a forthcoming picture, Babe would often respond, "Ask Stan." He was never as involved with the writing and cutting of the films as Stan was, which has prompted many to think that he just wasn't interested in those aspects of filmmaking. Actually, he wanted to direct, but he never pursued it because he felt he lacked the talent for it. He'd go through an L&H script and find a line which didn't fit him, but he'd never say anything to Stan about it because he couldn't think of a better substitute; besides, he was sure that Stan would see the problem on his own.

Babe belittled his own abilities as an actor. When other people praised him as a great comedian, he was genuinely surprised; he thought of himself merely as Stan's straight man. After Hardy had perfected his comic style, he rarely watched the day's rushes or attended previews of the pictures, because he dreaded watching himself on the screen.

Despite all of his shyness, he was much more social than Stan was, and had friends in a wide range of occupations. Stan's companions were almost all show folk, but Babe's friends included doctors, lawyers and other professional people, as well as a number of close associates in show business. At a social gathering, he tended to listen while others did the talking.

His greatest interest in life — which began January 18, 1892, in Harlem, Georgia — was people. As a child in nearby Madison, where his mother ran a hotel, he formed a habit of sitting in the lobby and observing the idiosyncracies of the patrons. He drew upon these observations in later years when he was asked to portray everything from leering brutes to haughty society ladies.

Childhood had its share of adventures for Norvell Hardy. His father, Oliver Hardy, died soon after Norvell was born, and in his honor the child adopted the name Oliver Norvell Hardy. The surviving family consisted of his mother, Emily Norvell Hardy, and four older half-siblings — Sam, Elizabeth, Emily and Henry LaFayette Tante.

The genteel customs of the Old South were a distinction of the household. His screen character's trait of politely extending his little finger while holding a cup was something he'd observed his Aunt Susie doing when the neighborhood ladies joined his mother for afternoon tea parties. As a very young child, he was raised by a black servant whom he called Mama; he referred to his mother as Miss Emily until he grew older.

Although nobody in his family was in show business, they loved music. Norvell's mother always encouraged her son's interest in singing; in 1900, when he was eight, Norvell toured the South as a boy soprano with Coburn's Minstrels. He soon longed for home, however, and returned there.

Music continued to preoccupy the young lad, to the extent that his school work suffered. Finally, his mother agreed to send him to Atlanta to take voice

Left: Oliver Norvell Hardy, circa 1900.
Right: Milledgeville, Georgia's first theater manager, circa 1910.

In Jacksonville, Florida, with his first wife Madelyn, 1916.

Hardy and Billy Ruge as "Plump and Runt," with director Will Louis, 1916.

lessons. A couple of months later she came to Atlanta and discovered that he hadn't attended classes for weeks. He had gotten a job singing to slides in a theater for 50 cents per day. That was the end of the music lessons; his mother tried to instill some discipline in him by enrolling him in Georgia Military College, a government-supervised military academy.

Babe did learn to play drums, however (a talent he displays in a 1926 Mabel Normand comedy, *The Nickel Hopper*). Co-workers remembered him strumming a ukelele and joining in impromptu barbershop quartets at Hal Roach Studios between takes. He loved all kinds of music, everything from spirituals to swing, but had a special fondness for old ballads like "You Are the Ideal of My Dreams." (He performs this at the beginning of *Beau Hunks*.)

Music was his primary interest during his youth; he did not become interested in acting until 1910, when at 18 he began running the first movie theater in Milledgeville, Georgia. He was so appalled at the acting he saw in the comedies he screened that — with typical humility — he decided he couldn't be any worse than *those* fellows, and headed for the then-burgeoning movie capital of Jacksonville, Florida late in 1913.

From early 1914 through 1917, Hardy made over 100 comedies for the Lubin and Vim companies. There was a brief trip to New York in 1915, but the young actor found the city to be harsh and unfriendly, and quickly headed back to Jacksonville. There was a real camaraderie among the players at Lubin and at Vim; the actors, crew and executives all socialized freely, often going for

Babe with star comic Jimmy Aubrey, Dixie Lamont and director Jess Robbins, on the set of *She Laughs Last* (1920) at Vitagraph.

outings at Pablo Beach, and dining together in local cabarets. (Hardy did some moonlighting as a singer in Jacksonville nightspots, especially Cutie Pierce's Roadhouse.)

Hardy's days in Jacksonville made a lasting impression in more than one way. While he was working for Lubin, he and the other young actors would get their daily shave at the local shop of a florid Italian barber. This gentleman took a fancy to the portly Georgian; he delighted in rubbing talcum powder into Hardy's chubby cheeks and cooing, "Nice-a babee!" The other troupers soon dubbed Hardy "Baby," later shortening it to "Babe," and it became Hardy's lasting sobriquet.

When fans and reporters would initially address him as Oliver, he'd ask them to please call him by his nickname; he was even billed as Babe Hardy in some early comedies. He changed his screen name back to Oliver Hardy only when a numerologist told him that the longer name would bring him success. (Babe's mother had always been interested in fortune-tellers, and her son seems to have been similarly intrigued.)

Although he starred in Vim's *Plump and Runt* series with diminutive Billy Ruge in 1916, Babe was clearly happier when supporting a star comic. The bulk of his work in the late Teens and early 1920s was as a comic villain or "heavy" for Billy West, Jimmy Aubrey and Larry Semon, all of whom were impressed by the work of his bulk. Hardy joked in later years, "my weight just automatically made me a heavy" — but even when encumbered by the outlandish beards

Larry Semon has — as usual — incurred Mr. Hardy's wrath.

and mustaches required for these roles, he was able to inject a sly, tongue-in-cheek humor and a remarkable expressiveness into his work.

Since he was a film actor from the start, Babe was capable of a subtlety that eluded actors who had been trained on the stage. In the L&H films, he speaks volumes with a tiny gesture or a brief glance, and he has a natural quality which few actors, dramatic or comic, have attained.

Many of Babe's most famous comic mannerisms can be seen in embryonic form in his early solo films. Especially notable is a 1925 comedy, *Stick Around*, co-starring Hardy and Bobby Ray as inept paperhangers. The derby, the toothbrush mustache, the flowery gestures and the disgusted looks to the camera are all there — it's as if Hardy had already created the "Ollie" character and was merely waiting for the right partner to come along.

He never expected to be a big star, but when the right partner *did* come along, he was eager to become Stan's teammate. (He was more enthused about the projected teaming than Stan, who was itching to get back to directing.) Although he was a world-wide celebrity and made $2,000 a week in the depths of the Depression, Babe never behaved like a movie star. Once, during a vacation in Seattle, Babe was invited to watch a horse race from the judges' stand; he politely declined, saying that he was having fun watching the races right where he stood.

He never forgot old friends. When he toured England in 1947 and learned that his Vim Comedies companion of 30 years before, Bert Tracy, was out of work, Babe created a job for him as the team's wardrobe man. Hardy worked with a cameraman named Glen MacWilliams on one picture in 1923; 18 years later, Babe heard that MacWilliams couldn't get re-established in Hollywood after working many years in England, and requested that MacWilliams be the director of photography on *Great Guns*.

During an especially long period of unemployment in 1923, Hardy was given a meal by a compassionate soda-fountain clerk named Charlie Barton; one day in the mid-30s, after Barton had become a director at Paramount, he opened his locker at the Lakeside Country Club and was surprised to find a brand new set of expensive golf clubs, accompanied by a note of thanks from Babe.

A lot of Babe's money went to the racetracks and casinos, and he lost a good deal more when he tried to manage his own stable of racing horses. His generosity and easygoing nature gave him a reputation as a soft touch, and he often found himself investing in ventures he really didn't want to support, just because the person asking for his money seemed like a nice guy.

He paid a good deal of alimony, too. In 1913, Babe married Madelyn Saloshin, a pianist who was a few years older than he, who helped him get his first movie work; they divorced in November 1920. On Thanksgiving Day the following year, Babe married Myrtle Lee Reeves, a film actress he'd reportedly known from childhood.

The marriage was turbulent, clouded by Myrtle's alcoholism, her placement in sanitariums and frequent escapes from those institutions. Although they almost divorced in 1929 and again in 1932, Babe kept hoping for a permanent reconciliation, until he couldn't stand any more and obtained a divorce in 1937. For a few years, he was frequently in the company of Viola Morse, an attractive divorcee with a young son; when Babe ended the relationship, she took some sleeping pills and then drove into three parked cars. She recovered, but a lot of noisy publicity ensued.

Babe found his lasting happiness when he married Virginia Lucille Jones, a script clerk whom he met on the set of *The Flying Deuces*. They remained a devoted couple for the rest of Babe's life, and settled into a near-idyllic existence on a three-acre ranch in the San Fernando Valley. Although the team's film career began to decline soon after Babe's marriage in 1940, his years with Lucille were unquestionably the happiest of his life. He began spending much more time at home, and less at the golf course.

Golf had been Babe's grand passion for most of the 1920s and '30s, though. He began playing under the tutelage of comedian Larry Semon, and went on to win dozens of cups and trophies; his skill was such that it was almost unnecessary to hold the annual Roach studio contest.

Hardy had a number of other interests. Card games had fascinated him from the time he'd learned to play as a boy in his mother's hotel, and provided a frequent diversion at the Lakeside Country Club; later, a weekly poker game was a tradition at the Hardy home. He loved to watch football; he'd played it in school, and was the Lubin studio's best player in his Jacksonville days. In his early fifties, he was a member of the 20th Century-Fox baseball team.

Hunting quail and deer was another frequent pastime until 1937, when he shot a deer and was so saddened by the dying animal's expression that he put away his guns for good. When Babe and Lucille began farming on their property during the war, they made such friends of the animals they had intended to kill and eat that they had to buy meat and poultry.

Cooking was another of Babe's great skills, too. He taught Lucille to cook, and they frequently and happily tried out new recipes. His specialties included spaghetti sauce, waffles, hamburgers and Caesar salad. He often told interviewers that he really didn't eat that much — he was simply big boned, and most of his excess weight had come from being induced to have a few beers with his friends at Lakeside. A number of the team's friends have remarked that Stan usually ate more than Babe, but an associate who worked at the Granada Club — which Babe frequented in the mid-'40s — recalls his favorite meal as being a 32-ounce New York steak, medium well, with up to two dozen new potatoes fried in pure ham fat, accompanied by a salad and coffee.

Despite his great weight, Hardy was always extremely agile; "I don't like to see heavy men lurching all over the place," he once said. He was an exceptionally graceful dancer, as well. The added weight made him extremely conscious of his appearance, and as a result he always wore specially-tailored suits. His girth was another reason for his shyness; he was so sensitive about it that if someone expressed their surprise at his height — he was 6'2" — he took it to be a comment about his weight.

Although he loved performing, he didn't have an urgent need to continually cavort in front of an audience. Occasionally he could be persuaded to sing a number or two in his clear, expressive tenor when he was recognized at a nightclub, and he would beam with delight at the thunderous applause he received. On a few evenings, he and his pal Bing Crosby gave impromptu concerts for servicemen.

Babe was always conscientious about his work, and studied his scripts faithfully every night before going to bed, even if he knew that his dialogue would be rewritten. Reading the scripts gave him the feel of a given scene, and prepared him for the ad-libbing that would almost certainly ensue during the next day's shooting.

February 7, 1925: Dorothy Dwan, Larry Semon, Babe and Myrtle Hardy at the premiere for *The Wizard of Oz*.

His tastes in comedy were somewhat broader than Stan's — he loved the Marx Brothers, for example, and golfed often with Chico. He enjoyed most of the radio and early television comedians, his favorites on the latter medium being George Gobel and Jack Paar. In the theater he built on his ranch he frequently rented and screened comedies and dramatic pictures, but he hardly ever watched his own films. He preferred the Laurel and Hardy movies which had "production" — another story line which would keep the comedy from being dull.

In contrast to Stan, Babe rarely wrote letters to fans; he appreciated their comments but didn't feel pressed to respond. He tried to get around the problem by having a stamp made of his signature, which others could apply to the photos that fans requested, thus freeing Babe from having to write his name over and over again. The ploy didn't work. Hundreds of pictures were returned to the Hardy home, accompanied by letters reading, "We want a *real* autograph!" Fans often stopped by his Van Nuys ranch, and on more than one occasion Babe and Lucille invited them in to chat and use the swimming pool.

Babe wasn't terribly political, but he was fond of FDR and Adlai Stevenson. While he and Stan were alike in their political views, they never actively supported any candidate publicly. Babe felt that an individual shouldn't be swayed by the endorsement of any celebrity, particularly when the celebrities were "two half-assed comics." He read a lot about current affairs, subscribed to the Hollywood trade papers, and although he had never been especially reli-

Why the Roach studio golf tournament was almost unnecessary.

gious, he read the Bible often during his last years. "I don't know very much," he would say, "but I know a little bit about a lot of things."

When asked to sum up his life, Babe Hardy once responded, "It wasn't very exciting and I didn't do very much outside of doing a lot of gags before a camera and play golf the rest of the time." This is the kind of answer you would expect from a shy man who wasn't given to talking a lot about himself. In truth, though, Babe Hardy's great talent as a comedian was matched by his talent for living.

THE LUCKY DOG

Production history: Written and filmed circa November 17-29, 1919. Released circa 1922 by Metro as part of the Sun-Lite Comedy Series. No copyright registration exists for this film. Two reels.

Produced by Gilbert M. Anderson. Directed by Jess Robbins.

With Florence Gillet.

Thrown out of his boarding house, Laurel befriends a stray dog. Thanks to the dog, he bumps into a robber (Hardy) who's pocketing some money earned in a stick-up. Stan outwits the portly robber, makes a shambles of a dog show and tangles with a top-hatted Swiss count — who turns out to be the robber in disguise.

The film comedy community was a small if well-populated one in the early days, and what with Stan Laurel making occasional comedies for a plethora of small companies and Babe Hardy doing the same thing, a meeting between the two young comics was bound to happen. You might say it was *destined* to happen.

Mr. Laurel's introduction to Mr. Hardy was arranged by producer Gilbert "Broncho Billy" Anderson and director Jess Robbins. Anderson did a bit in Edison's *The Great Train Robbery* (1903) and quickly became the first great cowboy star. He just as quickly became a multimillionaire, formed the Essanay Film Manufacturing Company, and signed Charlie Chaplin away from Mack Sennett in 1915.

By 1919, Essanay and much of Anderson's fortune were only a memory, but he continued to produce two-reel comedies. In mid-November that year — during Stan's two-week engagement at the Pantages Theater in Los Angeles — Anderson decided Laurel was funny enough to warrant a series of films. They agreed to make a pilot film, which Anderson would then show to the big New York distributors in order to get enough backing to make a full series of 26 pictures.

Anderson asked Jess Robbins, a friend from Essanay days, to direct the pilot film. Robbins was directing Vitagraph comedies starring Jimmy Aubrey, who had worked with Stan in the Fred Karno troupe. The "heavy" in the Aubrey comedies was none other than Babe Hardy, and since Robbins considered Babe a friend as well as an excellent actor, he brought Hardy over to work in the Anderson-Laurel picture.

The company shot the exteriors at various locations in Los Angeles, filming other scenes at the Selig Zoo studio near Eastlake Park. (It's now called Lincoln Park, but there's still a side street named Selig Place — the lone vestige of a past great civilization.)

Now that the Fates had finally gotten Mr. Laurel and Mr. Hardy together, did the two actors sense immediate indications of great things to come? Were there fireworks? Explosions? Nope. Not even sparks.

Stan recalled that during the filming of *The Lucky Dog*, he and Babe were "friendly, but there was nothing about the picture or our own personal relationship to suggest that we might ever become partners."

Truth to tell, Stan was probably less than enthused about working with Babe. The portly actor was a modest man who never deliberately upstaged the comics he supported — but his command of film acting technique was so masterful, he just couldn't help stealing scenes.

"Babe was a good actor, a good heavy; he was easy to work with," recalled director Jess Robbins. "Sometimes if something didn't look right, if I wasn't getting what I wanted, we'd stop shooting and talk it over. But he usually knew just what to do to make it look right."

In *The Lucky Dog* Babe very nearly acts Stan right off the screen. Stan obviously doesn't yet know what kind of a comic he wants to be — he's dumb and sympathetic in some scenes, brash and quick-witted in others. On the other hand, Babe is in his element as the villain, and clearly relishes every opportunity to sneer and snarl his way into our hearts.

The first film meeting of Laurel and Hardy is about as inauspicious a

At the mercy of some "Bolsheviki candy," 1919.

debut as one could hope for. The two men whose characters would become an international symbol of undying friendship begin their joint film career by playing a brash young man and a robber who is about to kill him.

Stan bumps into nasty Babe Hardy early in the film, just as Babe is pocketing some loot he's stolen from a man at gunpoint. Trouble is, Babe is pocketing the money into Stan's pocket. When he realizes where he's deposited the cash, Babe roughly whirls Stan around, thrusts his gun at him, and speaks (via title) the first line of Laurel-Hardy dialogue: "Put 'em both up, insect, before I comb your hair with lead." We obviously have a long way to go before we'll hear anything like "Well, here's another nice mess you've gotten me into."

There's some characteristic byplay between the boys in this scene. When Babe means to stick his gun in Stan's back, he barks, "Turn around!" and Stan turns a full circle, so he's again facing Babe when he comes to rest. Babe's exasperation at this, and Stan's uncomprehending expression, provide a hint of what was to come.

In a later scene Babe tries to do Stan harm with a pistol. But his gun jams, and Stan has to help him get it unstuck, nearly shooting Babe in the process. This scene reveals that L&H already have a great knack for anticipating each other's actions, and for reacting to those actions.

Babe then promises to blow up Stan with some dynamite, or what he terms "Bolsheviki candy." (This example of topical humor is vintage 1919, in reference to the all-pervasive Red Scare that followed World War I. It makes you wonder why so many film historians have mistakenly guessed that this film was made in 1917.)

About all that can be said for this film is that it shows how two comics with wildly contrasting characters and styles can still manage to show a rapport with each other. But *The Lucky Dog* was only a momentary flirtation with destiny. It would be seven more years before Laurel and Hardy would again appear in the same film. The Fates would have to be patient.

1920: The 28-year-old studio president is pictured with his staff.

The Lot of Fun

Those who were fortunate enough to work at the Hal Roach Studio will tell you the place was better than Paradise, if your goal in life was to make funny movies. At the major studios, everything was regimented, while the smaller comedy lots ground out films cheaply and prolifically with little thought given to quality. Only at the Roach studio was there enough time, and, most importantly, enough concern to ensure that every release would be as hilarious as humanly possible.

If the major studios could be likened to a huge chain of supermarkets, the Roach lot was a Mom-and-Pop grocery. "There's been no other studio to date like it," asserted Roy Seawright, who served as head of the optical-effects department. "MGM, Fox, Universal — they were nothing but machines. The Roach lot was very individual. And the people there had talent with a wonderful sense of humor. The Roach studio was nicknamed 'The Lot of Fun,' because it was a comedy studio — and it *was* a lot of fun.

"Mr. Roach would come in in the morning; he'd walk down the street, he'd greet everybody and everybody would greet him. He expressed so much warmth and love and affection for everybody that it was just contagious — it spread from him to other people within the organization. So much great talent emanated from that lot," said Seawright. "It took the Hal Roach Studio to nurture those people's talents and bring them to the fore."

Oddly enough, the man whose name graced the studio had no ambition to write or be funny during his formative years; however, he had a zest for life, a healthy ego, and a capacity for hard work. We're fortunate that Hal Roach was sidetracked from his original goal: he wanted to be an engineer on the Lehigh Valley Railroad.

Harry Eugene Roach was born in Elmira, New York on January 14, 1892, the grandson of Irish emigrants; he had his name legally changed to "Hal" as a young adult. One of his most vivid childhood memories was of sitting entranced in the living room with his older brother Jack, as their maternal grandfather spun all sorts of fascinating yarns. Later in life, Roach would attribute 90% of his success as a film producer to a storytelling ability inherited from his grandfather.

When he turned 17, his father told him now was the time to see the world. Young Hal went off to Alaska, where he spent a year loading six-horse pack teams. He then took a job in Seattle driving an ice-cream truck, but was soon fired for driving the vehicle "fast and hard."

Roach was all of 19 when his job with a construction company brought him to Los Angeles. One day he read a newspaper ad offering $1, carfare and lunch to anyone who owned Western-style clothes and wanted to work as a movie extra. He put on a Stetson hat and cowboy boots and took a bus to the 101-Bison Company.

Roach had the luck of the Irish his first day in Hollywood. The gambling hall scene being filmed called for the hero to win lots of money at roulette, then lose it all. Nobody knew which way the ball was supposed to spin in the roulette wheel — except Roach, who had seen his share of real gambling halls in Seattle. His salary was immediately jumped to $5 a day.

He found employment in westerns as an actor — not a very good one, by his own admission — then worked as a $30-a-week dress extra at Universal. Among Roach's fellow extras in 1913 were two men he would later employ — Harold Lloyd and future director George Marshall.

"At Universal there were five of us, all about the same size, so we could switch clothes rapidly," Marshall recalled of those early days. "Hal and I were very close friends; we were like brothers almost. As things went along, we bought a complete wardrobe — and then Universal would keep us, as we were very handy for them for any particular role."

Roach and other neophytes enacted a scenario of their own after hours. "Somebody would play the part of the director, another guy would have a cigar box and pretend it was the camera, and we made out like we were making pictures," Roach said. "And every one of the people who did this at night, did something great in pictures afterwards. This way we got rid of stage fright — not just for acting, but for learning to talk with other people." The skill would come in handy for Roach in a very short time.

The young actor was playing heavies in one-reelers when he was appointed an assistant director. He soon met an attorney who told him about a well-to-do acquaintance who wanted to get into the film business. Roach convinced the attorney he was "the best undiscovered director in the business" and his career took an upward turn.

In 1914 Roach recruited former fellow dress-extra Harold Lloyd and made six untitled one-reel comedies (at a cost of about $350 each) and three dramatic two-reelers. The comedies featured the broadest kind of knockabout; they were entirely improvised, shot outdoors at nearby locations, and co-starred people literally yanked off the street.

Roach sent the comedies to New York, where a middleman sold them to the Pathé Exchange, but "failed to tell Pathé who made the pictures so we didn't get any money." That ended Roach's first production venture. He was directing one-reelers at Essanay when he chanced to see one of his self-produced comedies in a theater, with the Pathé logo emblazoned on it; he got in touch with the company, who wanted more of the same.

Roach then began making "Phunphilms" for the new Rolin Film Company ("Ro" for Roach and "lin" for partner Dan Linthicum). He rejoined forces with Harold Lloyd; together they created a character called Willie Work, which they soon replaced with Lonesome Luke. In 1917, Lloyd donned a pair of horn-rimmed glasses and a winsome smile; his star — and Roach's — were on the ascent.

The young producer began building a new studio in 1919 on a 17-acre parcel of land, in the new Los Angeles suburb of Culver City. "The studio was an impressive looking thing," recalled a former employee. "The front of it

Left: Hal Roach, about the time he started his studio in 1914.
Right: At a convention in 1980.

looked like a mansion on a Southern plantation" — appropriate for a producer whose ancestors lived next door to Robert E. Lee.

In addition to features starring Lloyd, Roach gradually began developing other short-subject series, including a series of one-reelers with Lloyd's second banana, Harry "Snub" Pollard. Child actor Ernie "Sunshine Sammy" Morrison, who had played in support of Pollard and Lloyd, became the nucleus of the immensely popular *Our Gang* series which debuted in 1922.

Will Rogers began making two-reelers the following year, often under the direction of Roach's new director-general Charles Parrott. His brother, James (aka Paul Parrott), starred in his own series. By late 1923 the brothers had switched places, with Charles changing his billing to Jimmie Jump and finally to Charley Chase.

After Lloyd left Roach to form his own company, the Paul Parrott films were replaced with a series of one-reelers starring Stan Laurel, who had found filmmaking more to his liking than vaudeville. There were short-lived attempts to build comedies around Scottish comic James Finlayson and Australian comedian Clyde Cook. Roach also produced a series of Western features with Rex, King of Wild Horses.

Probably the most intriguing Roach series of the mid-'20s was the "All Star" series, which featured once-popular dramatic stars in two-reel comedies that verified their decline — sometimes in parodies of their earlier successes. What fun there was in these films was usually generated by the supporting comics. Two of these comics worked so well together that they became stars themselves — but more about that later.

Among the behind-the-camera talents who passed through the studio on their way to greatness were director George Stevens, who got his start as a cameraman; Frank Capra, who wrote briefly for the *Our Gang* series; and Leo

Trying to break into a Roach studio film vault.

McCarey, who began at Roach's as a gag writer in 1920 and wound up supervising, writing and directing many of the studio's greatest films.

Other staff members included writers Carl Harbaugh, who was head of the scenario department in the mid-'20s; Jean Havez, later one of Buster Keaton's best gag men; Frank Butler, who would gain fame for his work on films like McCarey's *Going My Way*; Tay Garnett, who later turned director; and Frank Tashlin, who went on to direct offbeat comedies, some starring Jerry Lewis.

F. Richard Jones, an alumnus of the Mack Sennett studio, supervised production of the Roach films in the early '20s. Jones was an intense, driven man, and although former co-workers described him as "aloof," he spent virtually every waking hour in pursuit of comic perfection. He lived solely for his work, with the result that it killed him at the age of 36. McCarey took over Jones' duties in late 1927.

Despite Jones' boundless energy, most of the folks who worked at the Roach lot were relaxed and easygoing. Given the kind of product the studio turned out, it's not surprising that nearly all the employees had a highly-developed sense of humor. Everyone who worked at the lot retained a special fondness for it.

"The Christie studio was close-knit, but there was something special at Roach's," said actress Anita Garvin, who found her niche in the studio's two-reel comedies. "I don't know anybody on the lot who wasn't easy to get along with. I can't tell you how happy the days were that I spent in that place. I loved every minute of it.

"There was never any pressure to get the pictures done in a hurry. That was one thing about the Roach studio," said Garvin. "It wasn't like working for other small studios; they used to take pretty good time in making the films. At

Will Rogers visits with Babe, Stan and Margaret Roach at the 1931-32 Academy Awards banquet.

most of the other studios, you'd adhere to the script more or less, but on the Roach lot we were quite informal, and everyone could speak their mind. You didn't have to be afraid to open your mouth to the director or anybody else."

Dorothy Granger, who was featured in three L&H films as well as Roach's mid-'30s series, *The Boy Friends*, recalled, "When I'd do a comedy, my dad would come out to visit me on the lot. Jack Roach, Hal's brother, who was casting at the time, would say, 'Hey, Pop, you want to work?' So in all the comedies, you'd see my dad and my brother, you'd see my co-star Mary Korn-man's mother and her uncle. It was a family thing. And, of course, you'd have practically the same crew all the time. It was very warm and friendly."

Working at the studio was literally a "family thing" as far as the Hal Roach clan was concerned. Jack Roach was also an assistant cameraman and location scout; their father, Charles H. "Dad" Roach, was the company treasurer until his death in 1936. Roach's parents and brother lived in a house on studio property.

There was never any caste system at the studio. Stars and grips considered each other as equals, united in their pursuit of the belly-laugh. "It was the friendliest lot in Hollywood," said actor Henry Brandon. "Everybody said hello, and good morning — by name. The studio commissary, The Our Gang Inn, where everybody ate, was right there on Washington Boulevard.

"And on the set, other actors would come and visit. Thelma Todd and Patsy Kelly — they were wonderful girls. Charley Chase was always coming in. Everything would stop — a lot of gags and funny stuff would go on, and then we'd go back to work maybe in half an hour. And the assistant director would be going crazy.

"The most heartbreaking thing of all was when I came back to Los Angeles from Europe, and I drove down to look at the lot — and found a big, empty space there. I just pulled up the car and sat there and cried — because they'd taken all those memories away."

While his studio was always a congenial place, Roach himself could be somewhat reserved. Roy Seawright asserted, "The only times I saw him laugh and have fun were in his office, when he'd have a group come in and they'd talk about something entirely divorced from studio matters — or at the lavish Christmas parties they'd have on the lot. Those were the only times when you'd hear him really let loose. He covered up his feelings very well — negative or positive. He's a wonderful man; I have all the respect in the world for him," said Seawright. "But I don't think anyone on the lot was really close to him."

Roach was a man who played as hard as he worked. "He was a terrific sportsman," observed Seawright. "He had his own polo field, where he kept his ponies; he was a very aggressive player. The heck with the pony and the heck with his own neck, he just wanted to hit that ball! If anybody got in his way, why, there'd go their horse and everything else."

Richard Currier, head of the studio's film editing department from 1920 to 1932, retained fond memories of his ex-boss more than 50 years after his departure from the lot. "The fact of the matter is, he's the best boss I ever had," he stated emphatically. "I've never heard of anybody that didn't like Hal Roach.

"I worked for him on a temporary job when he was at his first studio, up near Bunker Hill in Los Angeles. He had a half-assed band up there. He used to play a violin and a saxophone, and if they ever had any spare time, why, Jesus, the guys'd get their instruments and play a couple or three tunes. I played a banjo at the time, so I went up and joined them. When I got the job at the Culver City studio, it was the same thing. I could hear Roach playing the saxophone, alone in his office.

"He was friendlier than other bosses at the studios. He was the big boss, but he didn't show it. And he was smart, too — he did a hell of a lot of thinking that nobody knew about but Hal. He'd keep his ideas to himself, but he'd tell them to the right people.

"No bunch of people could live together as amicably as the gang at Roach's. Nobody was jealous, or yelling their heads off — it was a hell of a swell place to work. Over the years, I've dreamt many times about working back there. I have dreams of my same office, same gang around me and all. The people down there made such an impression on me, that my inner soul, or whatever you call it, keeps bringing it back to me all the time."

Hal Roach himself recalled that warm studio atmosphere: "If Charley Chase had something funny that the Our Gang kids could do, he'd tell Bob McGowan, their director, or tell me. And if Bob McGowan had a funny idea for Laurel and Hardy, he'd tell them — everybody was helping each other."

This spirit of cooperation and dedication, combined with a relaxed, familial environment, helped engender the creativity that made the Roach comedies so special. And it was only in an atmosphere like this that two comedians who heretofore had only minor success in their careers could stumble upon each other, create highly individual comic personalities and become the most popular comedy team of all time.

The Boss Meets the Boys

Hal Roach's association with Stan and Babe began years before the teaming. In May, 1918, Stan and Mae Laurel were appearing in Los Angeles. Their act was caught by Alf Goulding, an Australian ex-vaudevillian who was directing for Roach. The producer was desperate for a new comic. He had hired a famous clown named Toto the year before for a series of one-reelers. After completing 14 films, Toto quit, due to a nervous condition which affected his eyes. On Goulding's suggestion, Roach wired Stan to make a test with comedian "Snub" Pollard:

LOS ANGELES, CALIF.
MAY 24, 1918

STANLEY LAUREL
CARE PORTOLA THEATER
SANTA BARBARA, CALIF.

CAN YOU ARRANGE TO LEAVE TONIGHT FOR LOS ANGELES IN ORDER TO TAKE TEST WITH HARRY POLLARD WHICH WE WISH TO SHIP TO NEW YORK FOR PATHE APPROVAL FOR PERMANENT ENGAGEMENT WITH US.
YOU CAN RETURN IN DUE TIME FOR MATINEE SATURDAY. WIRE OR PHONE IMMEDIATELY.

HARRY BURNS, MANAGER,
ROLIN FILM CO.

The "permanent" engagement lasted from June 15 to July 13. Stan made five one-reelers, with Roach personally directing the first three (*Do You Love Your Wife?*, *Just Rambling Along* and *Hoot Mon*). Each was filmed in less than a week, for an average cost of about $1,800.

"They used to shoot mostly off the cuff," recalled Stan. "For one-reelers you just needed one idea, no stories. Just tell a little incident and that was it. I had no single character. If I did a baker, or a butcher, I dressed accordingly. After I finished the five pictures for Roach I was let out, because that's all there was."

Stan didn't work for Roach again for another five years. In the interim, Laurel made three films in support of Vitagraph's star comic, Larry Semon — an association which was abruptly terminated when Semon thought Stan was getting too many laughs. Despite a few detours into movie studios, Stan and Mae basically stayed on the road from October 1918 until the spring of 1922, playing Majestics and Bijous and Orpheums all across the United States and Canada.

Stan resolved to "settle down and really try for pictures" when producer Gilbert M. "Broncho Billy" Anderson found backing for a Laurel series in 1922. (Anderson had been shopping around the pilot film, *The Lucky Dog*, since 1919.) The Laurel-Anderson films, released through Metro, were often ambitious and hilarious parodies (one, *Mud and Sand*, featured Stan as the dashing toreador Rhubarb Vaselino). Good as they were, the films just didn't earn enough. Stan and Mae went back into vaudeville.

Hal Roach had been watching Stan's career, however, and decided to sign him for a new series of one-reelers on March 2, 1923:

LAUREL IS SIGNED BY HAL ROACH

———•———

Famous English Comedian to Start at Once on Series of One-Reelers

———

In line with his increasing production activities, Hal Roach yesterday signed Stan Laurel, one of  the foremost comedians before the camera, to a five-year contract.

Laurel is to begin immediately the production of a series of one-reel comedies, under the direction of George Jeske.

Stan Laurel.

The new Roach star has just completed a long tour in vaudeville, which he interrupted several times to appear in motion pictures, one of the best-known of which is his burlesque on Ibanez's "Blood and Sand."

Laurel comes from the same group of English comedians that gave Charles Chaplin to the screen. Ten years ago he came to this country with Fred Karno's "English Music Hall" company, of which Chaplin also was a member. He toured the United States, and then returned to England for a short time, coming back to America, where he has been for nine years.

Some of the resulting films were top-rate, among them *Kill or Cure,* in which Stan is a patent-medicine peddler who stops at nothing to make a sale; *Smithy,* a disjointed but hilarious comedy with Stan as a doughboy who ends up in the construction business; and *The Soilers,* wherein cowboys Laurel and James Finlayson periodically interrupt their barroom brawl to gape at an outrageously gay tenderheel.

Stan worked hard on the one-reelers — perhaps harder on the gags than

Left: Stan is a Chaplinesque chef in this Roach gag photo.
Right: Babe in character for *No Man's Law*, a 1927 Roach Western.

on his own character, which was still just an outline. He played a brash simpleton, a contradiction which neither he nor his audiences found terribly amusing. Ultimately, Roach had to let Laurel go, two years into the contract.

Stan and Mae moved in with Laurel's agent, Percy Pembroke, and his wife, comedienne Gertrude Short. Despite the bad reputation that Mae had given Stan (she kept pestering producers to let her play the ingenue in Stan's films), independent producer Joe Rock signed Stan to a five-year contract — with the provision that Mae could not work with him. After making two sample films with his own money, Rock obtained a distribution deal with Lewis J. Selznick. The production of the Laurel two-reelers went along happily, with Stan characteristically absorbed in every aspect.

"Stan was in everything — he was a dedicated comedian," said Rock. "He'd sit in on our gag sessions and make suggestions, he was there early in the morning, watched everybody work, never left until late. He always wanted to see the daily rushes. He'd sit there and make comments. Always sticking around, seeing if he could improve something and talk about it. You had to respect somebody who was that interested."

Joe Rock helped Stan in his personal life, as well. After a number of unsettling incidents, Mae Laurel agreed to return to Australia if Rock paid her way. Joe arranged for Mae's passage back home; the day she left, Joe introduced Stan to a young lady who had worked as an extra in some of the comedies (in fact, she'd also been an extra in Stan's 1918 one-reelers for Roach). Before long, Stan and Lois Neilson began dating; they married on August 13, 1926.

Then, according to Rock, Percy Pembroke told Stan that he would never get the 15% of the grosses which Rock had promised him. "Stan was convinced he'd never get his percentage," Rock said. "He started not staying late, not

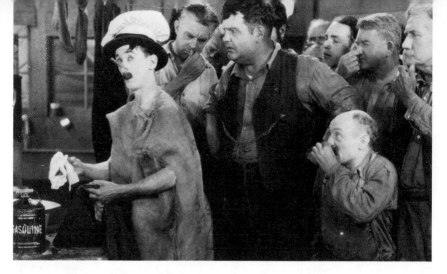

Australian comic Clyde Cook arouses the ire of Babe Hardy and little Sammy Brooks in *Wandering Papas* (1925), directed by Stan Laurel.

coming in the morning; he wanted to break his deal.

"People said he was going down to Hal Roach and talking about a deal with them. Then he told me he didn't want to make any more films with me. We had made our 12 films in seven months; my problem now was that the distributors paid me once a month, as each film was delivered. I said, 'Stan, look. I don't want to stop you from making a living, but if you make anything with Roach, and they're billed as Stan Laurel Comedies, what am I gonna do with my distributors, when *I've* got a deal to deliver Stan Laurel Comedies?

"Stan said he wanted to go back to the stage. I said, 'If you'll put that in writing, it'll be fine.' So he wrote me a letter saying that he wasn't going to make any more films. I notified my distributor that I couldn't deliver any more of his films after this. Well, down he went to Roach's."

Stan began working at the Roach studios in May, 1925, as a writer and director. Under the guidance of F. Richard "Dick" Jones, Stan learned the craft of comedy film directing — how to place the camera so that the audience could clearly see the important action; why a particular shot was most effective in a given situation. With Jones supervising, Stan directed a number of one- and two-reel comedies, some of them in association with Richard Wallace.

A couple of the shorts Stan directed starred an Australian eccentric dancer and comic named Clyde Cook. "We used to kill ourselves laughing," Cook recalled in 1980. "Stan used to laugh more than anybody else. When he was directing me, he'd say, 'What do you think of this?,' and I'd say, 'Well, let's try it.' In one picture, I had to get rid of a body, so I put it on my back and took it out in the country some place. We started to think about what we could do with it. I said, 'What do we do with the body?' And that became a gag with us. When we were stuck for a gag, we asked ourselves that."

Another performer in some of the films directed by Laurel was Babe Hardy. Babe's earliest known job on the Hal Roach lot came late in 1924, supporting Charley Chase in a one-reel short supervised by Leo McCarey, *Is Marriage the Bunk?* Hardy made some interesting films for other studios (notably Semon's version of *The Wizard of Oz*, and a pair of Laurel and Hardyish two-reelers for Arrow which co-starred Hardy with Bobby Ray) but Babe found himself returning to the Roach lot more frequently during 1925.

The portly free-lance comic became a useful foil to Chase and other Roach stars, with the result that Hardy signed a contract with the producer on February 6, 1926:

OLIVER HARDY SIGNS UP FOR ROACH COMEDY

Former Culver City Man Joins With Studio Here

Oliver Norvelle Hardy, known in Culver City as "Babe" Hardy, a comedian with varied experiences dating back to his juvenile aspirations with the old Lubin company in Jacksonville, Florida, in 1923, has been signed by the Hal Roach studios on a long term contract. He will play various types of supporting roles in Charley Chase and Mabel Normand comedies and featured roles in the all-star series, with the prospect eventually of being featured in his own right.

Recently Hardy, who used to live here, has played with Chase and Glenn Tryon, also in comedies of the all-star series. He is classed by F. Richard Jones, vice president and director-general at Roach's, as one of the most versatile comedians of the day, in spite of the type restrictions embodied in his 284 pounds of size.

In the old Lubin company in 1915 he worked alongside Edwin Carew when the latter was staring in three reel "features" directed George Nichols. Now Carew is a director and Nichols a character man.

Hardy's last completed role was in "Along Came Auntie," with Glenn Tryon.

Babe became more prominently featured in Roach comedies starring Glenn Tryon, Our Gang and others. Then, on July 24, 1926, one of the quirks of fate which helped bring Laurel and Hardy together was reported by Los Angeles newspapers:

One of the strangest sequences of hard luck in the annals of Hollywood put Oliver Hardy, Hal Roach comedian, and his wife on the sick list together this week.

Mrs. Hardy, visiting a friend in Laurel Canyon, climbed a path about 100 feet from the main road and ran directly into a coiled rattlesnake. She turned and fled, but fell two or three times on steep trail, tearing all the ligaments in her right leg, incapacitating the leg for several weeks to come.

Next night, while she was in bed and able to get around only with the aid of crutches, Hardy stepped into the kitchen to demonstrate a little culinary skill while the cook played nurse. Getting a frying pan of grease to the scalding point he lifted it, the handle slipped and the burning grease was spilled over his right hand and wrist, causing an agonizing injury. He tried to get out of the house quickly through the back door in order not to make any fuss before his wife, and in so doing he slipped and fell, twisting one leg and acquiring several bruises. His hand will be in bandages for several weeks and he will be unable to carry on the role which he was playing in Mabel Normand's comedy.

OLIVER HARDY

In addition to the Mabel Normand feature (*Raggedy Rose*), Stan had also been assigned to direct a two-reeler with "fading star" Harry Myers, entitled *Get 'em Young*. Babe was cast as a butler. When Hardy burned his arm while trying to cook a leg of lamb, Dick Jones asked Stan to replace him. Stan was reluctant. For one thing, he preferred writing and directing to acting; for another, Stan had gotten his release from Joe Rock with the understanding that he would not appear in the Roach comedies. (Rock and Laurel filed suit against each other over this matter during the same week in which Hardy burned his arm.)

Laurel in a role intended for Hardy: *Get 'em Young*, 1926.

Stan was finally convinced to act once again when Hal Roach asked him to do so — and offered a raise of $100 per week. As a result, Laurel played the butler in *Get 'em Young*, and the direction was taken over by Fred Guiol.

Throughout the following year, Babe Hardy and his new fellow-actor Stan Laurel appeared in Roach's comedies. Sometimes they were cast in the same picture, sometimes not. (Once, they just missed each other: *Eve's Love Letters*, a 1927 two-reeler, features Stan, with another actor portraying "Sir Oliver Hardy.")

Stan and Babe eventually found themselves in the roles for which they were best suited, evolving from two comics with contrasting styles into a perfect partnership. It could only have happened at one studio: Hal Roach's lot of fun.

Walter Long relaxes with the boys and an unidentified script girl on the set of *Any Old Port*, while director James Horne (kneeling) and photographer Art Lloyd focus the camera on assistant E.V. White.

The Method of the Madness

The Script on the Studio Floor

In theory, movies are supposed to be produced like this: The actors adhere to the script; the director firmly guides the actors and technicians; many takes are made of each scene, from different angles; and the film is shot out of sequence, with all scenes at a given location shot at the same time.

Laurel and Hardy movies, though, were produced like this: Stan and Babe routinely deviated from the script; Stan guided the actors, technicians *and* the director; they usually shot only one take of each scene, to capture the spontaneity of the first run-through; and they filmed in sequence whenever possible, because they never knew how their ad-libbing would change the story.

Stan Laurel and Hal Roach both felt that the story was of paramount importance. "You've got to start with a believable story" was Stan's credo of comedy construction; Babe Hardy echoed this with, "We did a lot of crazy things in our pictures, but we were always *real*." Stan and Ollie were believable, human characters, and they needed to be placed in plausible situations.

From the mid-'20s on, Roach's comedies got as many laughs from their situations as they did from the gags. This paid off with audiences, who were tiring of the gags-for-gags'-sake films of Sennett and other producers. "I was able to pass Mack Sennett because of stories," said Roach. "Mack was the best at that time in slapstick — broad comedy, knockabout, chases and things like that. And I began to put a bit of a story into my things, while doing really the same gags."

Those stories, oddly enough, were often not very funny in themselves. They provided a dramatic context which made the gags seem even funnier by contrast. "Many of our stories for shorts could have, and have, been used in feature pictures as serious material," Stan said. "We took the other line; the humorous side of it. You can visualize the situation and what *could* have happened might be very funny."

The main titles for the L&H short subjects usually give no writer credit. (Until mid-1932, H.M. Walker was credited for titles or dialogue, but he didn't play a major part in the development of the stories.) Hal Roach took an active role in preparing the plots, especially in the early stages of the team's development. He explained how the stories were conceived:

"We had about six or eight writers with Laurel and Hardy," Roach said. "When Laurel and Hardy were shooting a picture, I would bring the writers in and I would have an idea of what the next picture should be like. I'd say, 'All right, they're gonna be a couple of sailors,' or whatever the hell it was. After two or three hours, I would see that a couple of these writers knew what kind of a thing we were talking about. So I would say to these two writers, 'All right, you guys pick it up. Give me a treatment as soon as you can.'

"Now, they would write a treatment, not trying to put gags in, but writing the story line to see where it would go. Then we would have another meeting with all the writers to see if anybody had a gag that would go into that story," Roach continued. "So by the time that Laurel and Hardy were through with the picture they were working on, this story would be ready to submit to the director and to Laurel — Hardy never paid any attention — and as a rule, to a couple of gag men who worked on the set. They would try it out, and if it didn't work, we'd have another conference, and might even go into an absolutely different story."

Stan also helped develop the stories from the team's inception; he had been hired as a writer in early 1925, and remained busy in that capacity even after Roach asked him to go before the cameras again. By 1929, he was basically the head writer; he took the gag men's ideas, added his own, and distilled them into the final script. "I had some very fine boys who worked with me," Stan recalled. "We'd all have ideas. No one thought one was any better than the other. We'd just work out a script and get to shooting it as quick as we could."

The writing sessions were a gleeful chaos, with all of the gagmen joining Stan in a perpetual game of "Can You Top This?" Marvin Hatley, musical director of the Roach studios, was also on the payroll as a gag man in the early '30s. He remembered the writers' meetings thusly:

"Stan had three or four guys hanging around, you know, but he was the main one who did everything. He always had these other people to offer suggestions, and he'd twist them around. Then they'd get up in the projection room and they'd act out their ideas. If somebody had a gag where a character was choking, he'd demonstrate it; he'd put his hands to his neck and say, 'He's choking!' They wanted to show the other guys what they meant."

There was a high turnover rate among the Roach writers, but at various times the men who worked with Stan included Frank Butler (later the studio's head story editor), Carl Harbaugh, Lloyd French, Gordon Douglas, Wallace McDonald, Walter Weems, Stanley Rauh, Felix Adler, Jack Jevne, and James Parrott. Other gag men worked as actors, too, among them Billy Gilbert, Jack Barty, Don Barclay, Harry Langdon, Baldwin Cooke, Frank Terry and Eddie Dunn. The gag man who remained with the boys the longest — from about 1928 until their separation from Roach in 1939 — was a diminutive Englishman named Charley Rogers.

Rogers had toured in music halls with an act called *The Iceman*. Hal Roach commented, "I don't think Charley ever originated a damn thing, but he had a good memory. He remembered what they had done in pantomimes in England. He was a gag man; he never was a *writer*. I don't ever remember him being in a conference when we were starting out to write a new story, but he was always on the set when they were working. When they'd get into something that didn't work, he was the guy that helped them out of it. If Laurel wanted to discuss an idea, he usually did it with Charley. And Laurel most always figured a part in the picture for Charley, you know, something to keep him on the set anyway."

Left: Editorial department head and title writer Harley M. "Beanie" Walker.
Right: Carl Harbaugh, a Roach gag writer in the late '20s.

Stan and the gag men could gather at any place or time to dream up funny material. Often, they'd meet at Stan's home. (His daughter Lois recalls that Stan always joked around a lot at home — but the only time he'd get intense about it was when the writers came over to work on the script. Then, Lois would be sent out to play elsewhere. Joking around with her at home was *funny* funny, but working with the writers was *serious* funny.)

Gag sessions could often develop spontaneously, frequently after the shooting day was over, and could continue as long as the ideas kept flowing. Roy Seawright, head of the optical-effects department, had an office across the hall from Stan and Babe's dressing rooms.

Seawright recalled, "I'm inside my room, working on my camera at eleven, one, two in the morning. And through those two walls, I hear these guys over here going crazy. Now, how does one concentrate when you hear Stan and Babe laughing like hell? What do you do? You've got to cut the cameras off, walk around the corner and say, 'What's happening?' They were sitting there, screaming! Charley Chase would join them. Leo McCarey would come in. And they'd sit there, with maybe a little, shall we say, Seven-Up.

"So I'd take a break, go into their dressing rooms, and listen. Stan was saying, 'We'll do this, we'll do that.' Stan *was* Laurel and Hardy. I loved Babe, but Stan was a writer, a director, a cutter, he did everything. I don't care what the credits say; Stan was the power behind their whole enterprise, from the two-reelers on up to the features."

As the preceding comments indicate, Babe Hardy's contribution to the writing was minimal. His widow Lucille recalled that Babe could always spot a scripted scene that wouldn't play well, but felt he was unable to invent a funnier replacement.

George Marshall, who directed the team in 1932, recalled, "Babe was creative in a different form. He'd come in, he'd listen, he'd see the pattern of what you were doing, and while you were talking, he'd come up with a very good gag. We'd say, 'Pretty good, Babe,' and he'd say, 'Well, I'll see you all later,' and he'd be gone, off to the golf course. That was Babe — but whatever he came up with was good." Since Stan so obviously relished writing gags, Babe was more than happy to leave the job to his partner.

After Stan and the writers had worked on the story for a week or so, they would generally have a finished script — three to six legal-size pages, single-spaced, with a description of the action and sometimes a few brief dialogue sequences if they were especially funny or important.

The script was then sent to Harley M. "Beanie" Walker, head of the editorial department — which oversaw script and film editing. Walker, a former sportswriter, joined Roach in 1916 and began writing brilliantly witty titles. ("Neither Mr. Laurel nor Mr. Hardy had any thoughts of doing wrong. As a matter of fact, they had no thoughts of any kind.") Walker usually named each film, and wrote a critique of it before it was sent to the distributors.

Walker was a chain-smoking eccentric; he was crazy about cats, and usually had a few prowling around his office. This was beneficial to his friend George Herriman, who drew his "Krazy Kat" comic strip in the same office at the Roach lot.

Film editor Richard Currier said of Walker, "He was my immediate boss; he had a few odd things about him, but you'd get acquainted with him and just pay no attention to them. He never drove a car; his wife would drive him to the studio. He'd walk right to his office — I used to say, 'Good morning'; sometimes he'd answer, sometimes he didn't. He'd take the cover off his typewriter and wham it against his legs four or five times and fold it up and put it in a certain place. Then he'd come out the door and say, 'How are you this morning, Richard?' He never called me Dick, always Richard. That's how my name happens to be 'Richard' on the credits.

"Walker was a prince of a man," Currier continued. "He gave me a Webster's dictionary once; the note I got with it will give you an idea of how everybody at Roach's felt towards everybody else: 'Richard — having listened for years to your astonishing and, at times, highly-charged vocabulary, I hasten to add to your voltage.'"

Walker was the only writer to receive screen credit on the early films (probably because he was also an officer of the Roach corporation), but his contribution to the L&H films was relatively minor. In the sound era, Walker would write a few pages of dialogue after receiving the "action" script. Comparison of the two scripts with the finished film usually reveals that most of Walker's dialogue went unused, the important dialogue (such as the memorable wordplay in *Helpmates*) having already been written by Stan and the gag men in the first script.

While Roach and Laurel always agreed that a good story was essential, they often disagreed over whether or not a given story *was* good. In recent years, Hal Roach has expressed a somewhat controversial view of Laurel's writing ability:

"Stan Laurel, next to Charlie Chaplin, was the best gag man in the

The creative nucleus of the Hal Roach Studios, circa 1927. First row, seated: Roach, H.M. Walker, studio manager Warren Doane. Second row: Fred Guiol, Carl Harbaugh, *Our Gang* director Robert McGowan, writer Mauri Grashin. Third row: Art Duquette (with pipe), Anthony Mack and James Parrott.

business. That's for gags, or individual pieces of business. As for writing a story, Laurel wasn't worth a nickel. Somebody else had to do that, not him. The things that he thought would be funny as a picture, you'd think a little kid had written.

"Laurel was equally good as Chaplin in remembering many of the sight gags from English music halls. In writing visual comedy, approximately 50% of what you write, which sounds very funny on paper, does not work. When you get on the set and start to rehearse the thing, you realize that it doesn't come off. That was where Laurel's ability came in great. He would remember something that had been done; not necessarily by himself, but in one of the hundreds of different pantomime theaters all over England," Roach said.

A foursome: Roach studio general manager Henry Ginsberg, George Marshall, Babe and Beanie Walker, 1932.

George Marshall offered an intriguing viewpoint about Roach's ability as a writer in a 1974 interview. "When we saw Hal, he'd have a gag, and nobody could understand what he meant — because he would say, 'You know, they come in here, they go out there, you know what I mean.' And that would be the end of the gag! We picked it up from there, but that was sort of a standing joke on the lot; we'd all say, 'You know what I mean?'

"Hal would go through the script at first," Marshall recounted, "but then once the script was set up, I don't think I saw Hal two or three times during the shooting. After he'd look at his dailies, Hal was usually gone. There was never any producer interference. I know he and Stan often talked things over — that was probably business — but I had nothing to do with that.

"Stan was a pleasure to work with. He was so bright in story — we often worked on our story material together. That mind of his was always working, to piece things together; Stan was so creative. I learned a lot from him, rather than he learning anything from me."

Playing on the Set

After they became a team, Stan and Babe played the same characters for almost 30 years. As a result, they didn't have to prepare much to get into character — they were hardly method actors.

The work day began at 8:00. Before applying his make-up and getting into costume, Stan would often view the rushes to determine if any of the previous day's footage had to be re-shot.

Stan with director Lewis Foster and cameraman Art Lloyd, 1929.

By 9:00, everyone would be on the set. "We didn't have any 6:30 or 7:00 make-up call," said actress Dorothy Granger. "We'd start shooting at 9:00. You'd arrive at the studio a little before then for make-up — which you did yourself! You did your own hair, too. They *did* have a wardrobe department at Roach's; in those days, you had to have two or three dresses alike, because there was no telling when you'd have to go into the drink — or they'd wreck your dress, and you had to have a standby. And you needed another for your double." Occasionally some of the actresses — Anita Garvin and Thelma Todd among them — would wear their own clothes.

Stan and Babe both used a light pancake make-up, which gave them an innocent, pixieish look; Stan also made his eyes look smaller by lining the inner lids. The boys wore formal stand-up collars, to give their characters a sense of dignity. Stan wore a flat-brimmed Irish children's derby — appropriate for his childlike character — and he fastened his cuffs with string. His shoes had no heels, which made Stan look shorter and more vulnerable; this device also gave him his flip-flop walk.

The shooting day usually ended around 5:00 — according to Dorothy Granger, "You'd quit sort of early, and then Stan and Babe and the gag men would all go off and figure out gags for the next day." Before the unions came in, there were occasions when cast and crew kept shooting past the normal quitting time, to finish the picture. If they were shooting both day and night exteriors on the same set, they would occasionally work all day and continue through the night.

What went on between the director's first call of "Turn 'em!" and "That's a wrap!" was a strange combination of ad-libbing, conferences with gag men, practical jokes, throwing out old gags and trying on new ones, impromptu concerts from musically-inclined actors, reminiscing about vaudeville, and — somehow — getting the picture shot.

The Roach maxim of "50% of what is written will not play" was obeyed on the set, where the first order of business — apparently — was ignoring the script. "We did have a script," Stan said in a 1959 interview, "but it didn't consist of the routines and gags. It outlined the basic story idea and was just a plan for us to follow. Oh, a few gags were mentioned here and there in the script, but they were always *worked out* on the set."

"Of course, Stan was the brains," recalled Dorothy Granger, "but we never thought of him as the boss. It was a team effort. If the sound man got an idea, he'd tell Stan; everybody would contribute. But Stan usually came up with the original idea — and of course, he and Ollie would ad-lib, and it was just automatic.

"As far as rehearsal goes, you'd get your positions for camera, and sort of walk through the scene. But you couldn't tell how it would end up when you were in a scene with Stan and Babe, because when they'd start filming, they'd find all these little pieces of comedy business. They could do a whole show just on one scene. Now, when you had a scene with actors besides Stan and Babe, you were placed and just spoke your dialogue; but when you were with the boys in a scene, you placed it pretty loose."

Anita Garvin, who lent tremendously funny support to the boys in many silent and sound shorts, agreed that the process of shooting a Laurel and Hardy comedy was very informal. "Stan would talk it over with the rest of us," she said, "and once in a while we would run through something for the timing, but as a rule the rehearsal was practically nil. We just shot it after talking about it. And if it felt like it was going to be something funny, we'd just keep right on going, and the camera would keep right on grinding.

"After sound came in, the filming took a little more time, but the talkies were made in rather the same way," Anita recalled. "I would just look through the script or get the basic idea, and go in without learning the lines letter-perfect. It was easier. If you came in with your mind set that these were the lines, then tried to change them, it was very difficult. We ad-libbed more at Roach's than at other studios; we had more leeway to do what we wanted.

"Stan and Babe shared everything," Anita added. "They didn't try to hog every scene. If you had something that they considered funny, they'd allow you to do it without interruption."

This generosity characterized Stan and Babe's attitudes toward each other. Said Hal Roach, "I never saw Hardy at any time try to steal a scene from Laurel; and although Laurel was directing, he never tried to sneak in or steal a scene — if it was Hardy's scene, Laurel gave it to him.

"The gestures that Hardy did were *his*," Roach stated. "The tie, his looking into the camera, and the way he did things individually, nobody told him. I never heard anybody, including Laurel, direct him in anything. You didn't have to tell Hardy what to do; he was a hell of a good actor."

The atmosphere on the Laurel and Hardy sets appears to have been always very relaxed. "We never had a regular schedule," Stan recalled, "we just worked to get a good picture. The studio didn't mind because in those days the salaries weren't much money, there weren't any unions, and we never used a big cast." Anita Garvin concurred. "Roach used to take pretty good time in making the shorts; not that you'd make a lot of retakes," she said. "You pretty much had to get it the first time, unless it was something mechanical that had to be timed just right with the props — maybe you'd have to do that several times."

"We had a lot of mechanical effects," Stan recounted in later years, "like an explosion, where everything fell over — the walls fell down, the drapes and everything else. All that was wired, and sometimes it got fouled up. Or sometimes in the middle of a scene, a carpenter would look through the window and say, 'Did it work?'"

In addition to these problems, there could also be minor accidents on the set. Anita Garvin recalled, "They had these great big bulbs, these brilliant lights. And I used to paste my hair down flat with Vaseline hair tonic. So I'm doing a scene with Stan, and he's looking at me so funny — and all of a sudden, he starts pointing at me. I thought, 'What am I doing wrong?' I couldn't imagine what he was looking at. My *hair* was smoking! It was catching fire — from the heat of the lights and the Vaseline hair tonic. So I had to wash *that* out of my hair. Another time, one of those big bulbs exploded, and Stan pushed me out of the way; that glass just came down.

"You could get pretty bruised up doing some of the stunts, too," Anita said. "You'd fall down in the mud, or anything. That was all part of the job. I used to take these falls, and I didn't know that other people would go to wardrobe and get pads to put on — nobody told me! I'd go out there with just a thin dress on, and — whap!

"Stan and Babe had doubles for a lot of the crazy things that they did," Anita stated. "With Babe being so big, he couldn't very well do a lot of the hard physical stuff. And they didn't want the boys to get hurt, of course." Through the mid-'30s, the dangerous stunts were performed by Stan's double, Hamilton Kinsey, and Babe's, Cy Slocum. Later, the boys were doubled by Chet Brandenburg and Charlie Phillips.

Between takes, there was almost as much comedy on the set as when the cameras were rolling. Practical jokes kept the crew in a happy frame of mind, so they truly had a practical value. Some of the stunts were just as inventive as the gags which got on film. Roy Seawright recalled a prank which Stan pulled on a co-worker.

"Stax Graves was the head of our still department for years," said Seawright. "He was a very serious, sweet, dedicated man from the South — with no sense of humor at all. None at *all*. And you do not walk onto a Laurel and Hardy set with no sense of humor. Stan had rigged up a gag with our prop master, Harry Black, and they'd put a fine piano wire on the tripod of the still camera — naturally unbeknownst to Stax. So Stan says, 'Come on, Stax, let's get going and get those pictures!' Stax says, 'Yes, sir — yes, sir!' He puts his hood on, lines up the camera, checks the focus, and finally says, 'Okay, we're ready to go.' And as he's just about to flip the trigger on the lens, the camera collapses. It just slides down to the floor.

"Poor Stax. He's so nervous. 'Oh! God! I'm sorry, I'm sorry!' He puts the camera all back up again, and Stan's saying, 'Come on, come on, man — let's get going!' Stax has his camera all ready again, puts the hood on, looks through the camera and says, 'Okay, smile!' — and the tripod goes out again!

"Stax stands there and looks. He can't believe it. He picks up his camera

Director Leo McCarey — who put the team together — with the boys on the set of *Wrong Again*.

again, puts it back up — and now, Stan is really pouring it on. 'Stax *Graves*. Come *on*, man. You're getting paid a lot of money, here. Time is wasting, and time is money!' Poor Stax doesn't know he's caught in a trap. Believe me, there's no man more dedicated, more serious, than Stax Graves. And he's going out of his mind.

"So he sets the whole camera up again, gets ready to take the picture again, and he stops and looks right at his camera and says, 'Don't you fall down!' Stan knew he'd milked his gag, so he gave the sign to a prop man, Don Sandstrom, who was holding the piano wire, not to pull it. And Stax, with nothing going wrong — click! — got his picture!"

The Laurel and Hardy sets rang out with music as well as mirth between takes. In the '30s, the studio's musical director, Marvin Hatley, was a frequent visitor. "Stan Laurel used to have me come down to the set and play the piano, while he'd sing all those old English songs," said Hatley. "And Babe Hardy would join in — Babe sang tenor, you know. They enjoyed doing that while the crew was changing the lights."

Roy Seawright retained fond memories of these spontaneous songfests. "I always look back to the days when things were kind of quiet, when they'd roll a piano over to Stage 1, and Leo McCarey would start playing," he said. "And just like that, Charley Chase, Babe, Stan and Leo would start a quartet. It's unfortunate that we don't have a recording of their impromptu entertainment. You'd walk in and listen to them, and you'd be entranced.

"The whole studio would come to a complete stop, the minute word got around that they were singing. People would just flock around that stage. Stan and Babe and the others would have a whole group watching them, and they'd be completely oblivious to it. My God, how they harmonized; they all recognized each other's talent, and they loved it. They loved to get away from production — forget writing, forget directing. They'd just get around the piano, and they were completely free to express themselves. And that expression — that freedom — was manifested in their pictures. In everything they did, there was freedom."

Stan — The Director's Director

Stan Laurel never considered himself an *auteur*. "No one man can make a picture. That's silly," he said in a 1957 interview. And when his biographer asked him to assess his contributions to the direction and shaping of the films, all he could muster up was, "I guess you might say that I sort of stood on the sidelines and helped."

The people who worked with the team share a somewhat different opinion. Hal Roach stated flatly, "Laurel bossed the production. No question about that. Laurel worked hard; when they were making a picture, he was working all the time to make the picture as good as he could."

It's true that Stan was always accountable to Hal Roach. As Roach's close associate Richard W. Bann observed, "The simple fact is that Roach gave the orders. Everyone on the lot was working to please *him*. If he didn't like something, it was changed. A business trip or a trip to play polo had no impact on his control; he talked, privately, with the key people before he left. He saw the results when he returned. They did it the way he wanted, or they fixed it when he objected."

Stan's right hand man, gagman and director Charley Rogers, on the *Devil's Brother* set.

While all of Roach's films share certain traits (emphasis on story over gags, good production values, a stock company of talented supporting players), it seems that his most successful pictures were made in collaboration with other individuals who "bossed the production." Harold Lloyd virtually produced his pictures (and literally did after 1923). Roach's *Our Gang* series flourished under the direction of Bob McGowan; Charley Chase was the guiding hand of his films.

When Roach didn't have an employee guiding a series, the results were uneven. After George Stevens quit directing Roach's *Boy Friends* series, it faltered. The Thelma Todd—ZaSu Pitts films were alternately delightful or dull. The *Taxi Boys* series was an absolute disaster. The quality of the Roach features was just as unpredictable; wonderful films such as the *Topper* series were released alongside misfires such as *The Housekeeper's Daughter* and *Turnabout*. After 1941, the studio produced few films of merit.

In sum, Hal Roach was indeed a creative producer, and he had a definite concept for the style and content of his films. However, he needed other people to help realize that concept. Roach's films, like all films, were creative collaborations.

Roach was happy to leave many of the production chores for the L&H films in Stan's hands — until the late '30s, when the increased cost of the features caused stricter supervision. Anita Garvin recalled, "You'd see Mr. Roach on the lot walking up and down, but rarely on the set. I think he realized that it made people uncomfortable — if you saw him there, you were bound to stiffen up. You just wouldn't be yourself."

Roach himself concurred, "I would very seldom be on the set, unless I was directing. In fact, I would slow them down on the set, because they all knew I'd had more experience than anybody else. I knew more about the business, and unless I was directing — it was more of an embarrassment, you know what I mean?

"Now, I *always* saw the dailies. I would criticize the hell out of the dailies; if I didn't like them, I'd tell the people the way I thought the scenes should be. But as far as telling them on the set — I didn't believe in it. And that applied to practically everybody. You saw the results in the projection room. If you didn't have faith in the people that were making the picture, then they shouldn't be there in the first place."

Stan ran the L&H set no matter who was in the director's chair, but he never felt compelled to assert his authority. "Stan was never nasty, never said anything mean to anyone — never," said Anita Garvin. Likewise, the directors never tried to pull rank on Stan. As Hal Roach remarked, "With any director that was directing Laurel and Hardy, if Laurel said, 'I don't like this idea,' the director didn't say, 'Well, you're going to do it anyway.' That was understood."

Sometimes, the directors weren't aware that they were following Stan's instructions. "A lot of directors thought they were directing Stan," said Anita Garvin, "but believe me, Stan was the one who was directing. And the director was never cognizant of the fact. Stan was clever; he had a brain, in spite of that look. He would make suggestions in such a clever way. He'd say, 'You started to say...' And the director thought it was his own idea.

"He'd suggest different things to the actors, too. He'd say, 'How do you think this would work?' He wouldn't tell you what to do, but he'd ask your opinion. And 99% of the time, you'd say, 'Great!' — because he had a comedy mind like no one I have ever known, before or since."

Roy Seawright provided another example of Stan directing his directors. "One day, Stan went over to the script clerk, Art Duquette — a little guy with a mustache — and on this picture, Stan made him the director! There he was, sitting in the director's chair one day. I said, 'What are you doing here?' He said, 'I'm directing this picture!' He just sat there, and Stan told him, 'When you say "Camera," we'll go to work.'

"Stan would say, 'What do you think, Art?' and pull something from him — and Art would say, 'Yes, let's do it this way.' Then Stan would say, 'That's great. Hey, Babe — he just came up with a beautiful idea.'

"Stan was pulling words out of Art's mouth. But he did it with such tact that no criticism could ever be pointed at the director. Stan wasn't worried about not getting credit as a director; he wasn't egotistical in that way at all. He was very generous."

With Stan making so many suggestions, there wasn't much left for the credited director to do. Leo McCarey seems to have exerted more control than the others, although he officially directed only three of the team's comedies and shot retakes without credit on a couple of others. Even here, his work seems to have been a collaboration with Stan. In later years, McCarey recalled Stan starting another day's work after the shooting day was over, "working on gags and story with me or helping cut the picture."

Anita Garvin, who worked in several of the McCarey-supervised L&H films, asserted, "Stan was the one who was directing, even over Leo McCarey — and there was no director better in the world than he. But to give him all the credit for teaming Stan and Babe, and telling Stan what to do, well, that's ridiculous."

To give him his due, it *was* McCarey who first conceived the Laurel and

Stan and Babe with their frequent director from 1928 to 1933, James Parrott.

William Seiter directed the team only once — but well — in *Sons of the Desert* (1933).

Hardy team. Frank Butler, one-time head of the Roach scenario department, has stated that McCarey noticed the funny contrast between the fat man and the thin one, but the basic concept of the boys' characters — dumbness combined with invincible innocence — came from Stan. "He was the first one to bring that idea into play at the gag sessions," said Butler, "and Leo and the gag men took up that concept and spun out infinite variations on it."

McCarey had definite ideas about the style and pace of the comedies. "At that time, comics had a tendency to do too much," he told Peter Bogdanovich in 1969. "With Laurel and Hardy, we introduced nearly the opposite. We tried to direct them so that they showed nothing, expressed nothing — and the audience, waiting for the opposite, laughed because we remained serious." Laurel shared McCarey's view. He felt most comedies were paced too quickly; since Stan and Ollie were characters with slow-acting minds, the films needed to reflect that with a slow tempo.

Credited as the "supervisor" of the team's early films. McCarey was more influential in the creation of stories than directing. He supervised the Charley Chase and Max Davidson series as well as the L&H films, so his participation in the actual filming was limited. According to Anita Garvin, McCarey would occasionally be on the set as an observer.

The Laurel-McCarey collaboration was a happy one; Leo told author John McCabe that he worked with Stan "smoothly and sympathetically, and that made it very easy for us to meet the studio's rather demanding deadlines." Hal Roach summed up their relationship like this: "Stan *adored* Leo McCarey."

When McCarey left the Roach lot in December 1928, Stan became the man in charge of the films — although, of course, he still reported to Roach. Most of the team's directors seem to have been chosen for their malleability. Said Roach, "Many people who directed Laurel and Hardy weren't exceptionally great directors, but they got along well with Stan."

None of the team's directors had an especially commanding presence. Marvin Hatley recalled director James Horne primarily for his trait of swearing good-naturedly after a take went wrong; James Parrott is best remembered by his co-workers for his shyness. Dorothy Granger said of him, "Jimmy was on the quiet side, and Stan didn't need any direction, really. The smart directors gave him his freedom, and Parrott let the boys go like that."

The director who gave Stan the most leeway was Charley Rogers, who began working on the L&H films in 1928 as a writer and sometime actor; he started directing the team in 1933. Stan highly valued Rogers' talents as a gag man; as a director, however, Rogers' chief attribute was his ability to follow Stan's orders.

"To me, Charley was the ideal stooge," said Roy Seawright. "He was always on the set, and if Stan would laugh, he'd laugh. I don't think he contributed anything spectacular; Stan kept him on out of loyalty. When he was directing, Stan put the words in his mouth. But Charley would try to inject his own little ideas without conferring with Stan, see?

"Stan would say, 'What's this?' And Charley would say, 'Well, I thought I'd do this —' And Stan would say, 'I do the thinking, you sit in that chair!' Charley would sit in his chair and he'd sulk, and finally Stan would get him out of it, get him in a good mood again."

A frequent director for Stan and Babe in 1932 was George Marshall, who later piloted such classic features as *Destry Rides Again.*

"Stan never tried to take over the direction," Marshall told author Jordan R. Young in a 1974 interview. "We worked together. Either Stan or Babe might come up with something that made the routine work better. I could add to it, or Charley Rogers might add a gag to make it better. Things always developed; you could start with nothing and suddenly it would be a full-fledged routine.

"Stan would get into the gag, grab Babe maybe, and say, 'Babe, let's try it this way.' It wouldn't be a case of interference; more likely, he'd say, 'George, what do you think if we try it that way?'

"It was a very valuable experience for me; I learned a lot from Laurel," Marshall related. "It was like a big family, and everybody would talk to each other. There was a great relationship, and that was why we turned out good comedies."

McCarey and Marshall were the only directors who made many excellent films apart from their work with Laurel and Hardy; it's difficult to assess the talents of Clyde Bruckman, since he always worked with comedians who controlled their productions. George Stevens was the team's primary cinematographer until 1930; one wonders what he might have brought to the L&H films as a director. (Stevens did in fact direct the team's sequences in the 1934 MGM feature *Hollywood Party.*)

The strongest evidence to support the argument that Stan was truly the director of the films is the fact that Laurel and Hardy had two dozen directors during their tenure at the Roach studio, and the films have no discernible stylistic differences.

The pace is very slow compared to that of other comedies (even other comedies produced by Roach); this allows us to know the characters thoroughly. There's a preponderance of long shots, which lets us see the boys' pantomime fully. Takes are lengthy, so the team's performances are uninterrupted. Close-ups are limited almost exclusively to reaction shots after a gag; these give the audience time to laugh before the next bit begins.

Stan obviously wanted to approximate the experience of a live theatrical performance in the films. Rarely are there any showy effects with camera placement or editing, because Stan wanted the laughs to come out of the performances, not the cinematic technique.

Stan knew just how he wanted the films to look. He wanted bright, even lighting in each shot; it engendered a sunny, happy look which helped induce laughter. It also had a practical use: if Stan and Babe began improvising while the cameras were rolling, and their ad-libbing caused them to move to another area of the set, they would still be properly lit.

Laurel also knew how *he* wanted to be photographed, much to the chagrin of their perennial cameraman, Art Lloyd. Venice Lloyd, Art's widow, recalled, "Art would be dying to do something artistic, but it was very seldom that he got the chance. Stan wouldn't let Art put any contours into his face; he made Art photograph him so that he looked absolutely white — and you don't get any awards for photography that way. Stan would say, 'Now, wash me out, Artie. No shadows. I want to be flat-faced, and as long as you do that, you're my cameraman.'

"Art would take all kinds of time lighting the girls, and sometimes they'd go out on location and he could get some good photography. But as far as putting a shadow into the face on Stan and Babe, I'll tell you, they wouldn't have it. Still, Art was very fond of Stan. He'd say, 'Well, I'll never win an Academy Award, but I'll sure please Stan Laurel."

Not only did Stan pay attention to the individual shots; he wanted them shot in sequence, in the same order as they would appear in the finished film. This was an unusual procedure, but Stan had a reason for it.

"We shot our comedies right from beginning to end," Stan said. "The only place I could do it was at Roach's. Anywhere else, they wouldn't go for that. And many times, not shooting in sequence just ruined the picture, or the prospects for the picture. For instance, if we had a lot of scenes in a kitchen where we came back and forth at different times... when we left the kitchen, we never knew what we were going to run into. If we'd shot all the kitchen scenes at once... we couldn't come back with a black eye or covered with anything, because the scene was already shot."

While the methods of making movies became increasingly regimented at the major studios, Stan and Babe had a private oasis at the Roach lot, where they could give their creativity full rein.

Roy Seawright eloquently summed up the experience of working with Laurel and Hardy. "Everybody on the lot would go out of their way to see Stan and Babe, just to get the morning off right, with a laugh," he said. "Stan would mention something about an old stage play — completely irrelevant to what they were shooting — and then he'd start laughing. He'd be sitting there, just screaming — holding his sides, beating his knees. And of course, everybody on the whole stage was laughing. The whole atmosphere was very warm and convivial. But that's the way Stan ran the stage.

"I always remember the humor and love that developed in working with these two beautiful men," Seawright declared. "It could be windy, rainy, dull outside; you'd walk through the stage door — and it was warm. It wasn't the temperature; it was a human element. You knew that you were participating in something unique. You'd walk on the stage, and everybody's smiling. It was vastly different from other studios — I've worked at all of them. No comparison. The minute you walked onto the Laurel and Hardy stage, you were happy. You were grateful to be there."

Cutting Humor

The folks in the Roach studio's film editing department were also Stan's collaborators, just like the folks in the other departments.

Almost all of the Laurel and Hardy films made through 1932 bear the legend, "Edited by Richard Currier." Currier, who joined the Roach forces in 1920, received credit on hundreds of films. Although he was a skilled editor, he had relatively little to do with the cutting of the Laurel and Hardy pictures — as he freely admitted when interviewed in 1980.

"When I went down to Roach's in 1920, I took over the editorial department," he said. "I ran it; I had four girls working for me as a negative cutters, and I had Bert Jordan and a couple of other fellows cutting the pictures. So, down there, I didn't do a hell of a lot of cutting. I just supervised it." The blanket credit was given to Currier by his boss, Beanie Walker. "There wasn't much said about it," Currier related, "because in those days editors weren't getting any credit anyway."

The editor who received no credit (until 1932) for working with Stan was Bert Jordan, a thin, soft-spoken Englishman who had worked for the Lion's Head Film Company in England, and the Vitagraph studio in Hollywood before Currier hired him in 1921.

"I was officially named the Laurel and Hardy film editor," Jordan noted with pride. "I was the only one that Stan would have to cut his pictures, unless I wasn't available. He used to crab if he had anybody else cutting them — so I was flattered by that."

The editing process began during the shooting; Jordan would sit on the sidelines and take notes on what was being filmed. "I used to try and be on the set as much as I could," he said. "I used to see all the rushes; Babe didn't care whether he saw them or not, but Stan would always look at them."

The daily screening of the rushes is warmly remembered by the team's co-workers, primarily because Stan unfailingly flew into hysterics when he saw the new footage for the first time. "He used to just laugh like the dickens when he saw the gags," said Bert Jordan.

Roy Seawright concurred. "Stan was his own greatest audience," he said. "You'd go into the projection room, and at the dailies, he'd sit there and scream! He'd beat the goddamn table; he'd go nuts! But it wasn't ego.

"Stan lived in two personalities. When Stan performed in front of the camera, he performed just the way he felt it. He did not know how it would look, coming through the camera and onto the screen. In our projection room, he'd look at it, and he actually had no relationship to the guy in the dailies. He was

Left: Richard Currier, head of the Roach film editing department, in the '20s.
Right: Bert Jordan, the largely uncredited but "official" L&H editor, in 1967.

not that guy on the screen, but he sincerely reacted to what he *saw* on that screen. Stan was like a painter who would sit back with his canvas in front of him — maybe two days later, he'd look at his work and say, 'Hey, that's good!' He was a true artist."

It wasn't only his own performances that sent Stan into the aisles. George Stevens recalled, "I walked into the projection room once, when a film was being run for one man, and there's a fellow sitting on the edge of his seat, holding onto it to keep from falling down, and it was Stan Laurel watching Babe Hardy on the screen."

Once the filming was completed, the editing began in earnest. Richard Currier provided this general outline of the procedures involved: "Down at Roach's, we had our own laboratory," he said. "The negative was developed at night, and in the morning, we got a print from it. Then, I'd give it to one of the boys to sync up the sound track with the picture. Then we'd go down to the projection room, and I'd call Hal, and the director, and we'd look at the dailies. After that, the assistant would cut the individual takes, put them up on racks, and you'd start cutting the film. Some pictures took longer than others, but when they were through shooting it would take four or five days to cut."

According to Bert Jordan, Stan basically had the right of "final cut," and supervised the editing of each sequence. "The editing was just between Stan and myself," said Jordan.

"The process of cutting the Laurel and Hardy films was this. First, I'd read the script all through, then I'd look at the rushes. After Stan looked at them, I'd put the film together the way I thought it should be. Now, after I put together my version, the director and Stan would look at it, and they had the privilege of making changes — but the first cut was for me to decide.

"Sometimes, they didn't make many changes. Stan may have said, 'Well, I tell you, Bert, I think that would look better if you played it in the long shot.' But I always knew what they wanted.

"Mr. Roach would sometimes look at what Laurel did as far as the cutting was concerned, and he'd suggest some changes — but if Stan didn't agree with them, they weren't changed. Roach thought a lot of Stan Laurel, I think; he pretty near always agreed with what Stan said. When we were editing a picture, I used to get permission from Mr. Roach to go to Stan's house, Fort Laurel, and we'd go over all the changes to be made, over there."

Richard Currier recalled that there was no standard studio policy on the style of editing. However, there was a comedy philosophy which was reflected in the cutting. Currier explained, "In comedies, there's one thing you have to follow: Be careful to see that the audience is always in on the gag, but don't let your characters in on it. Guy comes out of a grocery store, and he's got a lot of bundles in his arms; he drops a banana, and it lands right on the steps. Well, he doesn't notice it. The audience sees it, and they *know* something's gonna happen with that banana there, so the next guy that comes out of the store, he does a 108 [a pratfall] off of that banana.

"Editing one of these pictures wasn't a proposition of just putting the film together," noted Currier. "You've got to pick out the best parts of the scene — get the reactions of both Hardy and Laurel, because that's what makes the pictures. If you cut away from them to something else, why, it spoils the comedy for you."

In keeping with Stan's desire to approximate the effect of a live performance as closely as possible, he and the editors cut the scenes so that the actors always managed to pause for the duration of the laugh, as they would if they were performing on stage. The effect is magical, but it was accomplished through a very practical method.

"We usually left a foot to a foot-and-a-half of film for the laugh," said Currier. "And then, when we took the picture on preview, if the laugh went over the amount of time we'd left for it, then we'd lengthen the scene a little bit, to give the audience a little more chance to laugh."

Hal Roach added, "If the dialogue was furthering the story, then if the audience laughed over it and didn't hear the line, it didn't mean anything. Sometimes you'd see the picture and the audience would be laughing so hard that you didn't want to come in with more dialogue — you'd have to put in another shot of Laurel to slow them down, so that your next line could be heard."

The Laurel and Hardy films were designed for large theater audiences, which lessens their impact on television. As Stan reflected in later years, "You watch any of the Laurel and Hardy pictures alone in a projection room, they look terrible. Doesn't seem to be a laugh in any of them, you know? But the reaction in a theater with an audience — they're laughing all through this. In the home, with just a couple or three people watching, they're wondering why the actors are standing still."

Once a film had been cut in accordance with Stan's and Roach's suggestions, and everyone thought they had it right, they asked preview audiences to prove them wrong. The Laurel and Hardy films were thrown onto the screen as a surprise before unsuspecting audiences, who were likely to be harsher critics and provide a more accurate assessment of the film's merit.

"A Laurel and Hardy picture was usually previewed at least three times before we ever let it out," said Hal Roach. "We'd preview it first, then re-cut it, maybe make some retakes, then look at it again."

Reflecting the care lavished over the films, a small army of Roach staffers attended these secret previews. Richard Currier recalled, "If we were previewing a Laurel and Hardy picture, they would be there. We usually had about 20 seats set aside in the theater for us. Hal Roach always went. And he always had one certain hat that he wore to the previews. He was a little superstitious; he thought it was a good luck hat."

Art and Venice Lloyd attended many of the previews, too. "Artie would come home and he'd say, 'Well, Friday night there's going to be a preview out in Alhambra,' Venice recalled. "They tried to preview the pictures in little outlying areas, to start with. Later on, with the longer pictures, they'd preview them in quite prominent theaters. It was really great fun, because it was all supposed to be very, very secret."

The studio kept the previews a secret from the supporting actors, possibly to spare them any disappointment if their scenes were received unfavorably and had to be deleted. Anita Garvin said, "They tried not to have the other actors see the previews. I really don't know why; I think I saw only two or three previews of Roach comedies."

One person who always attended them, though, was Roy Seawright. "I got a pass to all previews," he said, "because I could outlaugh Stan. He always had me sit way up in the front — first or second row — and I'd practically roll on the floor, watching those pictures."

The purpose of the previews, of course, was to gauge the audiences' reactions to the films before they were released. The Roach staff had an ingenious method of rating each film. "At the previews," said Roy Seawright, "the cutter, the director, and Stan and Babe all carried clickers, and they sat at different spots in the theater. Whenever they thought they had a legitimate laugh, they'd click the clicker." Richard Currier added, "The clicker was just a machine that turned one number every time you pushed the button. There were usually four or five of us doing it, and nobody would have the same number of laughs, so we'd take the whole bunch and average them off."

Sometimes unforeseen difficulties could arise during the preview. "We went to a preview one time in Pomona," said Bert Jordan. "We drove up outside the theater, and we heard a lot of laughing. They were showing a Laurel and Hardy when we got there! We were afraid it was going to kill our new show if we had two Laurel and Hardys in a row, but it didn't."

"When we previewed the early talking pictures," Jordan continued, "we'd bring two great big wax discs — one for each reel. And of course, the needle of the theater's phonograph had to be placed on a certain spot on this disc. Well, we had it out of sync more than once!"

Barring any of these minor catastrophes, Stan and Babe and the Roach staff would compare notes afterwards. "After the preview," said Venice Lloyd, "we'd wait in the lobby, and there's where the yakking started. Then we'd go out for a sandwich, and we'd all yak again. That would go on until 11:00 or 12:00. And Roach would generally lead the discussion; he was the Godfather."

Bert Jordan offered another perspective. "Stan and I would notice which gags didn't get very big laughs. And maybe the show ran over its usual length; something would have to come out. So we'd just make notes in there, and Stan would decide what to cut. Nobody interfered with what he wanted."

After the previews, Beanie Walker usually wrote a report telling how each film had fared. Despite all of the humor he displayed as a title writer, Walker was a harsh critic when he evaluated each comedy. After the whole studio had poured its combined talent into a film, Walker would grudgingly send the pictures to MGM with a concession like this: "It took four previews to pull this one under the wire. In finished form, it clicked 52 laughs."

Most Roach two-reelers averaged between 50 and 60 laughs; according to a 1929 newspaper article, *The Battle of the Century* held the record among early L&H comedies, earning 140 laughs. This is seven laughs a minute, which means that either this was a phenomenally good comedy or that you can't believe everything you read.

Hal Roach explained why he depended so much on the previews: "The comedies made for television today are not so good; whatever they make, that's it. But in those days, we could afford to do retakes. On most every picture that we made with Laurel and Hardy, we previewed the picture and then re-did the picture afterwards.

"If I went to a preview and it went great, I was on top of the world," Roach said. "If it went badly, I was as low as a snake. And never in my life was it, 'Oh, my God, the money I'm going to lose on this,' or 'The money I'm going to make on that.' The whole basis was either how good or how bad the picture was. That applies to everything I made. I never in my whole career paid any particular attention to the finances."

All of which explains why the Laurel and Hardy films produced by the Roach studio are still shown and loved today, while comedies dashed off by other studios were considered mere filler in their day, and have long since been consigned to oblivion.

The Hal Roach Silents

45 MINUTES FROM HOLLYWOOD

Production history: Written and filmed circa August 1926. Copyrighted December 13, 1926 by Pathé Exchange, Inc. (LU 23421). Released December 26. Two reels.

Produced by Hal Roach. Directed by Fred L. Guiol. Titles by H.M. Walker. Story by Hal Roach.

With Glenn Tryon, Charlotte Mineau, Theda Bara, Our Gang.

A country boy (Tryon) and his family head for Hollywood to pay off a mortgage. They do some sightseeing (the movie stars they meet are conveniently under contract to Hal Roach) and encounter a group of bank robbers masquerading as a film crew. Ollie is a hotel detective who spends most of his time in a bathtub; Stan has a bit as an unemployed actor staying in the hotel.

Stan Laurel and Oliver Hardy were both gainfully employed at the Hal Roach Studios by mid-1925, and over the next year they did a remarkable job of avoiding each other. One would think that with Stan working as a writer and director, and Babe snarling away in front of the cameras, they would've had ample opportunity to work together. But between May 1925 and January 1926, they put their combined talents to use on only three films: *Yes, Yes Nanette*, a Jimmy Finlayson one-reeler; *Wandering Papas*, starring the Australian acrobatic comic Clyde Cook; and a Theda Bara "All-Star" short called *Madame Mystery*.

While these shorts are unremarkable, there are hints of Great Things To Come in their later work together: Babe manages to upstage the frantic antics of his fellow players with his subtle facial expressions, and Stan keeps the direction simple and uncluttered, letting the gags speak for themselves. Laurel seems to have been well aware of Hardy's comic potential, giving him several choice bits as the rather dainty foreman of a bridge-construction crew in *Wandering Papas*.

After the third of these epics co-directed by Laurel and co-starring Hardy, the two were not to encounter each other on a movie set until another eight months had gone by. By now it was August 1926, and Stan had returned to the ranks of the thespians. And now, for the first time in history, Stan Laurel and

Oliver Hardy would both appear in a film produced by Hal Roach. Did this great and holy triumvirate of film comedy issue forth a masterpiece? And was there set loose in the nation, or even the Roach studio, excited conversation about the teaming of two glimmering new stars in the comedy constellation? Not quite.

45 Minutes From Hollywood is interesting today for about 45 seconds. True, Laurel and Hardy are both *in* the film; they just don't have any scenes together.

Stan is made up for this film with a bald wig and a mustache, so that he looks like Jimmy Finlayson. As Laurel is trying to sleep in the hotel policed by detective Hardy, Tryon and a young woman fight in the hallway. They break into Stan's room and continue tussling on his bed, evidently unaware that it's occupied. Meanwhile, Hardy and two cops are trying to batter down Laurel's door and stop the skirmish. They succeed only in accidentally battering down the door across from Stan's room.

For decades now, scholars have racked their collective brains trying to figure out why Stan was made up to resemble Finlayson. A possible reason: when Stan got his release from producer Joe Rock, it was with the understanding that Laurel could direct and write for Hal Roach, but not appear in front of the cameras. Rock and Laurel were suing each other over this point while this picture was in production. The suit wasn't resolved until December 29, 1926, by which time Stan had appeared without much makeup in a number of Roach comedies.

It had been seven years since *The Lucky Dog*. Laurel and Hardy were finally appearing again in the same film — but they didn't even exchange so much as a howdy-do.

And the Fates were thwarted again.

DUCK SOUP

Production history: Script finished September 15, 1926; filmed late September. Copyrighted January 13, 1927 by Pathé (LU 23526). Released March 13, 1927. Two reels.

Produced by Hal Roach. Directed by Fred L. Guiol. Titles by H.M. Walker. Story based on a sketch by Arthur J. Jefferson.

With Madeleine Hurlock, William Austin, Bob Kortman.

Two hoboes (Stan and Ollie) take refuge in the temporarily vacant mansion of Colonel Blood, who is on his way to Africa. The tramps are enjoying their new digs when a wealthy young couple drops by to inquire about renting the place. The two ne'er-do-wells are forced to masquerade as the owner and his maid — a ruse that goes awry when the colonel returns unexpectedly.

Great Britain, 1908. Arthur J. Jefferson, renowned theater manager and playwright, pens a deathless little farce entitled *Home From the Honeymoon*. This sketch is booked into the prestigious Moss Empire houses and plays all over England. All is jolly until one of the starring comics has a tiff with playwright Jefferson, who replaces the offending farceur with another up-and-

No, this is not Syd Crossley.

coming young comic, one Arthur Stanley Jefferson.

Flash forward to September 15, 1926. The same Arthur Stanley Jefferson, now going under the professional name of Stan Laurel, is sitting in his office at Hal Roach Studios. He gazes wearily but proudly at a script which he has just finished writing — a 19-page opus entitled *Home From the Honeymoon*.

Although Hal Roach is away in New York, Laurel is obeying Roach's orders to keep writing himself into the pictures. This new script — a cinematic reworking of his father's sketch — concerns two hoboes on the run from, of all things, a forest ranger trying to recruit men to help battle a blaze.

Stan cast himself as James Hives, one of the hapless hoboes. His partner, Marmaduke Maltravers, was to be played by Roach stock actor Syd Crossley. For some mysterious reason, Crossley never made the trip from script to screen. Instead, Stan's partner was played by Oliver Norvell Hardy, who had by now recovered from the burns inflicted on his arm by that nasty leg of lamb.

Just why Mr. Hardy was substituted for Mr. Crossley will never be known. Perhaps supervisor F. Richard Jones made the switch. Maybe director Fred Guiol preferred Hardy over Crossley. Maybe Hal Roach called from New York and said, "Put Hardy in the picture!" Maybe Crossley burned *his* arm while cooking a leg of lamb.

Or perhaps those ubiquitous Fates intervened. After seeing L&H work together — just once — in 1919 for Broncho Billy Anderson, then seeing them just miss each other when both worked for Larry Semon at Vitagraph in 1921, *then* seeing Stan flatly refuse producer Joe Rock's offer to make Babe the heavy in the Laurel comedies, the Fates looked down and said, "Enough, already!" L&H were predestined to be partners, and that was that.

At 19 pages, Stan's script was fairly detailed for a two-reeler, so there wasn't much room for improvisation (the later scripts generally ran three to five pages). But not all the gags in Stan's script were included in the film.

Stan's projected gag for the opening shows the hoboes enjoying a lavish breakfast in bed at a ritzy hotel. Just as Ollie is about to dig in, Stan suggests that he take a shower before eating, and Ollie agrees. As the water splashes over his robust physique, Mr. Hardy wakes up. He and Stan have been sleeping on a park bench, and now they're being drenched by a lawn sprinkler. Ollie turns to Stan and mutters, "Why didn't you let me eat my breakfast before I took my shower?" (Guiol filmed the "rude awakening," but the dream sequence was never shot.)

Another deleted gag: the hoboes' hunger is compounded when they see a little boy throw a loaf of bread into a lake, whereupon hungry fish attack the loaf from all directions and devour it immediately.

The most interesting thing about *Duck Soup* (which someone, probably Beanie Walker, decided was a more appetizing title than *Home From the Honeymoon*) is that Laurel and Hardy are instantly recognizable as the characters we know and love, and they appear as a team all through the picture. This debunks the usual story proffered by historians, scholars and Laurel himself — the story being that L&H started out with bit parts in some pictures, gradually got more scenes together and eventually became a team.

Between 1927 and 1974, *Duck Soup* was seen by virtually no one; by the early '60s it was considered a lost film. Film scholars theorized that it showed Laurel and Hardy together only briefly, or perhaps not at all. But in 1974 a 35mm print (with French and Dutch titles) was discovered in a European archive.

What *Duck Soup* reveals is that, in effect, L&H started out as a team, and then reverted back to just being two comics in the same film. There are rough edges (and most of them are on Hardy's unseemly unshaven chin) but the "Stan and Ollie" characters are there already, in all their glory.

Ollie — who wears a battered top hat instead of a battered derby — is pompous, domineering, Stan's "master." Stan is already the trusting innocent, clinging to Ollie, who will guide him through that cold, harsh, cynical world out there. (Stan is so trusting that it never occurs to him that he is usually a bit brighter than Ollie.)

During the film's production, the special chemistry between Laurel and Hardy was noticed by a few perceptive people at the Roach lot. Richard Currier, the head of the film editing department at Roach, recalled the first time he noticed the comic telepathy between Stan and Babe: "F. Richard Jones — Dick — was a supervisor at Roach's. He used to look at everything with me. I'd just call him up and tell him I was gonna look at so-and-so, and would he like to see it. Laurel had had trouble with Universal — I don't know what the hell kind of trouble it was, but anyway they had him under contract, and he couldn't make pictures for anybody but Universal until the end of the contract.

[Joe Rock shot his Stan Laurel comedies at the Universal lot.]

"So, he left Universal and came over to Roach's, and Hal put him on as a story man. And he worked as a story man for a few months — never in a picture, just writing gags and one thing or another. I remember looking at some film with Dick Jones one day, and Hardy was in the picture we were looking at. And I said, 'Dick, you know something? Laurel can work in pictures now.' I said, 'How about taking this guy, Hardy, and letting him be the foil for Laurel?' He said, 'You know something, I was thinking the same thing.' Well, the first one was a belly laugh from start to finish. So they just kept on going."

The publicity department was also starting to think of Laurel and Hardy as a team, as shown in this news item:

LAUREL AND HARDY TEAM UP IN FILM

As two perfect gentlemen who merely have been unfortunate enough to lose their wardrobe and razors, Stan Laurel and Oliver Hardy, Hal Roach contract comedians, have the best characterizations of their career in the latest Roach star comedy. Madelaine Hurlock provides the beauty to offset their tramp appearance. William Austin and William Courtwright have important roles and Fred Guiol is directing.

The Roach Star comedy series may be placed on an alternating unit system, in order to supply the number of short feature comedies, with good casts, demanded by exhibitors after the past year's reception accorded the series.

So, the idea of a Laurel and Hardy team was now a twinkle in the eyes of several Roach studio employees — with the probable exception of Syd Crossley.

The question is, if Laurel and Hardy already had their characters and their rapport with each other established in this film, how come it all unraveled? It would take several more films before L&H would reweave the seamless partnership they'd displayed in *Duck Soup*.

And the Fates looked down and said, "Damn!"

SLIPPING WIVES

Production history: Script finished October 18, 1926. Filmed circa October 1926. Copyrighted January 17, 1927 by Pathé (LU 23555). Released April 3. Two reels.

Produced by Hal Roach. Supervised by F. Richard Jones. Directed by Fred L. Guiol. Photographed by George Stevens. Edited by Richard Currier. Titles by H.M. Walker. Story by Hal Roach.

With Priscilla Dean, Herbert Rawlinson, Albert Conti.

A delivery man (Laurel) is hired by a woman to make her husband jealous. The husband is an artist who's so wrapped up in his work he neglects his spouse. A male friend of the wife suggests she hire someone to romance her, and thus arouse the ire — and the libido — of her husband. Stan gets the job; unfortunately he thinks the friend is the husband and the husband is the friend. Hardy is a butler to the artist and his wife.

October 1926 brought the gentle winds of fall to the Roach studio. Rumors that Roach was going to sever his distribution arrangement with the faltering Pathé company and instead release his films through Metro-Goldwyn-Mayer were wafting in the breeze.

Before the month was over, director Fred Guiol steered his sturdy "All-Stars" actors through another two-reeler. The cast consisted of Priscilla Dean and Herbert Rawlinson (former Big Names confirming their loss of popularity by appearing in two-reel comedies), Albert Conti (a discovery of Stroheim's) and hard-working comics Stan Laurel and Oliver Hardy. They had the help of cameraman George Stevens and the not inconsiderable assistance of Hal Roach — who had, after all, suggested the plot in the first place.

Slipping Wives was another entry in a seemingly endless procession of Roach comedies about jealous wives, angry husbands, unwitting gigolos, larcenous gold-diggers and the like. The relaxed state of modern mores has taken a lot of the shock value out of these comedies, so today's audiences are more likely to be bored by them than titilated.

The Laurel and Hardy relationship so painstakingly woven in *Duck Soup* is all but torn asunder in this picture. As Jarvis the butler, Hardy takes an instant dislike to Laurel, and spends most of his time devising ways to kill him. Their scenes together are few and brief.

The highlight of the film arrives when the artist's wife introduces her inattentive husband to Stan, explaining that he's Lionel Ironsides, famous writer of sea stories. Stan launches into a thrilling depiction of his latest epic, "Samson and Delilah." His extended pantomime of the whole hairy story provides the most amusing moments of the picture.

The craft of writing scripts for films which are purely pantomime is a lost art. Here's a brief excerpt from the Samson and Delilah routine:

Stan takes up the position again of Samson asleep. He than pantomimes Samson's awakening. He sees the imaginary hair on the floor — gives it a double takem — feels his head — gets over that his hair is gone — staggers to his feet — tries to walk but his knees wobble under him. He gets over that all his strength is gone and finally falls to the floor. He gets over his despair with intense dramatic emotion. He jumps to his feet out of character and speaks another title:

— THEN CAME TWENTY THOUSAND PHILADELPHIANS —

Stan makes a quick exit. He then runs in and out several times — waving his arms — shouting and gesturing others to follow — getting over the idea of a crowd of men....

NOTE....MAKE CLOSE UPS AND WHATEVER SHOTS MAY BE

NECESSARY OF HUSBAND, WIFE AND FRIEND WATCHING STAN WITH DEAD PANS AND WHATEVER EXPRESSIONS MAY BE NECESSARY TO HELP THIS SEQUENCE.

They don't write scripts with directions like *that* any more.

A few of the true L&H characteristics shine through in *Slipping Wives*, but not enough. Hardy is meticulous and self-important while Laurel is appropriately dumb. (He's still the old excitable, ready-for-a-fight Stan of the solo films, though.) The problem is that instead of being united together, they're working against each other — "bitter enemies," in the words of the script.

It was going to take a lot of work for everybody to get back to the right direction shown so clearly by *Duck Soup*. The next film didn't help matters any.

LOVE 'EM AND WEEP

Production history: Written and filmed circa January 1927. Copyrighted April 11, 1927 by Pathé (LU 23846). Released June 12. Two reels.

Produced by Hal Roach. Directed by Fred Guiol. Titles by H.M. Walker. Story by Hal Roach.

With Mae Busch, James Finlayson, Charlotte Mineau, Vivien Oakland, Charlie Hall.

Prominent businessman Titus Tillsbury (Finlayson) has his prestige in the community threatened by an old flame (Busch), who threatens to expose him as a two-timing womanizer; Mae has evidence of Tillsbury's purple past, a picture of them together in bathing suits. Since Tillsbury is giving a dinner party for other pillars of the community, he dispatches his aide (Stan) to keep her at bay until Tillsbury can make a settlement. Mae, however, storms over to Tillsbury's home, and causes a ruckus.

Hal Roach contributed the basic story for this domestic farce; Walker, Guiol, Laurel and the gag men helped turn it into a 12-page script entitled *Better Husbands Week*. The script deviates only in the final gag, a bizarre bit of business involving Finlayson's butler. The gag men tried to use this idea again when Stan and Babe remade the story as *Chickens Come Home* in 1931. (The gag, which wasn't used in either film, is detailed in the latter chapter.)

This picture is a showcase for Australian-born actress Mae Busch, who had appeared in a number of prestigious dramatic features before disagreements with MGM executives — and a nervous breakdown — sent her career into a tailspin in 1926. Although she had slipped from stardom, her work in this picture clearly proves her talent had not deserted her. Mae's vivacious personality dominates the film, and she holds her own against the strident mugging of her co-stars.

Two of these co-stars, like Busch, appeared here for the first time with Stan and Babe. James Finlayson (who called himself Jimmy, was known around the lot as Jim and is usually referred to today as "Fin") was a bald, mustachioed Scot who'd worked for Mack Sennett; as with most of Sennett's comics, his mustache was a prop.

Finlayson's special niche was the funny reaction; within this limited realm, he was a great original. He had several variations on his most distinctive "takem" — an outrageous reaction he called the "double-take and fade away." (In the 1929 *Men O'War*, Finlayson does about a dozen reactions in the same sequence, each of them different from its predecessor.) The script writers often referred to another of Jimmy's takes as "giving it the one-eye": when something has provoked his wrath, Finlayson squints with his right eye, while his left widens in an expression of surprise and disgust, and the eyebrow climbs toward his forehead.

The bit part of Finlayson's butler is essayed here by Charlie Hall, a diminutive British actor whose portrayals often belied the notion that good things come in small packages. While he's relatively benign in his first L&H picture, over the next 13 years he would rank among the nastiest of their nemeses — most of whom were far brawnier than he. ("We always called him the Little Menace," Hal Roach once observed.)

Speaking of bit parts, they don't get much bitter than the tiny role Babe Hardy plays in this movie. As Judge Chigger, his facial expressions are hidden under a bushy mustache and sideburns; he has little to do but express hilarity or dismay at the events surrounding him. (Hardy's role was originally scripted as "Chief of Police"; the role of Stan's wife, played in the film by Vivien Oakland, was slated for Gertrude Astor.)

Stan was given second billing in the original credits, with Babe listed fourth in the cast. Laurel's character, Romaine Ricketts, has surface resemblances to the mature "Stanley" persona; he's naive, an easy pushover for worldly-wise, gold-digging Mae, and he cries at the slightest provocation. But he does everything at the frantic pace established by director Fred Guiol; he acts too fast to be thinking that slowly.

Love 'em and Weep is a slick, frenetic comedy about cynical dames and brainless men. When Laurel and Hardy remade it four years later (with Hardy taking over as the businessman and Finlayson replacing Hall as the butler), they transformed it by the force of their unique personalities into a much more subtle film, based not on gags but on characters. Those characters are nowhere to be found in *Love 'em and Weep*.

WHY GIRLS LOVE SAILORS

Production history: Written and filmed February 1927. Copyrighted May 18, 1927 by Pathé (LU 23978). Released July 17. Two reels.

Produced by Hal Roach. Directed by Fred L. Guiol. Titles by H.M. Walker. Story by Hal Roach.

With Malcolm Waite, Viola Richard, Anita Garvin.

Stan is a rather bashful and brainless young sailor. His fiancée (Richard) is kidnapped by an old flame, a tough sea captain (Waite). Since Stan will be turned into flotsam if he tries to fight the burly captain, he hits upon the idea of disguising himself as a flapper girl. The captain is immediately taken with this young lovely — until his jealous wife (Garvin) arrives, and proves she can easily outmuscle her philandering hubby. During the fracas, Stan finds his sweetheart and they make a hasty exit.

Stan in early 1927, about to gain a teammate — and immortality.

Second Mate Oliver Hardy, in a reflective mood for *Why Girls Love Sailors*.

This film has been unseen in the United States for decades. French film critic Roland Lacourbe, who saw the only known print at the Cinematheque Française in 1971, has been the only person to offer a critique of it since the '20s. Lacourbe's verdict: "Le film est mediocre."

Thanks to the endless red tape engulfing the Cinematheque's collection, the film remained unseen until 1986. A California-based L&H fan and a devotee from Copenhagen independently obtained two copies — with French titles — thanks to a French fan who made a video transfer from the Cinematheque's 16mm print.

The most noteworthy aspect of this movie is that Malcolm Waite plays the heavy — not Hardy, as has been presumed. Babe has little to do in his role as the Second Mate, but he makes the most of his limited opportunities. Another surprise is the appearance of Anita Garvin, in her first film with Laurel and Hardy. Her presence in this movie was unknown until its recent rediscovery — although she dominates the last five minutes of the picture. Wearing a blonde wig and a heart-stopping sneer, she proves her mastery as a comic actress in this debut.

Anita first worked at the Roach lot in March 1926, nearly a year before this picture was made. "When Stan went to Roach, he tried to get Roach to call me. Nothing happened. Later I was hired for a picture with Mabel Normand... I was walking on the lot, and I saw Stan, walking with Mr. Roach.

"Stan gave me a big 'Hello, Anita!,' and he threw me in the air. He turned to Hal Roach and he said, 'This is the girl I've been *telling* you about!' And Roach looked at him, and he said, 'Well, why didn't you *tell* me?' It was so silly I had to laugh. And then I thought, 'Oh, he might think I'm laughing at him!' I was scared to death of the man."

If Anita Garvin had a certain timidity in the presence of Hal Roach, she could display a steely determination when playing opposite Laurel and Hardy. Her striking aquiline features, crowned by jet black hair smoothed straight back with vaseline, made her an imposing presence indeed. As a comic actress, she was never less than superb. Her command of timing and mastery of subtle gestures rivaled those of Babe Hardy.

Her performance in *Why Girls Love Sailors* is a highlight of a film which doesn't have many. There is a cute early scene where Stan bashfully proposes to his sweetie — and confirms their engagement by giving her a necklace made of gum wrappers. He then bounds onto the girl's bed, coyly and gleefully entangling himself in the bedspread. All of this is seen by the burly captain, who barges in and asks Viola, "Who is this herring?"

Miss Richard explains that her new fiancee is a mighty sailor, and asks Stan to show the captain his boat. Stan pulls down the front of his sweater to reveal a battleship tattooed on his chest. The captain tests its seaworthiness by pouring a pitcher of water down Stan's sweater.

Babe has a few brief scenes spotted throughout the film; in most of them, he struts around as though he's the man in charge, until he runs afoul of the captain. Stan and Babe have one scene together in the middle of the picture: Dressed as a blonde flapper, Stan has to get past Hardy before he can reach the captain's quarters, where his sweetheart Viola is trapped. Stan flirts outrageously with Babe, and promises to give him a great big kiss. Babe closes his eyes and puckers his lips — and Stan runs off.

Just then, Anita, the captain's wife, clambers over the side of the boat.

Babe, seeing her, thinks she's Stan, and tickles her leg. Anita responds by giving Hardy a mighty wallop.

In later years, Babe Hardy recalled that *Why Girls Love Sailors* contained the first use of his characteristic "tie-twiddle" and slow burn while looking into the camera. The scene which Hardy described is actually in a comedy made a few months later, *Sailors, Beware!* While he has no opportunity to coyly wave his tie here — mainly because he isn't wearing one — he does glance expressively into the camera quite often.

Much more interesting than *Why Girls Love Sailors* is an early, tentative script for the film, which was preserved among the papers of director Fred Guiol. At 21 pages, there's enough material here for a feature. Curiously, the story has little resemblance to the plot eventually used.

Originally, Stan and Ollie — playing a dumb young gob and Petty Officer Leggit — were supposed to be inseparable companions. Anna May Wong, one of those "fading stars" frequently employed by Roach, was slated to play Delamar, Stan's exotic heartthrob; Sojin, a Japanese actor who appeared prominently in several '20s features, was to portray an evil "money lender."

The original story has Sojin forcing Delamar's impoverished father to promise her hand in marriage to the evil financier. Delamar, however, is in love with Stan, and when Sojin learns about this, he sends his henchman to hold Stan prisoner until after the marriage has been performed.

While this sounds like a melodramatic plot, the script is enlivened by several amusing gags. Stan gets most of the material, but a few embryonic L&H bits highlight the middle of the script.

One gag has the boys at a Chinese restaurant. Ollie is starving, but Stan just wants a pot of tea. A waiter brings two menus; the boys can't read them, so Stan just points to a few of the Chinese hieroglyphics, while Ollie indicates with a sweep of his hand that he wants a whole section of the menu.

When the waiter brings the order, the boys discover that Stan has requested a huge feast, while all Ollie receives is a pot of tea. Ollie then pantomimes that he wants a hot dog — he barks and puts a match to his own foot. The Chinese waiter seems to understand; he grins wickedly, grabs a canine and heads for the kitchen. Stan and Ollie trade uneasy glances and scurry out.

Another gag occurs as the boys enter a general store. Ollie takes off his shoes before entering, in accordance with Chinese customs. Stan, however, just tramps right in. The proprietor throws Stan out. Ollie explains to Stan that he must observe these traditions. Later, the boys pass a jujitsu arena and spy a wrestler who, according to the script, "is naked except for a little coolie coat." Stan wants to make a proud and dignified entrance; he observes what he thinks is the custom and takes off his trousers, marching in barelegged to the horror of the spectators. Ollie hastily covers Stan and shoves him outside.

Laurel and Hardy have more of their usual characteristics in this unfilmed story than in some of the later shorts which actually were produced. This script may have been scrapped because several sequences required large exotic sets, a battleship and hundreds of extras. (The finale has Stan chasing Sojin around his palace and employing all sorts of Fairbanksian acrobatics, while Ollie and a huge squadron of Marines batter down the palace gates.)

Although it's by no means a classic, *Why Girls Love Sailors* is certainly worthy of rediscovery. It's a special joy to watch a newly-found' Laurel and Hardy movie, even if le film est mediocre.

WITH LOVE AND HISSES

Production history: Outline and final script written and filmed circa March 1927. Copyrighted May 18, 1927 by Pathé (LU 23978). Released August 28. Two reels.

Produced by Hal Roach. Directed by Fred L. Guiol. Titles by H.M. Walker. Story by Hal Roach.

With James Finlayson, Frank Brownlee, Chet Brandenberg, Anita Garvin, Eve Southern.

The first of the Laurel and Hardy army comedies: Stan is a dim-witted and somewhat effeminate buck private; Ollie is an ill-tempered sergeant. Hardy and Finlayson (as an equally ill-tempered captain) join in the attack on Laurel — giving him orders, watching in exasperation as he fouls up and then yelling at him. Both get into trouble as a result of following Stan's suggestions.

By March 1927, Roach and his gag writers were starting to notice that Stan Laurel and Babe Hardy worked well together. But nobody realized that if L&H were going to be a viable team, they'd have to have characters with a common bond, characters that worked with each other as friends instead of adversaries. Such is the wisdom provided by hindsight.

With Love and Hisses is yet another film that pits Stan against Ollie, thus affording them precious little opportunity to do anything funny together. Here Ollie is part of "the rest of the world"; subsequently, he would join Stan as part of the misfit squad. In later pictures, he would defend Stan against Finlayson's vitriol, but here he just joins in the attack.

The individual gags aren't much help, either. There's a crude and grimy atmosphere to them — maybe "aroma" would be a better word, since several bits of business depend on things like garlic, body odor and skunks for their pungency.

The original script had another fragrant gag wherein Finlayson walks down the aisle of the soldiers' sleeping car, and the aroma of their protruding feet makes him faint. Finlayson recovers two days later. This is followed by another questionable bit of business in which Stan is pacing very nervously in front of a small building at the army camp which appears to be an outhouse; finally his need to enter is so great that he pounds with tremendous force on the door. A quartermaster opens it, revealing that it's just a supply room; Stan merely wants to return a mop and bucket. Neither of these gags appears in the film.

The film's final gag has the earmarks of something written by gagman Carl Harbaugh, whose justification for outlandish and improbable gags was, "The prop got there because the goddamned prop man *put* it there!" Character motivation and logical plot development were not things which kept Mr. Harbaugh up late at night.

Here, a typical Harbaugh gag arises when the soldiers tire after marching miles from their camp. They find a lake and decide to indulge in a bit of skinny-dipping. Thanks to Private Laurel's carelessness and Sergeant Hardy's cigarette, the soldiers' uniforms are reduced to ashes. The troops have to get back to camp without exposing more than their stupidity. Fortunately, the god-

Eve Southern and Anita Garvin are both Captain James Finlayson's girls — but Sergeant Hardy hasn't found out yet.

damned prop man has put a billboard advertising Cecil B. De Mille's movie *The Volga Boatmen* smack in the middle of nowhere. The clever soldiers cut out the faces of the Russians pictured in the billboard, insert their own mugs through the artwork, and sashay back to camp, billboard and all.

Among the buck privates in *With Love and Hisses* was a 19-year-old Detroit native named Frank Saputo. In a 1974 interview, he recalled his experiences working as an extra at the Roach studio, for $7.50 a day.

"Most of the time we were on location; we went to wardrobe and put on our uniforms, then they took us in buses out on location.

"Jimmy Finlayson played a captain — I thought he was fantastically funny," said Saputo. "This whole uniform he wore was tailor made, and I envied it because even the officers in the National Guard didn't have a uniform that was as well cut. He also wore the high polished cavalry boots. And on Jimmy it was lost. When he walked, he walked with his feet out, almost like Chaplin. And they'd tell him, 'Keep your feet straight. Walk in a military fashion.' Those boots were too tight for Finlayson, and all he did was complain about them.

"He had that Scotch brogue, and he'd say, 'Why couldn't they make bloody boots that would fit me?' In between takes, he would take off his boots and just sit there and puff; the director [Fred Guiol] told him, 'You know, these boots are worth $50.' And Finlayson said, 'They're not worth 50 *cents* if you ask me!'

"I think we shot these military scenes near Griffith Park," recalled Saputo. "Finlayson came in for inspection, and Babe was the sergeant taking notes.

When they did this bit of inspection, Jimmy tried to take the gun away from Stan. And finally when Finlayson did get it away from him, he'd throw it back to Stan. The director said, 'Cut. Now let's do it again.' He'd call Finlayson aside while we were waiting for a take, and he'd say, 'I want you to cuss at him, get mad at him, and when you take the gun, *throw* it at Stan. Get at him until he gets so hot at you that he wants to kill you!' And Finlayson said, 'He bloody well *might* kill me!'

"So they did the scene two or three times — Finlayson would throw the gun, and Stan would grab it. Finally, Finlayson couldn't think of anything else to say, so he said, 'You, you, you — cockwalloper!' It was so funny that the cast just broke up. The director just leaned back in his folding chair and fell right back on it, just laughing.

"The director was one of the instigators of practical jokes on Stan. Jimmy Finlayson took delight also in getting him frustrated—and it would make the scene work better. Stan had a Star Coupe, made by the Durant Company. He was very proud of it. He also had a St. Bernard named Lady, and he kept the dog in his Coupe; he'd come over and give her some water in between takes.

"And one time they took the distributor cap off of Stan Laurel's car. He was so proud of this car, and the car wouldn't start. He got so frustrated, and Lady stood there barking because she wanted to eat. Stan said, 'Quiet, Lady! Quiet! I'm trying to get this bloody thing started!' And Jimmy Finlayson was laughing like hell because he had the distributor cap in his pocket. Finally he gave it to Stan. He was so mad he threatened not to work that afternoon. Finally, they promised to buy his lunch. They were always playing some kind of a practical joke on Stan," said Saputo.

With Love and Hisses was released by Pathé on August 28, 1927, to the accompaniment of moans from disappointed filmgoers and reviewers. Typical of the reaction was this review by Raymond Ganly: "When three extra good comedians like Stan Laurel, Jimmy Finlayson and Oliver Hardy are in a cast you naturally look for a higher grade of comedy than is to be found in this opus of the training camp. This trio is competent enough to put any gag over with plenty of gust, but the humor here fails to click because gag material is too weak."

With Love and Hisses isn't a bad film; it simply lacks the charm and extra dimension that would later be provided when L&H had fully developed their characters. The film marches along serviceably, but nobody's too disappointed when the two reels are up and the bugler sounds "Taps."

SAILORS, BEWARE!

Production history: Written and filmed circa April 1927. Copyrighted June 9, 1927 by Pathé (LU 24060). Released September 25. Two reels.

Produced by Hal Roach. Directed by Hal Yates. Titles by H.M. Walker. Story by Hal Roach.

With Anita Garvin, Frank Brownlee, Lupe Velez, Harry Earles.

Stan is a cab driver whose passengers — unbeknownst to him — are a lady jewel thief and her midget husband. Through one of those chain reactions that

Purser Cryder (Ollie) welcomes Madame Ritz and her "son" (Anita Garvin and
Harry Earles).

*happen only in silent comedies, they end up on a ship out at sea. Ollie is the
ship's purser, whose only interest in life is flirting with female passengers.*

Laurel and Hardy weren't much closer to becoming a team in April 1927
than they'd been since *Duck Soup.* True, their roles in the All-Stars films were
becoming more prominent, but they still had very little to do together. People
around the lot were starting to notice the rapport between L&H, but the gag
men weren't yet thinking of them as a team when it came to writing the stories.

Hal Roach, who wrote the story for *Sailors, Beware!,* also directed the film
— except for one day's worth of retakes which were directed by Hal Yates, who
got credit for the whole thing. This picture shows that Roach may have been
awakening to Stan and Babe's potential as a team. Laurel and Hardy have very
few scenes together in this picture, but these seem to have been included only
because someone — Roach, or possibly Leo McCarey — noticed that the two
comics worked well together.

There is a big difference between the Stan of *Sailors, Beware!* and the Stan
of the mature L&H films, as illustrated by a scene where he climbs out of his
cab — after being shanghaied out to sea — and demands to be put back on
land. The later Stan would placidly accept his new surroundings and figure out
how to adapt; *this* one marches over to the ship's captain and gives him a
harangue that would scorch our ears if this were a talkie.

A memorable moment comes when Babe is splashed with a bucket of
water. He waves his fingers in embarrassment, and casts a glance into the
camera. Although Hardy recalled this as his first "camera look," he had been
looking into the camera for years before this; there are some very funny

camera looks in *Stick Around*, a 1925 Arrow comedy starring Hardy and Bobby Ray. But *Sailors, Beware!* was the film that made Babe realize what a powerful tool the camera look could be.

Lupe Velez, a new contract player at the Roach studio, had little to do but display her hauteur and get thrown into a pool. Still, her presence did not go unnoticed. "Crazy Lupe!" said Anita Garvin. "She was a little, wild Mexican — with her little chihuahua. They'd get the chihuahua and hide the poor thing in the cameraman's sack that was on the tripod. And she'd go storming all over the place — 'Where's my ba-bee, my chi-wa-wa?'

"You know, in those days, I was very, very thin. And Lupe was tiny. And she says, 'A-nee-ta! You are so nice and *fot*! I am so skinny!' I may be a little *fot* now, but not then!"

Sailors, Beware! is an enjoyable film, but a frustrating one — it would have been much better if only L&H had been given more to do *together*. But the film made more people aware of Stan and Babe's possibilities as a team. Anita Garvin recalls, "*Sailors, Beware!* wasn't planned as a Laurel and Hardy picture; that was when they were just starting. I even remarked to Stan how well they worked together as a team. It was after this that they became 'Laurel and Hardy.' But this was the first inkling they had of pairing them; it just happened."

Better things were to come.

DO DETECTIVES THINK?

Production history: Written and filmed circa May 1927. Copyrighted July 8, 1927 by Pathé (LU 24157). Released November 20. Two reels.

Produced by Hal Roach. Directed by Fred L. Guiol. Titles by H.M. Walker. Story by Hal Roach.

With James Finlayson, Viola Richard, Noah Young, Frank Brownlee, Will Stanton.

Judge Foozle (Finlayson) has sentenced the Tipton Slasher (Young) to death for murdering two Chinamen. The Slasher vows revenge. The judge calls a detective agency and asks for their two best men — instead he gets Ferdinand Finkleberry (Stan) and Sherlock Pinkham (Ollie). The boys fail to recognize the Slasher when he arrives at the judge's home, posing as the new butler; despite their best efforts, they succeed in capturing the criminal.

In *Do Detectives Think?* Laurel and Hardy — at long last — are no longer two comics with conflicting styles. They're no longer cast as enemies. Nor are they doomed to spend most of the film in solo scenes, kept from joining each other by the borders of the frame. *Do Detectives Think?* is the first Laurel and Hardy movie since *Duck Soup* that looks like a Laurel and Hardy movie.

First of all, this film marks the debut of the rumpled-but-dignified suits which became the boys' standard outfits. Stan is wearing the bowtie which obeys only its own unique centrifugal force, so that it's continually tilted; and Ollie wears his four-in-hand tie, although he isn't yet too proficient at twiddling it. Because they're cast as detectives, they both wear the regulation detectives' derby, which turns out to be just the right headgear for these innocent-but-dignified characters. (Stan would later wear an Irish children's derby, with its

Two timid detectives... and their quarry (Noah Young).

tall crown and flat brim; here, in a standard silk derby, he looks a trifle too dapper.)

Some refinements need to be made in their appearance: Stan's hair still has a patent-leather shine; this flawless grooming is a flaw in itself. And Ollie's mustache needs to be trimmed down to the foolish bit of fluff that usually adorns his cherubic face. Here, he looks as though he's been eating a melted candy bar and half of it is still on his upper lip — which may well be the case.

The characters inside these costumes seem a lot more familiar. They may not be "Stan and Ollie," but they're blood relatives. Stan still has moments when he runs around like a jackrabbit, but the aggressiveness he used to display all too frequently has vanished; he's closer to the slow-witted, slow-moving Stan we love. And when he cries, we feel that it's really an expression of his personality, and no longer just a quick way to get a laugh.

The boys' relationship is fairly well defined here, too. Ollie clearly sees himself as the leader, and feels fully justified in delegating most of the dirty work to Stan; Stan is quite content to be the follower, and seems to admire Ollie for his ambition. (One senses that Stan would stay put, happy enough just to exist, if it weren't for Ollie's ambition. In the Laurel and Hardy partnership, Ollie has the drive, but neither of them has the brains.) There is a glimmering of something deeper; at one point, faced with a dangerous task, Stan holds onto Ollie's hand for reassurance, and there's no special attention called to it — it's the natural expression of two little boys lost in a grown-up world. And a nasty world it is.

There were a number of highly inventive gags in the script which never made it into the film. To wit:

The script proposes an opening scene in the outer office of the Hitchcock and Scratchit Private Detective Agency. Ollie is reading the *Police Gazette* when in walks Stan, severely mussed. Ollie asks if Stan got his man, and Stan describes in pantomime how he captured his quarry. He draws his gun, recounting how he told the criminal to stick 'em up — and then his gun gives an instant replay, knocking Ollie's derby off, and cutting the Chief's cigar neatly in half. (The Chief, naturally, has chosen just this moment to walk into the room.)

Another scripted gag that sounds like pure, unadulterated L&H was excluded from this film, but similar routines would crop up in later releases: at night, the boys are in bed, evidently feeling that the judge is well protected. Ollie, trying to read a newspaper, is continually annoyed by Stan, who is eating crackers. The boys notice a picture of the escaped Slasher in the paper and realize that he's the "butler"; they get up to put their pants on, and spend half the night getting their legs and trousers entangled.

Among the stuff that *did* get into the film is a bit that crops up in film after film: The Never-Ending Hat Routine. Through some happenstance, both boys have lost their derbies. Stan picks them up, and hands the wrong one to Ollie, who puts it on his head and looks ridiculous; Ollie angrily hands the hat back to Stan, who unthinkingly hands Ollie the wrong hat again. If the routine got to be old hat after a while, it never failed to work.

Inasmuch as this film belongs to Jimmy Finlayson almost as much as it does to Laurel and Hardy, it's interesting that he wasn't the original choice for the role of Judge Foozle. The script suggests a "type like Forrest Stanley," but evidently someone couldn't see the Forrest for the judge. Syd Crossley, who didn't play the Oliver Hardy role in *Duck Soup*, was slated to play the *real* butler in *Do Detectives Think?* but lost out on that role as well. He seems to have made a career out of not appearing in L&H comedies.

Do Detectives Think? features a bravura performance by Noah Young, an actor who knew no style *but* bravura. He'd been working at the Roach lot practically since its start, and figured prominently (at his size, he could hardly do otherwise) in Harold Lloyd comedies of the World War I era. Hal Roach recalled that when the war was declared in April 1917, Young tried to enlist. "Noah Young was the champion weightlifter of California, the strongest man I ever knew," Roach said. "But the board turned him down because he didn't have enough teeth."

Although it was shot in May 1927, *Do Detectives Think?* sat on the shelf for several months before Pathé finally released it on November 20. During the fall of 1927, the Laurel and Hardy films were beginning to attract notice, but by that time Roach had ended his contract with Pathé and had begun producing films for MGM. The Pathé Exchange, left with only a handful of films starring this hot new property, released them slowly in order to get the most exposure out of each film.

FLYING ELEPHANTS

Production history: Written and filmed circa mid-May 1927. Copyrighted September 2, 1927 by Pathé (LU 24347). Released February 12, 1928. Two reels.

Produced by Hal Roach. Directed by Frank Butler. Titles by H.M. Walker. Story by Hal Roach.

With James Finlayson, Viola Richard, Dorothy Coburn.

When the king of the cave people decrees that all men under his jurisdiction must marry, almost all the males are successful in finding mates — all except two. Ollie is Mighty Giant, who is given to boasting about his romantic prowess; Stan is the effeminate Twinkle Star. The two bachelor neanderthals "choose up sides" for the hand of a pretty cave girl, using a club as though it were a Louisville Slugger. Stan loses, but wins her hand when a goat butts Ollie over the edge of a cliff.

After looking at *Do Detectives Think?* one would think that Laurel and Hardy had finally found their niche. But every true L&H fan knows that for each step forward, the boys take three steps back. And here that rule applies to their career. In *Flying Elephants*, Laurel and Hardy spend 90% of the film doing solo turns, and when they finally do meet up, they try to kill each other. They appear to be as much of a team as Popeye and Bluto.

In May 1927, Stan and Babe, along with Hal Roach and a group of studio colleagues, trouped out to Moapa, Nevada, about 60 miles northeast of Las Vegas — which, in 1927, meant about 60 miles northeast of nowhere.

Roach had written a Stone-Age story for his All-Stars, and decided to make one of his infrequent appearances in the director's chair. Although the credited director is Frank Butler, Roach asserted that Butler only directed one day's worth of retakes.

Moapa was an appropriately desolate background for this caveman comedy which, unfortunately, is primitive in every sense. The seamless teamwork which L&H displayed in *Do Detectives Think?* has vanished with the Moapa winds.

All one can do is assess their work as individual comics. Hardy shows much more depth and finesse than he did in the preceding film. One senses that he has finally found his own unique comic identity — he knows all about this character who's alternately polite or pompous, but always naive. The shy smile, the dainty gestures, the elegant way he carries himself — everything is there.

Stan, on the other hand, plays a character far removed from the familiar Stanley persona. As Little Twinkle Star he flits around the hills with all the effeminancy he displayed in *With Love and Hisses*.

During its production, the film boasted the titles of *Were Women Always Wild?* and *Do Cavemen Marry?* But its lasting moniker was inspired by a gag in which Hardy, chatting with a girl, remarks that the elephants are flying south for the winter — and through the miracle of animated cartoons, we see them doing just that.

The animation was done by Roy Seawright, who had started working at the Roach lot in 1920 as an office boy. (Roach took young Seawright under his wing when Roy's father was killed while working on construction of the studio in 1919.)

Roy had just taken over the Roach cartoon department when *Flying Elephants* was made. In fact, he *was* the Roach cartoon department. Seawright had been working as a prop man, but the studio's general manager, Warren Doane, knew that Roy had been an art major at Manual Arts High School. He put Seawright's talent to use, temporarily, when the staff animator proved to be more fond of the bottle than his work.

One day, Hal Roach was showing some important Pathé executives around the studio. As he was about to escort them into the animation

These costumes were redesigned before the film became airborne.

department office, he paused outside the door and said, "All of the magic tricks in motion pictures happen in this little room. We call it our Den of Mystery." But the only mystery the group encountered was a drunken cartoonist sleeping on his animation table. Under that table were several barrels of wine, the product of Roach's Culver City ranch.

Doane replaced this animator with another who, it turned out, could drink the first one under the table any time. Since Seawright had the evidently rare combination of talent and sobriety, Doane chose the youthful artist to be the new staff animator. Eventually, Roy Seawright became one of the best special effects men in the business, devising the amazing optical work for Roach's *Topper* and *One Million B.C.* While he later dismissed his cartooning for *Flying Elephants* as "very poor, very amateurish," it is well done nonetheless, and is one of the most inventive gags in the picture.

Flying Elephants was the last L&H comedy to be distributed by the Pathé Exchange. Pathé's management was rapidly ruining the company with a number of inept decisions. One which hurt Roach in particular was that Pathé was also distributing Mack Sennett's comedies, and since the theaters could only afford to rent a certain number of shorts from a given distributor, Roach and Sennett found themselves in direct competition.

After considering a deal with Paramount, Roach elected to distribute his films through Metro-Goldwyn-Mayer. In April 1929, Roach sued Pathé for $1,866,000 for unfair distribution policies and for failing to make timely accountings of the receipts. Pathé countersued, claiming that Roach owed them $179,445. (The suit was settled out of court in April 1931.)

As was the case with *Do Detectives Think?* Pathé let this film sit on the shelf for months — which worked to the company's benefit since Laurel and Hardy's popularity kept growing. *Flying Elephants* was withheld from release until February 12, 1928, by which time the L&H comedies had so vastly improved that this film looked even more foolish than its makers intended.

SUGAR DADDIES

Production history: Written and filmed circa June 1927. Copyrighted August 17, 1927 by Metro-Goldwyn-Mayer Distributing Corp. (LP 24291). Released September 10. Two reels.

Produced by Hal Roach. Directed by Fred L. Guiol. Photographed by George Stevens. Titles by H.M. Walker.

With James Finlayson, Noah Young, Charlotte Mineau, Edna Marian.

Finlayson is a millionaire businessman who depends on his lawyer (Stan) and his butler (Ollie) to bail him out of romantic entanglements. Fin goes to a party and ends up married, inheriting his wife's gold-digging daughter and murderous brother. He hides out in a beachfront hotel with his butler and his lawyer but is forced to escape. Laurel climbs on Finlayson's back and dons a long cape, posing as Hardy's abnormally tall wife; Fin's newly-acquired kin chase the hapless trio through a boardwalk funhouse.

Hal Roach's negotiations for a distribution agreement with Metro-Goldwyn-Mayer, which began in November 1926, paid off when he finally formed an alliance with the biggest and most prestigious of movie factories in late February 1927.

The arrangement worked out just dandy for all concerned. MGM got some badly needed short subjects for all of its theaters, and Roach got some badly needed theaters for all of his short subjects. Major studios like MGM not only made films, but also owned the distribution exchanges and theaters in which those films were shown. It was hard for a studio *not* to make money when it controlled every facet of the film business. Thus, MGM films — and now Hal Roach films, too — were guaranteed to be shown everywhere, in some of the world's most prestigious movie palaces.

Freed of his obligations to Pathé, Roach began making films for MGM release in June 1927. The Roach studio was still an autonomous unit; there were no money men from MGM arriving in droves at the little Roach lot, breathing down the necks of gag writers. The Lot of Fun kept making comedies in its own unique, unhurried way, with quality the most important consideration. The only difference now was that the Roach films would be distributed and publicized more effectively, and Roach would get more money from his new partners with which to make those films.

The Roach-MGM-Laurel-Hardy alliance lasted for almost a dozen years and produced some of the funniest comedies ever made. A pity that it began with *Sugar Daddies* — which is much the same story as *Love 'em and Weep* and not much funnier.

James Finlayson was still the big star of Roach's All-Stars — but not for long.

While this is a pleasant film, there's little "Laurel and Hardy" comedy in it. If other people at the Roach lot noticed their potential as a team by now, Stan and Babe themselves still seemed blissfully unaware of it. Stan portrays roughly the same character he played in his films of 1918, and he's no funnier here. And he's aggressively stupid, which isn't nearly as endearing as being placidly dumb.

Stan's first encounter with butler Ollie at Finlayson's front door sparks an argument when Stan is anxious to keep his derby on his head, and Ollie is just as eager to yank it off his cranium. Stan then marches over to Finlayson's new brother-in-law and reads him the riot act, and while his energetic pantomime is amusing, one longs for the sublime, slow-paced bungling of the real Stan. Ollie has little to do but express dismay at the rude events going on around him, but he does it amusingly enough.

The film benefits from George Stevens' polished photography, some gorgeous sets and location shooting at the Pike amusement park in Long Beach. The extras in the boardwalk scenes seem to be actual park patrons, as they simply stand and gawk and register no amusement whatsoever; one little boy in overalls keeps following the camera crew as they dolly down the boardwalk. The fun house sequences invite a nostalgic pang for all the creative ways in which people had fun, in the days before they were all seduced into immobility by television.

They obviously weren't a team just yet.

The script for this film was a whopping two pages. Stan was originally cast as Finlayson's butler, with Ollie as his secretary. In the script, Finlayson marries a young tart, and is menaced by her mother and brother; this is given a kinky twist in the film by having Finlayson marry that old harridan of a mother. Kay Deslys and David Butler were slated for the parts of the daughter and brother, roles finally played by Edna Marian and irascible Noah Young.

The script was evidently written in haste — either that or the writers had great faith in the comics' ad-libbing abilities. The amusement park routines aren't detailed at all; they're hardly implied. The script says simply, "Play this routine through the lobby, from where they go through the rounds of concessions, the wife and family following; possibly bring a cop into it. Finally, the menace gets so close they have to duck into a dance hall. Play this routine here for what it is worth, with the menace following them through the dance hall. They come out and finally duck into the fun house, where we play another routine for what it is worth."

The next Laurel and Hardy film would be much sweeter than *Sugar Daddies*.

THE SECOND HUNDRED YEARS

Production history: Script finished June 10, 1927; filmed late June. Copyrighted September 21, 1927 by MGM (LP 24437). Released October 8. Two reels; black and white with tinted sequences.

Produced by Hal Roach. Directed by Fred L. Guiol. Edited by Richard Currier. Titles by H.M. Walker.

With James Finlayson, Tiny Sandford, Ellinor Vanderveer.

Stan and Ollie are two convicts who escape during a lunch break by turning their clothes inside out and posing as painters. To avert the suspicions of a cop, they whitewash everything in sight. They elude the cop by jumping into a passing limosine; the passengers, who happen to be visiting French prison officials, are disrobed and ejected. The tuxedo-clad jailbirds are driven to a banquet in "their" honor; afterward, they adjourn to the prison, where they meet two French inmates who've been arrested for running around in their BVD's.

Duck Soup provided Laurel and Hardy with the basic outlines of their characters. *Do Detectives Think?* gave them their costumes, and a glimmer of the "Stan and Ollie" relationship. Other early films showed them acquiring some of their characteristic traits. But there had been no consistency. They'd make one film in which they were a perfectly united pair, and in the next they'd be torn asunder.

But someone at the Roach studio saw clearly that L&H had great potential — which could only be developed if they were a team in all of their films together. That someone was Leo McCarey.

Leo McCarey was a free-spirited Irishman who had tried his hand at being a lawyer, a miner and a songwriter before becoming an assistant to director Tod Browning at Universal in 1918. Before long, McCarey found work at the Hal Roach studio; he began by writing gags for the *Our Gang* series, and quickly worked his way up.

Roach film editor Richard Currier recalled that McCarey got his big break from the head of the editorial department, title-writer Harley M. "Beanie" Walker. "Walker and McCarey's father were old friends," noted Currier. "Walker used to be a sportswriter under the name of 'Blinky Ben', in the *Examiner*, and Leo McCarey's father was a fight promoter; he had a stadium in Los Angeles. Walker would go down there and write up the fights, so he got acquainted with Mr. McCarey. And I think it was through Beanie that Leo got a job with Roach. At first he was kind of an assistant director, but Walker made him a director."

In April 1924, McCarey began directing a series of shorts with actor Charley Chase. Together they developed a style for Chase which concentrated on characterization and situation, rather than gags. McCarey later recalled, "I received credit as a director but it was really Chase who did most of the directing... he taught me all I know."

Their collaboration lasted until the start of 1927, when McCarey began working on scripts for the All-Star series and directing occasional shorts. The

❧ ❧ PRESS SHEET ❧ ❧

HAL ROACH Presents His ALL STARS in
THE 2ND HUNDRED YEARS
with OLIVER HARDY and STAN LAUREL

The Super-Comedy Arrives

Moving picture comedies have outgrown their infancy, and nobody is crying "Keep Him a Baby Still." The ancient humour dependent on custard pies, and ridiculous costumes now seem hopelessly stupid. It is the high standard set by such worthwhile comedies as "The Second Hundred Years," latest Hal Roach M-G-M offering, now regaling crowds at the _____ theater that has educated the public to the point where the better type of humor is demanded.

In this funfection, Jimmy Finlayson, as a diginfied governor, is largely responsible for the hilarious and hair-raising plot that engulfs the other members of the famous comedy trio, Oliver Hardy and Stan Laurel. Not the least pleasing feature of a notable supporting cast, is a host of beautiful women, who are modishly gowned. Fred Guiol directed.

HAL ROACH

presents

Oliver Hardy, Stan Laurel,
Jimmy Finlayson

Directed by
Fred Guiol

Photographed by
Geo. Stephens

Edited by
Richard Currier

Titled by
H. M. Walker

New starring team uncorks riotous performance in first picture as comedy duo.

STAN LAUREL and OLIVER HARDY
The new Hal Roach Comedy team

RELEASED BY
METRO-GOLDWYN-MAYER
1540 BROADWAY, NEW YORK, N. Y.
Any promotion suggestions or ideas should be sent to
HOWARD DIETZ
1540 Broadway, New York, N. Y.

SYNOPSIS

Stan Laurel and Oliver Hardy are in the penitentiary for a long term. In attempting to tunnel out, they wind up under the floor of the warden's office. In digging they break a water main and flood the jail. A chase starts. They turn their striped suits inside out, and take the place of two painters who have gone to lunch. They paint themselves out the gate, past the guard, who mistakes them for the workmen. A policeman outside becomes suspicious, but they evade him by jumping into a taxi. They forcibly change clothes with the occupants—two French criminal experts — and throw the Frenchmen out the window. The gentlemen are found in the street in their B.V.D.'s and are put in jail in the cell formerly occupied by Stan and Oliver. The jailbirds continue in the taxi to a banquet at the Governor's home, where they are received and entertained as guests of honor. The evening's entertainment consists of a trip through the penitentiary which Stan and Oliver cannot refuse, since criminology is their presumed interest. Although in tuxedo Stan and Oliver are recognized by their jail "buddies," and when the party pass the cell occupied by the embarrassed Frenchmen, the secret is out. Stan and Oliver are given an additional sentence and told to start making sand out of boulders.

In their first official comedy, Hal Roach's new team — Hardy and Laurel.

young director was especially intrigued with the comic abilities of Stan and Babe.

McCarey encouraged his All-Stars collaborators to give Laurel and Hardy larger roles, and recalled that the team kept evolving as "gradually, their parts grew longer and the parts of the other players grew smaller." But the films themselves indicate that McCarey — the Roach staffer who was most enthusiastic about L&H — began decisively guiding the construction of the films in June 1927, with *The Second Hundred Years*.

It's difficult to determine just how much Hal Roach contributed to the development of the team. "I would say McCarey was 50% of it," stated Roach in a recent interview. "I mean, I was the boss, I was the guy that told McCarey to do it. I think Leo set a standard for their kind of humor that was followed after that." Suffice it to say that Roach provided a cozy environment in which Laurel and Hardy's talent could develop, and McCarey came up with the inspiration to team them.

And how did Laurel and Hardy feel about all of this? Stan not only did not envision the team, but was very much against it when McCarey proposed it. The reason for Stan's disapproval was no personal or professional dislike for Babe Hardy; he simply wished to return to full-time directing and writing as soon as possible, and didn't want to be tied down to any long-term commitments as an actor.

Babe Hardy's reaction was entirely different. He had done well as a supporting character actor, but was eager to become a featured player. During the past year he had become friendly with Roach cameraman Art Lloyd and his wife Venice: when Babe visited them he would talk excitedly about the studio's plans.

"He was anxious to be part of a team," recalled Venice Lloyd. "They were grooming him for it. So he came over one night, and he was asking Art, 'Have you heard anything? Do you think I'll really get on steady, do you think I can really be part of a team?' He was so anxious to work with Laurel."

The Second Hundred Years is the first true "Laurel and Hardy" film. The boys don't quite look like their usual selves, thanks to their convicts' garb and shaved heads, but the inner qualities are starting to show through. They're well on their way to becoming the two little boys who never grew up, united in innocence and braving the terrors of a hostile world.

A script exists for the film, dated June 10, 1927. As with all L&H short-subject scripts, there's no writer credit, so it's impossible to discern who came up with the basic story idea. The gag sessions were so chaotic, with each gagman trying to top the others, that when the dust settled, *they* probably didn't know whose gag was whose.

The script has a different opening scene, with Stan going alone to tunnel under the prison; meanwhile, Ollie allays the suspicions of a guard by talking animatedly to a dummy, which is standing in for his absent cellmate. Later, when the boys are put in separate cells, they steal the guard's key; they use it not to escape, but just so they can be together in the same cell.

This was replaced in the film by a brief, charming vignette: Ollie has just enough tobacco and paper to roll one cigarette, but gives in to Stan's longing looks and splits it in half. But it's all to no avail, since neither of them has a match.

Laurel and Hardy exercised their ad-libbing skills throughout the filming.

The memorable scene in which they find new and creative ways to apply paint to objects that don't need it was entirely improvised. The script simply says, "A cop enters the scene. Stan and Babe take it and get all flustered and start painting promiscuously."

Likewise, Stan's extended routine at the banquet with a fruit cocktail was a product of on-the-set inspiration. The script tosses off this whole sequence with, "We then go for several gags of etiquette and conversation."

One nice gag which only appeared in the script occurs when the guests are touring the prison. Hanging on a prison wall is a reward poster, with Stan and Ollie's mugs conspicuously displayed. Ollie hastily tears it off and explains that he wants to take it back to France as a souvenir. Stan takes a whole *stack* of posters.

Some confusing stills exist, which show L&H working on a rockpile under the baleful glare of prison guard Tiny Sandford. No such scene exists in the film or the script. However, the official studio synopsis indicates that this may have been the original wrap-up gag: "Stan and Oliver are given an additional sentence and told to start making sand out of boulders."

MGM's publicity department issued a press sheet for each Roach short subject. These were sent to theater managers, and contained articles about the film which could be placed in the local papers. The press sheet for *The Second Hundred Years* is especially interesting, since it suggests that the studio wasn't quite sure how to promote the stars.

"New Starring Team Uncorks Riotous Performance in First Picture as Comedy Duo," reads a headline — then bills that team as "Oliver Hardy and Stan Laurel." About half of the articles bill them as "Hardy and Laurel," and a few stories call the stars a "famous comedy trio," with Finlayson the third member of the team.

Fred Guiol directed this, his ninth and last L&H film, although some of the publicity material listed James Parrott as director. However, the guiding hand behind the picture was Leo McCarey, with the support of Hal Roach and the not-inconsiderable assistance of Stan Laurel. And the assistance would be even more considerable before long.

CALL OF THE CUCKOOS

Production history: Written and filmed circa late June 1927. Copyrighted October 12, 1927 by MGM (LP 24501). Released October 15. Two Reels.

Produced by Hal Roach. Supervised by Leo McCarey. Directed by Clyde A. Bruckman. Photographed by Floyd Jackman. Edited by Richard Currier. Titles by H.M. Walker.

With Max Davidson, Lillian Elliott, Spec O'Donnell, Charley Chase, James Finlayson, Charlie Hall.

Mr. Gimplewart (Davidson) and his family are somewhat put off by the strange antics of their next-door neighbors — Laurel, Hardy, Chase and Finlayson — who supposedly attend a school for radio announcers, but act like they'd be better suited to a lunatic asylum. Gimplewart, in self defense, moves to a new home which starts to self-destruct immediately. When he wonders how any

Babe and Myrtle in their July 1927 passport
photo, for a vacation in Cuba.

*new calamity could befall him, Stan and Ollie and their friends happily
announce that they've moved next door.*

Laurel and Hardy's appearance in this Max Davidson comedy was not
much more than a cameo; it was inserted by Roach to publicize his new team.
Stan and Babe's scenes were shot a few days after they'd completed *The
Second Hundred Years*, and as a result they still have the shaved heads. "The
boys were just too good to be kept inactive, so they were put almost right away
into the next picture, brush cut and all," George Stevens later explained.

Their scenes have such a spontaneous air that they look like home movies:
The boys cavort outdoors with Chase and Finlayson around a home-made
microphone. Stan challenges Ollie to a reenactment of William Tell's stunt,
but Stan's arrow misses the apple atop Ollie's head and lands instead in the
Hardy posterior. Ollie scoots Charlie Hall across the lawn as if he were a
wheelbarrow.

This was a rather inauspicious debut for Clyde Bruckman, directing his
first film with Laurel and Hardy after a long association with Buster Keaton.
Bruckman fits the pattern of L&H directors in that he had no individual style at
all. He was certainly competent, however; his five films with the team include
two of their best, *Putting Pants on Philip* and *The Battle of the Century*. Since
Roach, McCarey and Laurel were jointly supervising the comedies, it's difficult
to determine just how much credit Bruckman deserves, but he certainly didn't
hinder the team.

Within a few months, Laurel and Hardy would be so popular and
recognizable that they would no longer need publicity devices like their guest
appearance in *Call of the Cuckoos*.

HATS OFF

Production history: Written and filmed circa late July-early August 1927. Copyrighted October 17, 1927 by MGM (LP 24509). Released November 5. Two reels.

Produced by Hal Roach. Supervised by Leo McCarey. Directed by Hal Yates. Edited by Richard Currier. Titles by H.M. Walker.

With James Finlayson, Anita Garvin, Dorothy Coburn.

Stan and Ollie are door-to-door washing machine salesmen. Anita is a prospect who lives atop a monumental flight of steps; the boys drag the machine all the way up the steps, only to learn she just wants them to mail a letter for her. The demoralized salesmen soon get into a tiff and start ripping each other's derbies. Passersby are drawn into the fray, losing their heads as well as their headgear. Soon the town is a sprawling mass of angry men bent on ruining each other's hats. Then a tractor happens by and demolishes the washing machine.

Hats Off is the Holy Grail of Laurel and Hardy movies. It was last screened publicly in 1928, whereupon it seems to have vanished without a trace. Given the unstable nature of nitrate film stock, we're lucky that any Laurel and Hardys have survived — but of the handful that are missing this is an especially sad loss. *Hats Off* was a hugely popular comedy which did a great deal to establish L&H with the public. It also further reinforced their characters and provided the genesis for their 1932 Academy Award-winning short *The Music Box.*

The basic idea for the film came to Stan Laurel one day in the person of a very persistent washing machine salesman who absolutely insisted on demonstrating his washing wonder for Stan and his wife Lois, even though they had no intention of buying one. The climbing-the-stairs gag came from one of the gag writers, who was driving down Vendome Street in the Silver Lake area of Los Angeles, and saw that ridiculously long flight of steps.

The climactic tit-for-tat sequence, the first of many in which innocent bystanders reveal their true animal nature, was hatched at a party when Mabel Normand untied Leo McCarey's bow tie with one fell yank. McCarey, who claimed he'd spent the better part of the evening desperately trying to get someone to tie his tie for him, was not amused, and thus began a chain reaction of tie-yanking and collar-ripping that would be remembered for decades — at least by Leo McCarey.

Hats Off not only brought back The Never-Ending Hat Routine from *Do Detectives Think?*, it brought back the boys' trademark derbies and and suits. Another lasting trademark born with this film was Stan's upraised hair. Stan and Babe's hair was still growing in, having been shorn for *The Second Hundred Years;* one day Stan tried to brush his hair back, but it stubbornly refused to lay down. People on the lot began doubling over with laughter at his appearance, which Stan, naturally, took as a compliment. The funny haircut was here to stay.

Somebody who was not here to stay was James Finlayson, who could see

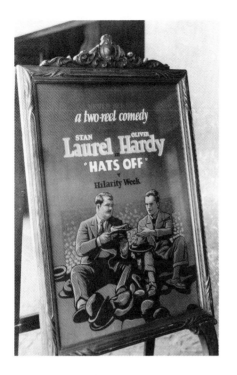

Hats Off was promoted in theater lobbies, in advertisements, and on Roach studio vehicles (including the "Our Gang" bus, foreground).

that he was no longer being groomed for stardom by Hal Roach. (In *Sugar Daddies* he'd been given footage just about equal to Laurel and Hardy's; in *The Second Hundred Years* he was clearly in a supporting role; and in *Hats Off*, judging from the story outline and existing stills, he had only a brief bit.) He left the Roach lot in late September 1927, about two months after *Hats Off* was filmed.

The *Los Angeles Times* noted, "So long has Jimmie Finlayson been working at the Roach studios that we are used to thinking of him as a landmark over there... Finlayson is going to strike out into the wide, wide world with a view to making feature comedies in some other studio. At present his plans are not definitely set, but it is understood that he has one or two tentative offers." Finlayson would be back at the Roach lot by mid-1928.

The shooting of *Hats Off* was fairly uneventful, except for the usual occurrence of Culver City bystanders being amused and/or annoyed by actors who were being paid to portray Culver City bystanders during the location scenes. The location the studio chose for the hat-fight scene was Culver City's Main Street, an unusually short Main Street but one with a small-town charm — which was appropriate, since Culver City in 1927 *was* a small town.

Main Street would be used repeatedly in L&H comedies. Sometimes footage shot there would be intercut with footage shot on the Roach backlot, thereby confusing generations of fans who have searched Culver City in vain for the Pink Pup nightclub and Ice Cream Cohen's drugstore. However, those who visit Main Street today will still find several familiar landmarks from Laurel and Hardy films.

Hats Off was completed sometime around early August 1927; although its official release date was November 5, it did not appear in the Los Angeles area until March 8, 1928, after several subsequent L&H films had already been shown there. Apparently Hal Roach decided this particular film was the best of their early efforts, and wanted to use it to publicize his new team.

The Roach studio mounted an incredible publicity campaign to herald the coming of *Hats Off* to the Metropolitan Theater in Los Angeles. One hundred billboards advertising the film went up all over the city. People emptying their shopping bags from Ralph's Grocery stores would find little slips of paper inside, reading "Hats Off to Ralph's Vacuum Coffee — Now see *Hats Off* at the Metropolitan!" Anyone buying Hollywood Dry Ginger Ale or Wurlitzer musical instruments would find Laurel and Hardy displays in the store windows, and soda jerks at Owl Drug Stores wore ribbons on their coats promoting the film.

The Metropolitan Theater had a special parade on the opening day of "Hilarity Week," with a car containing L&H doubles and a washing machine. Two thousand balloons promoting the team were released from the top of the theater during lunch hour, which caused havoc with the traffic on the street below.

Fortunately, the publicity paid off. Philip K. Scheuer of the *Los Angeles Times* wrote, "It is fairly obvious that the two-reelers in which Hal Roach is so felicitously presenting Laurel and Hardy are carefully mapped out from fade-in to fade-out before ever the camera-crank is turned; and the result is uproariously funny."

Raved Harrison Carroll of the *Los Angeles Evening Herald*: "I laughed so hard I cried ...It is no exaggeration to say that the entire audience bordered on hysteria at the climax of this two-reeler.

Babe and Stan kept their hats *on* for this promotional tie-in with the Stetson company.

"In my opinion, Hal Roach has the most promising comedy team on the screen today in Laurel and Hardy. It is to be hoped he withstands the temptation to promote them into five-reel features, a horrible example of which is on the Metropolitan bill in *Tillie's Punctured Romance*."

Hal Roach figured he had something special going, too. According to the Roach publicity department, "Roach shook each solemnly by the hand and told them they'd better get along well personally from now on, because they were to work together forever...."

Hats Off has been lost for decades, but every once in a while a new rumor of its existence surfaces. The latest one is that a 9.5mm copy of it — made for the home collector market — has been located in France.

PUTTING PANTS ON PHILIP

Production history: Written and filmed August 1927. Released December 3, 1927. Copyrighted January 3, 1928 by MGM (LP 25206). Two reels.

Produced by Hal Roach. Supervised by Leo McCarey. Directed by Clyde Bruckman. Photographed by George Stevens. Edited by Richard Currier. Titles by H.M. Walker.

With Harvey Clark, Dorothy Coburn, Sam Lufkin.

The respectable Piedmont Mumblethunder (Ollie) is more than embarrassed when he goes to the docks to meet his Scottish nephew Philip (Stan), a hyperactive, kilt-clad girl chaser. An attractive flapper (Dorothy) is the frequent object of Laurel's passions. When the uncle pulls his nephew into a tailor shop for a pair of trousers, Stan misunderstands the tailor's attempts to measure his inseam. He emerges from the fitting room looking disheveled and deflowered — but is out girl-chasing again before he can be put in pants.

In August 1927, while Laurel and Hardy's epic battle of headgear was still waiting to be released, the Roach studio sent out publicity releases about the team's next picture. "Stan Laurel and Oliver Hardy, following their sensational success in *Rough on Hats*, [evidently a working title for *Hats Off*] will henceforth be costarred in Roach's 'All-Star' unit.... In their next M-G-M production Laurel will appear as a knock-kneed kilted Scot fresh from the heather."

Just when L&H had finally become a comedy team — once and "forever" — things got botched again. The team's usual costumes and characters have been discarded, and the relationship between the characters in this picture is nothing like the "Stan and Ollie" relationship. *Putting Pants on Philip* is, however, a beautifully crafted comedy.

Roach considered *Putting Pants on Philip* one of his favorites among the pictures he produced, along with such films as Harold Lloyd's *Grandma's Boy* and the Cary Grant-Constance Bennett screwball comedy *Topper*.

MGM executives felt the picture warranted an unprecedented amount of ballyhoo. Jeff Lazarus, an MGM overseer, sent the following memo to colleague H. C. Arthur Jr.:

Standing by the Roach studio pool in summer 1927, Stan and Babe pose for their portrait...

...and so do their screen counterparts.

We have already notified your Division that soon they will be playing another LAUREL-HARDY comedy, the second one in the series, and one of the funniest things I have ever looked at...be sure that they have an intensive campaign on their screens and in their programs and lobbies one week in advance of the time they play the comedy. There are many other angles which they should and will use in putting over this LAUREL-HARDY picture, but I want to be particularly sure that they do it justice in the regular channels such as advertisements, program, lobby, trailers, newspaper stories...

Despite all the previous books and articles about Laurel and Hardy that proclaim *Putting Pants on Philip* as the first "official" L&H comedy, this conclusion fails to hold up, historically or aesthetically. It's the 15th film in which both comedians appear, and Roach press releases referred to it as "the second of their teaming vehicles." (Those press releases refer variously to *Hats Off*, *The Second Hundred Years* or even *Duck Soup* as the first of their teaming vehicles.) The frequent argument that it's the team's first "typical" film doesn't hold water, either. What's typical about an L&H movie where Stan plays a Scottish sex maniac?

Putting Pants on Philip is a great Laurel and Hardy comedy, but it's hardly a "Laurel and Hardy" comedy. The next film is both.

THE BATTLE OF THE CENTURY

Production history: Written and filmed late September-early October 1927. Released December 31, 1927. Copyrighted January 9, 1928 by MGM (LP 24848) Two reels.

Produced by Hal Roach. Supervised by Leo McCarey. Directed by Clyde Bruckman. Photographed by George Stevens. Edited by Richard Currier. Titles by H.M. Walker. Story by Hal Roach.

With Noah Young, Sam Lufkin, Eugene Pallette, Charlie Hall, Anita Garvin.

Stan is the world's worst prizefighter; Ollie, his optimistic manager, is grooming him for a championship battle. Stan is terrified at the very appearance of his beefy opponent, with good reason, since the burly boxer knocks Laurel out cold. Ollie buys an accident insurance policy on Stan, then tries to cause an accident with a banana peel in Stan's path. The peel instead fells the driver of a pie wagon; an argument escalates until the denizens of an entire city block are combatants in the biggest pie fight in movie history.

On September 22, 1927, boxers Gene Tunney and Jack Dempsey fought "The Fight of the Century" — which included the famous "long count" — at Soldiers' Field in Chicago.

Immediately thereafter, Stan Laurel and the Roach gag writers set about making a comedy based on the fight. Somehow, the idea of throwing a few pies got tossed around, and just as quickly got tossed out. "Pie throwing went out with Keystone comedies," was the general consensus. Still, Stan was intrigued. What if you made a joke out of the very *act* of pie-throwing? And the way to do

Stan and Ollie's little arguments have a way of escalating.

it would be to throw more pies. And still more. Not a couple of pies, not a dozen, not a baker's dozen but hundreds — thousands.

Stan took his idea to Roach, and since the producer was inclined to be generous with his successful new team, he okayed the idea, even though it would be costly. Thus, early in October 1927, production began on *The Battle of the Century*.

Roach authorized the purchase of a day's output from the Los Angeles Pie Company, whereupon more than 3,000 pies were flung on their merry way toward unsuspecting targets.

Two years after this film was completed, it already had a legendary status, and Stan explained the reason for its success to film critic Philip K. Scheuer. "It wasn't just that we threw hundreds of pies. That wouldn't have been very funny; it really *had* passed out with Keystone. We went at it, strange as it may sound, psychologically. We made every one of the pies count.

"A well-dressed man strolling casually down the avenue, struck squarely in the face by a large pastry, would not proceed at once to gnash his teeth, wave his arms in the air and leap up and down. His first reaction, it is reasonable to suppose, would be one of numb disbelief," said Stan. "Then embarrassment, and a quick survey of the damage done to his person. Then indignation and a desire for revenge would possess him; if he saw another pie close at hand, still unspoiled, he would grab it up and let fly."

One of the highlights of the film is a brilliantly executed throwaway gag featuring the queen of comic hauteur, Anita Garvin. It is one of the great moments in all of Laurel and Hardy, and it came about, typically, as one of Stan's on-the-set inspirations.

Anita recalled, "I was working with Charley Chase on a picture, and Stan came over on the set about 11 o'clock. He says, 'Anita, will you do a favor for me?' Of course, I'd break my neck for him... He said, 'I want you to do one little scene in the picture that I'm on. Go to wardrobe on your lunch hour and have them give you a dress that has a circular skirt. It'll only take 10 minutes.' So, I made the scene as a favor to Stan. I never got paid for doing that!

"The original [film] was so much better than the way you see it now. I'm sure that just yards and yards of footage has been lost... In the original cut, this pie comes in and plops on the sidewalk, and I come around and slip and fall on the thing. The skirt goes around. Now, I don't know that the pie fight is going on. And they came in on a great big close-up; apparently I got over the fact that I don't know what in God's green earth I'm sitting on, but whatever it is, I'm *afraid* to know what it is. And the close-up was the thing that got the biggest laugh.

"Then when I get up, they cut to an insert of just a wet spot — not the pie on the sidewalk, but just a damp spot in the shape of a pie. And then I walk away from the camera and, sort of daintily, shake my leg a little.

"I understand that when they previewed it, that scene was in the beginning of the pie fight. It got such a big laugh and all, they put it at the end of the picture." Although the sequence may exist only in truncated form today, Anita Garvin's mastery of timing and expression makes the scene a memorable one.

The publicity material for the film hailed L&H as a new sensation. Roach was quoted as saying, "I believe they will strike the note of public fancy to such an extent that within a year they will rank with Lloyd, Chaplin and other comic geniuses." This is one of the very few instances in which public-relations puffery has proved to be right.

The Battle of the Century exists today only in fragmentary form. In the late 1970s, a print of the long-lost first reel was found, but the classic pie fight sequence survives only in part. When Robert Youngson was editing his 1958 documentary *The Golden Age of Comedy*, all he could find was a 35mm negative of reel two, which had already started to decompose. Fortunately, the last 300 feet — about three and a half minutes' worth of footage — still remained in usable condition. Youngson didn't know that as he edited this film, he was also preserving it — no other complete negatives or prints of the second reel have been found since then.

In 1965 Blake Edwards staged a Technicolor pie fight in *The Great Race*. The dedication on the film — "To Mr. Laurel and Mr. Hardy" — made clear his inspiration.

"I worked with Leo McCarey, and I used to get him talking," said Edwards in an interview. "He talked about the early days, about Hal Roach and Laurel and Hardy and the great pie fight ...I would say I learned intellectually as much from McCarey as from anybody."

But Laurel and Hardy, Hal Roach and Leo McCarey had few equals when it came to creating comedy — as Edwards and other filmmakers have proved time and again.

LEAVE 'EM LAUGHING

Production history: Written and filmed October 1927. Copyrighted January 9, 1928 by MGM (LP 24847). Released January 28. Two reels.

Produced by Hal Roach. Supervised by Leo McCarey. Directed by Clyde Bruckman. Photographed by George Stevens. Edited by Richard Currier. Titles by Reed Heustis. Story by Hal Roach.

With Edgar Kennedy, Charlie Hall, Viola Richard, Dorothy Coburn, Jack V. Lloyd.

Stan has a toothache. After a number of futile, do-it-yourself attempts to extract the tooth, Ollie takes Stan to the dentist. Stan is terrified, and the anguished screams of the dentist's other patients are no help. Once inside the den of dental doom, Stan tries to escape; in the ensuing fracas, the boys are both overcome with laughing gas. They amble out to their car, whereupon they chortle and guffaw their way through the streets, creating havoc and igniting the ire of a traffic cop (Kennedy).

Although the previous three Laurel and Hardy films had not yet been released in October 1927, the Roach staff felt they had a success in this new series. Everyone involved in the production took great pains to ensure that each new picture would be a complement to the previous one.

These early L&H comedies were a collaborative effort between Roach, McCarey, Stan, the gag writers, and whoever the director happened to be on a given film. McCarey got official credit as "supervisor," a highly ambiguous term. Sometimes he wrote the stories, sometimes he directed, sometimes he just stood on the set and watched. McCarey, Roach and Stan all had definite ideas about the direction and crafting of the films; fortunately they all agreed with each other.

Roach himself came up with the idea for *Leave 'em Laughing*, which was originally titled *A Little Laughing Gas*. While it *is* a very basic comedy premise, the execution of the routines and the imaginative gags sprinkled liberally throughout make all the difference.

One of the funniest gags occurs in the opening sequence, when the boys are trying to sleep despite Stan's throbbing toothache. Stan tries to quell his pain with a hot water bottle, which begins to leak. In a close-up of Hardy's cherubic countenance, we can see that he plainly thinks the liquid is emanating from another source.

In a 1954 interview with critic David Robinson, Stan recalled that filming this sequence was more difficult than he'd anticipated: "We went on the lot the first day, got up on the bed and started laughing. We laughed so much we couldn't stop. So we weren't able to shoot anything that day. Next day we went back, got up on the bed, and the same thing happened again. So we weren't able to shoot anything that day either."

The same thing happened when they got out onto the Culver City streets and shot the traffic-jam scenes. Stan and Babe kept breaking up, and got so intoxicated on their actual hilarity they had to call it a day to give their stomach muscles a rest.

The new team was well promoted — as this billboard proves.

L&H trademarks continue to make their debuts in these early films; here we have the first appearance of the boys' usual mode of transport, the Model T. Like Stan and Ollie themselves, their Tin Lizzie was battered but beloved — and like them, it took unbelievable amounts of abuse.

"We had them specially made," Stan recalled. "We had one in a half circle that would go around and around, and then one that was squashed between two cars... There were no motors in them, you know, they were just breakaways; we had one that was all fitted together, and you pulled wires, and everything collapsed at one time."

Another perennial of the L&H stock company who withstood a lot of abuse made his debut in this film: Edgar Kennedy. Although his tenure at the Roach lot was fairly brief, Kennedy made a lasting impression on the people with whom he worked. His fellow actors remembered him as a truly nice man — despite his gruff on-screen persona — who was "a real pro." Film editor Richard Currier added, "He was a great actor and a great golf player!"

Onscreen, Kennedy was the polar opposite of Jimmy Finlayson. While Finlayson would delight in expressing his anger, Kennedy tried valiantly to suppress his rage — twisting his face and rubbing his bald head in determination not to let his emotions get the best of him. But they always did.

The Laurel and Hardy films were immediately popular overseas. When Roach went on a world tour during the first five months of 1928, he was invited by German MGM executives to see the great reaction that *Leave 'em Laughing* was getting.

At one point in the traffic jam sequence, Kennedy's trousers fall down while he's directing traffic, and he bends over to pick them up. "Right in the middle of this," Roach recalled, "they put in a German title which said, 'He looks like a washerwoman.' I said, 'What the hell, there's nothing funny about looking like a washerwoman.' Then they took me to the theater, and the audience laughed like hell at this title. Then I found out that there was a dirty saying in Germany about a washerwoman leaning over and somebody attacking her from the back. But the scene was very funny without any title, and I couldn't see why in the world they'd put a title in it like that."

THE FINISHING TOUCH

Production history: Written and filmed circa late November-early December 1927. Copyrighted February 25, 1928 by MGM (LP 25337). Released February 25. Two reels.

Produced by Hal Roach. Supervised by Leo McCarey. Directed by Clyde Bruckman. Photographed by George Stevens. Edited by Richard Currier. Titles by H.M. Walker.

With Edgar Kennedy, Dorothy Coburn, Sam Lufkin.

Stan and Ollie are maladroit carpenters who advertise themselves as "Professional Finishers." A man who owns a half-built home offers them $500 if they'll finish constructing his cottage by noon next Monday. Their attempts to finish the building are thwarted by the noise-sensitive residents of the sanitarium next door; a tough little nurse who keeps telling the boys to keep quiet; a tougher cop (Kennedy) who ensures that they do; and, mostly, their own incompetence.

L&H were now turning out comedies at the rate of one a month — at least. Their output during the late '20s was phenomenal, and the level of quality was remarkably good, for the most part. If *The Finishing Touch* isn't as memorable as the films which preceded it, it's a pleasant enough little picture.

Stan and the gag writers had a finished script in their hands by November 1927 — as usual, a script that differed substantially from the finished film.

The script has an opening sequence wherein the "nerve sanitarium" patients are going even nuttier, thanks to the racket caused by a construction crew. Fed up with complaints, the contractor calls his men off the job — that's why the house is left unfinished. The script also suggests that "perhaps" the homeowner explains he's being married the next day and wants the home ready for his wife.

The script proposes that the adversary from the sanitarium who keeps charging over and screaming at Laurel and Hardy and Kennedy the cop to knock off the racket should be a male physician. In the film, Stan and Ollie's innocent bumbling and Kennedy's ineffectiveness were emphasized by making this character a diminutive young nurse (Dorothy Coburn) who is the quintessential tough-cookie.

One nice sequence in the script didn't end up in the finished film: Ollie is in one room, Stan in an adjoining one; Ollie drives a nail into the wall and hangs his coat on it. On the other side of the wall, Stan tears his sleeve on the nail, so he pounds it back out. Ollie, wondering why his coat has fallen off, drives the nail home again. Then Ollie storms through the doorway to see if it might be Stan who's causing the trouble, but Stan has gone through another doorway to look for Ollie. (Great minds think alike. So do Laurel and Hardy's, but not at the same time.)

This Laurel and Hardy "one-sheet" poster, like most, captures everything except their likenesses.

Back on his side of the wall, Stan again hammers that pesky nail, but Kennedy steps into view to give Stan a lecture. As Kennedy stands with his back against the wall, Ollie (on the other side) puts the nail back into place and strikes a mighty blow, which sends Kennedy flying across the room.

When the basic premise of a film has L&H building a house, one can pretty well anticipate how the picture's going to end. Right; the house falls apart. But the script and the film offer two different means to this end.

In the script, the owner pays them for their splendid work as he surveys the completed cottage. Then Stan realizes that he's left his derby on top of the roof, and clambers up the top of the porch to retrieve it. The house begins its inevitable gradual collapse. As each component of the house self-destructs, the owner takes away more of the money, until he's taken it *all* back; he growls, "You don't get a dime!" This was made more concise and eloquent in the film: a cartoon bird alights on the chimney, which immediately crumbles. And, slowly, so does the rest of the house.

The Roach construction gang built the house on an empty lot on Motor Avenue, near the Fox studios. One of the men on the crew was Thomas Benton Roberts, who primarily worked on the *Our Gang* comedies, helping to build all the strange contraptions the kids supposedly created.

Originally, the house was to have been demolished by having the boys' truck go straight through it, leaving a gaping hole. But the Roach construction crew ignored Roberts' specifications while building the house. As a result, the final gag misfires; the truck comes to rest midway through the house, causing the structure to collapse upward. Stan was philosophical about the foul-up. "Oh, well," he told Roberts, "maybe it'll be funnier that way."

When you're working for a small comedy studio, you can't have everything.

FROM SOUP TO NUTS

Production history: Written and filmed late December 1927-January 5, 1928. Copyrighted March 24, 1928 by MGM (LP 25373). Released March 24. Two reels.

Produced by Hal Roach. Supervised by Leo McCarey. Directed by E. Livingston Kennedy. Photographed by Len Powers. Edited by Richard Currier. Titles by H.M. Walker. Story by Leo McCarey.

With Anita Garvin, Tiny Sandford, Edna Marian, Ellinor Vanderveer.

Stan and Ollie are waiters hired for a swanky dinner party given by nouveau-riche Mrs. Culpepper (Anita). Unfortunately, their experience has been in railroad eateries. Stan spills soup on the guests; Ollie has a habit of slipping and falling into large, gooey cakes. Not be to outdone, Mrs. Culpepper is continually exasperated by an elusive cherry atop her fruit cocktail. The evening comes to a climax when Stan is instructed to "serve the salad undressed" — and does just that.

As 1927 drew to a close, all was well with Laurel and Hardy. *Hats Off* and *Putting Pants on Philip* were in release in various parts of the country, and the

Stanley J. "Tiny" Sandford and Anita Garvin off-camera.

reviews were encouraging. And *The Battle of the Century*, the film which would really put them over, was to be released on December 31.

Stan and Babe's personal lives were going well, too. There had been some strain in Babe's marriage with Myrtle Lee Reeves Hardy, but for the time being the couple was amicable. And on December 10, Stan's wife Lois gave birth to a daughter, whom they named Lois Jr.

In the last week of 1927, the boys started filming a new comedy entitled *Let George Do It*. While evidently previewed under this name, it was eventually called *From Soup to Nuts*. A first-time L&H director was at the helm — E. Livingston Kennedy — known professionally as Edgar, and to everyone on the Roach lot as just plain Ed.

There was a new fellow behind the camera, too. Most of the L&H films up to this point had been photographed by serious, dedicated George Stevens. This one was shot by Len Powers, remembered by Roach staffers as an inveterate practical joker, but one who could retaliate violently if someone pulled a joke on him. "You couldn't pull a gag on him, because it may have backfired on you. He was a tough guy," says one Roach alumnus.

Despite the newcomers to the team, the creative reins seem to have been held by McCarey and Laurel, under the guidance of Roach. During the shooting of one of Ollie's mishaps with the cake, McCarey waited for him to fall, then yelled out, "Don't move! Stay just like that!" McCarey wanted to ensure that Babe milked the laugh for all it was worth before he got up.

Neither McCarey nor Kennedy gave Anita Garvin much direction for her fruit cocktail sequence, easily the highlight of the picture. Stan had used the gag a few months before in *The Second Hundred Years*, but by this time the pace of the films had been slowed down — Stan felt that a slower pace was necessary if the audience was to really know the "Stan and Ollie" characters. With the decrease in tempo, Anita was able to take her time; with her beautifully subtle expressions of uncertainty and disgust, she wrung every possible laugh out of the gag.

"Nobody told me anything," Anita recalled. "I was just told that I'm trying to get this cherry, and I don't know what instrument to use — that was about it... I pick up one utensil, and look to see who's picking up what, then I put it down and pick up something else — and I'm still wrong. And then there was the gag with the cherry going around the plate, and I'm trying to get it, and my tiara keeps falling. I don't know how I got it to fall over my eyes at just the right moment — I think I just gave my head a little shake. The tiara was set on there so that just a little nod would do it.

"When I was working on the pictures, I always went in and took a look at the dailies. But I didn't see the pictures all put together! Not even *From Soup to Nuts*. I never did see it, not until the last few years, since my so-called — ahem — rediscovery."

There is a mysterious still from this film which shows Anita as Mrs. Culpepper — bereft of her dress — glaring at a hastily-clothed Stan, who is now draped in the garment. While there is no such scene in the film, the press sheet suggests this was the original wrap-up (pardon the pun):

"Hardy enters with a third cake, this time on a tea wagon. He is horrified at Stan's appearance, seizes what he thinks is a Spanish shawl from the hostess's shoulders to cover Stan's nudity [Laurel having served the salad undressed]. The shawl proves to be the hostess's dress, whereupon Hardy faints, falling headlong into the third cake." (This scene was apparently shot and previewed, but ultimately scrapped.)

The film wrapped on January 5. Oddly enough, Babe was playing a supporting role in the Our Gang comedy *Barnum & Ringling, Inc.* at the same time. His role as a startled drunk was a minor one, though; he wouldn't make another film without Stan for more than a decade.

The week after production wrapped, Hal Roach and his wife Margaret sailed for Hong Kong as the first stop on an around-the-world tour. They didn't return until May 24. During Roach's five-month absence, the studio was run by Vice President Warren Doane. Doane now had another colleague on the board of directors: on December 27, Leo McCarey had been made a Vice President of the corporation.

The success of the team he put together probably had something to do with it.

YOU'RE DARN TOOTIN'

Production history: Written early January 1928. Filmed January 17-27. Copyrighted April 21, 1928 by MGM (LP 25251). Released April 21. Two reels.

Produced by Hal Roach. Supervised by Leo McCarey. Directed by E. Livingston Kennedy. Photographed by Floyd Jackman. Edited by Richard Currier. Titles by H.M. Walker.

With Otto Lederer, Agnes Steele, Christian Frank, Chet Brandenberg.

The effects of passing the hat too much.

Stan and Ollie play clarinet and French horn in an orchestra fronted by a tempermental conductor; inept and out of sync, they soon lose their jobs. They try to scrounge a few pennies by entertaining the passersby. Indignities mount until they begin to take their frustrations out on each other. Ollie punches Stan; Stan kicks Ollie. A stranger punches Stan, who retaliates — and soon the street is engulfed in a stomach-punching, shin-kicking maelstrom of men. When that grows tiresome, they begin to tear each other's pants off.

Stan Laurel, Leo McCarey and the Roach studio gag writers were brimming with enthusiasm as 1928 began. The "Stan and Ollie" characters had finally come into their own, and they were so appealing — and so much could be done with them — that story ideas began flowing like bootleg hooch at a speakeasy.

One day early in January, one of the gagmen watched some musicians perform in the band shell of a local park. He mentioned this to Stan and McCarey. They soon began shooting what they tentatively called *The Music Blasters*. Before the picture was released, Beanie Walker rechristened it with the American slang expression, *You're Darn Tootin'*. (In England, however, the film retained its initial title.)

You're Darn Tootin' is the first clear statement of the essential idea inherent in Laurel and Hardy. The world is not their oyster: they are the pearl trapped *in* the oyster. Their jobs hang by rapidly unraveling threads. Their possessions crumble into dust. Their dreams die just at the point of fruition. Their dignity is assaulted constantly. At times they can't live with each other, but they'll never be able to live without each other. Each other is all they will ever have. That, and the hope for a better day — which is about the most profound philosophical statement ever to come from a two-reel comedy.

It took the L&H crew 10 days to shoot this minor miracle of comedy. The picture was shot almost in sequence, with the first three days spent at a local park's band shell, the next five on the New York Street of the Roach studio backlot, and the final two days on the stage, shooting the boarding-house sequence.

Edgar Kennedy once again manned the director's chair, and again his professionalism earned him the respect of his actors. Rolfe Sedan, who played a friendly drunk in the picture, recalled, "Edgar Kennedy — there was a wonderful guy. He was a man who knew his business as a director." The chief cameraman was Floyd Jackman, who spent most of his career in movies as a backup cameraman; he later gave it up to become a dentist.

Until a copy of the shooting script surfaces, we won't know what sequences — if any — were left on the cutting-room floor. However, an existing still suggests one gag that was shot and scrapped: an elderly lady is about to give the two street musicians a coin, but grimaces and thinks twice when she hears a sample of their musical wares.

Did any of the extras think twice about getting their shins kicked, or standing around on the Roach backlot in their B.V.D.'s on those chilly January days? Frank Saputo recalled the experience vividly:

"We worked two days on that thing. The pants-ripping was probably toward the end of the second day. Truthfully, I don't remember Kennedy directing this one. But the director was on a platform truck with two cameras; then they had a camera over on the far side of this flatiron-shaped building, a camera on the left side of the scene, and one right by the curb. This fellow on the truck directed the whole thing, but he had two assistant directors who would get the people placed and tell them when they should come in.

"The first kicking would start it all, and we extras would be somewhere around the building," remembered Saputo. "Some of us were off out of the range of the camera. And the director would say, 'Action. Start coming in slowly now...you get in there...don't go too fast. Don't mob up. Then you walk in, you look, and you start kickin'!'"

You're Darn Tootin' is the film which asks the question, "If you strip everything away from Laurel and Hardy so that all that remains is their essence, what do they have left?" The answer: their affection for each other.

It's enough.

THEIR PURPLE MOMENT

Production history: Written early February 1928. Filmed February 11-24. New ending filmed March 7. Copyrighted May 19, 1928 by MGM (LP 25254). Released May 19. Two reels.

Produced by Hal Roach. Supervised by Leo McCarey. Directed by James Parrott. Photographed by George Stevens. Edited by Richard Currier. Titles by H.M. Walker.

With Anita Garvin, Kay Deslys, Tiny Sandford, Fay Holderness, Lyle Tayo, Jimmy Aubrey.

Stan and Ollie are two terrifically henpecked husbands who have been saving for a night on the town. Stan's wife discovers his stash of loot, and substitutes cigar coupons for the cash. The unsuspecting husbands end up at a swank cafe, where they offer to help two girls whose deadbeat dates can't pay their bills; true to form, the boys are soon in the same predicament. They battle it out with a burly waiter, their wives and a cantankerous chef in the establishment's kitchen, decorating each other with pie filling.

February 1928 was an especially happy time at The Lot of Fun. With the success of the initial L&H comedies — and the substantial increase in revenues resulting from the MGM distribution arrangement — the Roach studio had its most profitable period to date in the last quarter of 1927. Leo McCarey received a new contract giving him a percentage of the films' profits.

One would think that Laurel and Hardy also received a share of the profits, but they didn't. Stan was getting $500 a week, while Babe's pay was raised from $300 a week to $400.

Take-home pay figures prominently in the film they made during February. *Their Purple Moment*, the first of the L&H domestic comedies, is similar in plot to the early All-Star films. But here it's Stan and Ollie who get into domestic entanglements, not Jimmy Finlayson.

Available stills and scripts indicate that the original finale was markedly different from the sequence we see today.

A floor show featuring a troupe of midgets entertains the nightclub patrons as the boys realize they've got no money. The burly waiter (Tiny Sandford), wise to the boys' lack of funds, chases them; Stan and Ollie run into the midgets' dressing room, and the midgets offer to help. When the group returns to the stage in a "Floradora sextet" routine it has two new members, gaily attired in frilly dresses and hats, and carrying dainty little parasols. The new girls — er, boys — try valiantly to keep in step, but as they see the waiter, the cab driver, the wives and their dates glaring at them, they become a trifle nonplussed and make for the exit.

The wives pay the bill and run after their errant hubbies. A cop (Edgar Kennedy) is flirting with the two diminutive "girls"; Stan tickles him under the chin and laughs demurely. Then the wives give chase. Running as fast as their little knees can carry them, the boys pass over a sidewalk ventilator. Their dresses fly up, much to the amazement of the bystanders. The boys decide to run on their *feet* from this point on, passing the puzzled cop once more. Inevitably, the wives catch their prey, but as they march their sorrowful husbands home, they make the mistake of stepping off the curb into the street. They haven't yet learned that one *never* does that in a Hal Roach comedy, because there might be a six-foot mudhole just waiting to engulf them. There is, and it does.

The story was conceived and shot as outlined above. But the entire concluding sequence with the midgets, so dazzlingly funny on paper, didn't make it past the previews; the midget troupe of the Al G. Barnes circus, which was spending the winter in Los Angeles, was paid $50 a day for ending up on the cutting room floor.

So, the Roach crew went back to work. Stan and the gagmen hastily rewrote a new ending wherein the boys, the waiter, the wives and a cantankerous chef

Kay Deslys, Lyle Tayo, Leo Willis, Fay Holderness, Tiny Sandford and Anita
Garvin eye some ersatz midgets in a deleted scene.

(Jimmy Aubrey) battle it out in the nighclub's kitchen, and everyone is eventually decorated with pie filling.

Women do not come off as especially endearing creatures in this story.
Not only are the wives shrewish battleaxes; the boys' dates — played by Kay
Deslys and Anita Garvin — turn out to be pretty nasty too. Kay totes around a
Saturday Night Special and Anita carries a stiletto. While this is much the way
women are portrayed throughout all of the Laurel and Hardy films, most of the
other *men* in the films are equally rotten.

Their Purple Moment was the first L&H film to be directed by James
Gibbons Parrott. "I loved to work with Jimmy Parrott," says Anita Garvin. "He
was kind of quiet. Always walked around with a slight grin on his face. And he
was a very gentle man." Parrott, who was Charley Chase's brother, had worked
as a comedian for Roach in the early '20s; he would continue to direct many of
Laurel and Hardy's best shorts until 1933, and wrote for the team until 1938.

Soon after this film was released, an anonymous New York critic wrote,
"...it is a classic of the slapstick school. Actual howls go up all over the house...
The gags are unforced and logical. The two stars are master comedians."

Nevertheless, those two stars usually showed their mastery off to better
advantage than they did in *Their Purple Moment.*

SHOULD MARRIED MEN GO HOME?

Production history: Written early March 1928. Filmed March 13-21; added scenes and retakes filmed March 23, May 2, May 11-12. Copyrighted September 8, 1928 by MGM (LP 25603). Released September 8. Two reels.

Produced by Hal Roach. Supervised by Leo McCarey. Directed by James Parrott. Photographed by George Stevens. Edited by Richard Currier. Titles by H.M. Walker. Story by Leo McCarey and James Parrott.

With Edgar Kennedy, Kay Deslys, Edna Marian, Viola Richard, John Aasen.

Ollie and his wife are enjoying a rare moment of domestic bliss — until Stan arrives, dressed in golf togs. The Hardys reluctantly invite him in, only to have Stan wreck the Victrola. Ollie accompanies Stan to the golf course, where they form a foursome with two young beauties. After a detour to the soda fountain — where they try to buy four sodas for fifteen cents — they adjourn to the links. Their graceless attempts at golf are hampered by unpleasant encounters with a burly golfer (Kennedy). A mud fight erupts, with all involved.

Everybody at the Hal Roach studio loved comedy, and nearly everyone loved golf. Roach had an annual studio tournament, which was invariably won by Babe Hardy. Stan was often too busy working on story preparation or editing to participate, but on occasion he'd join his teammate on the links.

A friend of Babe's, Rodney Sprigg, recalled seeing the team together at Babe's beloved Lakeside Country Club. "Stan would show up at the club; he'd get out on the putting green, and he'd put on the doggonedest, funniest act you ever saw. He'd do more with that doggone golf ball — he'd just keep you in stitches. But I never saw him get out and *play* golf.

"The nearest Stan and Babe ever came to a quarrel would be when Stan would show up at the club, and he'd look at Babe and say something like, 'Well, I've been over at the studio doing your work.' I never knew two men who were more compatible."

It was only a matter of time before Leo McCarey and Jimmy Parrott would get together with Stan and concoct a story around Babe's favorite pastime. They originally called it *Follow Through* before Beanie Walker gave the film its final title.

Trouping out to the Riviera and Westwood golf courses with L&H were beauteous Edna Marian and Viola Richard, who did their best to smile and look perky even though they'd just been notified that their contracts were being terminated. (Edgar Kennedy, conversely, had just been placed on a five-year contract.) John Aasen, so memorable as the giant in Harold Lloyd's *Why Worry?*, returned to the studio to play a bit as a giant golfer. He stood 8'9" tall offscreen as well as on.

The crew, which included Lloyd French as assistant director, Morrie Lightfoot as prop man, George Stevens behind the camera and Hal Roach's brother Jack as his assistant, began shooting March 13 and wrapped on March 21 — only to return to location two days later to retake some of the golf scenes.

On March 26, the studio closed for its annual one-month vacation. The

James Parrott, trying to direct a golf ball.

cameraderie among Roach staffers extended to their lives away from the studio, and several of them, including Babe, Jimmy Parrott and film editor Dick Currier, vacationed together. Recalled Currier: "I remember one year, when Laurel and Hardy and Jimmy Parrott and Charley Chase and — there was damn near a dozen of us — all drove up to Vancouver and had a vacation together up there. It was a hell of a lot of fun." The Vancouver trip in April of '28 was especially happy for Babe and Jimmy Parrott, who took splendid advantage of the opportunity to buy some legal liquor.

After the studio reopened on May 2, Lloyd French shot some inserts; then Stan and the crew took the film around to a few theaters for previews, made notes, wrote some new scenes (evidently for the beginning of the film) and shot those on May 11 and 12.

By the time the film was released on September 8, L&H had become tremendously popular. MGM's publicity department began issuing billboard-sized posters to publicize the team. If this was an uncommon practice for a series of short subjects, MGM felt the team deserved the extra fanfare.

Laurel and Hardy made their stage debut during the production of this film. On March 21, 1928, they appeared at a midnight show at the Metropolitan Theater in Los Angeles — which had recently promoted *Hats Off* to the hilt. Stan, Babe and just about every star in Hollywood appeared in a benefit for victims of the St. Francis Dam disaster. The team's initial stage appearance was probably a brief walk-on, but live appearances would become their chief medium 20 years later — when neither MGM, nor any other studio, felt the team deserved any fanfare at all.

In Vancouver, there was no Prohibition — as Babe and Jimmy Parrott happily proved.

EARLY TO BED

Production history: Written early May 1928. Filmed May 21-29. Retakes directed by Leo McCarey June 18, 19 (Hardy only), 25 (Laurel only). Copyrighted October 6, 1928 by MGM (LP 25719). Released October 6. Two reels.

Produced by Hal Roach. Supervised by Leo McCarey. Directed by Emmett J. Flynn. Photographed by George Stevens. Edited by Richard Currier. Titles by H. M. Walker.

The boys are vagrants until Ollie inherits a fortune from his uncle. Mr. Hardy moves into a sumptuous mansion and shares his wealth by making Stan his butler. Ollie delights in heaping abuse on his new servant — until Stan rebels, and goes on a rampage, destroying the mansion's costly furnishings. He chases Ollie to a fountain, which is decorated with gargoyles bearing an amazing resemblance to Mr. Hardy. One of these gargoyles has trouble spouting water, and Stan hits it with a shovel until Ollie smiles and reveals his hiding place. "Let's forgive and forget and be pals again," he says.

While the Laurel and Hardy comedies had maintained a consistently high level of quality thus far, there was bound to be a clinker sometime, if only to satisfy the law of averages. *Early to Bed* was it.

This film does nothing more than examine Stan and Ollie's relationship; perhaps it *had* to be made, so the comics could clearly define their characters

Note the microscopic director's credit (bottom, right corner). No wonder Flynn
made only one Laurel and Hardy film.

for themselves and their audience. From this point on, Laurel and Hardy's undying friendship is pretty much a given in their work. But if *Early to Bed* is a necessary and meaningful film, it's not a particularly funny one.

The script lacks the redeeming features of the film's ending. Originally, Stan was to knock Ollie out, drag him from the fountain and pull his semi-conscious master upstairs to the bedroom. "Stan does not realize that he is at the top of the stairway," the script tells us, "and keeps on going to a footstool, cedar chest and window, making three extra steps to the open window. He is just about to pull Babe up the last step when Babe comes to and suddenly realizes they are both going out the window, but it is too late. He screams, and as they both fall out the window we fade out."

The director on this film was Emmett J. Flynn, a writer-producer-director whose most notable achievement was *A Connecticut Yankee in King Arthur's Court* (1921) starring Harry Myers. This was Flynn's only film with Laurel and Hardy, and he doesn't seem to have clicked particularly well with them. Leo McCarey directed retakes, including some newly-added scenes with Stan. (An opening scene in a park and the final ending may have been added by McCarey, since neither scene appears in the original script.)

In June 1928, Hal Roach returned from his five-month trip around the world. Roach found his comedies went over well in Europe, particularly in England, but that it was rather difficult to appeal to the Oriental sense of humor. He also noted happily that MGM's New York executives saw many prestigious theaters dropping vaudeville and stage presentations before the feature picture; they were replacing the live entertainment with Roach's short subjects.

All of this promised to make 1928 a highly profitable year indeed. But Roach, always alert to change, was protecting himself for the future by securing an agreement with Electrical Research Productions, Incorporated, for sound-recording equipment. The talkies were coming.

Meanwhile, Stan enjoyed his new prosperity. He and Lois sold their small house on Van Ness Avenue in Los Angeles, and on Stan's 38th birthday, bought a splendid new home on Bedford Drive in Beverly Hills.

Now Stan had his own mansion — and he didn't have to be the butler.

TWO TARS

Production history: Written early June 1928. Filmed June 22-23, June 26-July 3. Copyrighted November 3, 1928 by MGM (LP 116). Released November 3. Two reels.

Produced by Hal Roach. Supervised by Leo McCarey. Directed by James Parrott. Photographed by George Stevens. Edited by Richard Currier. Titles by H.M. Walker. Story by Leo McCarey.

With Thelma Hill, Ruby Blaine, Edgar Kennedy, Charlie Hall, Edgar Dearing, Thomas Benton Roberts.

Stan and Ollie are two sailors on shore leave; they rent a car, pick up two girls, and have a wonderful day. On the way back they become ensnared in a

Two Tars but three kindred spirits.

massive traffic jam. *Tempers flare amongst the motorists, and minor skir-
mishes become major ones. A motorcycle cop arrives to quell the riot; all
fingers point to L&H. As the mangled jalopies depart the scene, the boys can't
help giggling — the world has triumphed over them again, but it was fun while
it lasted.*

By mid-1928, the idea of a reciprocal destruction skirmish erupting into a
massive battle had become pretty well worn. L&H had gotten mixed up in
crowds throwing hats, pies, rocks, mud and trousers. Still, the device had some
laughs left in it, and it occurred to Stan that the way to get those laughs would
be to slow everything down. Just as Laurel and Hardy had slowed down all the
standard old comedy routines, they now slowed down their own invention. In
The Battle of the Century and *You're Darn Tootin'*, events come quickly to a
boil. In *Two Tars*, they simmer.

Leo McCarey was credited with writing the story, which bore the working
title of *Two Tough Tars*; in all probability, it was a joint effort between McCarey,
Stan, Charley Rogers and a few other gag men. In any event, McCarey was not
present during the shooting. The first scenes shot were an altercation between
the boys and pedestrian Sam Lufkin (who also plays one of the irate motorists
later in the film), and a squabble involving the sailors, their girls, a faulty gum-
ball machine and ill-tempered drug-store proprietor Charlie Hall. As usual, the
crew shot some of these scenes on the studio backlot, and others on good old
Main Street in Culver City.

On June 25, Stan went back and shot added scenes for *Early to Bed*. The

Prop man Thomas Benton Roberts borrowed Jimmy Parrott's glasses and
became an actor.

next day, the company headed out to Centinela Boulevard (now Centinela
Avenue), where L&H tore apart cars for four days on a remote stretch of pave-
ment (the road now borders the Santa Monica Municipal Airport). On July 2
they came back for more; the next day they wrapped after shooting the railroad
tunnel finale, near the Southern Pacific Railroad station at the eastern border
of Santa Monica.

Thomas Benton Roberts, who usually did construction work at the Roach
lot, found himself playing the part of a bespectacled gent who hurls tomatoes
at a truck driver, and has his own face washed with one of the red ripe beauties
by Stan.

Roberts recalled, "I'd made these breakaway cars for *Two Tars*; a lot of 'em.
I did the finishing touches on the squashed car that came out of the tunnel at
the end — the mechanics in the studio garage narrowed the chassis, but I did
the body work and built the hood. I had to re-seat the radiator, too, because it
was on an angle. Then we just towed it out of the tunnel, with an airplane cable
attached to a truck. The radiator's steaming on the car — that was easy; just
used a smokepot.

"Anyway, someone at the studio said, 'Bring your car in; we've got a traffic
scene tomorrow at noon.' Nothing else was shooting at the studio, so a lot of the
employees brought their cars and they all lined up out at Centinela Boulevard."

James Parrott and his assistant, Lloyd French, directed on horseback,
galloping along the two lanes of traffic while wielding the megaphones. "Of
course, they just did what Stan said," stated Roberts. "Jimmy Parrott knew what
Stan wanted, and he'd just call for the camera to roll or to cut.

"So, we're shooting, and they start the traffic jam. The studio had bought 10 cars to wreck; some of them were running, some of them weren't ...So I drove in, and I thought it was just by accident that I got up near the action — there was Laurel and Hardy's car, Ed Kennedy's car, a car behind that, and then mine. I didn't know I'd be in the picture, maybe just in long shots.

"A few days after we finished shooting, they had a preview in Glendale. They'd have counters, to count the number of laughs. That was one of Charley Rogers' jobs, to count laughs. Sixty was the minimum for two reels. If they didn't get 60 belly laughs, why, they didn't think much of it. They got more than that on *Two Tars*, but the audience had gotten such a big laugh out of it, they thought they could improve it with a couple more shots. So Stan, of course, had to ask Hal if he could spend the extra money on it.

"After the preview, Stan, Hal, Jimmy Parrott and George Stevens were standing outside the theater. I came out, and they said, 'Hey, Benton! Get the same outfit on and be out at location tomorrow. We're gonna make some additional scenes.' They brought back just four cars — my car, the car in back of it, the truck behind it, and in the background they had the car with Jack Hill and all the camping equipment.

"That shot where the tomato hits Stan in the neck — a prop man named Harry Black did that. Blackie, they called him. Oh, he was something — he had great aim, never missed on things like that. For my scene with Stan, they cut a tomato open and put catsup in it so it would photograph better; when he rubbed it all over my face, boy, I could taste catsup for a week after that!

"I'd worn my own clothes in the picture. I got paid $35 for a new suit, $15 for a new hat, $15 for the use of the car, and $15 for myself. I just took the clothes to the cleaners and had the tomato juice cleaned out, and kept the money."

Lunchtime: prop men Roy Seawright (extreme left) and Charley Oelze (in kerchief), Babe, Stan, Sam Lufkin (in derby), Ruby Blaine, Charley Rogers, Edgar Kennedy, Thelma Hill and director James Parrott.

Roberts has warm recollections of some of his *Two Tars* cohorts. "Jimmy Parrott was just like an old shoe; he knew what Stan wanted. Charlie Hall was pretty buddy-buddy with Stan. He helped them with some of the writing and detail, before they started shooting. Jack Hill, who played the camper, would kill himself for a Stan and Babe picture. When he fell against his car, he could've broken his back — but he kept going. He was a good stunt man and stunt driver; he'd do anything to get a day's work."

The boys' feminine companions in *Two Tars*, Ruby Blaine and Thelma Hill, contribute greatly to the film's charm. Blaine, the statuesque blonde who tangles with Charlie Hall, was reportedly a professional wrestler who was then appearing in nearby Pasadena.

Several members of the L&H stock company made their first appearance in this film. Short and stocky Harry Bernard, who plays the truck driver, was one of the more congenial inhabitants of the Laurel and Hardy world, but he could also be a formidable adversary. Baldwin Cooke, a former vaudeville partner of Stan's, appears as one of the mad motorists; he would do bits in the team's films for the next 10 years. Charley Rogers, Stan's right-hand man off camera, makes his on-camera debut with the team here as the fellow whose car door injures Ollie's proboscis.

No scripts seem to have survived for *Two Tars*, but stills indicate that a couple of scenes were shot, then deleted: one in which the boys, in their car, try to attract the attention of some young ladies, and another in which Stan gives Ollie a shoeshine before they go out on their day of revelry. Thomas Benton Roberts recalled that at the end of the traffic jam sequence, Stan wanted to show a truck carrying a pole, ramming into a limousine window and tearing the body from the chassis; this shot isn't in the film, but the end result is — a chauffeur walking on the road as he "drives" the chassis.

Editor Richard Currier recalled that a gag in which motorist Sam Lufkin slashed the tire of the L&H car ran into trouble with some regional censors, because it showed young people how to puncture tires.

The gag in which a truck rolls over officer Edgar Dearing's motorcycle presented a formidable challenge to the Roach prop builders. "One of our prop men, Don Sandstrom, took the motorcycle down to a guy with a steamroller; he told him he wanted to have it smashed for a picture," recalled Thomas Benton Roberts. "The guy said, 'Lay it down there.' And when he drove over the bike, it darn near upset the big steamroller!

"Don looked at the bike — the handlebars were bent, but it wasn't anywhere near what we wanted, for the real effect. So he brought it back to the studio, and we used part of it and another motorcycle; I took the engine out of it and built another one out of sheet lead, so the truck could squish it with those solid tires.

"So, we ended up using the motorcycle where the cop drove in — he was a real Culver City cop; he'd bring his own uniform and motorcycle, do a scene and go on about his business. We used his bike, the two motorcycles that we combined and crushed, and the one that he picked up and looked at was still another one. We used four motorcycles for one gag!"

Dedication like this was an everyday occurrence at the Hal Roach studio. Everyone, from Roach right on down to the people in the prop department, was passionately committed to the quest for the belly laugh — which is a big reason why people are still laughing uproariously at *Two Tars* while comedy films from other studios are largely forgotten.

HABEAS CORPUS

Production history: Written early July 1928. Filmed July 16-31 (production suspended between July 24-28 due to Laurel's illness). Released December 1, 1928. Copyrighted June 27, 1929 by MGM (LP 493). Two reels, silent with synchronized music and sound effects.

Produced by Hal Roach. Supervised by Leo McCarey. Directed by James Parrott. Photographed by Len Powers. Edited by Richard Currier. Titles by H.M. Walker. Story by Leo McCarey.

With Richard Carle, Charley Rogers.

Vagabonds L&H come begging for food at the mansion of Professor Padilla, a genial fellow as mad scientists go. He hires the boys to go to a graveyard and steal a corpse for an experiment. Stan and Ollie reluctantly enter a cemetery, where their efforts are thwarted by their own terror — and by the professor's butler, who is really a detective. The detective plays dead and climbs into the boys' body bag; when the "corpse" comes alive, Ollie runs off in horror. He lands in one of those ever-present mudholes, along with the corpse.

Less than two weeks after *Two Tars* wrapped, Laurel and Hardy were back before the cameras, shooting a brand-new comedy. Well, not exactly new. To be exact, it was another trotting out of one of the tried-and-truest comedy formulae: the Horror-Comedy. Harold Lloyd had used it in *Haunted Spooks*. Buster Keaton had used it in *The Haunted House*. Just about all of Harry Langdon's films were horror-comedies, because he was terrified at everything.

L&H had already done an extended "spooky old graveyard" routine in *Do Detectives Think?* But now, a year had passed, the Stan and Ollie characters had been more fully developed, and the team had a chance to do their own unique variation on the horror-comedy theme.

Leo McCarey again got credit in studio press releases for having written the original story, although as always the final script was a collaborative effort. It's a pity all the inventive bits proposed by the script weren't used in the film. To wit:

The professor is still working on a mysterious experiment in the script. So mysterious is it in the *film* that we never find out what it is. The script tells us that he wants to transfer a brain from one body to another. Now *that's* all settled.

When the two vagabonds are beckoned inside the professor's study, the professor asks them to partake of his spaghetti dinner. Stan starts to serve, but Ollie shoves his plate too far forward, and the noodles curl up in his portly lap. (This gag was later used in *Unaccustomed As We Are*. It's okay to waste spaghetti, but never a good gag.)

When the professor tells the duo that to earn $500, all they have to do is go to the local graveyard and pluck out a dead body, the boys do spaghetti spit-takes. They run away, but the genial old prof tells them to come back and sit down. The do — on a shiny black box with silver handles. The good professor tells them that he already has one body. Stan and Ollie look around, then realize that the box on which they're seated is occupied, and the resident isn't

Richard Carle greets the boys in a deleted wrap-up sequence.

going to come out any time soon. None of this coffin comedy was used in the film.

One sequence was shot and then deleted: Stan is unnerved by the graveyard — particularly when the hidden detective/butler sneezes from out of nowhere, loudly — and scurries out. Ollie orders his partner back in. Stan tiptoes back, and stands next to a grave with a particularly large headstone. He sees an eerie-looking monk (Lon Poff), carrying a large lantern and an even larger ring, on which dangles a single key.

The monk asks him what he's doing, and Stan cleverly replies that he's waiting for a streetcar. Since the streetcar doesn't run past this particular grave, the monk gently escorts Stan out of the cemetery and locks the huge gates. Stan gratefully turns to the monk, and through the bars hands him a cigar. The monk thanks him and departs.

Ollie is none too pleased, and when Stan explains that the monk put him out, Ollie puts him back in by tossing Stan over the wall. This last bit is one of those unreal, Mack Sennett-like gags that L&H hardly ever employ. (They couldn't use many impossible gags when the whole source of their comedy was the personalities of two very real characters.)

The scripted ending took place at the Professor's home, wherein the boys deliver their charge. The professor enthusiastically rips the bag open, and is more than mildly chagrined when he sees his butler (still a true-blue detective underneath the mud) pointing a grimy finger at him in accusation. On cue, four other detectives, sporting the regulation meerschaum pipes, haul the professor away — but he begs them to let him pay the boys for their hard work.

Stan and Ollie's countenances fall as the professor pulls out an imaginary roll of bills, and peels off five non-existent C-notes. He starts to leave, then pulls out one more piece of mirage money, and says, "Have another fifty!"

Then Stan remembers the indignities he suffered in that cold, clammy cemetery and shoves Ollie, who smashes into the coffin that tastefully decorates the Professor's study. As Ollie climbs out, a corpse's hand attaches itself to his person. The boys are terrified at this unwanted company, and they run out of the house — through the back wall.

(This ending may have been shot and scrapped, judging from existing stills. In the finished film, however, the Professor is taken away just as the boys are starting their work in the graveyard.)

Filming began on July 16, with James Parrott at the helm. The company shot virtually everything at night, in a local cemetery. (A street sign in the film marks the corner of Hunter and Third, but there's no such intersection in the Los Angeles area.)

The supporting cast of *Habeas Corpus* adds greatly to the fun. Richard Carle plays the Professor with just enough subtle lunacy to make one doubt his sanity. And dependable gag-man Charley Rogers gets an extended role as the detective in disguise. Rogers had worked as a comic in England and the United States; owing to their mutual background in British music-hall comedy, Charley and Stan were very close professionally and personally.

Although the editing of *Habeas Corpus* was completed in August 1928, it wasn't released until December 1. While it sat on the shelf, the demand for sound films continued to build, and on October 4 Roach made an agreement with the Victor Talking Machine Company for "synchronizing certain pictures and installation of sound equipment at the studio."

Hal Roach recalled, "Nick Schenck was the head of Loew's, which owned MGM, and he was very much opposed to sound. He thought it would soon die out. Well, I had a different opinion, so I went back to Camden, New Jersey, where Victor's office was. They damn near threw me out three or four times, but in a week, I ended up with a contract with the Victor company. They didn't want to get into the picture business; they were making records. But I had some pretty good arguments for them, why it wouldn't hurt them to get in. And until RCA bought Victor, they made all the sound in my studio."

Roach sent the head of the film editing department, Richard Currier, to Camden in October. There Currier learned the methods of sound recording, and put together music-and-effects scores for silent films that had yet to be released.

"We had about 8 or 10 pictures we were going to release, with sound effects," Currier recalled. "And I put the sound effects and music in 'em back there. There was a well-known musician there, I can't remember his name, but he said, 'Hell, I don't know anything about the picture business. You pick your own music, I'll make it for you, and you can handle it from there.' So, I cut the music tracks together, and then when we did the redubbing, I added a bunch of sound effects.

"I'll never forget — I wanted the noise of a big bump for one of the pictures. They had a big box filled with rocks, and you'd turn it over, and you'd hear the bumping against the side," said Currier. "Well, they didn't give me a rehearsal. I thought, 'What the hell, don't need any damn rehearsal' — all you had to do was dump it over and record the bumps. Instead of taking it easy, I gave the box a hell of a shove, and — bumpety bump, bump, bump, you really heard those damn rocks! So they had to do a retake."

Publicity material for *Habeas Corpus* heralded it as Laurel and Hardy's "first sound picture." Unfortunately, we're unable to hear the music and effects track for this film, because the discs on which it was recorded have been lost. *Habeas Corpus* will remain an entirely silent film until someone exhumes its soundtrack.

WE FAW DOWN

Production history: Written mid-August 1928. Filmed August 23-September 1. Retakes filmed September 7, 13. Copyrighted December 29, 1928 by MGM (LP 25994). Released December 29. Two reels, silent with synchronized music and sound effects.

Produced by Hal Roach. Directed by Leo McCarey. Edited by Richard Currier. Titles by H.M. Walker.

With Bess Flowers, Vivien Oakland, Kay Deslys, Vera White, George Kotsonaros.

Stan and Ollie want to get away from their wives, and play poker with some pals. So they invent a ruse: an appointment with their boss at the Orpheum Theater. En route to the game, they help two damsels in distress, and fall into a muddy gutter. As their clothes are drying in the gals' flat, the boys get boisterously drunk. A jealous boyfriend sends them out the back window, half-dressed — in view of their unforgiving wives. Back home, L&H tell their wives about the wonderful show they saw. But the Orpheum, it seems, has burned down that afternoon.

After functioning in the somewhat ambiguous role of supervisor, Leo McCarey finally directed an L&H film in August of 1928. But all that *We Faw Down* proves is that even McCarey could not always save a film from mediocrity.

There were all sorts of wonderful things in the script which didn't end up in this film. The unused material started at the point when the boys are crawling out of the flapper girls' apartment — with each other's pants on. Their jealous pursuer (identified in the script as the husband of one of the girls) gives chase. The hapless and ill-clothed pair run behind a large crate on a sidewalk elevator, and start to change their trousers. Their efforts are frustrated when the elevator and crate descend. Worse, a cop is casting a very dubious eye upon them.

The script proposes that Laurel and Hardy walk down the street, start around the corner and return immediately, with the husband after them. They pass the cop again with a nod, and enter a store, where a workman is cementing the floor. L&H walk by unnoticed, but the workman sees their footprints in the cement behind him and is perplexed.

"Cut to the corner. The cop walks on down, and the two boys come around again, nod to him and go back into the building, followed by the husband. The man on the inside has just finished covering up the last footprints when, in back of him, the three again walk through. As soon as they have gone, he turns and sees it again.

"The wives" off-camera: Myrtle and Babe Hardy...

"Repeat the action, passing the cop and the workman three or four times, each time the tempo increasing, and each time the boys nodding to the cop. Finally, the workman sees Stan and Babe go through, figures they will be coming through again, so he gets a big bucket of cement and gets ready to hit them as they come through the door. The husband comes through and gets it. The husband, enraged, picks up another bucket of cement and throws it at the retreating workman, just as the cop steps into the doorway and gets it. The cop grabs the husband and starts to take him off."

From here, the boys run to a taxicab where they attempt to change trousers, but a young man opens the cab door for his girlfriend, revealing the boys in all their pantless glory. They hastily hoist up their mismatched breeches and depart, casting coy and embarrassed glances at the couple.

The boys are equally unsuccessful in their attempts to change trousers behind a fish market; what's more, an angry crab has fallen into Stan's too-ample clothing. This causes him to go into wild contortions as he and Ollie walk down the sidewalk looking for another place to change. Stan's gyrations are especially distressing when the boys walk past a music store, and Stan topples a brand-new Victrola phonograph.

The ill-attired duo finally find refuge in a doorway, rid themselves of Stan's crustacean companion, and switch trousers. Meanwhile, the wives have been seething and fretting at home; they've called every hospital in town, and can't determine if their husbands have survived the Orpheum blaze.

From here on in, the script and the film are alike. If some of these lost scenes sound familiar, they should. More on that in a moment.

Most of *We Faw Down* was shot between August 23 and September 1; the company used both of the studio's stages, the New York Street on the backlot, the corners of 8th Street and Westlake and Western and 10th (now Olympic Boulevard), and various other locales in Culver City.

...and Stan and Lois Laurel, with "little Lois."

A week after they wrapped, McCarey and the L&H crew shot retakes on Stage One; a week after *that*, they shot more retakes, this time in Culver City and on Stage Two. One surmises that McCarey and Laurel edited the film, and discovered it was almost 10 minutes too long; when they previewed it to see what they could cut, they found the only expendable scenes were the changing-the-pants gags.

Unfortunately, these were the funniest scenes in the picture. But nothing else could be cut without hurting the story. So, reluctantly, Leo and Stan removed the film's funniest sequence; they slightly re-wrote the plot so that the wives *did* see Stan and Ollie emerging in disarray from the girls' apartment, and did retakes to cover their editing.

The film they ended up with was amusing but nothing to rave about. The changing-the-pants routine that ended up on the cutting room floor was the funny stuff — and the filmmakers knew it.

They found it so funny, in fact, that they built their next film around it.

LIBERTY

Production history: Written mid-September 1928. Filmed October 1-17 (directed by Leo McCarey). Retakes filmed October 26 (directed by Lloyd French), November 13-19 (directed by James Horne). Released January 26, 1929. Copyrighted January 28, 1929 by MGM (LP 57). Two reels, silent with synchronized music and sound effects.

Produced by Hal Roach. Directed by Leo McCarey. Photographed by George Stevens. Edited by Richard Currier and William Terhune. Titles by H.M. Walker. Story by Leo McCarey.

With James Finlayson, Jean Harlow, Jack Hill.

L&H are two convicts who escape from prison. They make the mistake of putting on each other's pants while changing clothes in the getaway car, and spend the remainder of the film trying to rectify the situation. They attempt to switch trousers in an alley, inside a taxi, behind a fish market and finally in the elevator of an unfinished skyscraper. Naturally, Ollie leans against the "up" switch and before they know it, the boys find themselves dangling precariously atop the girders.

After they assembled *We Faw Down*, McCarey and Laurel found themselves with a great sequence in search of a story — Stan and Ollie having somehow gotten into each other's trousers and trying to switch them without anyone noticing. All they had to do was come up with a beginning and an end, and they'd be all set.

Process shots and rear-screen projection were still in an experimental state in 1928 — in order to show L&H on top of an unfinished skyscraper, they had to actually go to the top of a partly constructed building and film up there. Sure, it was dangerous. Sure, they were risking the lives of Hal Roach's biggest stars. But it was the only way the scene would work. Anything for a laugh.

After McCarey directed the first day's work on location in Culver City, the filmmakers gathered at the Western Costume Company building on South Broadway in Los Angeles. It wasn't an unfinished skyscraper at all, just a nice tall building with a good view of the downtown area.

The Roach construction gang built a framework for Laurel and Hardy to clamber upon. Thomas Benton Roberts, recalled, "We had three stories of supposedly steel structure up on the top of the Western Costume building; actually it was all made out of wood. The roof of the building was 150 feet, and we were working three stories above that. Each time we changed the set-up for a shot, we'd have to move the camera platform around, and try to miss the flagpole on the corner of the building."

Even though Laurel and Hardy and the entire crew (including assistant director Lloyd French, cameraman George Stevens; *his* assistant, Jack Roach and prop man Morrie Lightfoot) were working almost 200 feet above the ground, the shooting went fairly smoothly. The crew spent the better part of 12 days filming the skyscraper scenes, without incident — except one, which McCarey recounted in 1954:

"One day, they were on this skyscraper, and Stan looked down and got panicky, and Babe tried to quiet him. He said, 'Look, there's nothing to worry about.' There was a platform down below him, and Babe said to Stan, 'I'm going to show you that it's perfectly safe,' and he jumped. Well, it wasn't safe."

Roberts added, "The studio had sent some sugar pine down to make a safety platform for them. I had complained about that, but I wasn't the head stand-by on the company, so I could only carry out orders. When Babe jumped down, the sugar pine, of course, broke. But I had a safety net below that — and that saved him." Babe only fell about 20 feet, instead of 200; he only suffered minor bruises, and quickly got back to work.

Now that Stan, McCarey and the crew had finished the arduous task of clambering around on a none-too-secure framework at high altitudes, they had to go through the equally arduous task of looking at what they'd shot, and whipping the film into shape.

Tom Kennedy risked his life for the cutting-room floor.

While an original script has yet to surface, studio records indicate that McCarey shot some scenes with a dog, which does not appear in the film. Neither does the Los Angeles County Hospital, where they filmed for a day. Some stills exist showing Tom Kennedy as a construction worker cavorting with Laurel and Hardy on the girders, but this footage was scrapped, and Kennedy was given a new role as a prison guard.

Come November, the next film had already been conceived, and preparations were being made for filming. But something was seriously wrong with *Liberty*. On November 13, Stan, Babe and the crew all went back to the top of the Western Costume building and crawled around on those wooden girders again. James Horne did the directorial honors for the next five days.

Fortunately, all of this tortuous work paid off. *Liberty* is easily one of the best L&H films. Even though the story was constructed in reverse — starting with the middle and *then* finding the beginning and end — everything flows in a logical progression.

True to form, Laurel and Hardy took a familiar comedy situation and reshaped it to fit their viewpoint. When Harold Lloyd, or any other comic, stumbled around a skyscraper, the laughs always came from his perilous predicament and his narrow escapes. But with Laurel and Hardy, the laughs derive from their characters. A case in point: Stan is hanging underneath a girder, and Ollie comes to pull him up. As he struggles, Ollie realizes that *he* is slipping to the underside of the girder, so he hastily shoves Stan back into danger, and offers up a prayer for help instead. A telling comment about friendships, indeed.

Liberty was Laurel and Hardy's only real excursion into "thrill comedy."

HAL ROACH
presents

STAN **LAUREL** AND
OLIVER **HARDY**

in **LIBERTY**

Directed by LEO MC CAREY

A Metro-*Goldwyn*-Mayer Picture

Due to the easygoing nature of their characters, and the fact that both comedians were middle-aged at the outset of their association, they pretty much kept their feet on terra firma for the rest of their careers.

A sidelight: Harlean McGrew II, the blonde who's startled when Stan and Ollie emerge from the taxi in semi-undress, soon became better known as Jean Harlow. After several brief try-outs such as this one in August 1928, she was placed under a five-year contract in December.

WRONG AGAIN

Production history: Written late October-early November 1928. Filmed November 21-December 1. Released February 23, 1929. Copyrighted March 5, 1929 by MGM (LP 187). Two reels, silent with synchronized music and sound effects.

Produced by Hal Roach. Directed by Leo McCarey. Photographed by George Stevens. Edited by Richard Currier. Titles by H.M. Walker. Story by Leo McCarey.

With Del Henderson, Josephine Crowell, Harry Bernard, Sam Lufkin.

L&H work in a stable where there's a horse named Blue Boy. When they hear that "Blue Boy" has been stolen from its millionaire owner, they assume the gentleman is missing the horse, not the famous painting of the same name. They take the horse to the millionaire's house and inform him that they've got Blue Boy. The unsuspecting millionaire tells them to "put him on the piano." The boys follow orders, albeit with difficulty.

One day in October of 1928, Leo McCarey had a toothache. He went to his friendly neighborhood dentist to have the tooth extracted, and noticed a print of Gainsborough's "Blue Boy" painting on the office wall. While the dentist went to work on McCarey's throbbing molar, the young supervising director envisioned the above story.

Stan and the gag writers added their own embellishments, ending up with a whopping four-page script. The script and the resulting film were virtually identical — save for one sequence.

The working title for the film was *Just the Reverse*, in reference to a gag among the studio staff — which Hal Roach recounted: "Leo McCarey was a great comedy thinker. And, for some reason or another, we'd see a dramatic picture and change it a little. It finally got to the point where if a writer had a funny idea, he would twist his hand around, and that meant that you switched the dramatic thing that was going on — you made it a little different, and that's what made it funny."

This gesture plays a prominent part in the film, when Stan can't understand why the millionaire wants Blue Boy on the piano. Ollie calmly explains that rich people are a little bit different — using the hand-twisting gesture for emphasis. As Stan begins to grasp the meaning of this, he twists his hand at Ollie again and beams at him, proud to have absorbed the intricacies of its symbolism.

The "just-the-reverse" gesture also plays a part in the film's best gag. As Ollie brings the horse into the mansion, he unwittingly topples a statue of Venus, breaking it in three pieces. Delicately, Hardy puts the statue back together; unfortunately, her posterior is now facing the wrong way. Later, Stan strolls by the statue, stops, does a take, looks again — and realization dawns. Stan smiles knowingly, does the "just-the-reverse" hand gesture, and strolls merrily on his way.

The one sequence not in the script may have been the result of on-the-set inspiration: A leg of the piano has broken off under the weight of the horse, so Ollie crawls under the piano to put the leg back in place. Ollie's back is now bearing the weight of the piano *and* the horse. He pleads with Stan to help lift up the piano and put the leg where it belongs. But Stan doesn't hear, because he's too busy telling the horse to stop nuzzling the precious Laurel derby off of his head.

After a week of struggling with the horse at the studio, the company had the film's final sequence completed. On November 30 they shot the middle sequence on location at the mansion of a wealthy gentleman named Milbank. Next, they journeyed to the Uplifters' Club, a Los Angeles sports complex, and filmed the opening scenes in which Stan and Ollie work as stable boys.

Normally, an L&H comedy was shot in sequence from beginning to end, but this one was shot from end to beginning — just the reverse.

George Stevens behind the (right) camera, Leo McCarey directing, and Stan and Babe having a spot of tea on the *Wrong Again* set.

THAT'S MY WIFE

Production history: Written early December 1928. Filmed December 11-16. Copyrighted March 11, 1929 by MGM (LP 201). Released March 23. Two reels, silent with synchronized music and sound effects.

Produced by Hal Roach. Supervised by Leo McCarey. Directed by Lloyd French. Edited by Richard Currier. Titles by H.M. Walker. Story by Leo McCarey.

With Vivien Oakland, William Courtright, Charlie Hall, Jimmy Aubrey.

Ollie's uncle is coming to visit, promising his nephew a large inheritance — as long as he's happily married. Unfortunately, Mrs. Hardy has just walked out, thanks to Mr. Laurel, a permanent household guest. Stan is elected to play the missus when uncle arrives, and is fairly convincing — he even draws the attentions of a flirtatious drunk when the three of them go to a nightclub. Then a waiter steals a necklace from a patron and drops it down the back of Stan's dress; attempts to find the jewelry reveal the ruse and cost Ollie his fortune.

The unusual delays in the filming of *Liberty* finally began to take their toll as 1928 drew to a close. December arrived to find L&H obligated to churn out two more films, with very little time in which to churn them. The studio was set to close for a month on December 29, so that sound recording equipment could be installed. The talkies were approaching ever more rapidly.

Fortunately, Leo McCarey's fertile mind had already concocted another story. It was good basic material, and made use of the Stan-in-drag routine — which they hadn't used for a couple of years.

There were a number of differences in the script. One gag makes use of a bunch of balloons gaily floating around the nightclub. One of the balloons attaches itself to Stan's wig, and lifts it off his head. Ollie does his best to keep Stan's hairpiece from flying around the room. The uncle conveniently turns away every time the persistent balloon tries to escape with Stan's wig, but *is* eager to know why Ollie always has his hands clamped firmly on his "wife's" noggin. Ollie replies that he's simply massaging his missus' itchy scalp. Stan remains oblivious. He generally is.

Another development in the script but not in the film: When uncle and the happy "couple" are seated at the nightclub, who should they spy at another table but Ollie's real wife. At first, she has menace in her heart and murder in her eye, but the uncle thinks she's a charmer and invites her to their table. Ollie tells her to keep quiet if she doesn't want to lose the promised inheritance; she agrees, and turns on the charm.

The ending sequence was markedly different in the script. When a matronly diner realizes her necklace has been stolen, the club manager orders everyone in the place to be searched. All of the women, including Stan, line up outside a dressing room, where they're to be individually scrutinized by a lady officer. As Stan is ordered inside, he puts up quite a struggle with the officer; after a tussle, Stan dashes his wig to the floor. He storms over to Ollie's table, tells him he's tired of playing wifey, and stalks out. Ollie explains that the young lady with whom Uncle Bernal has been flirting all night is his real wife. The uncle gets mightily apologetic. Outside as Stan is leaving the club, the drunk pours a bowlful of soup on *Stan,* salutes, and marches off.

The problem with this ending is that it's just too happy. Ollie still has his fortune and his wife, but he's lost Stan's friendship. In the film, he loses everything *but* Stan's friendship — which is more like it.

The obnoxious drunk was played by Jimmy Aubrey, who had worked with Stan in the Fred Karno troupe and later for producer Joe Rock; Babe had supported Aubrey in a comedy series at Vitagraph. Now Aubrey was appearing in a small role, supporting Stan and Babe. Aubrey lived well into his 90s; when asked about his former associates, his comments were uniformly outrageous and unprintable.

The direction of *That's My Wife* has been credited to Lloyd French, the assistant director for most L&H films of this period. (His father, L.A. French, was the studio's business manager; those on the Roach lot referred to him as "Los Angeles French.") Some studio files indicate that French remained the assistant director on this picture, with the actual directing done by Hal Yates. Shooting was completed in a fast six days.

In 18 months, Laurel and Hardy had developed their characters and techniques to a point where they were masters of silent film comedy. But changing technology would not let them remain silent much longer.

BIG BUSINESS

Production history: Written mid-December 1928. Filmed December 19-26. Released April 20, 1929. Copyrighted June 27, 1929 by MGM (LP 492). Two reels.

Produced by Hal Roach. Supervised by Leo McCarey. Directed by James W. Horne. Photographed by George Stevens. Edited by Richard Currier. Titles by H.M. Walker. Story by Leo McCarey.

With James Finlayson, Tiny Sandford, Lyle Tayo.

Stan and Ollie are Christmas tree salesmen in sunny California. They have been angrily rebuffed by two would-be customers when they meet a particularly surly prospect (Finlayson). A simple argument escalates into a full-scale war, as the boys destroy Fin's house and its furnishings, while he demolishes their car and merchandise. A burly cop halts the fracas; Stan's gesture of apology to the homeowner is an exploding cigar.

Although many writers persist in stating that this film takes place in the summertime, it was actually shot during Christmas week 1928, in the midst of a typically sunny Southern California winter. The studio was eager to get the film finished, before closing on December 29 for installation of sound-recording equipment.

Big Business was shot entirely on location; an early scene in which the boys have an altercation with customer Lyle Tayo — followed by a violent encounter with a customer wielding a hammer — was filmed at a duplex on Culver City's Caroline Avenue.

After the first day of shooting, the company moved to a house on Dunleer Drive in the Cheviot Hills section of Los Angeles. For six days, the neighboring

Big Business isn't quite as violent as this poster suggests.

Marion Byron, half of a "female Laurel and Hardy" with Anita Garvin, wishes the boys a Merry Christmas for 1928.

residents had to put up with the sound and the fury of L&H destroying a house, its contents and the surrounding shrubbery.

For years, Hal Roach has told a story about the *Big Business* house. This is the way he told it in February 1981: "They said they wanted a bungalow. So the location manager went out and he photographed five or six bungalows with a still camera. One of the bungalows he photographed belonged to a guy working at the studio. I made a deal with the guy to go on his vacation. We'd keep a guard at his house every night; we'd wreck the house, and we guaranteed to put the house back in order and pay him a fee.

"The director had a picture of the house, and the other cars were following him to the location. Another bungalow, which was a block away, looked exactly like the one in the picture. The director said, 'This is it, all right, stop.' Then the property man says, 'The key don't fit!' The director says, 'Well, hell with that, we're gonna break the door down anyway!' So they broke the door down. They did a lot of things that weren't in the script. Cutting down all of those trees, that wasn't in the script, but what the hell, they all knew this guy worked at the studio — they figured they'd buy a new tree. The next-to-last day, a man, his wife and two kids drove up in front of the house. The woman damn near fainted. We had the wrong house. So we had to pay for that house, as well as pay for the house that nobody used."

Laurel, however, remembered things differently. In the early '60s, after Roach told this story on a television program, Stan stated in a letter to a fan, "The anecdote Hal Roach Sr. told on the Les Crane show was definitely not true — the chap who owned the house was employed at the studio and worked on the film with us." (The house is still standing today.)

Although James Wesley Horne was the director, Leo McCarey was again credited as supervisor. But McCarey's days at the Roach studio were coming to an end. On December 28th, two days after this film wrapped, his contract as a writer-director was terminated. McCarey, who had received an offer to direct features for Pathé, resigned as a vice-president of the Roach studio in January 1929.

McCarey began his Pathé contract with the campus comedy *The Sophomore* and followed with *Red Hot Rhythm*, which co-starred Anita Garvin. ("I have the distinction of having appeared in Leo McCarey's only flop!" she recalled.) Soon, with films like *The Kid From Spain* and *Duck Soup* to his credit, McCarey would be recognized as a major creative talent.

Oddly, McCarey receives story credit in copyright listings for every L&H film released through *Hog Wild* (shot in April 1930), meaning either that whoever did the Roach studio paperwork mistakenly continued to give McCarey a blanket credit, or that McCarey had amassed a small stockpile of story ideas which the other writers drew upon after he left.

Note: In the silent days, most studios shot at least two camera negatives; this would provide an original negative for the domestic market, and another for the European market. (There was no adequate "copying" film stock yet available.) Prints of *Big Business* made from different negatives have many noticeable differences. One close-up of Finlayson, for example, is virtually a profile in some prints; in others he faces the camera directly.

DOUBLE WHOOPEE

Production history: Written and filmed circa early-mid February 1929. Copyrighted May 13, 1929 by MGM (LP 361). Released May 18. Two reels.

Produced by Hal Roach. Directed by Lewis R. Foster. Photographed by George Stevens and Jack Roach. Edited by Richard Currier. Titles by H.M. Walker. Story by Leo McCarey.

With Jean Harlow, William Gillespie, Captain John Peters, Charley Rogers, Tiny Sandford, Rolfe Sedan.

Stan and Ollie are the new doorman and footman at a swanky hotel. With their usual ineptness, they quickly run afoul of a haughty blonde (whom they manage to partly disrobe), a surly cab driver, a cop and most of the hotel guests — especially a pseudo-Prussian prince, who keeps falling into a muddy elevator shaft. Before the evening is over, the Prince is threatening to declare war, and the boys are once again unemployed.

Conversion of the Roach studio's stages for sound-film production went on during the January hiatus; even though all of the recording and playback equipment had arrived, the installation would take until early March.

Thomas Benton Roberts played an integral part in the conversion. "I was in charge of construction and design for the changeover to sound," he said. "Even though I had many superiors, I was the only guy in the middle ranks who'd had Class-A construction experience — instead of hiring an architect and a construction engineer, they could get me for a dollar an hour!

"Nobody gave us any advice on acoustics or anything — at the Roach studios, we didn't have the money to pay for the help. All I had were a few sketches from the Victor Recording Company, like floor plans which showed where to place the projection machines and so on. I had to design all the structural stuff around it."

Meanwhile, the L&H company made three more silent films. Late in the first week of February 1929, Stan and Babe began shooting *Double Whoopee*, a story that had sprung from the fertile mind of Leo McCarey (according to the film's copyright registration). While McCarey had left the Roach lot, and was obviously no longer "supervisor" of the Laurel and Hardy comedies, it could be argued that the team's real supervisor had always been Stan Laurel. In any event, with McCarey's departure, Stan assumed his place as the creative guiding hand — although his work was subject to Hal Roach's approval.

The new director of the L&H unit was 28-year-old Lewis R. Foster. A native of Missouri, Foster had trained to be a journalist, but left the newspaper business and joined the Roach studio in 1923. In the tradition of Laurel and Hardy directors, he had no particular individual style.

Because of his relative lack of experience at directing — which may well be why he was chosen to work with Stan — Foster was more than happy to give Stan and Babe their freedom in ad-libbing routines.

The cast for *Double Whoopee* was an especially good one, with arch-nemeses Charlie Hall and Tiny Sandford playing an abrasive taxi driver and an intimidating cop. Rolfe Sedan, one of those stalwart character actors one always recognizes except by name, played a nonplussed desk clerk. The reason for his befuddlement was none other than 17-year-old Jean Harlow — who is stripped to her underwear when Stan unwittingly slams a taxi door on the train of her gown. It was a memorable scene in real life, too, as Sedan recalled:

"We weren't told that she was going to come in naked; nobody knew. It was a shock for all of us... when she came up to the desk, for a moment I almost didn't say the words. Even though I'd been in burlesque, they didn't walk around *like that*. It's bound to throw you when you don't expect it. There was no rehearsal. You're standing behind the desk, you're waiting, and all of a sudden — there she is. When she got through, she covered up and went back to the dressing room." (Harlow wore an almost completely transparent slip in the first take, then donned one that was less revealing.)

"We had fun at Roach; I worked a lot there," said Sedan, who played a drunk in *You're Darn Tootin'* and later appeared in *The Devil's Brother*. "Those were bread and butter jobs — $25 a day. You didn't get big money, but you worked.

"Laurel and Hardy had directors, but those two men did all their own stuff. They were very relaxed performers; there were no problems, no temperaments. It was just fun, playing with them. Working with Harold Lloyd was entirely different. He said, 'I can't allow anybody to top me. I have to be the top banana.' He was already The Star. Everything was centered around him. With Laurel and Hardy, the emphasis was on the comedy situation."

Several gags in *Double Whoopee* involve the visiting Prince, whose continual misfortune it is to step into an elevator shaft after the elevator has already ascended. The Prince is a dead ringer for Erich von Stroheim, and no wonder: he's played by Captain John Peters, who was Stroheim's double.

In passing, it ought to be noted that the anonymous public-relations man

Jean Harlow's presence did not go unnoticed by the publicity department.

who wrote the film's press sheet had a wonderful grasp of the L&H characters. Listen to the way he describes their misadventures, and their personalities: "In their child-like eagerness to serve the hotel's guests, they create a hilarious havoc of destruction. From this the two grown-up children emerge, jobless but undaunted ...Together they depart for new fields, facing the rigors of the world with the naive wonder and eagerness of their child hearts."

Somebody give that man a medal. A publicity release like this may not seem important, but it shows how Laurel and Hardy's characters were affectionately thought of as "grown-up children" at the Roach lot. By contrast, publicity releases from 20th Century-Fox and Metro-Goldwyn-Mayer for the team's later features would consistently describe Stan and Ollie as "dopes," "idiots," "dumb-bells" and so on — a callousness reflected in those films' scripts. There's precious little "naive wonder" to be found in a film like *The Big Noise*. There's a whole heap of naive wonder in the Roach films, even in a minor one like *Double Whoopee*.

BACON GRABBERS

Production history: Written and filmed circa February 16-March 2, 1929. Copyrighted September 3, 1929 by MGM (LP 643). Released October 19. Two reels, silent with synchronized music and sound effects.

Produced by Hal Roach. Directed by Lewis R. Foster. Photographed by George Stevens and Jack Roach. Edited by Richard Currier. Titles by H.M. Walker. Story by Leo McCarey.

With Edgar Kennedy, Jean Harlow, Harry Bernard.

L&H are attachment officers from the county sheriff's office. They're dispatched to serve a subpeona to a surly homeowner (Kennedy) and repossess a radio he's neglected to pay for. They reclaim the radio but leave it in the street where a steamroller smashes it. Kennedy's wife arrives to tell him she's just paid for the radio; as Stan and Ollie howl at Kennedy's misfortune, the steamroller flattens their car.

In mid-February 1929, Stan and Babe began preparing yet another comedy. *Hollywood Filmograph*, a trade paper, reported that "this newest humor effusion deals with the activities of a group of rum-runners," but the rum-running idea was, shall we say, scotched. Much of the story they *did* use was thrown out before everyone was satisfied.

One elaborate scene was filmed, but cut from the beginning of the picture: as the boys get into their trusty old Ford touring car, which is parked at the curb outside the sheriff's office, a truck backs into it and punctures the car's radiator. Water sprays out, but the truck driver says he knows how to stop it. He dashes into a grocery store and returns with a package of Cream of Wheat. The boys pour it into the car's radiator, and the leak magically stops. They thank the truck driver profusely and depart. (Typically, they don't stop to think that he's also the guy who *caused* their problem.)

As the boys travel down the road, beaming with pride and lovingly polishing their new badges, mush starts to bubble out of the radiator. It spritzes

Top: Charlie Hall's Cream of Wheat was not served in the film. Bottom: The boys disguised as the Smith Bros., in a deleted scene with Edgar Kennedy.

the windshield; as soon as Stan cleans the glass off, mush sprays back onto it all over again. Worse, the mush is coming out of the exhaust pipe, and when a cop stops the boys' car at an intersection, the mush sprays a curious dog, two refined young ladies seated on a bench, an unfortunate manhole worker and, of course, the cop.

The original script had a rather soggy finish. After Kennedy's radio is demolished by the steamroller, *another* process server comes up to Kennedy, and he dashes back into the house. The boys then go to their mush-covered car and start it up — and it explodes. As they sit in the rubble, the truck driver from the beginning of the film walks by, and Stan and Ollie tell him that his Cream of Wheat wrecked their car. The truck driver says, "It wrecked mine, too!" Fade out.

The filming took place during the last week of February 1929. Most of the shooting was done on location in Cheviot Hills, although the scene with truck driver Charlie Hall (which survived in an abbreviated version) was shot on the studio backlot.

After having released the last two pictures in strictly silent versions, the studio decided to release this and the next Laurel and Hardy picture with synchronized music and effects scores. (These two films were scored with a pipe organ, instead of the orchestral scores used in the previous pictures.)

ANGORA LOVE

Production history: Written and filmed early-mid March, 1929. Previewed March 30. Copyrighted September 3, 1929 by MGM (LP 651). Released December 14. Two reels, silent with synchronized music and sound effects.

Produced by Hal Roach. Directed by Lewis R. Foster. Photographed by George Stevens. Edited by Richard Currier. Titles by H.M. Walker. Story by Leo McCarey.

With Edgar Kennedy, Charlie Hall.

An affection-starved goat runs away from a pet shop and attaches itself to Stan and Ollie, after Stan has given it part of a doughnut. The goat follows them everywhere, and they are forced to bring it into their boarding house. The resultant noise — and odor — arouse the suspicions of the landlord. When the boys attempt to bathe their new-found friend, it results in a water fight in which Laurel, Hardy, the landlord and a neighbor are drenched.

Angora Love was the team's last silent film, and far from their best effort — but it's amusing enough. Everything seems familiar in this short, probably because the basic plot and several gags were reused in *Laughing Gravy* and *The Chimp*, with incidental routines repeated in *Be Big* and *Beau Hunks*.

If most of the routines seem well-worn, there were some fresh gags planned for the film which never made it past the script. For example:

As a cop chases the boys (because he thinks they've stolen the goat), Stan and Ollie run by a music store, and stuff their fragrant friend into a piano crate.

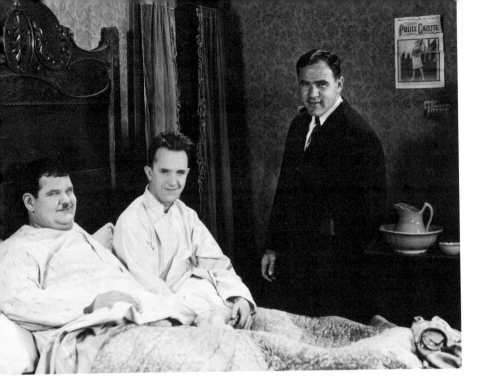

The boss pays a visit to the *Angora Love* set.

The cop looks at them suspiciously, sees no goat, and exits. The boys exit, too. Then two piano movers lift the crate into the shop. The bottom falls out, and so does the goat, which follows Stan and Ollie again.

An incidental gag which may have been rejected as a trifle gimmicky occurs when landlord Kennedy notices a peculiar odor in his boarders' room and asks, "Are you cooking anything?" The boys shake their heads, but we cut inside a closet, where the goat is hiding. The goat looks at us and says, via title, "Even my best friends won't tell me." Kennedy mutters something about cauliflower and storms out.

Typically, the whole water-fight finale was improvised on the set. The original scripted finish was somewhat tentative, with Kennedy discovering the boys washing the goat, yelling at them and throwing an as-yet-undetermined something at them. The prop was to go through a window and land upon the cranium of a cop, conveniently stationed outside the boarding house. The cop comes in, growls at Kennedy, takes the goat, and hauls the landlord off to the pokey. Finis.

During the filming of *Angora Love*, Babe's life was complicated by a lawsuit from Tyler Brooke, a comic with whom Babe had appeared in some earlier Roach comedies.

According to the *Los Angeles Times* (March 14, 1929), Babe supposedly got reckless with a pool cue and poked Brooke in the arm, causing a fracture, while they were playing pool earlier that month. Brooke got himself a hotshot lawyer and sued Babe for over $100,000. While the outcome of the suit is unknown, Babe was obviously learning that his newfound fame carried an expensive price tag.

Cameraman George Stevens refuses admission in this gag photo.

As always, *Angora Love* was previewed extensively before release; one such preview was held late in March at the Ritz Theater in Los Angeles. The film then languished on the shelf for over eight months, until it was finally released on December 14, 1929. By that time, seven Laurel and Hardy talkies had already been issued, and the silent era had come to an end.

When Boyd Verb interviewed Stan for *Films in Review* and asked if he had any preference between silent and talking films, Stan replied tersely, "Well, frankly, I preferred the silents." Making silents had been relatively easy, compared to talkies — as Laurel would find out very soon.

Sound recording brought new constraints.

The Hal Roach Talkies

A Sound Future

Talking films had been a gleam in inventors' eyes since the inception of motion pictures. But it was only when radio became a national craze in the mid-'20s, and audiences began to miss the sound of human voices at the movies, that studio heads began to take the idea of "talkies" seriously. Then, on October 6, 1927, Warner Bros. released *The Jazz Singer*, with Al Jolson not only singing, but talking and joking in an entirely natural, spontaneous way. Although the film's sound sequences were few, audiences thought they were sensational.

By the spring of 1929, virtually everybody realized the talkies were here to stay. Harold Lloyd wrote, "Sound is going to help the comedian. Before, he had to depend on pantomime alone. Where before we had great difficulty in finding some bit of action to start off a film, we now can easily get our effect with a word or a line. We can fade out a picture on a clever remark." Hal Roach simply stated, "The day of the silent comedy has passed."

Anita Garvin remembered her first experience with talkies vividly: "I was watching the dailies on the Fox lot, for a picture I was making with the comedy team Clark and McCullough. And I thought, 'Oh, my God, here I am *lisping* all over the place! I'm ruined; I'm finished.' But fortunately, the next person in the scene did the same thing, so I knew it was the sound track and not me. But for a few minutes there, wow! I could see my whole career, everything down the drain."

Comics were having a particularly tough time of it. The Mack Sennett style of surreal, frantic comedy which had seemed so dynamic in silent films looked hokey and leaden with the new, slower pace and realism of the talkies. Comedy was changing with sound, with more emphasis on dialogue, much less on pantomime. Things looked a bit uncertain for Laurel and Hardy; now that they'd finally achieved success, the talkies threatened their careers.

Stan was a bit concerned about his voice; even as a teenager it worried him. "I had quite a lisp at that time," he told an interviewer in 1957. "My voice was kind of broken, and I was just ill-fitted for anything but a comic." Stan's accent, and the sibilant sound of his s's, would eventually become two of his most endearing traits.

The sound track was now of primary importance, and everyone had to answer to the sound crew. At the Roach lot, the crew had to answer to Elmer Raguse, head of the sound department. Editor Richard Currier, who accompanied Raguse on the train from Victor's headquarters in Camden, New

Jersey to Los Angeles, recalled, "I used to have many arguments with him — Jesus, yes. In pictures, if you can't get an effect one way, you figure out another way of getting it. But with Raguse, there was only one line you could follow, and that was that.

"For example, he wouldn't let me shoot off a revolver near a mike," said Currier. "On the recorder, there was a thing called a light valve — two ribbons on a magnetic pole, and this caused the vibration that made the recording. A loud noise would break that. So, I said to Raguse, 'Well, how much does this cost — $150, $200?' He says, 'Oh, no — hell, it only costs probably 20 cents.' So I says, 'The hell with it, then. We're gonna shoot the gun right near the mike.'"

Marvin Hatley, Roach musical director from the department's inception in 1930 until 1939, recalled, "Raguse was a powerful man there. Even Roach had to rely on him, because Raguse was the only man who knew how to run all the sound equipment, and Roach knew nothing about it. I felt the same way! I was dependent on Raguse, and I did everything I could to make him like me, but I didn't succeed too well." Another Roach staffer says simply, "Elmer Raguse was antisocial. He was totally technical — in his own little world."

Harvey Wasden was one of Raguse's crew members in the first days of sound. "I started at the Roach studio in September of '29," he said. "Most of the crew came from Victor in New Jersey, but three of the nine were local boys, and I was one of them. I worked a lot on the location sound trucks; we usually stayed around the neighborhood, in Culver City.

"We could handle the sound effects if we knew what was coming. We

Edgar Kennedy, Stan, Babe and Our Gang greet the new sound crew (Elmer Raguse, standing on rail) and a new location recording truck.

usually rehearsed, because the light valves would break if we didn't. Those light valves would snap if there were any loud sounds — hands clapping, gun shots. The Roach studio recorded sound electrically with the sound-on-film system, and we also had the sound-on-disc system. We had both recording systems going at the same time, to cover — if we got a bad take on one, maybe we'd have a good take on the other."

Not only did sound create problems with the logistics of recording — it constrained the visuals as well. "The first sound cameras were in a big box, and you needed five men to move it — you couldn't hear the noise of the camera motor that way," asserted Richard Currier. "If you wanted a master shot and a close-up shot at the same time, you needed two cameras, with two of these big clunky boxes cluttering up the stage."

Direction changed markedly when sound came in. "In the silent days," said Hal Roach, "the director kept talking all the time. And many of the funniest things that happened in comedies were things that were never figured on. Something would go wrong, but it was funny. When sound came in, of course, as soon as things went wrong, you had to cut and do it over again.

"We had the top people [Victor] as far as sound was concerned. But the first three or four pictures we made, we had to make for the microphone. We had one microphone sitting still, so the sound men would say, 'No, this guy has got to come closer, and that guy has got to go farther back,' in order to get the sound — nobody thought about moving the microphone!

"Every once in a while, I would direct a picture just to keep my hand in, and when sound came in, I did one of the first sound pictures at the studio," recalled Roach. "When we ran the dailies, the projection room was packed. The first scene came on, and it was fine. At the end of the scene, somebody from off-screen said, 'That's good.' And the next scene came on; at the end of the scene, somebody said, 'That's good' again.

"The third scene came on. The guy said 'That's good' again. I jumped up and said, 'Stop the projection machine! I'm directing this picture. I'll decide what's good and what's bad! Now, who the hell is it in this organization that decided *they're* gonna say whether it's bad or good? And there was a lull. Finally one little voice spoke up. A script girl very quietly said, 'Mr. Roach, that's *you*.'"

In this atmosphere, work began on the first L&H sound comedy in mid-. March, 1929. Roach exercised even more authority than usual while the first talkies were made. As *Hollywood Filmograph* noted, "Roach has laid aside his polo mallets and assumed the duties of supervising director for the all-talking pictures of the four production units of the Hal Roach Studios."

UNACCUSTOMED AS WE ARE

Production history: Written mid-March 1929. Filmed March 25–early April. Previewed April 20. Released May 4. Copyrighted December 10, 1929 by MGM (LP 902). Two reels.

Produced by Hal Roach. Directed by Lewis R. Foster. Photographed by George Stevens, Len Powers, John McBurnie and Jack Roach. Edited by Richard Currier. Titles by H.M. Walker. Story by Leo McCarey.

With Mae Busch, Thelma Todd, Edgar Kennedy.

A 1929 newspaper ad invites us to *hear* the boys.

Ollie invites his pal Stan over for a home-cooked meal, but Mrs. Hardy is tired of cooking for her husband's freeloading friends. A pretty housewife who lives across the hall offers to help the boys make dinner, but before long her dress is on fire. The woman's husband — a cop — investigates the commotion; since his wife is now clad only in her underwear, the boys hide her in a trunk. When the husband realizes there's a lady in the trunk, he confides to the boys that they should be more careful with their affairs of the heart — like he is.

L&H purportedly took several liberties with the original script for *Unaccustomed As We Are*, which studio publicity material credited to Hal Roach. According to the press-sheet: "Using only a skeleton script, the two funsters, aided and abetted by H. M. Walker... developed their comedy gags of speech and action at the time of the actual shooting of the picture."

Beanie Walker's job changed with the coming of sound, from title writer to dialogue writer. For most of the Laurel and Hardy sound shorts, until Walker's departure in July 1932, there would be *two* scripts — an action script written by Stan and the gag men, and a dialogue script by Walker. Walker's script was often just a more polished version of the dialogue already contained in the "action" script. But neither of the scripts was adhered to very much.

On March 25, 1929, Stan and Babe walked onto the newly-renovated *sound* stage and began shooting their first talking footage at the Roach lot. "Their voices recorded perfectly, sounding even funnier than the two clowns look," proclaimed a studio press release. "The English accent of Stan's speech brings an additional note of hilarity to his words."

Hilarity or no, Thomas Benton Roberts recalled, "Stan was worried sick before sound came in about whether he'd be finished or not. He was afraid he wouldn't be able to talk. And every take we'd make, he wanted to hear a playback on it."

Hal Roach had no doubts about Laurel and Hardy's future in talkies. "You lost a lot of comedians when sound came in," he said, "but with Laurel and Hardy, almost from the first picture in sound, they were good."

Other Roach players had some difficulties, however. When Roach directed the studio's first talkie, *Hurdy Gurdy*, he discovered that "Edgar Kennedy sounded like a fairy!" Kennedy concentrated on speaking in a gruff, more masculine manner; as a result he sounds just fine in this film, his second Roach talkie.

The cast also included Mae Busch, making her first appearance with the boys since *Love 'em and Weep*. Her strident bark worked beautifully; it would pierce the ears of Stan and Ollie, and their audiences, frequently in years to come. Another fondly-remembered actress made her debut with Stan and Babe in this film: Thelma Todd.

There were *four* cameras on the stage filming *Unaccustomed As We Are.* George Stevens, Len Powers, John McBurnie and Jack Roach each climbed into one of those big boxes and braved the perils of suffocation. One camera covered long shots, another took care of medium shots, and the other two filmed close-ups. This was necessary to capture spontaneous, ad-libbed action from several angles at once.

The working title for this picture was *Their Last Word,* but by the first week of shooting the film had been re-christened. Much of the film was shot at night, because the Roach studio only had one set of sound equipment, and Our Gang's first talkie, *Small Talk,* was being produced at the same time. Because the Gang could only work until 5 o'clock — and Roach had invested a lot of money in recording equipment — the studio went to a double shift.

Stan and Babe planned to make their new sound pictures the same way they'd made the silents. As Stan related in a 1960 interview: "We had decided we weren't talking comedians and of course preferred to do pantomime, like in our silents. So we said as little as possible — only was was necessary to motivate the things we were doing. If there was any plot to be told, we generally would have somebody else tell it... as time went on, we became a little more accustomed, and did more talking than we first intended."

Unaccustomed As We Are is a very talky talkie nonetheless; it's a situation comedy, and the situation is conveyed primarily through dialogue. Other gags depend on sound; for example, while Ollie and his wife argue, Stan turns on the phonograph, and Mrs. Hardy's speech gradually takes on the ha-cha-cha rhythm of the recorded dance band.

Thelma Todd is clearly unhappy with hubby Edgar Kennedy.

The most creative use of sound is reserved for the film's final gag, and it was such an innovation in 1929 that Roach studio alumni warmly remembered it decades later. "Hardy brings Laurel home to dinner, and the wife gets mad," recalled Richard Currier. "So Laurel leaves, and he starts down the steps and falls. Well, you don't see him falling; you just hear the noise! And that is the one scene in the one picture they made that I'll never forget, because I was on the set. Just the *sound* of him falling made me laugh. We didn't use the real sound of him falling, though; we put in our own sound effects."

This type of gag — with the sound of an off-screen catastrophe allowing the audience to imagine what's going on — soon became part of the common vocabulary of sound comedies. (Incidentally, the film originally began with Stan falling *up* the same fight of stairs, but the gag was cut before the film was released.)

Even though the process of editing was made slightly more difficult with the addition of the sound track, Stan and the Roach staffers retained the time-consuming procedure of previewing the film, re-shooting, re-cutting and previewing again until they were satisfied. Said editor Bert Jordan, "I'd be in the projection booth raising the volume of the sound at certain points, because the dialogue always got drowned out by the audience's laughter at the previews."

Richard Currier related, "I would arrange for the preview; I had to get the sound department to make a sound track on records. Only half of the theaters had sound-on-film equipment, but all of 'em had turntables. It wasn't too difficult — you put a start mark on the disc and a start mark on the film, and you're in sync."

Unaccustomed As We Are was previewed in mid-April 1929; if Stan and Babe had been worried about their future in talkies, reviews like the one in *Hollywood Filmograph* put those worries to rest. The critic wrote, "If these two can continue along these lines in their talkers, there is no danger of them losing any of their popularity... If anything, as time goes on, and the makers become more acquainted with the possibilities of the talkies, you can gamble that the Laurel-Hardys will remain the best of the two-reel comedies."

MGM confidently exhorted its exhibitors to "spread the news of the showing of *Unaccustomed As We Are* at your theater far and wide... Every picturegoer is a Laurel-Hardy fan, and when they know that they can hear and see this pair in their new all-talking series, your box-office is due for a stampede. By all means, give this comedy all the advertising effort that you would put behind a feature. It's a box-office natural such as you seldom get."

Hal Roach realized that he had a surefire success on his hands, and rushed the film into release through MGM on May 4, 1929. (The last three Laurel and Hardy silents sat on the shelves and were parceled out gradually.)

"We were on the market with sound pictures six months ahead of Metro," recalled Roach. "And you never saw so much adjustment in your life — for two-reel comedies in sound, they were paying us more than they were paying for features. Metro didn't know what to charge for 'em, and the theaters didn't know what to pay for 'em. The theaters were paying enormous amounts of money for our comedies. That was the first time we changed from our original idea of selling the whole year's package at one time; we started selling these sound comedies by themselves. But we had to make hundreds of adjustments later on, because exhibitors couldn't afford the prices they were paying."

In mid-April, Roach planned 12 more silent comedies for the 1929-30 season — three for each of his four series. Roach did not produce these additional silents, but he did make silent versions of some talkies, for small town and overseas exhibitors whose theaters were not yet equipped for sound. (Silent versions of *Berth Marks* and *Brats* still exist.)

Nevertheless, sound was here to stay. And, fortunately, so were Laurel and Hardy.

BERTH MARKS

Production history: Written early April 1929. Working title: *In Vaudeville*. Filmed circa April 20-27. Released June 1. Copyrighted December 9, 1929 by MGM (LP 891). Two reels.

Produced by Hal Roach. Directed by Lewis R. Foster. Photographed by Len Powers. Edited by Richard Currier. Story by Leo McCarey. Story edited by H.M. Walker.

With Harry Bernard, Charlie Hall, Baldwin Cooke.

L&H are a big-time vaudeville act — at least in their estimation — en route to an engagement in Pottsville. They almost miss their train; once aboard, they inadvertantly cause the other passengers to engage in a clothes-ripping battle. The boys keep getting entangled as they try to change into pajamas in an upper berth. After they finally bed down, the conductor calls out the next stop: Pottsville.

In mid-April 1929, Stan and the gag writers began kicking around ideas for the team's second talking film. The film's press sheet claims the story was semi-autobiographical:

"Many times during his long and varied traveling career, Stan suffered the trials and tribulations endured by the two vaudevillians of *Berth Marks*. His memory of the days of crowded journeys in narrow upper berths formed the basis for this laugh fest of a night in a Pullman car."

Ere long, the studio craftsmen were making preparations for the shooting of this "laugh fest." Because this was a talkie which took place on a train, it was going to need the sound effects of a train. Elmer R. Raguse and his crew placed two microphones inside a real sleeping car, with the recording equipment perched precariously on a flat car at the rear of the train.

Shooting had begun by April 20, when a reporter for *Hollywood Filmograph* noted, "Laurel and Hardy making scenes at the Santa Fe Depot, a large crowd getting a kick out of their antics." Translation: L&H had their first encounter with a new problem engendered by this newfangled sound equipment. When shooting on location with a silent camera, a crowd giggling and hooting at the actors' comic cut-ups caused no problems. But with a sound camera, all of that giggling and hooting would be captured on the soundtrack. And since this was long before television sitcoms, where laugh tracks were necessary to inform the viewer what was funny, lots of retakes were needed.

The location scenes are remarkably well photographed. By this time, someone had figured out that you didn't need four cameras filming every scene in order to have a choice of angles *and* synchronized sound. Thus, Len Powers was the sole cameraman on this picture.

At the Santa Fe depot (*not* Pottsville) in a gag still.

The team's dialogue in *Berth Marks* appears to have been entirely impro-vised. There are sections when some pre-planned dialogue would have helped immensely. During the sequence in which the boys undress in the upper berth, Ollie keeps saying "Will you stop *crowding*?" until one wishes Stan's tangled clothing would strangle him. To be fair, though, the boys do sound entirely at ease in front of the microphones in this second talkie.

One reason why the upper-berth sequence doesn't come off too well may be the unforeseen problems that Laurel and Hardy encountered in shooting it. Thomas Benton Roberts recalled, "It took 'em three days to get that scene. They'd get to laughing, you know; Stan would get his foot in Babe's underwear! He didn't do it on purpose — he just couldn't see what he was doing. And as he went to stretch out, his foot went in and goosed Babe, see?

"They'd get to laughing, and then they'd go out and play golf — to get it off their minds. And, of course, we were wasting film. So they'd come back the next day, set up, shoot it again, and they'd break down and laugh again. Three days they worked on that thing!"

The Curse of the Unwanted Giggle, having first afflicted the crowd watch-ing Laurel and Hardy at the Santa Fe Depot and now causing the boys to break up, next spread to the man behind the camera, Len Powers. As he told *American Cinematographer*: "Sometimes, I can't do a thing for laughing as they start to ad lib... in *Berth Marks*, most of the very funniest stuff was abso-lutely devised on the spur of the moment by Stan and Oliver. They got started and we couldn't stop them. And that sequence was side-splitting."

Most existing prints of *Berth Marks* derive from the 1936 reissue. In these

A promotional poster heralds the team's second "All Talking" film.

copies, the opening scenes are accompanied by an arrangement of the team's signature tune, "Coo Coo," recorded in August 1932 by Van Phillips and the Columbia Orchestra. (The original 1929 prints had music over the main titles only; "Coo Coo" hadn't yet been written.)

Although well received in its day, *Berth Marks* is as bumpy and uneven a trip for its audiences today as it was for Laurel and Hardy. But the next film would be smooth sailing.

MEN O'WAR

Production history: Written early May 1929. Filmed circa May 11-18. Released June 29. Copyrighted July 29, 1929 by MGM (LP 550). Two reels.

Produced by Hal Roach. Directed by Lewis R. Foster. Photographed by George Stevens and Jack Roach. Edited by Richard Currier. Dialogue by H.M. Walker. Sound by Elmer Raguse.

With Anne Cornwall, Gloria Greer, James Finlayson, Harry Bernard.

Stan and Ollie are sailors on shore leave, enjoying a day in the park. They find a pair of panties, and then encounter two girls who are looking for an article of clothing described as "white... and easy to pull on" — a pair of gloves that are soon found. The foursome adjourn to the park's soda fountain, where the boys attempt to buy four sodas for fifteen cents. When Stan wins a slot machine jackpot, the boys rent a rowboat and escort the girls around the park lake; collisions with other boaters prompt the inevitable free-for-all.

With their third talkie, Laurel and Hardy appear so comfortable with sound that one would think they'd been making talkies for years. The first two sections of *Men O'War* depend primarily on dialogue. Fortunately these scenes are wonderfully funny, perfectly in keeping with the boys' characters, and free of the slight self-consciousness that marred *Unaccustomed As We Are*.

The opening scene with the missing "gloves" mines a new vein of comedy for L&H — the innocent double-entendre. The soda fountain sequence is a reworking (and vast improvement) of an episode from the silent *Should Married Men Go Home?* In the earlier film, the scene was amusing; with the addition of sound, it became one of the classic L&H routines.

The only sequence which doesn't entirely come off, ironically, is the one which depends most on visual comedy — the climactic rowboat battle. It's a valiant attempt to duplicate the reciprocal-destruction battles of the silent films, but it just doesn't work. New limitations on shooting and editing, imposed by the soundtrack, result in a sluggish tempo; the sequence doesn't build, it only clutters. The scene isn't helped by an abundance of cutaways to James Finlayson, standing on the dock and mugging stridently at Laurel and Hardy's antics.

Despite the soggy finale, *Men O'War* is a first-rate short — and solid evidence of how quickly and successfully Laurel and Hardy adapted to sound.

Director Lewis Foster, assistant director Lloyd French and cameramen George Stevens and Jack Roach began work on or about May 11, 1929, at

On location with Beanie Walker (in straw hat), Lewis Foster, and that newfangled sound equipment.

Hollenbeck Park, near downtown Los Angeles. The entire film was shot at this location, except for the soda-fountain scene, which was done at the Roach studio. The sight of the studio's sound truck, and the long microphone booms which followed Laurel and Hardy, attracted even more attention than usual; a horde of school children descended on the company, forcing them to return to the studio.

"The youngsters stayed out of camera range, but not out of the territory of the microphones," recounts the film's press sheet. "Their applause and laughter at the hilarious antics of Laurel and Hardy drowned out the voices of the players. When the comedy pair staged the boat fighting scene of the picture, the laughter of the onlookers sounded like thunder in the ears of the sensitive 'mikes.'"

Note: the "buzz saw" sound effects behind the main titles — taken from the soundtrack of *Busy Bodies* — were added for the Film Classics reissue.

THE HOLLYWOOD REVUE OF 1929

Production history: Written and filmed Spring 1929. Laurel and Hardy signed June 1. Previewed June 15. Copyrighted September 23, 1929 by MGM (LP 800). Officially released November 23 (reviewed in Los Angeles late June, New York mid-August.) 120 minutes; black and white with color sequences.

Produced by Harry Rapf. Directed by Charles F. Riesner. Photographed by Maximilian Fabian, John M. Nickolaus, John Arnold and Irving G. Ries. Edited by William S. Gray and Cameron K. Wood. Dialogue by Al Boasberg and Robert E. Hopkins.

With Jack Benny, Joan Crawford, John Gilbert, Cliff Edwards, Buster Keaton.

Magicians Laurel and Hardy are still arranging their props when the curtain opens on their act. Stan begins by acknowledging the audience; he tips his hat and a dove flies out. The boys' other feats of legerdemain are similarly ruined — despite Ollie's best efforts — by Stan's ineptitude. Ollie falls into a gooey white cake at the end, and pitches it into the wings; the emcee (Benny) appears, covered with frosting.

Once the studios had all converted to sound, they were anxious to flaunt their new equipment and display the versatility of their stars — even if none existed. As a result, a number of plotless musical "revues" hit the screen, showcasing the singing and dancing talents of performers who had never before sung or danced.

The Hollywood Revue of 1929 — two hours of All Singing, All Talking, All Dancing tedium — brings us such questionable delights as John Gilbert and Norma Shearer reciting the balcony scene from "Romeo and Juliet" in modern slang, and a miniature Bessie Love hiding in Jack Benny's pocket. The L&H sketch, though not much more than adequate, easily emerges as the highlight of the film for today's audiences.

Stan and Babe were added to the film at the very last moment. The picture was evidently already in the can when producer Harry Rapf realized that the film had virtually no real comedy in it — an Egyptian dance sequence with Buster Keaton in drag, while amusing, wasn't really an out-and-out comedy bit — and asked Hal Roach for the loan of his two biggest stars.

Just two weeks after *Hollywood Filmograph* reported Laurel and Hardy's addition to the film, the paper reviewed a sneak preview, applauding the "giggles and guffaws planted in this act by the screen's most popular comic pair." While the shooting of their routine may have been hastily arranged (made obvious by the extremely static camerawork), the boys appear to have been given a large measure of freedom in their first outing away from the Roach studio.

Charles F. Riesner, once a gag writer for Chaplin, directed the boys (he received director credit for Keaton's *Steamboat Bill, Jr.* the previous year). While there's no writer credit for the L&H sequence, its tone suggests the other brief sketches Stan wrote for the team's public appearances.

Metro-Goldwyn-Mayer was eager to publicize the team's appearance in the film. On Saturday, June 15, 1929, Laurel and Hardy were the guests of honor at a "Midnight Matinee" stage presentation at the Grauman's Chinese theater.

When the picture was released on June 21, the team was singled out for praise in its first feature-film appearance. *Hollywood Filmograph* noted, "Then we had two magicians, Laurel and Hardy, and what they didn't do to the opening nighters! Whether in talk or silent, there are few operating for fun's sake to vie with them."

With a 35-year-old Jack Benny, producer Harry Rapf, and director Charles Riesner.

The *New York Times* reviewer, Mordaunt Hall, was less impressed. He wrote, "When one of them flops on a great cake covered with icing, an otherwise promising piece of work winds up as mere slapstick."

Although viewing this movie is a trial for even the staunchest film addict today, it was phenomenally popular in its time. Astonishingly, it was even nominated for an Academy Award for "Best Picture, 1928-1929." (For the record, it lost out to *Broadway Melody*.)

PERFECT DAY

Production history: Written late May-early June 1929. Filmed circa June 8-15. Released August 10. Copyrighted August 12, 1929 by MGM (LP 589). Two reels.

Produced by Hal Roach. Directed by James Parrott. Edited by Richard Currier.

With Edgar Kennedy, Kay Deslys, Isabelle Keith.

Stan and Ollie's efforts to spend a pleasant Saturday picnicking in the countryside — with their wives and Uncle Edgar — are thwarted from the start. First, a fight between the boys ruins a mountain of sandwiches. Then their car finds all sorts of creative ways to keep from running. Laurel and Hardy's frustration is matched by the gout-ridden uncle, and a neighbor who partici- pates with the boys in a window-smashing fracas. The perfect day ends when the car plunges into a mudhole.

The copyright registration for this film gives story credit to Hal E. Roach and Leo McCarey. But Roy Seawright, head of the studio's optical-effects department, remembers the genesis of this film differently:

"It all came from Stan saying, 'I just thought of something this morning that was kind of cute.' I think he got the idea, actually, from some neighbors of his. The neighbors' problem wasn't quite as extreme — but it got Stan thinking about it, and he said, 'Wouldn't it have been funny if they never did get to the picnic?' He came in and threw the idea on the table, and in no time he and the gag men just tore it apart and added their ideas, and that was the picture right there. That's an example of the ingenuity and the brilliance of that man."

An outline running barely three pages was put together as Laurel and Hardy were finishing their brief sketch for *The Hollywood Revue of 1929*. The script differs considerably from the final film.

Perhaps the most surprising difference between script and film is that the role of the grouchy uncle was originally intended for James Finlayson. While the role is beautifully played by Edgar Kennedy, one wonders how Finlayson, with his more florid, explosive style, would have essayed the part.

The entire opening scene, with the wives trying to convince the uncle to go along on the picnic — and the boys accidentally ruining the sandwiches they've just prepared — is nowhere to be found in the script. One brief gag with the car, however, exists only in the script:

"While talking to the neighbor, Babe strikes a match and throws it out of the scene. The lighted match goes into a spot of oil on the driveway under the motor. A lot of smoke starts coming from the motor. Babe takes it [does a reaction], opens the hood and looks in, then looks underneath and sees that the oil is still burning. He puts it out and crawls under the car to see if any damage was done.

"As Babe crawls under the car there is still some smoke coming from the motor. Stan enters from the garage, takes it, thinking the motor is on fire, grabs a pail of water and pours it over the motor. Babe comes up sopping wet and bawls Stan out."

The ending proposed by the script reworks a gag intended for, but not used in, *Bacon Grabbers*. Through a Laurel mishap, the car's radiator is punctured. The next-door neighbor suggests that the boys put some corn meal in the radiator to stop the leak. Just as all seems right with the car, the radiator cap blows off, and corn meal mush sprays all over the neighborhood, prompting a mush-throwing fight amongst the residents. A cop steps in and breaks up the fight, ordering Stan and Ollie and their families to go to the picnic. But the radiator gag went unused in this film, too.

One of the great moments in *Perfect Day* is a beautifully choreographed and executed scene wherein Stan manages to smack Edgar Kennedy's gouty foot four times in rapid succession. The script scarcely mentions the running gag: "Somebody steps on Jim's foot and he lets out a howl." That Laurel and Hardy could have mined such a superbly executed running gag from this barely-suggested idea is a testament to their creativity.

While sources have stated for years that the film was supposed to end with the family picnicking in the country (and predictably making a mess of things), there's no mention of any such sequence in the script. Several articles published during the filming mention that "50 windows were smashed in one morning's shooting...in a general neighborhood free-for-all, the company

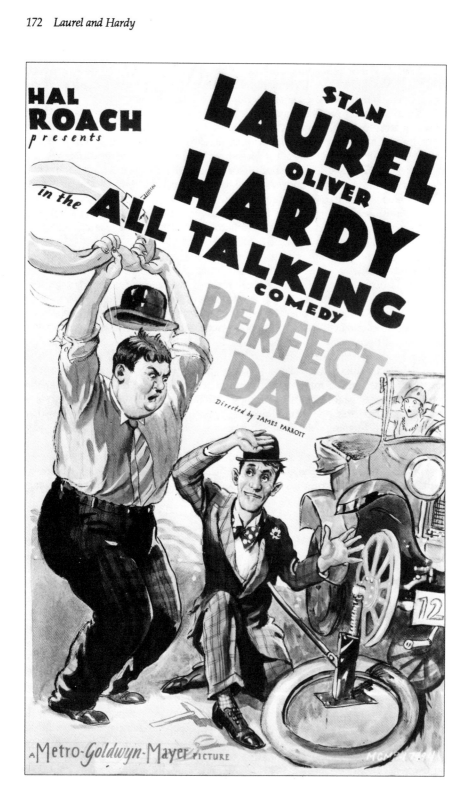

hurled rocks, wrenches and missiles of all kinds." There is a *brief* window-smashing fight in the film, but neither the script nor the film suggest anything on this large a scale.

Filming began during the first week of June, 1929, with an old friend in the director's chair — Jimmy Parrott. Parrott, who hadn't directed a Laurel and Hardy film since *Habeas Corpus* the previous year, had been absent from the Roach lot for several months. (Lewis Foster was transferred from the L&H unit to Roach's new Harry Langdon series.)

Most of the film — apart from the opening sequence — was shot in front of a bungalow on Vera Avenue in Culver City. The house, conveniently, was owned by Baldwin Cooke, who played the boys' next-door neighbor in the film. Cooke, a former vaudeville partner of Stan's, played bit parts in 30 Laurel and Hardy films.

The working title for this picture was *Step On It.* Sound department head Elmer Raguse would've liked to add *But Not Too Loudly.* "Comedy recording requires a technique all its own," he told a reporter for *Hollywood Filmograph.* "It is far easier to make a smooth reproduction of ordinary voices in conversation than of fun-making sounds. But we have been able to construct a controlling apparatus which enables us to prevent the thundering blasts usually recorded by smashes, falls, bangs and loud voices. Laurel and Hardy comedies give us more trouble than any of the other pictures. "

One loud noise which drew special attention from critics emanated from a gag where Ollie hits Stan on the head with the car's clutch. (Stan has taken Ollie's order to "throw out the clutch" a bit too literally.) As the clutch smacks the Laurel cranium, a loud, hollow clanging sound indicates the emptiness of Stan's skull. *The Film Exhibitor's Herald* called this "the funniest sound effect yet recorded."

As usual, the L&H crew had to guard against unwanted noises getting onto the soundtrack. In fact, they found it necessary to call out a squad of Culver City's mounted police to keep onlookers out of range of the microphones. Having learned their lesson during the filming of *Men O'War,* the company quit filming each day at 3 o'clock, before hordes of squealing schoolchildren could descend upon them. A few gags involved a bull terrier named Buddy, and a way had to be devised for the dog to hear its trainer's commands without those commands getting picked up by the mikes.

Perfect Day relies less on dialogue than *Men O'War.* "When Laurel and Hardy are on the screen, the audience is laughing so hard that it doesn't have time to listen to what they are saying," dialogue writer Harley M. "Beanie" Walker explained to the press. "With each of their talking pictures, we have written less dialogue, only using enough conversation to carry the thread of the story." The problem of pacing the dialogue to suit the audience's reaction would soon be solved through the preview-and-edit procedure.

Among the lines of dialogue is the first of the Hardy catch-phrases: "Why don't you do *something* to *help* me?" Granted, this isn't very funny in itself, but when given the plaintive Hardy tones in many successive films, it becomes hilarious.

By far the most curious line is uttered by Edgar Kennedy. Stan and Ollie have been fighting with their next-door neighbor, but the battle is suddenly terminated when the boys look off and see someone walking toward them — it's the local pastor, and of course the family doesn't want him to know that

A gag still with Isabelle Keith, Edgar Kennedy and Kay Deslys suggests a scene in neither the film nor the script.

they're picnicking on the Sabbath. They all have to hurriedly climb out of the car and run back into the house, and as Uncle Edgar tries to maneuver his gouty foot out of the cramped back seat, he mutters, "Oh, shit!" (This is one line which was definitely not in the script.)

The film's glorious finale, with the boys' car descending into a mudhole until only the five occupants' floating hats can been seen, was an example of the Roach technicians giving their all for the sake of a good gag. It took a small army of technicians — men who were particularly attuned to the peculiar problems presented by comedy films — to help get such gags across to audiences.

The press sheet for *Perfect Day* tells how the gag was accomplished: "A huge mudhole was excavated and filled with water in one of the Hal Roach studio streets... The mudhole, 8 feet deep, 20 feet long and 12 feet wide, was fitted with pulleys, so that the automobile could be lowered to the bottom without accident."

This gag is actually a repeat of the final gag for the team's *Leave 'em Laughing*. Kennedy shared the mudbath with Laurel and Hardy in that film, too.

No wonder he was swearing.

THEY GO BOOM

Production history: Written late June 1929. Filmed circa July 7-13. Edited circa July 27. Copyrighted August 26, 1929 by MGM (LP 642). Released September 21. Two reels.

Produced by Hal Roach. Directed by James Parrott. Edited by Richard Currier.

With Charlie Hall, Sam Lufkin.

Ollie has a severe head cold, but the worst of his problems is Stan's efforts to cure him. Hardy has to endure a very long night, during which Laurel applies a mustard plaster to his derriere, swabs his throat with cough medicine (losing the cotton swab down Ollie's throat) and deflates their air mattress. After an altercation with the landlord, they use the gas outlet to re-inflate their mattress, over-inflating it until it rises almost to the ceiling. A Hardy sneeze causes the mattress to explode.

The working title for this picture was *Coughing Up*; James Parrott's assistant director was Morrie Lightfoot, and the cameraman was Art Lloyd. Midway through the shooting, George Stevens took over the photography, and Hal Roach's brother Jack became the assistant director on the film, which now boasted the working title of *The Sniffles*.

About the only things which remained consistent during the shooting of this film were Laurel and Hardy's costumes (nightshirts and robes) and the one set used throughout the whole picture, a not very well furnished boarding-house bedroom. After the exhilirating, fluid outdoor photography of *Men O'War* and *Perfect Day*, the claustrophobic setting and static camerawork of this film make it seem more like a typically creaky early talkie than its predecessors.

Wearing those flannel nightshirts all day long was no picnic for Stan and Babe. After about the fifth day of shooting, Stan remarked to a reporter, "After working all day in a night-shirt, I feel like going home, getting dressed up and going to bed."

On the last day of shooting, Jimmy Parrott called Jack Roach aside and told him to find three men who were crack rifle shots. There was nothing in the script to suggest such a need, but Roach rounded up a carpenter, a prop man and a film cutter who were handy with the shooting irons. They were to fire upon the overly-inflated mattress which was to explode in the film's final gag.

Stan, Babe and Parrott stood well out of camera range as George Stevens got ready for a close up of the mattress. Then, Parrott called out, "Lights! Camera! Action! Ready! Aim! Fire!" And the poor mattress was executed as the camera rolled. Noted the studio publicist in his obituary for the mattress, "The set for the scene was built in the interior of a stage, and fire regulations prevented a real explosion from being made. So the mattress was filled with air, and the rifle shots punctured it sufficiently to suggest an explosion."

The film was rushed through the editing process; it had to be fully completed by July 27, when the studio shut down for its annual one-month vacation. Babe Hardy's vacation was not an entirely happy one. On July 24th his wife, Myrtle Lee Reeves Hardy, filed for divorce. She charged him with

seven years of "cruel treatment," alleging that Babe occasionally returned home "refusing to explain the evidence of his close proximity to persons using powder and cosmetics." Babe and Myrtle reconciled before long, but their relationship would continue to be a stormy one.

Things were noticeably brighter at the Hal Roach Studio, which was posting a very healthy profit on the L&H comedies. The 11 silent films made during the 1928-29 season made a total profit of over $35,000, while the five sound films made a collective profit of over $43,000. This reflected Laurel and Hardy's increasing popularity as sound-film stars — as well as the markedly higher rentals Roach was charging for sound pictures. Business was booming at the Hal Roach lot in the summer of '29. Unfortunately, within a couple of months, They Go Boom threatened to become They Go Bust.

THE HOOSE-GOW

Production history: Script finished August 29, 1929. Filmed August 30-September 14. Copyrighted November 11, 1929 by MGM (LP 840). Released November 16. Two reels.

Produced by Hal Roach. Directed by James Parrott. Photographed by George Stevens, Len Powers and Glenn Robert Kershner. Edited by Richard Currier. Sound by Elmer Raguse.

With Tiny Sandford, James Finlayson, Dick Sutherland, Ellinor Vanderveer.

Stan and Ollie are escorted to prison via a paddy wagon, despite their protests that they were only watching a raid. A failed escape attempt does not endear them to the warden. The boys are sent to a labor camp, to help dig a roadway; Stan's pick is forever entangling itself in Ollie's clothing. When a cook tells them to chop wood, they axe the tree that holds a lookout platform and a sleeping guard. The afternoon ends in a gooey melee when Laurel tries to plug a leak in the radiator of the Governor's car, by filling it with rice.

The Hoose-gow was one of Laurel and Hardy's best early talkies, and one of their most elaborate. It was shot entirely on location. Work on the script began as soon as the Roach lot re-opened its gates in late August 1929.

While the film's titles give no story credit, Stan almost certainly worked on the final script — an outline of the action running barely four pages. Assisting him were the Roach gag writers, which then included Mauri Grashin, Carl Harbaugh, Frank Holliday, Eddie Dunn and the ubiquitous Charley Rogers.

The final script has a number of touches which do not appear in the film. One sequence occurs when the boys are unwittingly lunching at the warden's table:

> On the table there is a freshly cut white cocoanut cake. Babe takes a large piece and is about to eat it as the warden returns and stands behind him. Stan tries to pantomime to Babe that the warden is behind him. Finally Babe looks up, sees the warden and shoves the piece of cake into his pocket. The warden orders the boys away from the table...

Follow Stan and Babe into a setup where there is a couple of large rocks [sic] against some trees. They enter and sit down. Babe reaches into his pocket and gets the piece of cake. Stan watches him, getting over that he is hungry. As Babe is in the act of taking a bite of the cake, a fly lights on it and Babe has some difficulty trying to keep the fly off the cake. Stan watches this and finally gets an idea. He suggests to Babe that if he gave the fly a little piece of the cake he wouldn't bother him...

Babe turns to Stan and says with a smile, 'That's the first spark of intelligence you have ever shown.' As he is speaking, cut to insert of the piece of cake Babe is holding and show a large bee light on it. We also hear the buzz of the bee.

Cut to closeup of Babe. Not noticing the bee, he quickly takes a large bite of the cake... As he is about to take another bite we hear a faint buzz. Babe gets over he has swallowed something and starts feeling his stomach, realizing that the bee is inside. Stan jumps to his feet and by this time Babe is going through all kinds of contortions, the bee presumably flying around inside him. Stan gets a shovel and starts hitting Babe, trying to kill the bee.

As Stan swings back with the shovel, the warden enters and gets it in the face, knocking him to the ground. Stan realizes what he has done and Babe forgets about the bee for the moment. The warden jumps to his feet and is about to beat up Stan and Babe when we hear sirens.

James Parrott again wielded the megaphone, with Lloyd French as his assistant. A number of mysterious locations were used; the script informs us that the "gates to the County Hospital" were to be used in the film's opening shot as stand-ins for the gates to the County Jail, but the rest of the opening sequence was shot in the "interior of the real county jail yard." The road camp sequence was filmed at the Roach studio's ranch, now part of busy Arnaz Drive near Beverly Hills.

Babe Hardy's widow Lucille recalled that Babe had a number of scars and marks all over his body as a result of the punishment he endured during the making of the films. One of those scars was received during the filming of *The Hoose-gow*, according to the press sheet:

"The comedy business of the scene called for Laurel to nick Hardy in the seat of his pants with his pick — a real pick being used, as the rubber pick looked 'fakey' in action.

"The 'nicking' was to occur on Laurel's uplift of the pick, but unfortunately for Hardy, his huge bulk moved too close to Laurel's downward swing of the heavy pick, and he received a very real 'nicking' in his flesh. The microphone recorded a yell of pain that burst the light valve as Hardy jumped out of the scene. Everyone on the set but Laurel and Hardy roared with laughter. Only they knew what had really happened."

The climactic rice-throwing melee which had been proposed for *Bacon Grabbers* and then *Perfect Day* finally ended up in this picture. There are some beautiful touches in this sequence — notably a close-up of Ollie in which he receives a faceful of rice mush, turns to us, and daintily and symmetrically flicks the goo from his eyes. All of this was ad-libbed. The script says merely:

The boys and Finlayson share coffee — and rice — during a break.

"Go into the mush routine, winding up with the Governor, guests, wardens and convicts getting into the mess."

The script proposes a slightly different wrap-up. Originally, Stan and Ollie were to escape during the rice-throwing fight; they come to a fork in the road and argue about which path to take. Finally, Stan takes the route suggested by Ollie, but the boys are met instantly by other escaping convicts, and guards escorting them back to camp.

Ellinor Vanderveer, a statuesque, dignified-looking woman whose purpose in life was being the target of various missiles thrown by lowbrow comedians, played a guest of the governor. In a 1976 interview, she recalled, "That was a lot of fun making this picture, but it took two weeks to get the rice out of my hair and my clothes. That rice really *was* cooked, right onto my lovely clothes."

The Hoose-gow was released on November 16, 1929. With a running time of just over 18 minutes, it was one of the team's shortest shorts, but also one of their most concise. Stated *Motion Picture Magazine*, "Slapstick pure and simple, but if you don't laugh yourself silly, you must have lockjaw... An antidote for any prison picture — and a satire on all of them."

THE ROGUE SONG

Production history:: Written and filmed circa July–September 1929. Laurel and Hardy signed circa September 19. Released January 17, 1930. Copyrighted March 26, 1930 by MGM (LP 1176). 115 minutes. Two-color Technicolor.

Produced (without credit) by Irving G. Thalberg. Directed by Lionel Barrymore. Photographed by Percy Hilburn and C. Edgar Schoenbaum. Edited by Margaret Booth. Story by Frances Marion and John Colton. Based on *Gypsy Love* by Franz Lehar.

With Lawrence Tibbett, Catherine Dale Owen.

Yegor, "the singing bandit of Agrakhan" (Tibbett), is an insurgent against the powerful Cossack soldiers. Ali-Bek (Laurel) and Murza-Bek (Hardy) are his sidekicks. Despite Yegor's hatred of the cossacks, he falls in love with young Princess Vera, whose brother commands a Cossack region. Yegor and Vera alternately romance and berate each other, while the sidekicks provide comic relief.

In the late summer of 1929, Lawrence Tibbett, the star baritone of the Metropolitan Opera, was signed for his film debut by Metro-Goldwyn-Mayer. A prestigious talent like Tibbett deserved a prestigious vehicle for his film debut. Fortunately, the producer of his first film was Irving G. Thalberg, whose middle name was Prestige despite the initial G.

Thalberg hired writers Frances Marion and John Colton to concoct an original story, based on a "suggestion" by another writer named Wells Root, which in turn was based on *Zigeunerliebe* or *Gypsy Love*, an operetta written by Franz Lehar in 1910. Much of Lehar's story and music was considered too sophisticated for mass audiences; two songwriters were called in to pen some new tunes, including an out-and-out pop ditty entitled "When I'm Looking at You." This "class" production was filmed entirely in two-color Technicolor.

The film was well into production by mid-September when MGM announced that it had borrowed L&H from Hal Roach to play "two burlesque desperadoes" in the film. Roach recounted his meetings with the MGM executives:

"Metro had made this picture and it was too somber. At the previews, the audiences apparently didn't like it. They wanted to know if Laurel and Hardy could work in the picture to lighten it up. And I said, 'Well, Laurel and Hardy are two funny men. If you've got any really funny things for them to do, I'll listen.' A couple of weeks later, Irving Thalberg called me again and I came down, and this was the first time I really got the idea of yes men. There were three or four writers in the room with Thalberg. Thalberg said, 'I've got it, it's great.' I says, 'Fine, what is it?' He says, 'Laurel and Hardy are the coachman and the assistant coachman on a coach.'

"Now, before I can open my mouth, these guys say, 'Mr. Thalberg, how did you *think* of that *marvelous* idea? Oh, hell, Roach, that's gonna make it! That's just the thing!' All of them, like a chorus! Thalberg always had to have a big chorus. So, when this thing quiets down, I says, 'Uh, wait a minute. What's funny about a coachman?' And they said, 'Oh, well, Laurel and Hardy — ' I said, 'Laurel and Hardy are two comedians. Now tell me what they're gonna do that's funny.' Thalberg says, 'Can't you make them funny?' I said, 'Maybe I can, but *you're* supposed to.'

"The story that I wrote for Metro for this thing, I made afterwards with Laurel and Hardy as *Fra Diavolo*. Lawrence Tibbett played a bandit in Metro's picture, and we had a bandit in *Fra Diavolo*. When I sent the story down to Thalberg, he said, 'Oh, Roach, you bastard. We've got a story for Tibbett, but you're written a story for Laurel and Hardy. They're the whole damn thing! You want Tibbett to play in a Laurel and Hardy picture! So I said, 'Well, you don't have to use all of it.'"

Roach wrote several sequences for the film, and also directed — probably at the behest of Thalberg, who was a close friend of his. Stan and Babe were somewhat constrained at Metro; whatever creative contributions Stan could make were limited to improvising and exercising his skill at controlling his director — who in this case was Roach, his employer. Actors did not give orders at Metro, as Buster Keaton was learning. (*Free and Easy* was the title of the concurrently produced Keaton film, but it surely did not describe the way movies were made at MGM.)

In a 1959 interview, Stan recalled that Tibbett had returned to New York, figuring that the film had been completed, but that the singer "had to fly back to Hollywood to shoot a scene with us — the only scene in which he and we appeared together."

For the record, Lawrence Tibbett Jr. stated that L&H were a part of the film from its inception. "You mean to say they had a whole complete cut without Laurel and Hardy to begin with? No, I don't think so. I don't remember Dad flying back and doing a whole series of scenes with Laurel and Hardy," said Tibbett Jr. "But I know that Dad liked working with them. He loved doing that picture; it was a happy memory for him."

The boys have eight scenes spotted throughout the 115-minute film. Most of them are little more than blackouts — in a scene, Ollie tries to mount his horse by stepping onto a water-filled barrel, and crashes through. The team's

Grand opera meets low comedy: L&H with Lawrence Tibbett.

connection to Tibbett's character, and to the plot, is barely enough to suggest that they belong in the picture. (They play two members of Yegor's bandit gang, *not* two coachmen as Thalberg had suggested.)

Two of the scenes are quite lengthy. The first is a reworking of a gag written for but not used in *The Hoose-gow*: Stan is trying to eat a piece of cheese, which is covered with flies. Eventually, he does take a big bite, but then emits a strange buzzing sound every time he opens his mouth.

The second extended scene has Stan giving Ollie a shave, with predictably disastrous results. As Stan applies the lather to Ollie's jowls, some pretty girls saunter by. Distracted, Stan accidentally jams the brush into his friend's mouth. Next, Stan decides to sharpen the razor by scraping it on a large rock — which, through a Laurel accident, lands on the Hardy toes.

The world premiere of *The Rogue Song* was held on Friday, January 17, 1930, at Grauman's Chinese Theater in Hollywood. The premiere was touted by the *Los Angeles Times* as "the social as well as motion-picture event of the season," and Tibbett and Laurel and Hardy appeared on a live broadcast of the premiere, direct from the forecourt of the theater.

Reviews were decidedly mixed. Mordaunt Hall of the *New York Times* applauded Tibbett's singing, but had a condescending attitude toward the comedy scenes. He wrote, "The comedy of that clever team, Stan Laurel and Oliver Hardy, may slip from quiet fun to slapstick, but so long as you know that soon again Mr. Tibbett's stentorian singing is to be heard, one laughs with the crowd."

Variety was less than charitable toward the scenes Roach wrote and directed; the paper's reviewer wrote, 'the comedy registers as if Barrymore had assigned an assistant director to put Laurel and Hardy through some hoke sequences, and then had simply picked the spots to cut them in. Those Laurel and Hardy names will likely help a draw, but there can be no question that the supposed laugh footage is awkward and deplorably weak."

Despite lukewarm reviews, the film did well. In 1933, Tibbett (in an article for a book called *The Glory Road*) remembered that the film was quite popular, despite the MGM executives' nervousness about selling a film with an opera singer. "The film played for five months at the Astor Theater in New York, and I was advertised there as a Metropolitan Opera star," he wrote. "But in all other theaters throughout the country my supposedly shameful connection with the grand opera was carefully suppressed... Any conceit that I might have had regarding my box-office value as a movie star was quickly eliminated when, passing through a small Western town on a train, I saw on a theater canopy: 'Laurel and Hardy in *The Rogue Song*.'"

About a year after its American release, the film was released in France as *Le Chant Du Bandit*. All of the dialogue, except for Tibbett's songs, was eliminated, and replaced with titles in French and English. Despite this truncation, *Variety* reported that the film "was nicely received, the audience appreciating Tibbett's voice, the Laurel and Hardy gags, and the fine color work."

And, from that point on, *The Rogue Song* bid us all adieu and disappeared over the mountaintops, with a smile on its lips and a song in its heart. It has been a lost film for decades, and remains frustratingly elusive. MGM's print was destroyed by a fire in the storage vaults; the Technicolor Corporation disposed of their check print and negative years ago; and no domestic or foreign archive has any record of the film, despite the efforts of scholars and fans to retrieve it. (One especially dedicated fan, Bob Stowell, has been leading a one-man crusade for years to locate a print.)

Fortunately, the sound-track discs still exist. Selections from them, including several L&H scenes, have been issued commercially on an album. In the spring of 1982, a three-minute clip was discovered by New Hampshire college professor Larry Benaquist. Luckily for Laurel and Hardy fans, the retrieved sequence is a complete L&H gag, in which the boys run into a cave on a stormy night, and Ollie asks Stan where he got his fur coat — only to be met by the growl of a bear. (We see a lot more of the dark cave than we do of Stan and Ollie, but any footage is better than none at all.)

The Rogue Song was the team's first real experience with making films at a major studio. It was not an entirely happy one. Laurel and Hardy movies had to be designed specifically for Laurel and Hardy, *by* Laurel and Hardy — with the help of writers and technicians who understood all of their characters' nuances. Stan and Babe didn't have the freedom to experiment when working for a big studio like MGM — even when their director was someone as sympathetic as Hal Roach.

It would be good to get back to what Metro's executives termed "that little studio down the street" — the Lot of Fun.

NIGHT OWLS

Production history: Written and filmed circa mid-October-early November 1929. Released January 4, 1930. Copyrighted January 6, 1930 by MGM (LP 977). Two reels.

Produced by Hal Roach. Directed by James Parrott. Photographed by George Stevens. Edited by Richard Currier. Dialogue by H.M. Walker. Sound by Elmer Raguse.

With Edgar Kennedy, Anders Randolph, James Finlayson.

Officer Kennedy is on the outs with his chief — 42 burglaries have been committed in his neighborhood recently, with no arrests. He hires vagrants Stan and Ollie to rob the chief's house; the alternative is a jail term for vagrancy, so they go along with the unorthodox plan. The burglary is accomplished, but none too stealthily; frightened by the racket they've caused, the boys escape out a window. Kennedy bursts in and picks up the bag of loot, just in time to be blamed for the robbery — and all the others.

Night Owls seems very much like a vaudeville sketch — in fact, the boys' 1952 stage sketch *A Spot of Trouble*, written by Stan, was based on this film. *Night Owls*, in turn, seems to have its roots in the vaudeville sketch Stan performed in 1914, *The Nutty Burglars*.

Night Owls is one of those films in which Laurel and Hardy take a simple situation and milk 20 minutes' worth of gags from it. This film probably has the least dialogue of any Laurel and Hardy talkie; it's also one of their noisiest, thanks to the astounding array of crashes, booms and bangs that the would-be burglars unwittingly cause. But Stan was convinced that the team should tell their stories chiefly in pantomime. He told *Los Angeles Times* film critic Philip K. Scheuer, "We did talk too much at first. If you have seen us in our latest, *Night Owls*, you will have observed that most of our talk is limited to 'shushes.'"

This was indeed a wise position to take, especially in an era when other formerly silent comedians — notably Buster Keaton — were being compelled by studios to break forth with a barrage of one-liners.

Though *Night Owls* is a lesser L&H comedy, it was a popular one. One publicity release noted that the Grauman's Chinese Theater, the most prestigious film house in Hollywood, booked the movie "before the film was dry on the racks." But Stan was not entirely happy with the picture when he'd finished the final cut.

As he explained to Scheuer: "We are very anxious to send out out pictures in whatever length they reach when they are completed. Nineteen hundred feet is the usual length for a two-reeler, and it necessitates some regrettable cuts. We were compelled to eliminate much of the business leading up to the big laughs in *Night Owls*, and the laughs themselves suffered by it. Comedy, especially our type of comedy, must be cumulative in effect, not abrupt.

"So it may be that we shall make arrangements to release our comedies in whatever footage they show to best advantage, from 1900 up to 2500 feet. The early Harold Lloyd films varied in the same way. Perhaps we shall do a five-reeler feature eventually. I am not in favor of it, myself."

Laurel and Hardy had been hugely popular overseas, and understandably Roach wanted to maintain the team's following in the lucrative foreign market. The solution to the language barrier created by the talkies was for the boys to film their comedies in a variety of tongues. *Night Owls* was the first of their films to be remade this way. In Italian it became *Ladroni*; and in Spanish, *Ladrones*. Eventually, the team would make films in German and French as well. Stan explained the procedure of making the foreign-language films to Bill Rabe in a heretofore unpublished interview:

"We'd make the picture first entirely in English, naturally, then we'd preview it. Then we'd get it cut and all ready for shipping. That way, we knew exactly what we were going to use of the film. If we hadn't previewed it, we may have reshot a lot of stuff that we weren't going to keep, you see.

"So, then we brought in French, German, Italian and Spanish interpreters. And they translated our dialogue into each language. Each interpreter brought his own company... Then we'd set up a camera for the first scene. He'd tell us what our dialogue meant in English, then he'd tell us in French, for instance, and we'd write it phonetically as it sounded to us. And knowing the meaning of it, we got the correct intonation, which was helpful.

"We'd set up the camera, and we'd do the French version of the first scene. After the first scene, we'd hold the camera, and we'd do the German scene. And each scene we did four times, before we moved the camera for each different change. But [the foreign audiences] understood us perfectly, and I think that's what made it so popular. So when we finally went over there, they were amazed that we couldn't speak their language."

The foreign versions of *Night Owls* necessitated a few cast changes. Robert O'Connor — a bilingual actor who had played in Roach comedies for five years — tutored Stan and Babe for the Spanish version, and played a supporting role in both the Spanish and Italian versions. The role of the police chief, played by

The boys relax with Fred Karno and James Parrott on the set. Karno was canned shortly thereafter.

ex-Broadway stage actor Anders Randolph in the English edition, was taken over by E. Acosta, a Mexican customs official, in both remakes. Other actors working in the Spanish L&H films were Rina de Lignoco, Linda Loredo, Vera Zouroff and Benito Fernandez. Edgar Kennedy and James Finlayson were irreplaceable, however, so they endured the agonies of speaking phonetic Spanish and Italian in those versions of *Night Owls*.

New technical people were needed at the studio for the foreign remakes, too. Louis McManus was hired to design the title cards for the foreign films, and also did the English-language main titles — all at a rate of $10 per card. McManus soon became film editor of the Spanish editions, remaining in the editing department long after the foreign-language releases had been discontinued.

All of this was extremely costly. The foreign versions took much longer to shoot than their domestic counterparts. "It was a long, drawn-out process," recalled editor Richard Currier. "You'd start in on a scene, and it was probably a half hour's worth of rehearsal on each one of 'em with each language coach before the boys got their lines down, so they could say them the way they should sound."

Nevertheless, to Hal Roach the cost was well worth it. "It *was* an expensive operation to do every scene four times," he said. "It cost us three times as much. But the prices we got in South American countries and Spain were fantastic. A Laurel and Hardy short in the Argentine would be like a feature picture. They'd run some other picture with it, but the big attraction was the two-reel comedy.

"There's a very funny thing that happened in Buenos Aires. When I went there one of the Metro foreign executives said to me, 'You've *got* to go to a theater to see this Laurel and Hardy picture.' And I said, 'Well, I've seen the picture, I know it already.' 'Oh,' they said, 'you've *got* to come and see it.' And I couldn't figure why they were so anxious... So I go to the theater, and Laurel said something in Spanish, I don't know what the hell it was, and the audience roared with laughter! He had mispronounced a Spanish word, and the word he used meant 'to pee.' We didn't mean that at all, but it worked perfectly in that particular spot."

The foreign-language films played a tremendous part in endearing Laurel and Hardy to audiences overseas. If the team was well-received in the States, their popularity in foreign countries was little short of phenomenal. In a 1959 interview, Stan noted that the team's success was always greater in foreign markets. "We're *still* big stuff abroad," he said proudly. "In Germany today they're running pictures we made 28 years ago, and they play in a theater for six months — with no other picture! Our pictures still line them up — that's right, today!"

An additional 28 years have passed since that interview, and their pictures continue to do so.

A number of interesting things occurred at the Lot of Fun in the fall of 1929. In October, Hal Roach signed Stan Laurel's mentor — and Chaplin's, too — Fred Karno, to a five-year contract as producer and writer. Karno had created the legendary "Karno's London Comedians" troupes and had nurtured and developed some fine comedic talent. Since the early '20s, Karno's fortunes had been on the wane; he'd sunk most of his sizeable fortune into an ill-fated resort hotel called the Karsino.

Still, Karno had his reputation. Richard Currier remembered the excitement that accompanied the English producer's entrance to the studio: "He was supposed to be the one guy in the world that knew comedy A to Z and backwards." Hal Roach had been hearing about Karno since 1915, when he directed Essanay comedies starring the supporting comics from Charles Chaplin's company.

Said Roach, "I hired Karno after working with Chaplin and Laurel and always hearing them talk about Karno, Karno, Karno. I thought, hell, this guy must know a lot of gags. But I never knew he was just the businessman. He just hired guys that were funny, and he hired other guys to write for them. I finally let him go; I wanted him to be a gag man." Karno's contract was terminated in February, 1930, less than four months into the five-year pact.

In late November, 1929, the team made an unusual move by doing a week of personal appearances at the new Fox Theater in San Francisco. James Parrott accompanied the boys, as did Babe's wife, Myrtle, with whom he'd recently reconciled. The timing of the trip may have been influenced by the concurrent match between the Stanford and California football teams. "Queer that the booking came just at Big Game time, isn't it," Babe remarked to a reporter.

But the big news of Fall 1929 concerned the stock market, which crashed much more loudly than anything in *Night Owls*. Stan lost about $30,000, although he later recovered $6,000 or $7,000. As a result of this setback, he invested in annuities — a wise move, which kept him financially solvent during his retirement years.

A newspaper ad for the team's engagement at the Fox, San Francisco, November 1929.

The effect of the Crash was not immediately devastating to the Hal Roach Studios. Before much longer though, the Depression would have a powerful effect on the studio, and on Laurel and Hardy's films — just as it would on everything else.

BLOTTO

Production history: Written and filmed December 1929. Released February 8, 1930. Copyrighted February 13, 1930 by MGM (LP 1089). Three reels.

Produced by Hal Roach. Directed by James Parrott. Photographed by George Stevens. Edited by Richard Currier. Dialogue by H.M. Walker. Sound by Elmer Raguse.

With Anita Garvin, Tiny Sandford, Frank Holliday.

Ollie, a carefree bachelor, invites his henpecked pal Stan out for a night on the town. Mrs. Laurel (Garvin) eavesdrops and learns their plans; she finds out Stan is planning to bring the precious bottle of liquor she's saved since Prohibition. She pours the liquor down the drain and refills the bottle with cold tea, pepper, mustard and other condiments. The boys have a great time at the nightclub, getting riotously drunk on the non-alcoholic "liquor." Their mirth evaporates when Mrs. Laurel visits the club with a double-barreled shotgun.

Blotto is one of the team's most skillful milkings of a basic situation. It's also one of their most visually elegant films, thanks to the elaborate Rainbow Club set.

This was an expensive comedy despite the fact that almost all the humor derived from Laurel and Hardy's pantomime. Two hundred extras were used for the nightclub scenes, and jack-of-all-trades Jack Roach (whose job this month was casting director) had to work until 3 o'clock one morning rounding them all up.

The gags in *Blotto* are few but memorable. One that would recur in future films is the incredibly rapid wiggling of Stan's ears when he tastes the potent concoction whipped up by Mrs. Laurel. Generations of L&H fans have marveled at Stan's ability to ear-wiggle, but it was simply another product of the Roach studio prop men. A thread was attached to each ear with adhesive tape and pulled back and forth while the camera ran at 8 or 12 frames per second.

The highlight of the film is unquestionably Stan and Ollie's drunken laughing jag, which is a beautifully controlled and paced piece of acting. It's punctuated with the wonderfully subtle reactions of Anita Garvin as Mrs. Laurel, who drums her fingertips and sneers with an expression that could curdle one's blood.

"I think that's one of the greatest scenes of all time, I really do," Anita stated. "Isn't it marvelous? When I see those two together, and especially Stan, when he's holding his sides — Oh! I think they were acting to a certain extent — but after you start laughing so much, you do go into it. But I just love that scene. I could look at that every day of the year and still laugh at them. And it was all I could do to look mean, you know.

"As for my own reactions — it just seemed to be the thing to do. When your face is on that screen in a close-up, it's magnified hundreds of times, so you don't have to be broad. In a long shot, you'd play it more broadly — you had to get over the point in a very short period of time."

Blotto had so many laughs that it became the team's first three-reeler. Roach would produce a number of three-reel shorts in the coming years starring Laurel and Hardy, Charley Chase and others. The three-reelers were brought about by artistic decisions, not financial ones. "We made the three and four-reelers because the stories went that far," said Roach. "Now, the theater circuits bought our complete product. They couldn't buy Our Gang, or anything else, separately.

"They paid a set price for the year at so much a week. They could run the pictures as much or as little as they wanted. But we knew by the first of October what we were going to get for our pictures. And if we made a picture with Laurel and Hardy that was four reels long, we didn't make any dough on the thing because we only got a two-reel price — we'd already made this deal."

Anita Garvin, Linda Loredo and Georgette Rhodes kept Stan from getting *Blotto* in *any* language.

Blotto, like the team's preceding film, was also shot in two foreign-language versions. But all three versions of *Blotto* were shot simultaneously — unlike the procedure used with *Night Owls*. In Spanish it became *La Vida Nocturna* — with Linda Loredo playing a hot-tempered Latin Mrs. Laurel — and in the boys' first French-language film, Georgette Rhodes did her best to foil *Une Nuit Extravagante*. Gene deBriac taught Stan and Babe their French, and also played "important parts in the French version," according to the press sheet. (He plays a bit in the American version as the shopkeeper who sells Anita Garvin a rifle.)

Laurel told reporter Mollie Merrick, "We're funnier if our French isn't so good. But they must understand us. No audience likes to sit and laugh and not know what it's laughing about. These are being made into longer releases for the foreign market than for America. That, too, is an experiment."

Available records indicate that all versions of *Blotto* ran three reels. However, the foreign versions of *Night Owls* were twice as long as the two-reel domestic print, and subsequent foreign-language shorts would include sequences missing from the American editions.

The sight of L&H helpless with laughter induced the same reaction in preview audiences. The press sheet noted that one preview was shown immediately following Harold Lloyd's feature *Welcome Danger*, which "made it rather dubious as to how the people would receive it. But they laughed just as loud and long as they did at Harold Lloyd...and long after it was finished the audience snickered in remembrance."

The press sheet hints at a scene which did not survive the preview-and-edit process:

"An entertainer, singing by Laurel and Hardy's table, receives a drink as reward. 'Rotten,' says he. 'So's your singing' yells Oliver at the retiring singer, and at Stan's suggestion proceeds to show him how to correctly sing 'The Curse of an Aching Heart.' Oliver Hardy's whisky tenor would make a confirmed drunkard tear at his hair with envy, and Stan Laurel's ditto alto would be the pride of a Limehouse rummy."

James Parrott won high praise for his direction of this short — which was fine with Laurel, who was too modest to take credit for his behind-the-scenes work. However, when Stan signed a new contract with Roach, commencing December 23, 1929, it was as "Actor, Director, Writer."

Note: The background music today's audiences hear in *Blotto* was added for a 1937 reissue; it was culled from T. Marvin Hatley's score for *Way Out West* (1937) and LeRoy Shield's compositions for *Our Relations* (1936). One can scarcely conceive of this film without those delightful background themes, although that's how it was originally issued.

BRATS

Production history: Written and filmed January 1930. Released March 22, 1930. Copyrighted March 31, 1930 by MGM (LP 1190). Two reels.

Produced by Hal Roach. Directed by James Parrott. Photographed by George Stevens. Edited by Richard Currier. Dialogue by H.M. Walker. Sound by Elmer Raguse.

L&H spend an exasperating evening at home with their sons, who look exactly like their respective fathers. The grown-up boys' attempts at recreation are thwarted by the noisy antics of the little boys. The children manage to leave the water running in the bathroom as the grown-ups attempt to put them to sleep; the kids agree to settle down if they can have a glass of water. Stan starts for the bathroom, but Ollie stops him: "Just a moment — you might spill it!" The apartment, as well as Ollie's dignity, is dampened in the ensuing flood.

There's not a single dull moment in *Brats*, which shows Laurel and Hardy fully surmounting any obstacles the sound revolution may have presented. It is also one of the team's most skillfully edited pictures.

The script supplies a number of interesting tidbits, and a few scenes which did not survive in the final print.

Generations of film critics have speculated upon the kinky possibilities hinted at in this movie, since it gives the impression that two families live together in one house. The story, however, takes place in "the living room of Mr. Hardy." Interestingly, the script differentiates between the grown-up children and the small children by calling the "adults" Laurel and Hardy, and the kids Stan and Babe.

A couple of scripted gags were never filmed, either because they were too technically complex or too violent: After a bit in which the kids' battle with building blocks has literally upset the adults' checkers game, Laurel and Hardy were supposed to stomp over to the kids, pick them up and shake them. Hardy discovers that he is shaking little Stan, and Laurel realizes he's shaking little Babe. The adults switch kids, then shake them again.

This gag was repeated later in the bedroom scene, after the kids have a skirmish with boxing gloves. Babe tells his father that little Stanley has hit him,

What's more fun than *one* Laurel and Hardy? Just guess.

so Mr. Hardy puts Stanley over his knee and spanks him. Mr. Laurel retaliates by punching little Babe in the chin — and Mr. Hardy, alarmed, cries, "Don't you hit my son!"

The children's shenanigans were also somewhat different in the script. When the boys (the little ones) decide to play hide and seek, Babe gets to choose who's "it." He does this by spitting into the palm of one hand and smacking a finger into the expectorate. It files into Stan's eye, and Babe proudly announces, "You're it." Stan decides to try this trick himself, but the spittle just flies into his other eye.

Babe blindfolds Stan with a handkerchief, then clambers up the chimney to hide. Some tattle-tale soot billows out, and Stan decides to flush out his quarry by lighting a fire. Babe's howls bring the fathers running to the scene of the fire. While Mr. Laurel rushes off to get some water, Mr. Hardy stamps out the fire and extricates his son. Just as Hardy *père* has everything under control, Mr. Laurel dashes in and flings a dishpan full of water in the vicinity of the fire. Unfortunately, it's a lot closer to Mr. Hardy. Dead on target, in fact.

One scene which was shot and deleted after previews was an extension of the boys' routine at the pool table. Thanks to a Laurel mishap, the felt on Hardy's pool table has been ripped. There's nothing for Hardy to do but take off his coat, roll up his sleeves, and glue the felt back together. Unfortunately, Laurel knocks the can of glue over, which oozes all over Hardy's coat, which is lying on the pool table. Hardy, oblivious to all of this, daintily puts the final touches to the repairs. He then picks up his coat by the collar — but the collar

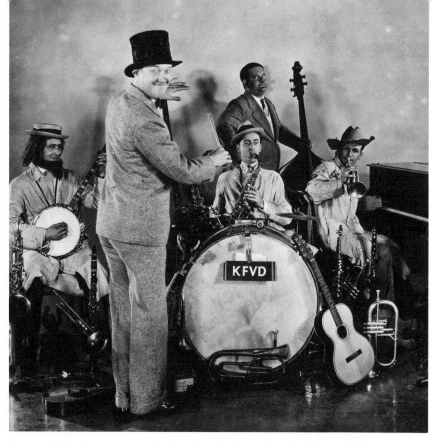

Stan and Babe join the Happy-Go-Lucky Trio — Vern Trimble (banjo), Art Stephenson (sax), and T. Marvin Hatley (piano, cornet and anything else).

is *all* he picks up. Laurel pulls away not only the remainder of the Hardy coat but also the entire covering of the Hardy pool table.

The film's glorious final gag is one of the best examples in all of Laurel and Hardy of "telegraphing" a joke. There are cutaway shots of the rapidly-filling bathroom spotted throughout the final five minutes, and you just *know* what's going to happen. But the scene was not set up nearly as well in the script. Originally, the boys (the grown-up ones) were to *accidentally* open the bathroom door, mistaking it for the hall door. The line, "Can I have a drink of water?" — as well as Hardy's "You might spill it!" — are nowhere to be found in the script.

Given the premise of *Brats*, one would think that there would be all sorts of tricky double-exposure shots. However, there are only two such shots, and precious little gimmickry. Which is just fine, because the comedy *shouldn't* derive from optical-effects trickery or the special large-scale sets; it should come from Laurel and Hardy. "We built everything — all the props — three times scale," recalled Thomas Benton Roberts, who helped construct the massive sets. "And it was made out of real wood — we only used balsa wood in the props they were going to use when they were in a fight. In those days, everything was less expensive. I was working for a dollar an hour!"

Optical-effects wizard Roy Seawright recalled how the split-screen shots were accomplished: "You just had the original set, and built the second one three times scale, exactly. After that, it's just a case of positioning your camera.

If it's six feet from the wall to the camera with your normal-sized set, then you multiply the distance three times, and make it 18 feet for your oversized set. Everything's tripled, and it just fits together in your final shot."

The opening titles of *Brats* herald the coming of an enduring (and endearing) L&H trademark: their theme song, "Coo Coo." It was written by a 25-year-old musician from Oklahoma named T. Marvin Hatley. Hatley, who could play any musical instrument "except the harp," was putting his talents to use at KFVD, a radio station located inside the Roach studio. With fellow musicians Vern Trimble and Art Stephenson, Hatley formed the Happy-Go-Lucky Trio, and they played popular tunes in a variety of styles on a weekday morning program. Hatley composed a dissonant little ditty for a time signal — a sort of musical cuckoo clock that would play on the hour.

Stan recalled, "We heard it one morning in a restaurant and thought it was funny-sounding music that would be good to start our pictures off with. So, somewhat as a gag, we had a copy of it made and had it recorded for our next picture. The preview audience laughed at it, everyone thought it seemed to fit, and we decided to continue using it."

Hatley remembered Stan telling him just why he thought "Coo Coo" was so appropriate for the team's signature tune: "Stan said the top voice, or the melody, represented Babe Hardy — it sounded like a bugle call, very dominant. And the other part represented Stanley — it's only two tones, very limited — and it's cuckoo, because Stanley's always doing the wrong thing. And when you put them together, the clash of the major second intervals makes it sound funny." Hatley sang both parts to Trimble and Stephenson (who, unlike Hatley, couldn't read music), and they played the tune on clarinets for its first official recording.

Music is a universal language, but English unfortunately isn't. Thus, Laurel and Hardy not only had to each play two roles in this picture, they had to play those roles four times — because the *Brats* of the American version became *Les Bons Petits Diables* in French, *Gluckliche Kindheit* in German, and something either unknown or unmentionable in Spanish.

A *Variety* reviewer noted that the German version was similar to the American one — maybe a little too similar. "Laurel and Hardy's German," he observed, "occasionally possesses a decided American twang."

The twang of Laurel and Hardy's voices was heard in a new medium soon after filming was completed. On January 27, 1930, the boys performed along with Charley Chase, Harry Langdon, Thelma Todd and Our Gang on a network radio program entitled *Voices of Filmland*. Crowded into the KHJ studios with these luminaries were the members of the Earl Burtnett orchestra. They should've hired the Happy-Go-Lucky Trio.

BELOW ZERO

Production history: Written and filmed late February-early March 1930. Copyrighted April 14, 1930 by MGM (LP 1220). Released April 26. Two reels.

Produced by Hal Roach. Directed by James Parrott. Photographed by George Stevens. Edited by Richard Currier. Dialogue by H.M. Walker. Sound by Elmer Raguse.

With Tiny Sandford, Frank Holliday, Leo Willis, Blanche Payson, Bobby Burns.

With Bob O'Connor as the policeman in *Titemba y Titubea*.

The winter of '29 is an especially bleak one for street musicians L&H, who are doing their best to cheer the ill-tempered citizens of a slum neighborhood. Their talents are unappreciated by the residents. The boys' luck changes when they find a wallet; unfortunately, it belongs to a cop, whom they try to treat to lunch with his own money. The "pickpockets" are left to the wrath of a restaurateur and his burly waiters.

Below Zero is a strange, sad little film, but one which defines Laurel and Hardy's relationship with each other — and all the nasty people who populate their world. Once again, people who seemed to be friends (the cop, a burly waiter) end up deserting them and doing them physical harm. All that Stan and Ollie have to sustain themselves is each other.

The film's most touching moment comes near the end: Ollie has been thrown out of a restaurant and into the snow-filled streets, while Stan has been dunked head-first into a rain barrel. Unable to find his friend, Ollie cries out for Stan with great anxiety edging his voice. (This is played with absolute seriousness, and it's evidence of Hardy's gifts as an actor that he can so convincingly inject such a dramatic note into a two-reel comedy.) Stan finally emerges from the barrel, with a gigantic stomach — he drank all of the water. This soon causes an even more urgent concern.

Until a shooting script turns up, it is impossible to know what, if anything, was cut from the final release print. An extant still suggests the boys did The Never-Ending Hat Routine yet again, this time confusing Officer Frank Holliday's cap along with their derbies.

Be-Nice-to-People-on-Your-Way-Up Department: among the supporting actors in this picture is Robert "Bobby" Burns, who played bit parts in many subsequent L&H films; Burns had starred (with Walter Stull) in the *Pokes and Jabbs* comedies made at the Vim studio in Jacksonvlle, Florida in 1916-17 — which featured a supporting actor named Babe Hardy.

At the time of this film's release, the Roach studio declared its financial outlook was "exceptionally bright." The studio had produced 40 silent comedies a season toward the end of the silent era; by 1930 it was turning out 32 talkies, but each of these was re-shot as many as three times for foreign-language theaters. (*Below Zero* was re-filmed twice, in a German version, and in a Spanish edition entitled *Titemba y Titubea*. The latter featured actor and interpreter Bob O'Connor as the policeman.)

While the studio was producing much more film, the profits unfortunately took much longer to materialize. "We consider 80 weeks the life of a talkie, which is half its estimated period of productivity," Hal Roach noted at the time. "At the end of the 80 weeks' run of each picture, we compute the profit or loss. As a result, we will have to [produce] talkies not exceeding 80 weeks, under the present plans, before profits show up constantly along with production."

Unlike most films produced in 1930, *Below Zero* is still turning a profit — and it has almost certainly been more than 80 weeks since its release.

HOG WILD

Production history: Written late March 1930; Dialogue script by H.M. Walker finished March 31. Filmed early April. Released May 31. Copyrighted December 3, 1930 by MGM (LP 1782). Two reels.

Produced by Hal Roach. Directed by James Parrott. Photographed by George Stevens. Edited by Richard Currier. Dialogue by H.M. Walker. Sound by Elmer Raguse.

With Fay Holderness, Dorothy Granger.

Despite Ollie's protests that he has a date with Stan, Mrs. Hardy insists that he put up that radio aerial today. Ollie wearily climbs up the ladder to the roof, only to come crashing down when startled by the horn of Stan's car. Laurel offers to help, but inadvertently sends Hardy sliding down the roof and into a conveniently located garden pond several times. With the ladder mounted in the seat of Stan's car, Ollie makes another ascent — only to wind up gyrating atop the ladder as the car speeds through the downtown streets.

Stan and the gag men came up with another epic three-and-a-half page script this time, one so well done that the boys adhered to it very closely during the shooting.

Examining the "action" script — as opposed to Beanie Walker's dialogue script — one notices only minor differences, such as this cute gag which was supposed to come after one of Ollie's many headlong dives from the roof into the garden pond: "Cut to Babe getting out of the pool. He looks back and realizes there is very little water in it. There is a faucet near the pool and Babe turns it on, filling the pool with water in case he falls in again."

On the *other* side of the radio, at the KFVD studios.

The only deleted sequence is a brief gag in which Ollie is on the roof, waiting for Stan to connect the aerial wire to the radio inside. "Connect that wire to rheostat A-9, and hurry up!," yells Ollie. Soon he hears "some lousy music," and is very pleased. He hollers, "That's fine! Now try KFVD!," but Stan replies that he hasn't found rheostat A-9 yet. Ollie looks around from his rooftop perch, and sees an organ grinder entertaining passersby on the street.

The action script landed in the hands of Harley M. Walker, who wrote additional dialogue for the film. Walker, a brilliantly witty writer of subtitles, was not as skillful when it came to writing dialogue for the team. He couldn't resist the temptation to put snappy one-liners in the boys' mouths, though he knew caustic comebacks and putrid puns were out of character for them. For example, he came up with the following for Ollie in the scene where Hardy is looking for the hat which is perched atop his head:

MRS. HARDY:	You must've put it somewhere! Hats don't walk!
OLLIE:	Why not? They feel, don't they? You've heard of felt hats, haven't you? *(Savagely)* Haw, haw, haw!
MRS. HARDY:	Well, well. America's greatest humorist is in again.

The dialogue in the finished film is far less "gaggy," and much more amusing. As Babe told an interviewer about this time, "The minute you wisecrack, you're fresh. People resent it. Comedy must be believable." And Stan, too, insisted on "No wise cracks." As a result, L&H dialogue often seems pedestrian — but it is exactly right for their Everyman characters.

Filming began on *Hog Wild* in early April, with Stan, Babe, director James Parrott, cameraman George Stevens, and various grips and prop men all clambering around on the roof. Since no homeowner in his right mind would have allowed all these people to run around on his roof, the studio rented a lot on Madison Avenue in Culver City and built a prop house designed specifically for this picture.

Among the supporting players in the picture is Dorothy Granger, who began working under a new contract at the Roach lot on April Fool's Day, 1930. She plays Tillie, the bubbly maid, and also does a bit (with her back to the camera) as a leggy flapper girl who tries to navigate a mud puddle and nearly causes Stan to have a car accident. "They used me in two roles — they always tried to get their money's worth at Roach's," said Miss Granger with a laugh.

The film was called *Hay Wire* all during production, and even while publicity material was being prepared. But at the last minute, for some unknown reason, someone changed it to *Hog Wild*. The British distributors for Metro-Goldwyn-Mayer didn't care for either title, and re-christened the picture *Aerial Antics*.

After the boys were done risking their necks by falling off rooftops for English-speaking audiences, they went back and did it all over again for French fans (in *Pele-Mele*), and Spanish-speaking devotees (in *Radio-Mania*). The film featured an added treat for all the boys' fans, in that it was the first to use the catchy and endearing background music. One of the songs was written by Hal Roach; another, entitled "Smile When the Raindrops Fall," was written by Alice K. Howlett. The other tunes were composed by T. Marvin Hatley, who, almost against his will, had just become the new musical director of the Hal Roach studio.

"I had played at a dance at Hal Roach's home," Marvin recalled. "So, I told my girlfriend Josephine there was going to be an opening for a musical director at the studio. She said, 'Well, I'd like to see you have that job.' I said, 'Oh, I'm scared. I'm afraid to try.' She said, 'Why don't you take me down to Hal Roach's — I'd like to see his home.' So I drove her down there. I was chewing gum, and she said, 'Now, spit your gum out, and get in there and meet Mr. Roach, and tell him you want the job!' I said, 'I'm afraid.' She said, 'Do what I tell you, or I won't marry you.' So I went.

"Pretty soon, Roach drove up with one of those old Stutz automobiles, with an engine as long as a piano. He said, 'Hi, Marvin.' It was about the first time he'd ever spoken to me.

"I said, 'I understand you're gonna go in for sound, and you'll need a music director, and I'd like to apply for the job.' Probably stuttered when I said it. And he said, 'Well, come around to the studio tomorrow, and talk to Ginsberg. He takes care of those things.' Henry Ginsberg was the manager of the studio. So I went around, and they offered me $100 a week. I was glad to get it."

Hatley went on to compose hundreds of specialty tunes for the various Roach series, while his wife Josephine managed the music department and hired the musicians. "I'd sometimes score two or three shorts at one time," Hatley related. "When the picture was finished, that's when I went to work on it. The director, or Stan Laurel or Charley Chase, would give me the general idea of what they wanted — where they thought the music ought to be — and then I'd work out the details.

"Every time Stan worked on a picture, he'd say, 'I want music everywhere.' He said, 'I do lots of pantomime, and I've got to have something going back there. A good, fast-paced music makes my stuff go better; if you take the music away, I don't move so fast. The fast beat excites 'em.'

"Stan Laurel never complained about anything I ever wrote; he was perfectly satisfied with it. And Mr. Roach never spoke to me in all the years I was there. One morning I was walking down the lot, and I said, 'Good morning, Mr. Roach.' And he bowed, politely, and looked at me out of the corner of his eye — that's as far as I got with Mr. Roach.

"Many times I'd write a score specifically for a certain short subject; other times I'd just write stock themes. What determined that was money. Everything was money! Henry Ginsberg was a money man; that's all he thought about, how to handle money. I'd write the music for a picture, and they'd figure, 'All right, we'll use this in another picture to cut down on hiring those musicians.' So they'd just splice the tracks in, put 'em in a new film. The editors wouldn't even consult me. A song I wrote called 'Honolulu Baby' was used to death. They'd just use it anyplace they felt like it.

"Each tune had its own title. To remember where to put the music, we'd just use the dialogue for the title. So, if a character said, 'I'm gonna hit that guy with a pie,' we'd call the tune 'I'm Gonna Hit That Guy With a Pie,' see?"

Hog Wild marked the end of the 1929-30 season of L&H films. The shorts cost $303,916.28 and earned $447,594.63 (in their initial domestic release), for a profit of $143,678.35. This would be the last profitable season for two years, given the state of the nation's economy.

THE LAUREL-HARDY MURDER CASE

Production history: Written early May 1930; Dialogue script by H.M. Walker finished May 6. Filmed mid-late May. Copyrighted July 16, 1930 by MGM (LP 1419). Released September 6. Three reels.

Produced by Hal Roach. Directed by James Parrott. Photographed by George Stevens and Walter Lundin. Sound by Elmer Raguse.

With Fred Kelsey, Del Henderson, Dorothy Granger, Frank Austin, Tiny Sandford.

Vagrants Stan and Ollie are fishing at the pier when their financial outlook is suddenly brightened: Ollie learns that the wealthy Ebeneezer Laurel has died, and his heirs are being sought for the reading of the will. The boys arrive at the spooky Laurel mansion on a stormy night, only to be told that Ebeneezer was murdered, and all of his relatives are suspects. Eventually, the boys capture the culprit, but it's all for naught: the whole thing has been a shared dream.

The Laurel-Hardy Murder Case — its title reminiscent of Paramount's Philo Vance films with William Powell — is a dull and unamusing little film.

The only differences between the script and the film are some cute touches for the opening scene at the pier. When Ollie is trying to determine if Stan is an heir to the Laurel fortune, Stan tells him that he had an uncle at Cambridge University. "What is he, a professor?," asks Ollie. "No, he's in a glass bottle," Stan replies. (In the film, Stan remarks that his uncle fell through a trap door and broke his neck. When Ollie asks if he was building a house, Stan says, "No, they were hanging him!")

The script contains some byplay for this sequence wherein Stan elabo-

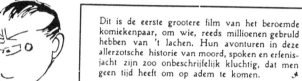

STAN   OLIVER
LAUREL EN HARDY

spelen op de hun eigen, onnavolgbare wijze
in de geheimzinnige moordgeschiedenis, getiteld:

NACHTMERRIES

met

100 °/₀ Duitschen
dialoog.

Dit is de eerste grootere film van het beroemde
komiekenpaar, om wie, reeds millioenen gebruld
hebben van 't lachen. Hun avonturen in deze
allerzotsche historie van moord, spoken en erfenis-
jacht zijn zoo onbeschrijfelijk kluchtig, dat men
geen tijd heeft om op adem te komen.   ♪

They didn't make a Dutch version, but *Murder Case* played in Holland anyway.

rately swings his fishing-pole line around his head, accidentally hooks onto Ollie's hat and flings it into the water. Ollie angrily snatches it back and clamps it down on his head, as water pours over his brow. At the end of the scene, Ollie was to have stalked off and stepped on a loose plank, hurling him into the water; Stan, on the other end, was to be thrown into the air, landing head first in some sand. (Incidentally, the background music for this scene — "The Cuckoo Waltz" — was taken from the music and sound-effects track created for *Wrong Again*.)

Walker's dialogue script indicates that the film originally ended with detective Fred Kelsey nabbing the murderer. Kelsey was to have said, "Well, boys, I solved this just like I knew I would from the very first. That's all for tonight; you can go home. That's that!" However, in the film, Kelsey meets the same fate as most of the Laurel heirs — he's told by the scheming butler he's wanted on the telephone, and when Kelsey picks up the receiver, a trap door opens and he's hurled into a yawning pit. Which is appropriate, since the audience is probably yawning, too.

Kelsey's line about "That's that" provides a clue to the solution of a mystery that's more interesting than the one in the film. Sometime in late 1936 or mid-1937, film editor Bert Jordan assembled a reel of bloopers, trims, shots from foreign versions and other odds and ends, and gave it to Stan as a present. Most of the footage is from *Way Out West* and *The Laurel-Hardy Murder Case*, and the title of this bizarre little reel is *That's That*. I suspect *That's That* was another working title for *Murder Case* (in addition to *The Rap*) and the title was changed along with the end of the film.

The shooting of the picture was delayed slightly, due to a tragedy in Stan's personal life. On May 7, 1930, Stan's wife Lois gave birth to a son, Stanley Robert Jefferson; the delivery was two months premature, and the baby died on May 16. The morbid story and setting of *Murder Case* probably didn't help Stan recover from the loss, and this may well be a reason why the film is largely devoid of the inventive gags common to L&H films.

Three foreign-language versions were shot at the same time as the English-language one. *Feu Mon Oncle*, *Der Spuk Um Mitternacht* and *Noche de Duendes* were the christenings given to the French, German and Spanish-language releases.

Dorothy Granger, who appeared in all three, recalled, "To play my English-language part, they had a French, German, and Spanish gal. And there were three different interpreters on the set with Stan and Babe. So, they did the English version first. I'm always curious, and I try to learn; I asked the German interpreter, 'How do you say my line in German?,' and he'd say it. I said, 'Write that out phonetically for me.' And I did the same with the French interpreter. I had just enough of an American accent so that it was cute to them; so, they paid off the three girls, and used me in the foreign versions."

The foreign releases were all one reel longer than the American counterpart; they included a new scene in which the boys travel by train to the Laurel mansion. This was a reworking of material from *Berth Marks*, which, come to think of it, wasn't very funny either.

PARDON US

Production history: Script written during May-June 1930. Filming started June 24, 1930. Previewed (as *The Rap*) during August-September 1930. Retakes on American version and shooting of Spanish, German, Italian and French versions from mid-September to December 1, 1930. Film receives new working title, *Their First Mistake*, January 1931. Released as *Pardon Us* August 15, 1931. Copyrighted on September 10, 1931 by MGM (LP 2460). 56 minutes.

Produced by Hal Roach. Directed by James Parrott. Photographed by George Stevens. Edited by Richard Currier. Dialogue by H.M. Walker. Sound by Elmer Raguse (final mix), with uncredited assistance by John Whitaker (mixing of English version), John Harrison and Ralph Butler (location sound recording), and S.C. Baden (mixing of all foreign versions).

With Walter Long, Wilfred Lucas, Tiny Sandford, James Finlayson, June Marlowe, Charlie Hall.

During Prohibition, L&H make some home brew; when Stan inadvertently sells a bottle to a policeman, the boys are sent to prison. Their contacts with the warden, and their cell-mate, The Tiger (Long), are not bettered by Stan's loose tooth, which makes a buzzing "razzberry" sound. After a prison break the boys

Fire engine foolishness deleted from the film.

escape to a cottonfield, but before long they're thrown back into the clink. The hapless pair foil another breakout attempt planned by The Tiger, and are pardoned for their valor.

By May 1930, Laurel and Hardy were more popular than many feature film stars. Their short subjects were frequently billed on theater marquees over the feature picture, and Hal Roach undoubtedly realized that the team had enough drawing power to succeed in features — which would bring much more revenue to the studio than the shorts. Yet when he finally put Stan and Babe into their first feature, it was with reluctance.

Roach had produced only one comedy feature since Harold Lloyd's *Why Worry?* (1923) — *Raggedy Rose* with Mabel Normand — and with good reason. "The greatest comedies that were made by anybody were made in two reels, I don't care who it was," Roach says. "It's a simple damn thing. If you can stop after 20 minutes, you've only got to go up to this peak for your last laugh. But if you've got to go clear to 60 minutes, the last laugh is three times harder. It's that simple. And I don't care how funny a guy is, if you listen to him long enough, you're going to be bored to hell with him."

Neither Stan nor Babe were particularly eager to go into features, either. Anita Garvin recalled, "Stan said he was sorry they ever made the features. He loved the shorts; he said they were much funnier than the feature pictures." When Dorothy Spensley interviewed the team for *Photoplay* magazine in mid-1930, she wrote, "They have no desire to make feature-length pictures unless

Stan Laurel, Walter Long and Oliver Hardy in
THE RAP—Because they decided to sell what they couldn't drink, Laurel and Hardy are put in the big house. An attempted prison break increases the sentence twenty years. Brimming with laughs, this burlesque on prison life is Laurel and Hardy's first feature length comedy.—*Hal Roach.*

A 1930 review for a 1931 release.

they find a sure-fire story. They have seen too many comedy teams hit the rocks in seven-reel specials." But by the time the article was published in July, Laurel and Hardy were already making their first feature.

"As far as I can remember, *Pardon Us* was supposed to be a two-reeler," said Hal Roach. Roach had asked the Metro-Goldwyn-Mayer executives for the use of the massive prison set for *The Big House,* a recently completed Wallace Beery drama, and they agreed. While the L&H prison story was being written, MGM suddenly notified Roach that his popular team would have to star in a film at the domain of Leo the Lion. Roach wouldn't hear of this.

As June approached, Roach hired set designer Frank Durloff to create the prison interior and exterior sets; Durloff based his designs on photographs of San Quentin and Sing Sing. The sets proved to be so elaborate, and so costly, that Roach decided to make the film a feature to recoup the expense.

Thus, Stan and the gag writers found themselves with a script for a two-reeler which had to be inflated to feature length. They didn't have a particularly easy time with the expansion, which is evident from the highly episodic construction of the film. Stan once remarked, "You can't take a whole, long series of things we do and stick them all together in eight reels, and expect to get a well-balanced picture out of it." *Pardon Us* is the film which proves that.

The first cut, entitled *The Rap,* had a number of scenes which didn't survive the previews.

One deleted scene takes place in the prison courtyard. Stan and Ollie have just watched a convict quartet sing "I Want to Go Back," and one prisoner asks

Stan what he thinks of the group. Stan's razzberry reply is, "Great! Bzzzzzz!" The prisoner is just about to sock him, but Ollie explains that his friend has a slight affliction. The con offers to yank out the offending molar; he ties a string around Stan's tooth, hands the other end to a group of prisoners, and tells them to pull. On the first try, Stan falls flat on his face, but the second time he convicts yank out the tooth — and fall backward onto a couple of guards. The guards think they've been jumped, and the prisoners, including Stan and Ollie, are sent to the Dungeon. As they march off, Ollie remarks, "Well, we won't be bothered with that noise anymore." Stan says, "No," punctuating his reply with a louder-than-ever razzberry.

Another deleted courtyard scene has a group of convicts planning a break. Stan and Ollie saunter by, and the other cons think they're eavesdropping. One convict sneers, "If I thought you'd squeal, I'd knock your block off." Ollie protests, "Knock my block off? Why, you couldn't even knock *his* block off!" The block in question is Stan's. Laurel tries to back away from an altercation, but the con sticks out his chin and says, "Go ahead! Hit me right there and make me good and mad!" Stan tries to sock him any number of times, since the con keeps demanding it, but his featherweight blows have no effect.

Much to Ollie's discomfort, a guard is watching the whole thing. Ollie tries to calm Stan down, but by now Laurel has taken off his coat and is dancing, weaving and doing scissors kicks. In his zeal to bop the con on the button, Stan swings, pivots around and smacks the guard. Ollie tries to revive the guard and tells Stan to get some water; Stan finds a fire bucket nearby, but his aim is a trifle off and Ollie gets the benefit of the water. Ollie throws the bucket at Stan, but his aim is also a trifle off, and the bucket is intercepted by the Warden's head. Back to the Dungeon.

After the first round of previews, the tooth-pulling scene was replaced with a reworking of the dentist's office scene from *Leave 'em Laughing*, and the fight sequence was modified. (This modification was also deleted later.) The Tiger breaks up the fight and tells the boys that he's overheard the Warden speaking well of them. It might be nice to show their appreciation, the Tiger says, and what better way than to give the Warden a present? He just happens to have a gaily-wrapped package of cigarettes, and the boys are only too eager to deliver the little surprise. (What they don't know is that the Tiger has actually gift-wrapped a bomb, and when the Warden pulls the string on that package, it's lights out.)

They find the Warden in the prison yard, speaking to a guest — the Governor. Ollie delivers the present with regal aplomb: "Would it be asking too much for you to accept this with our compliments?" Stan chimes in with, "Just a little surprise." The Warden promises the boys that they'll get good marks in his weekly report.

Beaming with pride, Stan and Ollie stroll back to their friend the Tiger, who is anxiously awaiting news of the package's delivery. "What did he say?" he asks. Stan replies, "He says he's going to give us a great big report." At that moment, another great big report is heard offscreen. When the smoke clears, the Warden staggers out from a huge hole in the prison wall, still holding the little piece of string.

The film originally had a different ending, which took place after the final prison riot sequence. We dissolve to a picturesque river setting, where Laurel and Hardy — now bearded old men — are talking to a couple of small boys.

"The Tiger" was played by a pre-*Frankenstein* Boris Karloff in the French version.

Ollie is in a wheelchair, while Stan is fishing. Stan has been recounting the story of his misspent life to the boys, and sums it up with, "It all goes to prove that you can't be too careful." As he says this, he removes the brick that's keeping Ollie's wheelchair from rolling off the embankment. The wheelchair and its occupant sail majestically into the river, and as the hapless Stan watches Ollie thrashing in the water, we fade out.

Laurel and Hardy's first feature ran 70 minutes when a reviewer for *The Exhibitor's Herald-World* caught a preview on August 9, 1930. He remarked, "It is a screamingly funny takeoff.... The outbreak itself slows up the comic action, as it is too long and the din is overwhelming. But this doubtless will be cured by further cutting." (The film was 14 minutes shorter when finally released.) Another preview in early September went well; a critic for the *St. Louis Star* noted: If the preview audience the other night can be taken as a standard, the two comics have nothing to worry about."

But Stan still wasn't fully satisfied with *The Rap*, and by October 7, he had collaborated with Roach and Beanie Walker on a new scene wherein the boys disguise as black cotton pickers. "There had been four or five feature pictures made where people were escaping from prison; these noisy bloodhounds were always chasing them. We were doing a satire on that kind of a picture," said Hal Roach.

"My particular idea was that after Laurel and Hardy escape, the bloodhounds are going through the swamp, chasing them. Then you cut to a close-up, and Laurel and Hardy are wearing blackface, sitting by a mailbox and talking about what they're going to do. As they walk away, Hardy turns around and says, "Come on, boys." And you cut, and the two bloodhounds are their pets. Well, I thought that was a hell of a funny gag. And the audience didn't get a smile out of it — it went way over their heads. They couldn't visualize the idea that Laurel and Hardy had tamed these bloodhounds." (Following the previews, Roach dictated memos to "shorten these scenes since the pay-off isn't worth the time we are taking to set it up.")

One scene which was shot and deleted had Stan and Ollie rescuing the Warden's daughter (played by our Gang's Miss Crabtree, June Marlowe) from a prison fire — and from the lecherous advances of Walter Long. Rodney Sprigg, June's husband, was on the set during the filming. "Walter Long was a friend of mine," Sprigg recalled. "He had a face like a bulldog, and he was the heavy in this film. And he was leaning against a door of the prison set; just waiting, because nothing was going on. Behind him, the crew was working. They had flame throwers; they were going to have a big fire scene.

"Jimmy Parrott had told the crew that he was going to pull his handkerchief out of his pocket — that was the signal for the men to turn on the flame throwers. Well, everything was quiet, Walter just standing in the door — and Parrott forgot all about the signal, and pulled his handkerchief out of his pocket. The guys turned on the fire, and it burned all he hair off the back of Walter's head. You could hear him screaming and cussing for a mile." Unfortunately, Long lost his hair for naught; stills are all that exists of this sequence.

When Roach, Stan, Babe and Parrott all agreed that the feature was shot and cut just as they wanted it, the boys had to go film it all over again — four times.

According to a studio press release, the foreign-language versions were shot only after the English version received several previews and the final stamp of approval. The foreign versions were filmed simultaneously; a scene would be shot four times, each time in a different language, before the next scene began.

The film became *Sous Les Verrous* in French (with a young Boris Karloff taking Walter Long's place), *Hinter Schloss und Riegel* for the German market, *Muraglie* to the Italians and *De Bote en Bote* for Spanish-speaking audiences. The "big report" gag and the ending sequence with Stan and Ollie as old men were apparently retained in the foreign editions while excised from the American print.

The Prohibition aspect of the story didn't translate well. As Babe told a reporter at the time, "How can you blame them for forgetting that we have Prohibition over there, when we can't remember it *here*?" Accordingly, the boys' crime was changed for the foreign versions: instead of selling home brew to a cop, the boys are arrested for somehow acquiring some stolen money and trying to put it in the bank.

On December 1, 1930, the foreign versions were finally completed. By the following month, the American edition been retitled, from *The Rap* to *Their First Mistake*. But by the time Roach made a distribution agreement with MGM on May 25, the feature was called *Pardon Us*. (The British didn't care for that title, either, and changed it to *Jailbirds*.)

The picture was released on August 15, 1931, and received lukewarm reviews. Mordaunt Hall, the stodgy old *New York Times* reviewer who had barely tolerated the team's antics in earlier films, begrudgingly admitted that *Pardon Us* "aroused no little merriment" in its audience, but added, "It seems a pity that the clever acting of this team was not rewarded by a keener and less robust variety of humor."

Outlook was brighter: "Some of their business is tremendously funny, and some of it is only moderately amusing, but all of it is way ahead of any other film comedy of this period."

After spending more than six months writing and shooting *Pardon Us*, Laurel and Hardy were glad to be back making short subjects. But the financial success of their first full-length comedy guaranteed that it wouldn't be long before the team made their next feature film.

ANOTHER FINE MESS

Production history: Action script written mid-September, 1930. Dialogue script completed by H.M. Walker September 19, 1930. Shot circa late September-early October. Released November 29, 1930. Copyrighted December 8, 1930 by MGM (LP 1790). Three reels.

Produced by Hal Roach. Directed by James Parrott. Photographed by George Stevens. Edited by Richard C. Currier. Sound by Elmer R. Raguse.

With Thelma Todd, Charles Gerrard, James Finlayson.

Vagrants Laurel and Hardy, running from the police, hide in the basement of a temporarily deserted mansion belonging to big-game hunter Colonel Buck-shot (Finlayson). When a dignified British couple inquire about renting the place, Stan assumes the roles of Hives the butler and Agnes the maid, while Ollie becomes "the last of the Kentucky Buckshots."

Another Fine Mess is a reworking of *Duck Soup* (1927), which, you'll recall, is a reworking of *Home From the Honeymoon*, the sketch written by Stan's father in 1908.

A number of scripted scenes, as usual, never made it to the screen. One lengthy sequence has Lady Plumtree trying to become accustomed to the new home which Ollie has just leased to her husband. She asks Stan — who is attired as Agnes, the maid — to show her to the bedroom, so that Agnes can help her change her clothes. Of course, Stan gets very nervous and tries not to look as Lady Plumtree disrobes. (She holds up some dainty lingerie and tells him, "Agnes, I think these will just fit you. Try them on, and if they do, you may have them!")

Next, Lady Plumtree decides she wants a bath. As Stan tries to draw the bath — and gets soaked when he turns on the shower — his mistress is seated at her vanity, apparently in the nude. She calls for Agnes, and Stan, mad with panic, runs around the bathroom in utter confusion. Finally, Lady Plumtree puts on a kimono and goes into the bathroom. She finds Agnes in the bathtub with "her" head underwater. When she pulls Stan out and he finally realizes that Lady Plumtree is clothed, he gives her the alibi that he was looking for the soap. (This scene was reworked in *Come Clean.*)

In the film, Lord Plumtree, having leased the house from Ollie, admires a picture of a gleaming Rolls-Royce and inquires if it is for sale. The film just drops the gag there, but in the script Ollie replies that he'd sell it for a couple of

Colonel Buckshot and Agnes relax with a French film magazine.

thousand. Lord Plumtree is astonished at this bargain, and instantly hands over a roll of bills to Ollie.

Stan — now dressed as the butler — has watched this transaction. Lord Plumtree next asks Ollie if he has any horses, and he replies, apologetically, "I'm sorry, your Lordship, but I am just out of horses at the present time." Stan leans over to Ollie and whispers, "Go on, sell him one!"

Stan then asks for his salary as the butler in advance. When he asks Lord Plumtree for $2, Ollie hurriedly explains that he's been paying Stan $200 a month.

Ollie then tells Stan to have the maid come in. Stan is sick of changing clothes, but when Ollie says it's so Agnes can receive *her* salary, Stan brightens noticeably. After a moment, Agnes walks up to Lord Plumtree, holds out her hand and says, "$200." Stan nearly gives away the ruse when he pulls up his skirt to put the money in his trousers pocket.

Lord Plumtree then compounds his error by asking Ollie if there's any *more* help. Ollie quickly tells Stan to bring in "faithful old Remington," the gardener; Stan bursts into the room in grubby work clothes, dragging a lawn mower. Stan collects Remington's salary, then exits — the mower cutting a path through the rug as he goes.

The film's bizarre ending — wherein Stan and Ollie escape from the real Colonel Buckshot by hiding in an animal skin and pedaling away on a bicycle with the police in hot pursuit — was slightly different in the script. The boys, attired as "a crazy-looking cow," run past the cops, out of the neighborhood and past a pasture, where a bull rushes toward them. The boys clamber onto a fence, but Ollie is gored by the bull before they can escape. Back on a city street, they move their hooves just quickly enough to escape an oncoming trolley, but crash headlong into the end title.

Beanie Walker's dialogue script has a nice Hardy line at one point that could've applied to virtually any conversation with Stan: "I don't mind telling you things, it's the *explaining* that wears me down."

The original action script gave Lord Plumtree's first name as Leopold, but Walker changed the name to Ambrose in the dialogue script. Evidently, Thelma Todd was using both scripts during the shooting — because she calls her husband Leopold in some shots, Ambrose in others. Midway through the filming, there was a half-hearted attempt to correct the mistake; in one shot, Lady Plumtree calls for her husband with, "Leopold Ambrose..."

Todd, making her first appearance with the team since *Unaccustomed As We Are*, has a wonderful (and largely ad-libbed) scene with Agnes in which they talk about Colonel Buckshot's servants. When Stan tosses in an un-scripted line about the other maids leaving because they had "housemaid's knees," Thelma very nearly breaks up. "She had a wonderful sense of humor," recalled her frequent co-star, Dorothy Granger. "She'd just start to laugh — for no reason! And sometimes we'd have to shoot seven or eight times before she'd simmer down enough. It got so that we'd just start to look at each other, and we'd start giggling!"

The last shot of the film shows just what happens when two men attired in an animal skin ride a tandem bicycle into a railroad tunnel — when a train is approaching from the other end: Each man emerges wearing half an animal skin and pedaling a unicycle down the tracks. For this shot, the studio located Joe Mole, a former vaudevillian whose specialty was doing stunts on bicycles.

"That's me and my brother in those goat skins," Mole recalled in 1974. "That scene was shot down at the old Hill Street tunnel, and we had a heck of a time trying to ride those unicycles, because of the gravel and rocks between the tracks. Boy, we worked about two days, and then Laurel said, 'Okay, give it up for now. We'll fix it.' They hired a dozen carpenters to put boards in between the tracks, and paint them to make it look like the gravel — so then there was nothing to it; we just rode our unicycles over the boards. But oh, boy, they spent a lot of money in getting that shot."

Another Fine Mess is the first L&H film to feature the background music of LeRoy Shield, who came to the Roach studio to score the concurrently-filmed *Pardon Us*. It was Shield's job with the Victor Talking Machine Company that brought the former concert pianist into contact with the Roach studio. Shield wrote dozens of breezy, engaging little tunes which were inserted repeatedly into Roach talkies at the whim of the studio's film editors. Some of them, such as "Bells" and "Here We Go," have become virtual standards among Laurel and Hardy buffs. One written specifically for this film was aptly titled "Colonel Buckshot."

Stan's father had some harsh words for the filmed version of his sketch. In an article for the British magazine *Picturegoer Weekly*, Arthur J. Jefferson noted, "I sent him [Stan] a little sketch of my own, which they filmed under the stupid title of *Another Fine Mess*, and I didn't like the American angle they got on it one bit."

The ironic thing about the film's title is that it misquotes Ollie's catch-phrase. Ollie's frequent lament to Stan — as aficionados know — is "Well, here's another *nice* mess you've gotten me into."

Thanksgiving 1930 looks more like 1621.

BE BIG

Production history: Script written circa late October-early November 1930. Dialogue script by H.M. Walker completed circa mid-November. Filmed circa late November-early December. Previewed late December. Released February 7, 1931. Copyrighted under the working title, *The Chiselers*, February 9 by MGM (LP 1959). Three reels.

Produced by Hal Roach. Directed by James Parrott. Photographed by Art Lloyd. Edited by Richard Currier. Sound by Elmer R. Raguse.

With Anita Garvin, Isabelle Keith, Baldwin Cooke, Charlie Hall.

Just as the boys are about to take the train for a vacation with their wives in Atlantic City, their friend Cookie calls Ollie to tell him that he and Stan are being honored that night at a stag meeting of their lodge. Of course, the wives would begrudge the boys a night out, so Ollie feigns illness. They send the wives off and promise to meet them in Atlantic City the next morning; unfor-

tunately, the boys never get to their meeting, because in putting on his official club uniform, Ollie has gotten his feet stuck in Stan's small boots.

Early in 1959, Stan told interviewer Boyd Verb, "We'd do what you call a milking routine...If, from the audience reaction, we felt they could stand more, we'd go back and add more and more to it....Sometimes our pictures were what you call 'over-milked.'" *Be Big* is one of those pictures.

The film's chief flaw is an excruciatingly protracted sequence which has Stan trying to pull his boot from Hardy's foot for damn near 20 minutes. Fun is fun, but there are limits.

The five-page script differs only in a couple of individual gags. The repeated use of the phrase "Be Big!" may have been improvised on the set; it's nowhere to be found in the action script. This script *does* tell us that when Laurel and Hardy borrowed a gag from a previous film, they did it deliberately. When the boys are to change into their club uniforms, the script reads, "They go into the door routine, as they did in *Angora Love*, hanging the clothes up on a nail. At the finish of this gag, cut to the depot." (Stan didn't hesitate to borrow from the team's silent comedies — the early films were then out of circulation and unavailable for comparison.)

One rather risque gag didn't survive: As Stan determinedly tugs at the too-tight boot, he drags Ollie by the foot into the living room. Ollie's cries of "Cut it out! You're hurting me!" arouse the curiosity of a bellboy who's strolling down the hall of the apartment building. He gets out a key and opens the door to find Stan and Ollie in what the script terms "a very funny position," struggling and groaning. Embarrassed, the bellboy says, "Excuse me!" and makes a hasty exit.

The script proposes a "high and dizzy" gag at the finish. Ollie, in his struggle to remove the boot, has taken *two* falls into his sunken bathtub. (Stan locked the bathroom door after the first tumble, but Ollie crashed right on through.) He asks Stan to help him take off his sopping sweater, and predictably the boys become entangled in each others' sweaters. Blindly, they stumble around the living room, somehow ending up inside the belt of a reducing machine. Stan accidentally turns it on, and they stand there, trapped, not knowing what's jiggling them.

The machine is next to the window of the Hardys' fourth-floor apartment; as the boys blindly struggle, the belt breaks and they fall backwards, hanging over the ledge. They climb back inside, but they're not safe for long — the wives soon return, see the uniforms, and wield their shooting irons.

There is a final gag at the end of the script, written solely for the entertainment of the writers. Either they knew they had a dud on their hands — *Be Big* is generally regarded as one of L&H's weakest shorts — or they honestly thought this one was a gem. Or maybe they just felt silly. In any event, the final shot is described as follows:

> 36. Cut to close up. Stan and Babe come up out of the debris, and we Fade out amid riotous laughter and deafening applause, the audience leaping to their feet with wild shouts of "Run it again! Run it again!"

Ollie's boot wasn't the only uncomfortable piece of costuming. "Mrs. Roach — Roach's first wife, Margaret — decided she was going to be a designer," said Anita Garvin, who played Mrs. Laurel. "So she designed the outfit I wore, which had stripes running vertically, up and down the jacket and skirt. And the thing was made of wool — it was itchy, scratchy and thick. She'd made it on a form in the wardrobe department, and when I got it on, she looked at me and said, 'Oh, if I had known you were so thin, I would have made the stripes running the other way!' Running around, horizontally! Oh, Lordy."

Be Big was Anita's last L&H film until 1938. She married bandleader Clifford "Red" Stanley soon after this picture, and although she continued to make occasional film appearances, she devoted most of her time to her family from then on. "Stan would call for me, many times," she said, "but I was busy raising my kids during that period. Mae Busch did several pictures they wanted me for."

When the American version wrapped, the boys began filming *Les Carottiers* and *Los Calaveras*, the French and Spanish editions. Isabelle Keith's role as Mrs. Hardy was taken over by Linda Loredo in the Spanish version, and by Germaine de Neel in the French one. Anita Garvin was used in all three, but her voice was not. She explains: "I'd learn the line in a kind of pigeon-Spanish, and I'd just move my lips; another girl speaking Spanish stood on the sidelines. She had the microphone off the set, and she'd speak the real words."

Curiously, although the film's titles credit James Parrott and Art Lloyd for the direction and photography, all the publicity material for the picture credits James W. Horne and Jack Stevens.

Stan's salary for 1930 totaled $74,716.67, in payments ranging from $1,000 to $2,000 per week. Babe received $52,716.67 for the year, with weekly paychecks of $1,000 to $1,500. While the comics were receiving the same amount at the start of the year, Stan's extra hours in the writing sessions and the editing room were soon verified by his paycheck.

CHICKENS COME HOME

Production history: Script written mid-late December, 1930. Dialogue script by H.M. Walker (entitled *Sweeties*) completed December 29. Shot early-mid January 1931; previewed circa January 24. Released February 21. Copyrighted March 3, 1931 by MGM (LP 2019). Three reels.

Produced by Hal Roach. Directed by James W. Horne. Photographed by Art Lloyd, Jack Stevens. Edited by Richard Currier. Sound by Elmer R. Raguse.

With Mae Busch, Thelma Todd, James Finlayson, Norma Drew.

Businessman Ollie is running for mayor. A gold-digging old flame bursts into the Hardy office and threatens to spill the beans about Ollie's high-living past. Ollie and his winsome wife are giving a dinner party for some very influential guests that evening, so business partner Stan is dispatched to the gold-digger's home until Ollie can slip away and pay her off. Naturally, the old flame heads for the Hardy home, whereupon events occur that do not bode well for Ollie's political career.

Chickens Come Home is a virtual twin of the 1927 silent *Love 'em and Weep*, except that Ollie has taken over the James Finlayson role, and Finlay-

Gordo y Flaco, dealers in *Spanish* fertilizer.

son has been demoted to playing Hardy's butler. Thelma Todd, who was slated to play the gold-digger, wound up playing Mrs. Hardy, with Mae Busch reprising her vamp part from the earlier film.

A glance at the script reveals that it was planned to be almost a scene-for-scene remake, but new bits of business, reflecting the growth in the Stan and Ollie characters, were introduced during the filming.

One gag which was planned for both films — but used in neither — occurs at the dinner party, after Mrs. Hardy learns the awful truth about her husband's purple past. She was supposed to run down a hallway, grab the butler, wrestle him to the floor and unfasten his wooden leg, and use it to club her formerly philandering husband into insensibility. Perhaps someone thought this joke a bit tasteless, or there was a shortage of butlers with wooden legs.

Reading Walker's dialogue script reveals that he may have been brilliant when writing titles, but he seemed to be lost when writing dialogue for Laurel and Hardy.

Here's an example of a Walker line that's too glib for its own good: When a policeman comes to the Hardy doorstep because he's found a box of cigars outside, Walker has Ollie telling the cop, "I thank you, inveterate sleuth that you are, I thank you."

L&H made only one foreign-language version of this film. In *Politiquerias*, Rina Liguoro took over Mae Busch's role, with Linda Loredo as Ollie's wife and Carmen Granada as Mrs. Laurel. Jack Stevens, who had photographed portions of the American version, left the Spanish edition to Art Lloyd; James Horne remained as director.

There was a new austerity at the Roach studio; several former mainstays, such as Edgar Kennedy, had had their contracts terminated. Roach was borrowing frequently from the Bank of Italy to keep production going. The Depression was reflected elsewhere at the Lot of Fun as well — even the publicity department stinted on promotional material.

THE STOLEN JOOLS

Production history: Produced early 1931 as a special promotional short; presented by National Variety Artists by arrangement with Chesterfield cigarettes, as a fund raiser for the N.V.A. tuberculosis sanitarium, Saranac Lake, New York. Released April 1931 by Paramount and National Screen Service. Released in England in 1932 as *The Slippery Pearls*, possibly by RKO. Two reels.

Produced by Pat Casey. Supervised by E.K. Nadel. Directed by William McGann. With Buster Keaton, Our Gang, Joe E. Brown, Edward G. Robinson, Joan Crawford and other stars, all in cameo appearances.

In this "All-Star" short, L&H make a brief appearance as two of detective Eddie Kane's best assistants. The boys escort Kane in their faithful Model T to the home of Norma Shearer, the fate of whose "jools" is in question. As Ollie parks the car in front of the Shearer abode, Stan pulls a lever and the car falls apart. After Kane scampers away, Ollie turns to Stan and remarks, "I told you not to make that last payment!"

The team's brief scene is one of the highlights of this film, which is more amazing than it is amusing. Equally amazing is the fact that in 1931 nobody thought it strange that a cigarette company should co-produce a film to raise money for a hospital which specialized in treating a respiratory disease.

LAUGHING GRAVY

Production history: Script written late January 1931. Dialogue script completed by H.M. Walker January 30, 1931. Working title: *True Blue*. Shot early-mid February. French, German and Spanish versions shot mid-late February. Released April 4, 1931. Copyrighted April 16, 1931 by MGM (LP 2141). Two reels.

Produced by Hal Roach. Directed by James W. Horne. Photographed by Art Lloyd. Edited by Richard Currier. Sound by Elmer Raguse.

With Charlie Hall, Harry Bernard.

On a bitterly cold and snowy night, Stan and Ollie attempt to keep their dog, Laughing Gravy, safe and warm in their room — and hidden from the dog-hating landlord. They fail. After the boys noisily and messily retrieve the dog, the landlord is about to throw them all out. Suddenly he is met with the news that the boarding house is under quarantine for two months. The landlord makes a dramatic exit, two shots ring out, and Stan and Ollie bow their heads.

The script for *Laughing Gravy* ran a whopping (by L&H standards) five and one-third pages. Included was a lengthy sequence shot for all editions, but retained only in the foreign-language versions.

Stan leaves his pal, in a scene cut from the American version.

The landlord, having been soaked with water intended for the dog's bath, tells the twosome to pack up their belongings and clear out. Ollie keeps tripping over Stan's suitcase. He chases Stan around the room; while in hot pursuit, Ollie uncovers a birthday cake which Stan has hidden for him. Touched by this gesture, Ollie apologizes — then asks Stan how he could possibly afford to buy the cake. Sure enough, Stan has borrowed their life's savings of $1.33. Ollie's rage is renewed. "Never speak to me again!" he yells.

Meanwhile, a registered letter has arrived for Stan, and the landlord goes upstairs to deliver it. Ollie is pacing around the room haranguing his one-time friend, but he trips over the suitcase again and falls into his cake. He hurls its gooey remains at Stan, but his aim is off — he decorates the landlord, who has just opened the door.

Wiping the frosting from his eyes, the landlord hands Stan the letter, and looks over his shoulder as Stan reads. From their reactions, Ollie realizes that it must be an important letter indeed. The letter is from a law firm, notifying Stan that his uncle has left him a fortune; an enclosed check for $1,000 is just the promise of further riches to come. But Stan will receive this immense wealth, the letter states, only on the condition that Stan leave Ollie forever. Stan's uncle considers Ollie a "nitwit," who has kept Laurel from achieving his rightful place in society all these years.

When Ollie asks to read the letter, Stan refuses; it's a private matter. "Oh," says Mr. Hardy a little too forcefully, "I don't want to read your mail. If it's private, that settles it. It's no business of mine. But I never kept anything from *you*." Ashamed, Stan offers Ollie the letter. Ollie is indignant at the very sugges-

tion that he should violate the sacred trust of Stan's privacy by reading his mail
— but when Stan agrees with him and pockets the letter, Ollie snatches it away.

Ollie is crestfallen when he finishes reading, and realizes that Stan was
only trying to spare his feelings. He apologizes to his tearful friend, and insists
Stan claim the fortune. "You'll be better off without me," Ollie says. "When
you're riding in swell cars, and living in big mansions, all I ask is that you think
of your old pal once in a while." Stan, resigned to his fate, picks up his dog
before leaving. But Ollie can't bear to lose his friend *and* the dog, and pleads to
keep the pet.

Reluctantly, Stan agrees, and heads for the door. He pauses, sees Ollie
sobbing, and decides he can't stand it any longer. Dramatically, he tears up the
letter, and the check. Ollie is overcome at this show of true friendship, and
beckons Stan over with outstretched arms. "My pal!," he cries. Stan runs toward
him — *past* him — and to the dog, which Stan hugs with joy. Ollie flies into a
rage again as the end title looms into view.

Why this whole sequence was deleted in the American print remains a
mystery; it was definitely an artistic decision, since it cost the studio more to
shoot the new finish. An official synopsis for this film, written for the press
sheet, exists in the Roach studio files; the original ending has been crossed out,
with the notation "new finish" written in the margins. This indicates that the
ending of the film was changed at the last minute, while the publicity for it was
being prepared. (Late in 1985, a 35mm work print of the original finish — in
English — was discovered at the British Film Institute.)

Laughing Gravy was re-filmed in French and Spanish, and possibly in German. An existing French print shows that it was tacked onto *Les Carottiers* (the
French edition of *Be Big*), and released under that title as a six-reel feature.
This was the last film L&H shot in a foreign language. Hal Roach explained
why:

"Those foreign pictures were extremely successful. The prices we got in
South American countries and Spain were fantastic. But finally, Metro-
Goldwyn-Mayer made us quit, because the other countries immediately said,
'We don't want dubbed pictures from Metro; we get them not dubbed from
Hal Roach.'

"They wanted Garbo and Gable and everybody else to speak German.
Well, hell, that was all right as far as comedy was concerned; if Laurel and
Hardy spoke lousy, it didn't make any difference, you know? But you could
imagine with these other people, like Gable, trying to speak German, and saying just yes or no — it would be impossible. So, I stopped — because the Metro
people were 100% right. And it was amazing; the people in the Argentine were
very indignant, but then they began dubbing the pictures, as they did in the
other countries."

OUR WIFE

Production history; Script written mid—late February, 1931. Dialogue script
completed by H.M. Walker March 3, 1931. Shot early — mid March.
Copyrighted by MGM April 27, 1931 (LP 2171). Released May 16, 1931. Two
reels.

Produced by Hal Roach. Directed by James W. Horne. Photographed by Art
Lloyd. Edited by Richard Currier. Sound by Elmer Raguse.

With *their* wives: Stan, Babe, Myrtle and Lois at the Los Angeles Coliseum, 1931.

With Babe London, James Finlayson, Ben Turpin, Charley Rogers, Blanche Payson.

Ollie's plans to marry his hefty girl friend, Dulcy, are torn asunder by her father, who absolutely forbids the marriage when he gets a good look at what Dulcy plans to wed. With Stan's questionable help, the couple elope; after barely squeezing into the tiny Austin car Laurel has rented, they repair to the home of a cross-eyed Justice of the Peace — who, because of his affliction, marries Ollie not to Dulcy, but to Stan.

The four-and-one-half page script for *Our Wife* bears a striking resemblance to the film. There is an additional reason in the script why Dulcy's father doesn't want Ollie to marry her. When Dulcy shows her father a picture of Ollie, the script reads, "Finlayson does an extra big takem and gets over his utter dislike for Hardy, and swears that no fortune hunter will ever marry the Finlayson millions."

The script also proposes a strange running gag. During the elopement, Finlayson was supposed to crawl out of Dulcy's bedroom window and halfway down the ladder, in an effort to to stop his defiant daughter. Stan sees this, and since Dulcy has already joined the boys on terra firma, Stan removes the ladder, leaving Finlayson hanging on the ledge. All through the rest of the film, we cut back to Finlayson, hanging desperately on the window ledge. At the very end, when the cross-eyed Justice has married Ollie to Stan, the door of the

Justice's home bursts open and there stands Finlayson, with his arms outstretched — about six feet.

The script has one line which reads, "Go for ad lib business trying to get Babe and the girl into the car." That's all it says — but this became the longest scene in the picture.

Babe London, who played Ollie's fiancee, retained happy memories of her experiences working on the film. "It wasn't hard work, it was play," she said. "Stan was the backbone really of Laurel and Hardy. He directed and wrote most of the material — at least in *Our Wife*. On the credits there's another man, but Stan did all of it.

"We didn't rehearse it any; they pulled surprises on you that they had in mind, and they'd ad-lib sometimes — things that came to them. One of the things that amused me is where I'm getting into the car, and Stan pushes me and Babe — just knocks us in!

"I got bunged up pretty badly doing that car scene — I got my face all pushed out of shape. It wasn't as uncomfortable as it looked. We all played it up, made it appear that the car was smaller than it was. There weren't many takes. In fact, I think we shot that automobile sequence in about a day or two. Everything went very smoothly."

When filming was more or less completed, the film was duly previewed. *Los Angeles Times* writer Paul F. Moreine reported on a studio conference that took place the following day:

> Principals, director and story editor form a little group. The picture starts and everybody quiets down.
>
> After a moment Stan Laurel speaks up: "Now watch this and see if you get it like I do. If we cut about eight feet it oughta double the tempo."
>
> Everybody watches and when the scene is over most of them agree with Stan. Somebody makes a note to cut the eight feet, and the show goes on.

Moreine went on to describe the L&H method as "a structure built and torn down, revised and built up again. Bit by bit and piece by piece, fitted and dovetailed and joined, slowly, tediously and with great labor. All with one purpose in mind — to entertain and amuse and lift, even if for only a few short moments, the weighty cares of the world from tired shoulders."

COME CLEAN

Production history: Written and shot circa early-mid May, 1931. Copyrighted September 1, 1931 by MGM (LP 2431). Released September 19, 1931. Two reels.

Produced by Hal Roach. Directed by James W. Horne. Photographed by Art Lloyd. Edited by Richard Currier. Sound by Elmer Raguse.

With Mae Busch, Gertrude Astor, Linda Loredo, Charlie Hall, Eddie Baker, Tiny Sandford.

The Hardys' quiet, romantic evening at home is disrupted by the unexpected — and unwanted — arrival of "those Laurels." While the wives make small talk, Stan and Ollie go out to satisfy Stan's craving for ice cream. On the way home, they discover a floozie who's about to jump off a bridge. They save her, only to be told that if they don't take care of her from now on, she'll accuse them of trying to kill her. A frantic evening ensues, with the husbands trying to conceal their house guest from their wives.

The script for this hectic little two-reeler differs from the film only in a few minor instances. The major change is that the script starts with both couples having dinner together — the film's lengthy sequence of the Hardys trying to keep the Laurels from interrupting their blissful evening was worked out during shooting. (This scene is a reworking of a similar sequence in *Should Married Men Go Home?*)

There's an amusing unused gag in the script's dinner party scene: Mrs. Hardy asks her guests if they'd like more to eat; all decline except Stan, who takes another helping of everything. Ollie turns to Mrs. Laurel to comment on Stan's appetite. Cut back to Stan, and he's already wiping his plate clean with a piece of bread.

The ice-cream parlor scene, with soda jerk Charlie Hall getting mightily exasperated when Stan keeps asking him for the flavors he *doesn't* have, was scripted virtually as played — except the sold-out flavors were originally "orange, walnut and chocolate." Someone changed this during the shooting, prompting one of the great Charlie Hall lines of all time: "We're out of orange, *gooseberry*, and chocolate!" It's hard for anyone to sound menacing when they're saying "walnut," but when Charlie Hall hisses "gooseberry" through those gritted teeth, you know he means trouble.

This scene originally had a cute wrap-up: Charlie is about to give Ollie his $4.25 change when he notices that Ollie has inadvertently smashed a bowlful of

Harry Bernard with Mae Busch and the boys in a deleted scene.

eggs on the soda-fountain counter. Hall counts the broken ones, and calculates the cost; oddly enough, it comes to exactly $4.25. Ollie takes the last unbroken egg and smashes it on the floor in disgust.

One gag was excised from the scene wherein the boys save the Mae Busch character from drowning. Mae is stretched out on the pier, unconscious, while Ollie works her arms up and down. Stan's knee accidentally presses against her stomach, and Mae spouts a stream of water into Ollie's face. She then mumbles something about being at peace, seeing a beautiful face — and then she sees Stan. The shock of it wakes her up and makes her realize she's still alive. From here on in, the changes between script and film are minimal.

Stan and Babe were no longer making foreign-language versions of their comedies, but they found a role in this film for Linda Loredo, who had appeared in most of their Spanish pictures. Miss Loredo's slight accent adds a distinctive touch to her rather undemanding part as Stan's wife. Eddie Baker, who played one of the lawmen in this film (and in the team's earlier opus, *Bacon Grabbers*), later gave up his film career to become a *real* detective.

ONE GOOD TURN

Production history: Script written late May, 1931. Dialogue script completed by H.M. Walker June 3, 1931. Shot mid-late June. Previewed circa July 11. Copyrighted October 5, 1931 by MGM. Released October 31, 1931. Two reels.

Produced by Hal Roach. Directed by James W. Horne. Photographed by Art Lloyd. Edited by Richard Currier. Sound by Elmer R. Raguse.

With Mary Carr, Billy Gilbert, James Finlayson, Dorothy Granger, Snub Pollard.

With Art Lloyd (wearing cap) behind the camera, James Horne directs.

"Victims of the Depression," Stan and Ollie beg for food at the home of a kindly old lady. While lunching they overhear a dastardly villain threaten to throw her out because someone has stolen the money due on her mortgage. Overcome, the boys sneak out and try to auction their car. A drunk bids $100, and absently sticks his wallet in Stan's pocket. When Ollie finds the money on Stan, he presents him as a thief to the elderly woman — who explains that the boys simply overheard a rehearsal of the Community Players. Stan directs violent retribution toward his portly partner.

One Good Turn has more plot than most of the shorts, and accordingly there wasn't much room for L&H to ad-lib. The script and the film have only minor differences. (For example: the action script refers to James Finlayson's character as Silas Hemingway; Beanie Walker's dialogue script calls this dastardly villain Hector Hammerhead; and the film calls him by the most evil-sounding name of all — James Finlayson.)

The script does propose a different finish, however. Just after the boys learn that the old woman and the "villain" were merely rehearsing a play, the script notes, "Babe takes it big, and at this point the drunk staggers in and says, 'Sorry I'm late for rehearsal, folks. I was trying to save an old lady from losing her home.' The drunk looks over and sees Babe with the wallet and says, 'What are you doing with my money?' He grabs it from Babe and hollers, 'Help! I've been robbed! Police!' Stan and Babe take it big and run out of the house. FADE OUT."

The new finish, with Stan unleashing his anger in the most violent outburst since *Early to Bed*, was indirectly brought about by Stan's daughter, Lois. After seeing so many movies in which her father took abuse from his rotund partner, Lois had become fearful of her "Uncle Babe," and shied away from him whenever Stan brought him home. Stan wrote a sequence which demonstrated that his screen character could easily protect himself if the occasion warranted it.

One Good Turn is the first L&H film which features their frequent co-star, Billy Gilbert. As Gilbert recalled, Stan saw him perform at the Mayan Theater in Los Angeles, and was impressed. Laurel went backstage and chatted with Gilbert; when he found that Gilbert wrote his own material, he got Billy a job at the Roach studio. Gilbert was signed as a writer and actor on October 19, 1931, and co-starred in Roach's *Taxi Boys* series as well as making films with Thelma Todd and Zasu Pitts, and Our Gang.

Dorothy Granger, who has a microscopic role as one of the Community Players, recalled an hilarious incident with Jimmy Finlayson that occurred during this period.

"On my 21st birthday, my folks gave me a party," she said. "I invited Jimmy Finlayson, and Mickey Rooney, and the Gumm sisters — Judy Garland was still Frances Gumm then. It was during Prohibition. I had gotten a recipe for bathtub gin from Mary Kornman's uncle. And he got me a gallon of alky, and we made five gallons of gin. My dad and one of his buddies put on false noses, and they were the bartenders. No matter what anybody ordered, they'd get gin and ginger ale.

"So, we got in a card game; they decided they wanted to play strip poker. Well, nobody ever really got stripped down. But Jimmy Finlayson got down to his shoes, and got his sock off; he had a toe missing, and every time he'd bet, he'd reach down and put his thumb where the missing toe was — he'd say, 'I bet my toe!'

"Oh, those days are gone; you can't have fun like that anymore. There was no dope, no marijuana, it was just good, clean — drunken fun!"

In August 1931, the Roach studio reported a loss of $25,005.64 on the 1930-31 series of L&H films; it was the first year the series failed to turn a profit. Not that the team was slipping in popularity — in 1930 and '31, hardly anything was turning a profit. On August 25, Roach borrowed $75,000 from the Bank of America, and put up all rights to *Pardon Us* as collateral. The Roach studio was a victim of the Depression, too.

BEAU HUNKS

Production history: Written and filmed September 1931. Copyrighted by MGM on November 3, 1931 (LP 2607). Released December 12, 1931. Four reels.

Produced by Hal Roach. Directed by James W. Horne. Photographed by Art Lloyd and Jack Stevens. Edited by Richard Currier. Sound by Elmer R. Raguse.

With Charles Middleton, Broderick O'Farrell, Harry Schultz, Abdul Kasim K'Horne.

Ollie is heartbroken when his beloved "Jeanie-Weenie" jilts him, and he joins the Foreign Legion to forget — bringing Stan in tow. The strict discipline and punishing exertion of marching all day in the hot desert sun does not agree with Laurel and Hardy, but the stern commandant has already given them a tongue-lashing. The legionnaires are sent to another outpost, Fort Arid, to defend it from an attack by the dreaded Riffs. The boys ingeniously thwart their barefooted attackers with barrelfuls of tacks.

The script for this film features a number of intriguing differences from its celluloid cousin. An opening scene, with Ollie singing and playing the piano while Stan reads the paper and excitedly cuts out an ad for fertilizer, was the start of a proposed running gag — in which Stan is forever using Ollie's penknife, and Ollie is forever snatching it back. Stan then asks, "What do they use fertilizer for?" Ollie responds, "Oh, they use it for lots of things. Some people put it on their strawberries." Stan thinks for a moment and remarks, "I always put sugar and cream on mine."

As per the film, the script then contains a lengthy dialogue exchange wherein Ollie enumerates the charms of his beloved, but is interrupted because Stan wants to know what "levity" means. Ollie then receives the fateful telegram which tells him that Jeanie-Weenie loves another, concluding, "B.S.: It's best we never see each other again." Stan surmises that "B.S." must stand for "Big Sucker."

The script then suggests that *Stan* pull a photo of Jeanie from his pocket; he castigates her with, "You vampire, you temptress, you wrecker of men, you levity!" Ollie is doubly devastated. "I see it all," he sighs. "So you're the another. That B.S. meant we're both suckers!" But Stan evidently wanted to keep his screen character asexual and dropped the idea of his being one of Jeanie's amours.

The march to the fort was markedly different in the script. At the point where Laurel and Hardy become separated from the other soldiers, the

Captain sees them and halts the company. Stan and Ollie hastily get back in line. The Captain orders everyone to lie down, since the storm will only last about 10 minutes.

After the wind subsides, mounds of sand are covering the soldiers. Stan and Ollie's derrieres are quite visible, though, and when the rest of them emerges, Stan hits his head, and sand cascades out of his ear. Ollie blows into it, but sand sprays out of Stan's other ear and into the Captain's eyes. Seeing the Captain's rage, Ollie puts a finger to *that* ear to stop the spray, but the sand backs up somewhere inside Stan's cranium and sprays back into Ollie's face.

Now, we cut to Fort Arid, but all the script suggests is that the Arid soldiers cheer as the reinforcements march proudly through the gate. There's no menacing speech by the chief Riff, no wonderfully hammy portending of doom by the Fort Arid commander, no soldiers jubilantly opening the gates to reveal only Stan and Ollie who, being lost, got there before the well-ordered regiment. All of this was apparently on-the-set inspiration. There *is* a scripted scene at the Arid barracks, in which Stan and Ollie are ordered to sentry duty just as they're getting ready for bed.

The battle between the Riffs and the Legionnaires was also different in the script. The commander needs a volunteer — one man who will go forth and silence the Riffs' machine-gun nest. Here they do the old gag where all the other soldiers in line take a step back, making it look like Laurel and Hardy have stepped forward. Since he needs only one brave man, the commander selects Ollie — naturally.

Ollie is to take some dynamite into the Riffs' hiding place, whereupon some other plucky Legionnaire (guess who) will push a plunger and precipitate an earth-shattering *kaboom*. Before Ollie goes out to meet his almost certain death, he gives Stan the penknife he always admired. Stan tries to peer over the gates to see how Ollie's doing, but he can't see, so he steps up onto the plunger box. Ollie miraculously plants the dynamite and starts to crawl back to the Fort, but Stan still can't see him, so he takes just one more step — which is one step too many. Ollie staggers back inside the fort, attired only in black powder and rags.

The commander orders the boys to hold those gates closed so the Riffs can't storm in. So they both stand against the left side of the gate. The right side opens up, unopposed, and the Riffs storm in.

At this point, the writers hadn't figured out just how the Legionnaires were going to conquer the Riffs. The script says only, "A battle ensues, winding up with the Legion victorious." We can assume the scene where the boys attack their attackers with tacks was a new tack taken on the set and tacked on during the shooting.

The ending proposed by the script strays further off the beaten path than Laurel and Hardy do while marching. The commander tells his troops that he's proud of them for putting off the Riffs, and now it's time to march home. The men grumble; they're not going to march all the way back across that hot sand. A mutiny breaks out, and Stan and Ollie run off to hide. But ere long the inspiring oratory of the commander has convinced everyone to stick together and march home. Everyone except Stan. So all of the others, including Ollie, march off and sing a spirited marching song.

Stan decides to join their ranks again, and scampers across the desert, finally catching up to the regiment. He puts his arm in Ollie's. Ollie smiles, and puts Stan's too-heavy knapsack on his own shoulders. Ollie hugs his old buddy, but when he sees Stan cleaning his nails with the beloved penknife, Hardy shoves him and grabs it back. Stan marches in bewilderment and the fade out comes rolling along.

In the film, they eliminated this sequence in favor of a wrap-up gag which brings Jeanie-Weenie back into the picture. Turns out that her picture is carried by not only most of the soldiers, but by the chief of the Riffs as well.

Stan and Babe had to drill for two days under a broiling September sun, dressed in heavy woolen outfits and carrying military backpacks and rifles. Two physicians on location treated the comedians for sunburn, and several extras reported to the field hospital for various burns, blisters and eye injuries caused during the shooting of the sandstorm scene.

The studio wanted all the costumes, props and locations to appear authentic, so they hired ex-Legionnaire Louis Van DeNecker to act as technical advisor. Van DeNecker oversaw many of these details, and drilled the extras so they would handle their "regulation LaBelle French Foreign Legion rifles" properly.

James Wesley Horne, director, rechristened himself Abdul Kasim K'Horne, actor specializing in Arabian Riffs. Three actors reportedly rehearsed for the role of the Riff chieftain, but none of them came up to Horne's expectations. So he donned a suitable costume, pasted on a beard, and stepped in front of the camera. He played the part beautifully — but as all jazz aficionados know, beauty often results when a Horne plays a Riff.

Charles Middleton, who would ultimately gain his greatest fame by playing Ming the Merciless in Universal's *Flash Gordon* serials, made his debut with the boys in this film. His glorious sneer and ultra-theatrical voice were put to good use in several subsequent L&H films. He repeated his role as the commandant in the team's 1939 reworking of this movie, *The Flying Deuces.*

The most intriguing bit of casting in *Beau Hunks*, though, was for the role of the femme fatale, "Jeanie-Weenie." Hal Roach explained, "Jean Harlow, who started with me and then went to Metro, gave me the permission to use her [photo] for free... the whole thing was, everybody in the Foreign Legion was there because they were stuck on Jean Harlow. I got a very nice leading lady for nothing!"

Beau Hunks is a *four*-reeler — twice as long as most of the team's comedies, but not quite a feature. Exhibitors profited from this — it was advertised as "Their Second Extra-Length Comedy" — but Roach lost money.

"It was already sold as a two-reeler; we couldn't get any more dough out of all the circuits because they'd already bought it," explained Roach. "But it was just one of those things; it was intended to be a two-reel comedy, but it kept getting funnier, and it ended up as a four-reeler. And it was so good that we didn't want to cut it, you know what I mean?"

There aren't many producers today who would willingly lose money on a film just because it was too good to cut. There weren't many producers *then* who would do that.

ON THE LOOSE

Production history: Written and filmed circa September 1931. Released December 26. Copyrighted February 15, 1932 by MGM (LP 2853). Two reels.

Produced by Hal Roach. Story by Hal Roach. Directed by Hal Roach. Photographed by Len Powers. Edited by Richard Currier. Dialogue by H.M. Walker.

With Thelma Todd, ZaSu Pitts, Claud Allister, John Loder, Billy Gilbert, Charlie Hall.

Stan and Babe did a cameo appearance in this Todd-Pitts short as a favor to their Boss, who was making a rare appearance in the director's chair. The story has Thelma and ZaSu depressed because their dates take them only to Coney Island. The girls brighten when they meet two British gentlemen who offer to take them somewhere novel and exciting — Coney Island. After a very hectic day, the girls are happy to spend a Saturday home, alone. Suddenly the doorbell rings; at the door are Stan and Ollie, who coyly ask if the girls would like to go to Coney Island. ZaSu and Thelma answer by hurling kewpie dolls at them.

HELPMATES

Production history: Action script and Dialogue script by H.M. Walker written early October, 1931. Shooting began October 19. Copyrighted December 21, 1931 by MGM (LP 2714). Released January 23, 1932. Two reels.

Produced by Hal Roach. Directed by James Parrott. Photographed by Art Lloyd. Edited by Richard Currier.

With Blanche Payson, Robert Callahan, Robert "Bobby" Burns.

Ollie calls Stan for help: his wife is due in from Chicago at noon, and the house is a shambles after a "wild party" the night before. L&H work together as efficiently as they always do — which means nothing gets cleaned up until Ollie goes to meet his wife at the depot. Stan decides to leave a nice cheery fire burning in the fireplace of the now-spotless house, but when he pours gasoline on the logs the fire gets a bit out of hand. Mr. Hardy returns home — alone, with a black eye — to find his friend hosing down the tattered remains of his house.

Helpmates, in my humble opinion, is the finest short film Laurel and Hardy ever made. *Big Business* and *The Music Box* are the usual contenders for this title; they may be masterpieces of comedy construction, but *Helpmates* has more soul.

Interestingly, there are fewer differences between script and film than for any previous L&H comedy; Stan and the gag men evidently knew they'd written a good script, and didn't want to tamper with it. There are occasional unused gags in the script — after an accident has decorated the floor with flour and soot, Stan sweeps up the mixture, puts it into the flour can and places it on the shelf — but most of the changes are microscopic.

The start and finish are slightly different: The film begins with Ollie castigating someone for throwing the wild party, and as the camera pulls back we see that he's berating himself while looking into a mirror. There's no mention of this in the script.

The ending was scripted like this: As Stan starts to leave Ollie's charred home, the phone rings. Ollie tells the caller, "Never mind; let it go," and hangs up. When Stan asks what happened, Ollie replies, "My fire insurance ran out yesterday."

Stan leaves, to the accompaniment of thunder. It scares him and sends him back inside — or what passes for it. Ollie is huddled in his chair, with an umbrella; he motions to Stan to come over. As they sit together, Stan slips his arm into Ollie's, and gives him a big grin. Ollie smiles as best he can. The thunder crashes again, and the rain pours down even heavier on the two friends.

This scripted ending is cute — maybe too cute — and it certainly conveys the idea that Stan and Ollie's friendship survives when everything else falls apart. But the filmed ending — with Ollie sitting stoically in his roofless home as the rain pours on him — has more power; it's probably the most poignant scene in any of the team's films.

A number of surrealistic dialogue routines permeate this picture. The script offers one more such exchange during a scene in which Ollie comes in to dry his soaking suit:

STAN: What did I say to you before you went out of here?
OLLIE: Why, you said if you had any sense, you'd walk out of here.
STAN: Then what did you say?
OLLIE: I said it was a good thing you hadn't any sense.
STAN: Then what did I say?
OLLIE: You said it certainly was.
STAN: Now, here's what I wanna find out. Do you agree with you, or me?

An example of the spirit of cooperation in *Helpmates*.

OLLIE: Why, I agreed with you.
STAN: Well, that's different.
OLLIE: Suppose I hadn't agreed with you, what then?
STAN: I'd have walked out on you.
OLLIE: Here, take these pants and wring 'em out....

The L&H company (which included assistant director Morrie Lightfoot and prop men Harry Black and Ed Brandenberg) began filming on October 19, 1931. They shot the opening sequence — in which Hardy gets his wife's telegram — at 1645 LaBonia, an address which has vanished from the environs of Los Angeles. According to the press sheet, the studio built "a regular five-room bungalow...on the edge of the studio property within a few yards of an adjoining home," so the house could be burned during the closing scenes.

"In order to get the desired results from the ruins of the burned building, the studio fire department stood by and took charge of the blaze when the director considered enough of the house had gone up in smoke," says the press sheet.

Although the studio could still spend lavishly enough to build a house and then burn it down, there was an economy drive during October and November 1931, which prompted the dismissal of many employees. George Stevens, erstwhile L&H cameraman who had been promoted to director of Roach's *Boy Friends* series the year before, was one of those fired.

With "The Expediter," Henry Ginsberg, who was anything but a helpmate.

In late November, after a month-long reshuffling of the executive board, the studio named Henry Ginsberg as the new general manager. Ginsberg had been affiliated with the distribution end of the film business: according to one source, he was installed because Roach's creditors, primarily the Bank of America, were concerned about the producer's ability to repay several recent loans. In any event, Ginsberg sought to cut costs wherever and however he could, and he didn't make many friends in the process. Said one former Roach employee, "I sure do remember Henry Ginsberg — I was scared to death of him. Cut, cut, cut, cut!"

Anita Garvin, who still worked occasionally at the Roach lot, recalled, "Stan used to call Henry Ginsberg 'The Expediter.' He was always trying to get everyone to work as quickly as possible. One day, Ginsberg came down to the Laurel and Hardy set to see how things were moving along. Well, Stan virtually called a halt to the production — he slowed everything way down, delaying everything as much as possible, until Ginsberg finally got the message and left."

There were creative conflicts as well, according to editor Richard Currier. "Everybody hated Ginsberg," he said, "because his attitude was just the opposite of Roach's. You'd go to a preview, and he'd come out with a sour face — probably one scene he didn't like, said it should be cut out — and I'd get into an argument with him about that. I'd say, 'That scene is the build-up for what follows. You pull that out, you've got nothing.' 'Well,' he'd say, 'that's the way you look at it. That ain't the way I look at it.' And I'd say, 'What the hell are you, a motion picture man, or are you a financier, or what? If you're a financier, I'll excuse you for the suggestion.'"

For Stan, the arrival of Ginsberg signified the first real constraint on his control of the pictures. Ginsberg's budgetary limitations — and his attitude that the films could always be made faster and cheaper — meant that the Laurel and Hardy unit wouldn't be allowed to build houses just to burn them down much longer.

ANY OLD PORT

Production history: Script and H.M. Walker's dialogue script written circa mid-November 1931. Shot circa late November. Copyrighted February 4, 1932 by MGM (LP 2818). Released March 5, 1932. Two reels.

Produced by Hal Roach. Directed by James W. Horne. Photographed by Art Lloyd. Edited by Richard Currier. Sound by Elmer Raguse.

With Walter Long, Jacqueline Wells, Harry Bernard, Charlie Hall, Robert "Bobby" Burns.

On shore leave, sailors L&H check into a fleabag hotel and discover that the proprietor, Mugsie Long, is trying to trap his slavey girl into marrying him. After a violent set-to, the girl escapes, but Long vows vengeance if he ever sees Stan and Ollie again. The boys are without funds until Stan is enlisted to fight a preliminary boxing match for $50. His opponent, naturally, turns out to be Mugsie Long. Stan wins the match when Mugsie's loaded glove somehow ends up on Stan's hand. But victory means defeat, because Ollie has bet the $50 on Mugsie.

Any Old Port is moderately amusing at best. Its curiously clumsy direction, punctuated by unnecessarily violent sight gags, gives it the look of a comedy made by the Three Stooges' frequent director, Jules White.

Ten minutes' worth of footage was shot but deleted after previews. The film might well have been funnier and more cohesive had this original first reel been retained. While the scrapped footage evidently no longer exists, a shooting script provides the original opening sequences:

The good ship Breadpoultice has docked, and Captain James Finlayson and First Mate Tiny Sandford are watching sailors stroll down the gangplank. Many of them carry monkeys, parrots and other pets they've picked up at some exotic port. As Finlayson hands the sailors their pay envelopes, he mutters something about a floating zoo.

The Captain and First Mate then see Ollie and Stan emerging from the hatchway; Ollie bears a small empty cage, and Stan is furiously pulling on a rope. At the other end is a fully-grown ostrich. Finlayson does one of his patented "takems," and asks how on earth the boys managed to get that thing aboard. Ollie explains, "A man in Port Said sold it to us in this cage." Incredulous, Finlayson barks, "In *that* cage?" Stan replies, "Yes, sir. He told us it was an African canary."

Stan gets his pay envelope, and leads his tethered feathered friend down the gangplank. Ollie holds his hand out for his pay, but Finlayson sneers that

Sandford, Finlayson and the African canary were cut adrift from *Any Old Port*.

he blew all of his money in Shanghai. Ollie's request for an advance on next month's salary does not put him in Finlayson's good graces.

The sight of Stan sitting on a crate and counting his money brings a smile to the Hardy countenance. Ollie explains his plight, and big-hearted Stan pulls out his bankroll and counts out a lot of bills — but gives Ollie only one. Mr. Hardy disgustedly says that he can't do much with one dollar; the least Stan can do is share it with him. "What, the dollar?," asks Stan. Ollie means that Stan should share the whole bankroll of $15, and, generously, he'll show Stan how it's done.

Ollie counts out the money. It starts out innocently enough, with Ollie counting out one dollar for Stan and one for himself. But then he counts one more for Stan — "That's two for you" — and *two* more for himself — "That's two for me." Another bill for Stan is "three for you," but Ollie takes one, two, three bills for himself to achieve parity. He continues in this way until finally he takes the five meager bills in *Stan's* pile, pockets them and says, "That's five for me. See how simple it is?"

Stan is a little confused, and expresses this in a twist on a then-common expression: "There's a woodpile in the nigger somewhere." Ollie suggests that Stan count out the money, which he does, and ends up with all of it on *his* side. Still perplexed, Stan then shoves the money back over to Ollie and admits, "You're right."

A lengthy scene which still exists in the film, with the boys majestically signing the hotel register, was supposed to have been topped by Stan asking if they can keep their African canary in their room — according to the script. "All right," says Long, "as long as he don't sing at night." Stan replies, "He don't even sing in the daytime." Before this threatens to become yet another remake of *Angora Love*, Stan finds that the ostrich has escaped from its hitching post.

The boys react wildly as a cartoon shot shows the ostrich flying off into the sunset — where presumably it meets up with a flock of flying elephants.

The script details a new wrap-up, with the boys going back to the hotel, after having thwarted Long's marriage plans by sending him over the pier and into the ocean. A nice young sailor, the slavey's fiancee, arrives on cue, and Stan and Ollie deliver the girl to him. The lovers embrace and skip away as Laurel and Hardy blow kisses at them. Then, the boys look into the other direction and see Long, drenched, stalking toward them with murder in his eye; they run over and push Long back in the water. They stand at the pier to make sure that he can't get out again, but a big truck rolls into view and honks its horn, frightening Laurel and Hardy and sending them over the pier and into the ocean, where a predator named Mugsie Long awaits.

While all this scripted material was evidently filmed, the original first reel and the wrap-up of the boy-girl subplot were scrapped. The second reel became the first, and a new second reel (containing the boxing sequence) was added.

The press sheet informs us that the scrapped opening sequences were photographed at San Pedro Harbor, where the comedians were besieged for autographs by the sailors stationed there. Similar events occurred when Stan and Babe shot the boxing sequences at Culver City Stadium. "Enough extras to fill a portion of the seats were hired," says the press sheet. "Interested spectators who learned of the affair soon filled the remaining 500-odd seats, however, and many of them appear in the picture."

Any Old Port is enjoyable, but it's a bit of a letdown after the classic film which preceded it. The film which followed it was good in its way, too.

THE MUSIC BOX

Production history: Action script and H.M. Walker's dialogue script written circa early December 1931; shot circa mid-late December. Copyrighted March 14, 1932 by MGM (LP 2914). Released April 16. Three reels.

Produced by Hal Roach. Directed by James Parrott. Photographed by Walter Lundin and Len Powers. Edited by Richard Currier. Sound by James Greene.

With Billy Gilbert, Lilyan Irene, Sam Lufkin, Charlie Hall, William Gillespie, Gladys Gale.

L&H are dispatched to deliver a player piano to a hilltop home. The boys make several trips up the redoubtable flight of steps, and just as many down. En route, they encounter a haughty nursemaid, a grouchy cop, and the blustery Prof. Theodore von Schwarzenhoffen (Gilbert). The boys make a shambles of the house while trying to bring in the piano; they are interrupted by the arrival of the professor, whose home this is. He insists that this piano can't be his — he hates them — and to prove it, he hacks it to pieces with an axe.

This is the one everybody remembers. The image of Laurel and Hardy forever pushing a piano up a tremendous flight of steps seems to have stuck in the public consciousness, a tribute to this movie's beautifully controlled milking of one basic gag.

It's a partial reworking of *Hats Off*, and the company used the same monu-

With Gladys Gale and Billy Gilbert at the end of a discordant day.

mental flight of steps. (For you sightseers, they're located in the Silver Lake district of Los Angeles, between 923 and 937 Vendome Street.)

It would seem that Stan and the gag men had the earlier film in mind when they fashioned this story. For the record, though, Billy Gilbert told an interviewer in 1969 that he and Stan jointly developed the idea after driving around Silver Lake, seeing the steps, and figuring that the boys would have to deliver "something huge and cumbersome but also delicate" to the hilltop home. Gilbert also stated that he was supposed to direct the film, but he was so convincing in demonstrating the von Schwarzenhoffen role that he ended up playing it.

Hauling that piano up those stairs was actually just as arduous as it appeared in the film. That's because Stan and Babe really were hauling a piano. Said Roy Seawright, "There was a real piano in the crate. It was something you'd never buy — but they needed it to be there for the weight."

When Stan and Babe weren't being stymied by the piano, the film crew was frustrated by the weather. Roy Seawright recalled, "We had a very serious climatic situation on *The Music Box*. Cloud coverage. That wasn't in the days of fast film — and the scenes had to match, because they were all interlocked in this one sequence which ran for two reels, with the boys going up and down the stairway. On the days with cloud coverage, you couldn't shoot; that cut the schedule down. And finally, when we got it all wrapped up and got to the cutting room, Stan really had to work to meet the schedule. He'd be in the cutting room, have a sandwich brought in, maybe sleep in his dressing room for a couple of hours, and then back to work. He really was a dedicated man."

Fortunately, the team didn't have to worry about the climate when they

Celebrating their Oscar win with Hal Roach and Walt Disney.

shot the sequences involving the Professor's house, because it was comfortably situated on a Roach studio sound stage. (That huge flight of steps actually leads to a cul-de-sac, not a hilltop home.)

The voice of the music box was supplied by the talented fingers of T. Marvin Hatley, who played a piano just out of camera range while the boys did their little dance. "I was playing 'Turkey in the Straw,' Marvin remembered. "I played with a lot of tremeloes, like a player piano, as fast as I could play it. And finally, when old Billy came in with an axe and chopped it all to pieces, I played that right on the set. There wasn't any special recording, I was just watching Billy Gilbert, trying to catch all of his axe hits.

"The piano he chopped up was just an old broken-down upright; it was a fake piano, built out of balsa wood and parts from another piano — it was made so it could be chopped to pieces easily. I remember one gag where some of the keys were on the floor, and Billy was running around trying to hit them with the axe, and I'd play a note for each key. But they cut it out of the picture."

When Stan finally emerged from his non-stop marathon in the cutting room — with assistance from editor Bert Jordan, who thought this the best L&H short — he knew he had a winner. This was confirmed on November 18, 1932 at the Ambassador Hotel's Cocoanut Grove, when *The Music Box* won a certificate as the Academy of Motion Picture Arts and Sciences' choice for "Best Short Subject (Comedy)" of 1931-32.

And just in case you're wondering, I counted 131 the last time I walked up those steps.

THE CHIMP

Production history: Script written early January 1932. Dialogue script completed by H.M. Walker January 13. Filmed late January-circa February 7. Released May 21. Copyrighted May 26, 1932, by MGM (LP 3055). Three reels.

Produced by Hal Roach. Directed by James Parrott. Photographed by Walter Lundin. Edited by Richard Currier. Sound by Elmer R. Raguse.

With Billy Gilbert, James Finlayson, Charles Gemora, Tiny Sandford.

L&H work in a threadbare circus which is soon flat broke. The manager gives each of the employees a part of the show in lieu of back pay; Stan wins a flea circus, and Ollie's prize is "Ethel, the human chimpanzee." The boys rent a room for the night, and have to sneak their new companion past the landlord — who is agitated because his wife, conveniently named Ethel, hasn't returned home. When the landlord overhears Ollie reprimanding the rambunctious simian with, "Ethel! Will you stop that and come to bed?," fireworks ensue.

Only a few gags perished on the trip from script to screen this time around. One gag illustrates how Ethel immediately takes a liking to Stan while disdaining Ollie: Ethel motions Stan over to her and gives him part of the banana she's eating, then gives Ollie the peel. In disgust, Ollie throws it away, then slips on it, does a high fall and lands on a porcupine's cage, getting quills all over his back.

The script suggests some gags of dubious taste during the scene where the boys are trying to put the frisky chimpanzee to bed. As scripted, the landlord in his adjoining room hears the boys yell some entendres far more double than those in the film: "See what you can do with her. She likes you better than me... Here, you put these clothes on and stop dancing around... Maybe she would rather sleep in *your* bed." At this point, Stan and Ollie tussle with the monkey, and the sound of squeaky bedsprings is supposed to elicit the biggest takem from the landlord. All of this was replaced in the movie with a hilarious and somehow poignant scene in which Ethel (the chimp, that is) overhears a phonograph record and dances the night away with Stan.

A rather silly wrap-up is proposed in the script: After the landlord discovers that the boys' companion is a monkey and not his wife, Ethel was supposed to climb out the bedroom window and say, "If this is civilization, back to the cocoanut trees for me. You're the dumbest thing I ever saw this side of a jellyfish." The filmed ending, with Ethel grabbing the landlord's gun and sending all and sundry scurrying away, is much improved.

For the filming of the big-top scenes, Roach rented and erected a circus tent on his ranch near Arnaz Drive in what is now part of Beverly Hills. Charles Gemora, a Philippine-born make-up artist and part-time gorilla impersonator, gave an inspired performance in the title role. Another cast member was especially dear to Stan — his daughter Lois, who appeared as a member of the circus audience.

Original prints of *The Chimp* have an elaborate opening-title sequence: We see a drawing of two clowns holding a round trampoline, which rips open to reveal each ensuing title. Subsequent comedies also had inventive gags during the opening titles. In *The Midnight Patrol* a windshield wiper sweeps each title

Charles Gemora gave a remarkable performance as *The Chimp*.

away; *Busy Bodies* uses a buzzsaw's circular blade to obliterate each title; and in *Dirty Work*, test tubes bubble over and wash each title away.

These marvelous scenes, which are sadly missing from most available prints today, were the creations of Louis McManus and Roy Seawright. McManus had been hired to edit the Roach studio's Spanish-language films; he stayed on after the demise of the foreign versions, editing the comedies and designing title cards — for which Roach paid him $10 apiece. Seawright worked his optical-effects wizardry with a stop-motion camera to animate the transitions between titles.

This film's title (which was mercifully changed from the working title, *Monkeydoodle*) was a play on MGM's popular Wallace Beery-Jackie Cooper prizefight drama, *The Champ*. The press sheet made the connection explicit when they billed this comedy as one in which "Box Office Champs Pack a Record Laugh Wallop."

As this picture went into production, the Hal Roach Studios issued its annual financial statement. It made a net profit of $91,750 for the fiscal year 1930-31, which was an increase of 48% over the previous year's profit. (The studio lost $25,000 on the 1930-31 Laurel and Hardy comedies, its most popular product — such are the vagaries of Hollywood accounting methods.) Stan made a healthy salary of $104,333.33 during 1931, while Babe received $77,333.33.

COUNTY HOSPITAL

Production history: Script and H.M. Walker dialogue script written early February 1932. Shooting began circa February 20. Copyrighted May 31, 1932 by MGM (LP 3060). Released June 25. Two reels.

Produced by Hal Roach. Directed by James Parrott. Photographed by Art Lloyd. Edited by Bert Jordan and Richard Currier. Sound by James Greene.

With Billy Gilbert, William Austin, May Wallace.

Ollie is in the hospital, recuperating from a broken leg. His stay is interrupted by a visit from Stan, who within a matter of minutes has Hardy's physician angrily ordering them both out. Stan attempts to drive Ollie home; unfortunately, he has accidentally sat on a hypodermic needle and injected himself with sedative. A hectic ride through the crowded streets ends with Stan's car smashed into a semi-circle by two streetcars. As a cop tells him to "pull over there," Stan drives around — and around and around.

Laurel and Hardy stories were often conceived in a roundabout way. This one reportedly had its genesis while the comedians were enjoying an evening of recreation together at a popular Beverly Hills club, when somebody asked 'Did you ever hear about my operation?'

In any case, Stan and his writers soon fashioned a hospital story, which originally bore the title *Forty Winks*. As always, some excellent gags went unfilmed.

A gag in the film has Stan trying to crack a walnut with the weight that keeps Ollie's broken leg suspended. Ollie is thus yanked to the ceiling by his leg, and doctor Billy Gilbert, in trying to right Mr. Hardy, is thrust out the window of the top-story room. The script suggests that, after calm is restored, the weight should "land on top of the main door in a balancing position."

Cut to the reception room, where Ollie's fluttery English roommate is finally being discharged after an eight month-bout with hay fever. He bids the desk clerk "Cheerio," and strolls out the door. The weight falls and conks him on the noggin, knocking him cold. Two attendants enter, place him on a stretcher, and carry him back to his room.

The final sequence was much more elaborate in the script. During their troubles in traffic, the boys' car was supposed to roll backwards down a hill and lock bumpers with a car that's parked facing the other way. Stan and Ollie then unwittingly pull the car and its grouchy driver backwards up the hill.

After they rectify this faux pas, Stan sleepily releases his foot from the brake, and the car careens backwards into a fire hydrant. Ollie sits on it to stop the gushing water; the force throws him into the air, and he lands in the gutter. Gritting his teeth, Ollie gets back into the car and tries to drive up the hill; he just misses several cars, and finally turns onto a streetcar track, whereupon he collides not only with a streetcar but a steamroller as well.

This would have been much funnier than the actual film, which has Laurel and Hardy in their car and reacting frantically to dull rear-projection footage of traffic. Roy Seawright and his crew usually did amazing special effects on a very limited budget; one suspects efficiency expert Henry Ginsberg wouldn't allow

James Parrott directs the team at Culver City's City Hall.

the L&H unit enough money to film the elaborate sequence suggested in the script, so the boys had to make do with the less expensive rear-projection.

Said Seawright, "The minute a script was written, the production office would mark the special-effects scenes with red lines in the margins, then they'd come to me and say, 'Roy, what do we do?' Then I would analyze it, and figure out the best and most *economical* way to do it. We had to have the ingenuity to solve each problem as economically as possible — if you needed a lot of money, they'd say, 'Forget it! We'll write something else!' We just didn't have the money — the production department would hammer you over the head with that until you were black and blue, that you had no money."

Despite the weakness of the final scene, *County Hospital* was well received. *Motion Picture Magazine* called it "one of their brightest, fastest and funniest," and New York's famed Roxy Theatre chose it for the first two-reel comedy ever screened there.

If Laurel and Hardy's career was flying high, so was Hal Roach — literally. From January to mid-March, he and MGM foreign manager Arthur Loew flew to various cities in South America, visiting all the film distribution centers, and setting speed records in Roach's private plane.

Roach found the South Americans to be avid movie fans. Possibly because Laurel and Hardy were extremely popular there, he soon announced that they would be "starred in two feature-length comedies" during the next year. Preparations for the team's next feature began immediately.

County Hospital on location at 48th St., Los Angeles, with crew and extras.

PACK UP YOUR TROUBLES

Production history: Script and H.M. Walker's dialogue script written April 1932. Filmed early May-circa June 1. Released September 17. Copyrighted September 23, 1932 by MGM (LP 3270). 68 minutes.

Produced by Hal Roach. Directed by George Marshall and Raymond McCarey. Photographed by Art Lloyd. Edited by Richard Currier. Sound by James Greene.

With Donald Dillaway, Jacquie Lyn, James Finlayson, George Marshall.

During World War I, Stan and Ollie become friends with another doughboy, Eddie Smith. Eddie is killed in battle, and after the Armistice, the boys take care of his motherless little girl. They endure many misadventures in trying to locate the girl's grandparents, a "Mr. and Mrs. Smith" who live somewhere in New York. When a stern welfare officer threatens to take the girl away, Stan and Ollie reluctantly rob a bank to finance a getaway. They are soon captured, but all is forgiven when the bank president turns out to be Eddie's father.

The Roach studio was closed for its annual "vacation" during April 1932; everyone took leave except the writers, who were busy concocting stories for the 1932-33 program of 40 shorts and two features. A press release noted that "if negotiations are successful, the studio will make several other feature-length

Ray McCarey puts in a rare appearance on the set, with the boys and George Marshall.

comedies." Yet the same time, Roach general manager Henry Ginsberg was quoted in the trade press as saying that short comedies would eventually conquer the new vogue for double-feature programs.

The second L&H feature was to be directed by a new resident of the lot: veteran director George Marshall. While Leo McCarey's 28-year-old brother, Raymond, was credited as co-director, Marshall later stated, "I don't think Ray did anything more than come in and say 'Good morning,' and go out again. He may have done some of those second-unit things like the battle scenes; but nothing at all with Stan and Babe. To this day, I don't know how his credit got in there."

Another associate of both McCareys remarked, "Ray lived on the coat-tails of Leo. He got his job at Roach's through Leo. But he wasn't creative, he was just run-of-the-mill." Conversely, two men behind the camera who contributed without receiving credit were the assistant directors, Lloyd French and Harry Black.

Soon after the story was written, Roach casting director Lawrence Tarver and his assistant Gordon Douglas (who would eventually direct L&H in *Saps at Sea*) found a three-year old London-born moppet named Jacquie Lyn. The child had appeared in a Marie Dressler feature; Roach was evidently captivated by her, and thought she could be a star with Spanky McFarland's potential. The script was reportedly altered to give her more footage.

The filming went smoothly with always-professional George Marshall at the helm. The elaborate war scenes were accomplished with the help of the 160th Tank Corps of Salinas, California, which loaned the studio a vintage

An early version of the wedding scene, with Grady Sutton, and Frank Brownlee (extreme right), who was later replaced by Billy Gilbert.

World War I tank. Reportedly, many of the extras for these scenes were vintage World War I soldiers.

As always, there was a lot of improvisation during the filming. Some of the best scenes paired Stan and Babe with Marshall, who found himself suddenly in front of the cameras, much as James Horne had in *Beau Hunks*.

"One morning there was a little scene at the back of the cook shack," Marshall recalled in a 1974 interview. "A mess sergeant was supposed to come out and dump something in the garbage can, and as he did Stan and Babe were there discussing the garbage — and they asked him, 'What do we do with this?' In the army, there was that balance of sarcasm; the mess sergeant said, 'Give it to the General, what the hell you think you do with it?!'

"The fellow we had hired to do this part hadn't shown up; it was somebody who'd been hired for the day. And we were ready to go to work, so I said, 'Oh, gimme the damn cap and the apron, which'll cover the fact that I haven't got a uniform on, and I'll do the mess sergeant; let's get on.' We often did that to keep things moving.

"Then at lunchtime, Stan got thinking about it — the fact that the boys had to go to jail for dumping the garbage in the general's quarters, and who was responsible? The mess sergeant was responsible, so if they went to jail, I should be in there with them. That was completely Stan's. That mind of his was always working, to piece things together.

"So I did the jail scene with them, where I said, 'Someday I'll catch up with you two, look out.' And *that* led into the finish of the picture, where the boys had delivered their dead buddy's baby to the grandparents and everything was

WELCOME HOME BOYS!

Sure, we heard how you took Europe by storm!

THAT'S GREAT! But we've got much better news! About your new feature length comedy!

"PACK UP YOUR TROUBLES"

It was previewed last week in New Rochelle. The audience howled from the first foot of film to the fade-out! Boys, it was a panic and a riot rolled into one! After the success of your first full length comedy *"Pardon Us"* exhibitors demanded another one. Will they be thrilled, delighted and jubilant about *"Pack Up Your Troubles"*! Dunt esk!

Leo takes off his hat to Hal Roach and his World's Funniest Comedians!

Hooray for Laurel and Hardy!

METRO-GOLDWYN-MAYER

MGM heavily publicized the team's new feature — and their European "vacation."

happy... then the grandfather said to his butler that there'd be two more for dinner, and the cook came in to complain — and saw Stan and Babe."

Marshall's laconic performance is easily the most memorable of a film just chock-full of heavies. His minimalistic style is much more threatening than the florid villainy of Charles Middleton, Rychard Cramer, Frank Brownlee and Billy Gilbert.

The film contains a memorable sequence with the ultimate florid villain, James Finlayson. "Jimmy loved to chew the scenery," Marshall said fondly. "He had a distinctive element which you could get by with then — you couldn't do it today, of course. He was very broad — even when we had a pretty straight story line. For instance, in *Pack Up Your Troubles* they load the garbage in his living room and he's trying to have his breakfast — and the odor of the garbage starts to come through to the dining room. I can still see Jimmy. His expressions were — not sedate."

While the shooting script has yet to surface, extant stills indicate that some scenes were shot and deleted. Among them was an alternate version of the gag where Stan and Ollie arrive with the child at a mansion where a wedding is commencing. The first version of this scene had Frank Brownlee as the father of the bride; in the film, he plays a put-upon drill sergeant. The scene was rewritten and re-shot with Billy Gilbert as the bride's father.

Although her scenes with Stan and Babe were brief, Muriel Evans warmly remembered portraying the bride. Miss Evans recalled, "Stan and Ollie managed to make their work joyful, never losing the fact that movie making was serious business to them — and as you well know, they were masters of their craft."

One sequence was cut from all reissue and television prints because of violence. It shows nasty Rychard Cramer, the temporary guardian of Eddie's baby, physically abusing his wife — and not being too nice to the kid, either. When Laurel and Hardy come to claim the child, Cramer sends a couple of his grimy buddies after them. A chase leads into Cramer's kitchen, where Laurel and Hardy thwart the brutes with boiling water. A print of this scene does survive — but it's dubbed in French.

Business was brisk but reviews were mixed when the picture opened in September. *Variety* dismissed it as "one of those hokum war farces" and growled, "After a while it becomes as tiresome as it is inanely obvious." Mordaunt Hall was more tolerant in the *New York Times*, calling it a "boisterous and sometimes funny picture" and allowing that "there are several good bits while Laurel and Hardy are in uniform."

Marguerite Tazelaar in the *New York Herald-Tribune* had the wisest observation: "The gags, if now and then somewhat moth-eaten, kept the Capitol audience in gales of laughter yesterday. Or rather, it would be more accurate to say the use of these gags by Mr. Laurel and Mr. Hardy."

SCRAM!

Production history: Script and H.M. Walker dialogue script written mid-June 1932. Filmed June 18-circa July 1. Released September 10. Copyrighted September 12, 1932 by MGM (LP 3237). Two reels.

Produced by Hal Roach. Directed by Raymond McCarey. Photographed by Art Lloyd. Edited by Richard Currier. Sound by James Greene.

With Arthur Housman, Vivien Oakland, Rychard Cramer.

Vagrants L&H are told to "Scram!" by an ill-tempered judge. Walking out of town, the boys help recover the missing car keys of a well-to-do inebriate; in thanks, the drunk invites the vagabonds to stay the night in his palatial home. The boys gain entrance despite a missing door key. They frighten the lady of the house; she faints, but they revive her with what they think is water — it's actually gin. They have a jolly time; meanwhile the drunk has departed, having realized he's in the wrong house. The real owner is a certain vagrant-hating judge.

Scram! and its script are remarkably faithful to each other. Most of the gags that went unfilmed were from the scenes in which the playful wife is laughing, dancing and otherwise whooping it up with Stan and Ollie in her boudoir.

In the script, after the boys have revived her with some very intoxicating water, the judge's wife hiccoughs and says, "Excuse me; I always do that when I get nervous." Ollie reassures her with, "That's perfectly all right." She hiccoughs again and says, "Pardon me; it's most embarrassing." To which Stan disgustedly adds, "It sure is!" Ollie kicks him.

The revelry was supposed to awaken the butler, who was to charge into the bedroom and snap, "I will have to leave if this noise keeps up. How do you expect a man to sleep?" He punctuates this with a gesture that knocks down the lid of a player piano; it crashes onto his head and knocks him out. Stan revives *him* with the 180-proof "water" too; the butler giggles and does a sprightly jig out the door. Before long, he encounters the judge, coming home from a hard night of sentencing drunks and vagrants. "Hi, judge!," slobbers the butler. "Alice is upstairs entertaining a couple of your pals!" The judge stalks upstairs.

The resolution of the story is fairly uninteresting as proposed in the script; all it suggests is that Ollie, trying to put the wife to bed, turns and sees the judge, who takes off his coat as Stan and Ollie run frantically around the room. Fade out, and fade in to reveal the boys, bandaged and with black eyes, in a prison quarry — where they're making little rocks out of big ones.

The filmed finale, however, is a genuinely inspired sequence, in which shots of the happy trio — laughing helplessly and bouncing around in their pajamas on the bed — are intercut with close-ups of the judge glaring hatefully at them. Although Richard Currier got the editor's credit in the opening titles, and Bert Jordan did the first cut (without credit), Laurel was probably the creative guide in the beautifully-timed editing of this scene.

This sequence shows Laurel and Hardy using the film medium itself to generate comedy. While they didn't call attention to the special properties of film as often as Keaton did, Stan and Babe did much more than simply let the camera record their performances.

This film was Arthur Housman's first with Stan and Babe; he would also play genial drunks in *The Live Ghost, The Fixer-Uppers, Our Relations* and (very briefly) *The Flying Deuces*. Housman's special comic niche may have been a result of art imitating life. "I never saw him sober," Stan recalled. "But not the way he was in the pictures, of course. That was wonderful acting and really good comedy."

George Marshall worked with the team during the preparation of this picture, but was assigned to direct a Thelma Todd-Zasu Pitts short (*Alum and*

Eve); in his stead was Ray McCarey. Jack Lloyd, the assistant director, was replaced midway through the shooting by the team's perennial A.D., Lloyd French.

The post-production of the film, typically, didn't take long; it couldn't, because on July 12, about ten days after the shooting wrapped, Laurel and Hardy went on vacation. They had been working with very little pause for more than five years.

A Busman's Holiday

At the start of 1932, Stan decided to visit his father and stepmother in England during July, while Babe planned to see Canada. Then, Babe began to realize that the golf courses in Scotland and England were among the world's finest. He talked it over with Stan, and the comedians decided to take a vacation to the British Isles together — or what they thought would be a vacation.

July 28, 1932: In Tynemouth, England, with Mayor J.G. Telford (center).

Stan's father, stepmother Venitia and sister Beatrice see them off at Victoria Station, London, August 10, 1932.

In February, word got to the foreign press that Stan and Babe would be visiting England in the summer for a music-hall tour; by March it was clarified that their trip would be "purely in the nature of a holiday." But holiday or no, the head of publicity for MGM's British distributors had other ideas.

By July 20, *Cinema*, a trade paper, was voicing concern; the press was already devoting a great deal of space to the team even before they'd stepped on British soil. "Officially, Stan and Olly are coming over for a well-earned holiday," the paper observed, "but so great is the publicity their visit is certain to arouse, that it is feared they will be given little rest by their thousands of fans. Co-incident with their stay, Metro-Goldwyn-Mayer have arranged a 'Laurel and Hardy Month,' from July 25 to August 21, during which time thousands of exhibitors will seize the opportunity of playing and plugging their comedies, and take full advantage of the publicity resulting from the visit."

Just to make sure their exhibitors got the hint, MGM took out full-page advertisements in the trade papers:

LEO BRINGS LAUREL & HARDY TO ENGLAND
Every live showman will cash in on the great publicity boost that is in store for the screen's comedy champs! Have you set your dates during "Laughter Month" July 25 to August 21? Gather your Laurels (& Hardys) while the going's good!
METRO-GOLDWYN-MAYER

Laurel and Hardy were obviously not going to tour England as inconspicuously as they hoped.

Still mugging for photographers while sailing for home on the S.S. Paris.

While it seems preposterously naive of Stan and Babe to have expected to travel unnoticed, they simply underestimated their hold on the public's affections. They gradually realized this during their four-day train journey from Los Angeles to New York. While changing trains in Chicago, they were mobbed by fans, reporters, photographers. In New York, MGM arranged a farewell reception; the team rode down Broadway, with newsreel cars following them. The crowds were so large, so enthusiastic, that police had to shove the bewildered comics into Minsky's Music Hall to avoid being smothered.

They arrived in Southhampton on the Aquitania on July 23, where Stan, Babe and his wife Myrtle met Stan's father and stepmother, Venitia. From there, the team went to Waterloo Station, where they were swallowed up by the throng. *Today's Cinema* noted, "Any exhibitor who may have queried the drawing power of these expert clowns should have been at Waterloo on Saturday afternoon when the boat train steamed in. The reception from a crowd of fans hundreds strong was overwhelming... Chaplin, in his heyday, hardly received such a welcome. The pair were mobbed from the moment they left the train until they struggled into a car to take them to the Savoy Hotel [for a press conference] attended by practically every special writer on Fleet Street."

Stan and Babe were prevailed upon to make a brief personal appearance at the Empire in Leicester Square, where *Any Old Port* was playing. Babe made a brief speech and indulged in some impromptu clowning with Stan. As they emerged from the theater, 2,000 fans came rushing toward them; the seven policemen trying to control the crowd were no match. Once the comics were inside their car, the mob surged toward it and tore off a door.

The reception was just as intense everywhere they traveled. The team's itinerary took them to the small North Country towns of Stan's boyhood, places which just weren't frequented by movie stars. In North Shields, Stan tried to sneak out late at night to see his old home at 8 Dockwray Square, but the crowds still caught up with him. In Tynemouth, the comedians lunched with the mayor, and gave toys to impoverished children, with hordes of admirers looking on.

At the Central Station in Glasgow, a crowd of 6,000 surged around the team and their bodyguards — six policemen. Stan almost lost one of his shoes; Babe nearly collapsed. As they struggled to the Central Hotel entrance, a stone balustrade guarding one side of the hotel door collapsed from the weight of people clinging to it. Two people were crushed by stones; several people fainted, others fell into a manhole. Nine people were hospitalized.

Blackpool, Manchester, Leeds, and Sheffield were much the same — crowds, hastily-arranged luncheons with town officials, and precious little sightseeing. The team planned to see Paris, Deauville, Berlin, Antwerp, Brussels and Madrid, but in Paris the attention from press and public was just as relentless as it had been in England — and so they returned there.

In London on August 18, they made their only commercial record at the Columbia Graphophone studios. In this sketch, Ollie tries to thank the British public for their warm reception — while Stan continually interrupts. On August 24, the team, exhausted, sailed for New York on the S.S. Paris.

They were back in Los Angeles on September 12, and got a brief rest from their "vacation," since the studio was closed for its annual one-month respite. It had been a wearying yet exhilarating journey. To their astonishment, Laurel and Hardy learned that they were full-fledged Movie Stars. For the rest of their days, they never ceased to be amazed at the intense devotion they inspired in their fans.

Ironically, although MGM and the Roach studio got a tremendous amount of profitable publicity from the team's "tour," it was hardly remunerative for Stan and Babe. Henry Ginsberg saw to it that Stan was docked $19,200 for going on the trip, while Babe had $15,200 of his salary taken away.

Stan and Babe were learning that fame could be costly in many ways.

THEIR FIRST MISTAKE

Production history: Script written mid-September 1932. Shot circa September 24 to October 1. Released November 5. Copyrighted November 22, 1932 by MGM (LP 3426). Two reels.

Produced by Hal Roach. Directed by George Marshall. Edited by Richard Currier. Sound by James Greene.

With Mae Busch, Billy Gilbert, George Marshall.

Mrs. Arabella Hardy is mighty angry at her husband for spending so much time with his friend Mr. Laurel, who lives next door. Eventually the boys decide to adopt a baby — Stan explains that it would keep the wife occupied while he and Ollie go out at night. The boys return with a bouncing baby, only to learn from a gruff process server that Mrs. Hardy is suing Ollie for divorce, and Stan for alienation of his affections. The boys spend a long, sleepless night trying to care for their new charge.

The boys with two more mistakes whose scenes were cut from the film.

Stan and Babe found some changes around the Roach studio when they returned from their much-publicized "vacation" in England. For one, Harley M. "Beanie" Walker, who had been with the Roach organization since 1916 and had written titles and dialogue for virtually all of its films, had resigned on July 25. By October, he was writing dialogue for comedies produced by ex-Roach general manager Warren Doane at Universal. (Two years later, he was at Paramount working on W.C. Fields' *The Old-Fashioned Way*.)

The studio's general manager, Henry Ginsberg, was becoming more involved in the day-to-day operations, leaving Roach free to fly his private plane to MGM conventions in Chicago and New York. And Ginsberg continued to cut costs, because the L&H series posted a loss on the 1931-32 season of $166,447.88.

The script for *Their First Mistake* offers a couple of subplots and some interesting gags that don't appear in the film. An opening sequence has Ollie sneaking over to Stan's next-door apartment to tell him not to come over for breakfast that morning, because the wife is angry. Ollie stands on a small table and peers through the transom of Stan's front door; he's holding the morning milk, having gone to get it as an excuse to see Stan. After Stan gets the message, he closes the transom, accidentally hitting Ollie on the head and causing him to crash through the table and spill the milk.

The wife sees Ollie sprawled on the floor. Another lodger across the hall has stepped outside after hearing the crash; Ollie turns to him and says, "Never push me again like that!" The Hardys exit hastily into their apartment. Their door opens slowly in back of them, revealing the lodger, as Ollie huffs, "Why, the dirty thief! I caught him in the act of stealing our milk!" The wife goes to the kitchen; Ollie turns and gets a punch in the nose, courtesy of the lodger's fist.

Breakfast fares no better for Hardy in the script. He pours syrup over his hotcake, but lays his newspaper on top of it after the phone rings. It's Stan, who says, "I want to talk to you," and hangs up. Ollie goes to meet him in the hallway. "Are you alone?" asks Stan. "No, my wife's here," replies Ollie. "Oh, I wanted to talk to you privately," says Stan. He goes back into his room, leaving Ollie bewildered.

Ollie goes back to his paper — which, unbeknownst to him, is now decorated with a hotcake — and the phone rings again. Whereupon Stan asks Ollie if he's there and Ollie replies that of *course* he's there; Stan says he wants to talk to him, Ollie says "All right," and Stan hangs up. As Ollie fumes, there's a knock at the door. Stan wants to know if Ollie's alone, and when Hardy replies that his wife is also at home, Mr. Laurel again says, "Oh, I wanted to talk to you privately." Slam goes the Laurel door. This threatens to go on for seven or eight eternities.

After Mrs. Hardy has, expressed her unhappiness and Stan encourages Ollie to adopt a baby, the boys return with a baby boy. The script suggests another altercation with the lodger at this point, but in the film the boys simply offer their neighbor a cigar, and he gives them his congratulations. (This brief bit was played by director George Marshall, who is much more genial here than in *Pack Up Your Troubles*.)

After Ollie learns that his wife has left him, the script proposes that we cut to Mrs. Arabella Hardy at her parents' home. She cries, "I want a divorce!," but her parents suggest that she needs a baby in her house; it would occupy Ollie's mind and keep him home nights. This advice sounds mighty familiar. Fade out.

As per the film, the script now shows the boys struggling to take care of the baby late at night, and failing spectacularly. At the point where the film ends, however, the script suggests that Arabella returns. She wants to reconcile. The Hardys embrace. The wife thinks they need a baby in their house; Ollie agrees, and motions to Stan to bring the baby over. But before he can show off this new addition to the family, Arabella calls to her mother, who proudly wheels in a perambulator carrying twins!

The script ends with, "Short finish to be added," but Stan made the finish even shorter by scrapping the reconciliation scenes. They *were* filmed; stills exist, showing May Wallace as Arabella's mother. There was very little time spent on the film's post-production — it was rushed into release just over a month after the shooting finished. Evidence of this is the lack of a musical score; Bert Jordan didn't have time to splice together a music track.

Their First Mistake had been a working title for *Pardon Us*, so, to be accurate, this picture was really Their Second First Mistake.

TOWED IN A HOLE

Production history: Script written mid-late October 1932. Shot circa November 1-10. Released December 31. Copyrighted January 18, 1933 by MGM (LP 3577). Two reels.

Produced by Hal Roach. Directed by George Marshall. Photographed by Art Lloyd. Edited by Richard Currier. Sound by James Greene.

With Billy Gilbert.

Fish peddlers L&H are surviving comfortably enough — and then Stan gets a "million-dollar idea." They'll catch their own fish and eliminate the middleman. The boys buy an old boat at a junk yard, and have great difficulty in repairing and painting it. Finally, though, the boys are ready to tow their gleaming new craft to the pier. Their car can't pull the boat — so Stan suggests they put up the sail. The sail billows, the boat hurls proudly into the car and pushes it through a fence, whereupon both vehicles are smashed.

Towed in a Hole is one of the team's finest comedies. Ironically, it was made at a time when Stan and the gag men had run out of ideas. Henry Ginsberg had announced that the L&H unit would start shooting a new picture on Monday, October 17 — but on the 22nd, Stan and director George Marshall were still struggling to write the story.

Among the surviving Laurel and Hardy scripts is a fragmentary outline written by Stan, entitled *Live Bait*. While this story is undated, it appears to be an embryonic version of the *Towed in a Hole* plot line.

In Stan's script, Ollie is married to Mrs. Phyllis Hardy, a domineering clubwoman who is preparing a luncheon for the Political Rights of American Women group. Mr. Hardy and his friend are ordered to peel potatoes and onions, and Ollie is repeatedly spritzed in the eye by Mr. Laurel's onion. The wife sends them out to get 50 pounds of halibut. En route, Stan spies two fishing poles in the window of a sporting goods store. He convinces Ollie that they should catch the fish instead of buying it, so it will be *really* fresh.

Making a suggestion to director George Marshall.

The two would-be fishermen cast their lines from the deck of a live-bait boat, and get not a nibble. Then a salty old codger suggests that their luck might be better if they used some bait. Disgustedly, Ollie mutters to Stan, "And that man we bought these poles from said they were ready to use!" Ollie asks the old gent what they should use to attract the fish, and he replies, "Fish." This develops into something akin to an Abbott and Costello routine:

OLLIE: But how do we get them?
MAN: Get what?
STAN: Fish!
MAN: Fish!

Soon, a couple of young lovelies stroll by and tell the boys, "You need some live bait, and we'll show ya where to get it!" Stan, horrified, tells Ollie that the girls are "a couple of freshies," but Ollie, man of the world that he is, follows the damsels over to the live-bait tank. And at this tantalizing juncture, the script comes to an end.

"We'd been stuck for four or five days or a week maybe," recalled George Marshall. "We hadn't come up with any particular story outline that seemed to progress or have any base to it. So I drove to the studio one morning, and in Culver City I passed one of these little fish wagons; and this fellow was touting his wares with a long horn as he drove down the street. So I thought, 'Well, maybe that could be the answer, with the boys selling the fish, but to make more money, catching their own fish.'

"I had about that much when I got to the studio. Stan was sitting in his room. I told him about the idea and he said, 'Yeah, that just might work.' We went to work on it there in the room; we started kicking it around, just the two of us that morning, making some notes. Charley Rogers [was there], he was making notes and possibly interjecting a gag of some kind as we talked, and out of it came the idea that if you're going to catch fish you have to have a boat, naturally. The boat they get is pretty dilapidated and has to be fixed up before it'll even float, and that's the way it went."

The script is most interesting for what it doesn't contain; most of the film's best scenes are nowhere to be found in the written outline. The script proposes that at one point, Stan and Ollie get angry at one another for their mutual transgressions while trying to clean the boat, and throw bucketfuls of water at each other. In the film, this has been transformed into a rather elegant tit-for-tat skirmish, in which the duo daintily find creative new ways to pour water on each other.

Nor does the script offer any trace of a lengthy scene wherein Stan has been incarcerated in the boat's cabin by an angry Ollie, and amuses himself by drawing a picture of Ollie on the cabin wall and poking it in the eye. Next, he plays tic-tac-toe with himself; finally, he traps himself behind the base of the boat's mast, and has to saw his way out.

"I think Stan played that scene for — it must have been two or three minutes," Marshall said. "I don't know of any comedian today who could play that kind of scene and hold the audience. But that was the creative value of Stan, which I loved; I learned so much from him, and I think I became a better director because of Stan.

"On those pictures we had to work pretty much in continuity, because the sales and releases depended on a certain amount of footage, at that time about 1800 feet for a two-reel short. Other gags developed as we were working — like Stan putting his finger through the side of the boat, and leaving the soap on the deck so that Babe would slip and fall into the cabin full of water. It developed so that the routine we'd written for the finish, we never got to shoot.

"In the film, they put the sails up and the boat crashed into their car right there. But the routine we had would've been funny: They put up the sails and the boat took off. We had a wild routine with the two of them going through traffic, Babe out in front with the car, and Stan in the back with the sailboat, trying to throw out the anchor. He throws it out and it catches a fireplug. We never shot that scene because we had enough footage.

"That's how those films were built. You'd think of many things beforehand in story construction, but then you got on the actual set, and the props would often lead into better things than we had written."

The unfilmed ending — which bears some resemblance to the unfilmed "wild car" finale intended for *County Hospital* — was followed by a coda: After a fade out and in, we're back to the street where Laurel and Hardy were driving their fish wagon at the start of the story. Only now, the boys are minus their car and are *walking* fish peddlers. Stan has one arm in a sling, and Ollie is hobbling along on crutches. In between choruses of "Fresh Fish!," Ollie glares at Stan and mutters, "Eliminate the middleman!"

Just as this film finished shooting, on November 9, Henry Ginsberg signed a new two-year contract as the Roach studio's general manager. Two days later, he demonstrated his cost-cutting abilities by terminating George Marshall's contract. Marshall went on to direct other comedies with Bob Hope, Martin and Lewis, and W.C. Fields, as well as some excellent dramatic features. But he always retained happy memories of his work with Stan and Babe.

"I was so fond of those two fellows," he said, shortly before his death in 1975. "They say that a director is supposed to teach other people. But I learned so much as a director from Stan and Babe because of their talents. I thought I knew a lot, but I found I wasn't too damn smart. And because of their experience, I learned a great deal which helped me through the years. I'm very grateful for what those two did for me."

TWICE TWO

Production history: Script written circa November 12-20, 1932. Filmed late November. Previewed late December. Copyrighted February 20, 1933 by MGM (LP 3668) Released February 25. Two reels.

Produced by Hal Roach. Directed by James Parrott. Photographed by Art Lloyd. Edited by Bert Jordan. Sound by James Greene.

With Baldwin Cooke, Charlie Hall; May Wallace and Carol Tevis (voices).

Oliver Hardy, M.D., is — incredibly enough — a brain specialist. Mr. Laurel runs the office switchboard. Each has married the other's sister, and tonight is their mutual anniversary. While preparing for a grand dinner at home, Mrs. Laurel and Mrs. Hardy prove to be as inept as their husbands. The evening turns into a shambles; tempers flare, and the evening collapses as the couples bicker.

Mrs. Laurel and Mrs. Hardy demonstrate their culinary skill in a deleted scene.

Twice Two is a not-too-funny reworking of the duplicate-identity device used in *Brats*. The occasional good gags are overshadowed by several overly talky scenes which crawl at a funereal pace. The "wives" are interesting characters, but they don't have much to do; possibly the boys' ad-libbing was hampered by the technical limitations imposed upon them in having to play two roles. In any event, *Twice Two* is truly a comedy where they "tried to get laughs from the make-up." And even that's not as effective as it should be, because Stan had already made earlier and funnier appearances in drag.

The team was in the headlines during the preparation of this short. On November 16, it was reported that Stan and his wife Lois had separated. Laurel told reporters, "We got to a point where anything that either of us did didn't please the other and we got on each other's nerves. So there wasn't anything left for us to do." One wonders if this turn of events might have prompted Stan to write this story about marital disharmony.

The *Twice Two* script is longer than most, and unlike most of the scripts, virtually all of the dialogue is fully written out. (Usually, the scripts left it up to the actors to get the story across in their own words.) There's one scene early in the script wherein the wives try to prepare a roast and mashed potatoes, and through some violent slapstick, "Fannie" (Babe) ends up with most of the food decorating her person.

Most of the climactic arguing between the two couples in the film was developed during the shooting; it replaced an elaborate scripted scene which would have let us in on a surprise Mrs. Laurel planned for her brother — Fannie has bought Ollie a movie projector.

The girls wash dishes in the kitchen while the boys set up an impromptu movie screen. Stan asks his sister for a tablecloth, and she pulls one out from under a stack of dishes, breaking them all. Ollie tries to hang the tablecloth over a curtain rod, but Stan inadvertently upsets the chair that he's standing on, sending Ollie crashing through a window.

Finally, the projector is set up, and Ollie confidently starts the film. But first the image is upside-down. After a brief pause, Mr. Hardy has fixed everything. The lights go down again. Now the image is backwards. This causes no end of merriment among Stan and the girls.

At last, Ollie gets the film running correctly. They watch some thrilling scenes of jungle life, but when a lion charges onto the screen, Stan gets scared and screams, "Look out!" Mr. Laurel and the ladies jump up and run, upsetting the projector; the lion seems to be following the trio wherever they run. Film spews onto the floor.

Ollie turns on the lights and kicks Stan in the rear. Stan's sister comes to his defense, prompting a free-for-all. The couples show that their marital bonds aren't as strong as their family ties, because Stan and his sister threaten to leave. As they stand at the front door bickering with Fannie and Ollie, a delivery boy enters, bearing a cake. "Will you see that Mr. Hardy gets this?" asks the boy. "I certainly will," says Stan. Mr. Hardy's cherubic features are soon adorned with frosting.

The movie-projector scene was probably scrapped because of the expensive optical work required to keep both couples in each shot. (Only a few of these split-screen shots are left in the film; typical of Roy Seawright's special-effects work, they're absolutely flawless.)

Although George Marshall had been given notice of termination, he worked on this picture during pre-production and was initially slated to direct. By the time Laurel and Hardy got before the cameras, James Parrott was in the director's chair. Although he would later work on the team's feature-film scripts, this was Parrott's last film as their director.

"Jimmy Parrott was a wonderful director," said Marvin Hatley. "But to take it in all its complexity, he'd get drunk periodically, and he'd stay drunk for three months. And after that, he wouldn't take another drop all year long. That's the way he was: he'd behave perfectly, and then he'd just get in one of those moods where he wanted to get drunk. They liked Jimmy's ideas, but they were afraid to trust him with the responsibility of running the whole thing."

In light of this, it's poignant to read the rave review for *Twice Two* that appeared in *Hollywood Filmograph* after a preview in late December:

> Beyond a doubt, Hal Roach's comedy titled *Twice Two* with Laurel and Hardy is one of the best that these comedians have done... James Parrott's direction shows that he understands these comedians to perfection, and he is deserving of a hand, along with the stars.

THE DEVIL'S BROTHER

Production history: Script completed early January 1933. Filmed February 4-March 4. Previewed March 22. Copyrighted May 4, 1933 by MGM (LP 3866). Released May 5, 1933. 90 minutes.

Produced by Hal Roach. Directed by Hal Roach and Charles Rogers. Photographed by Art Lloyd and Hap Depew. Edited by Bert Jordan and William Terhune. Adaptation of the Daniel F. Auber comic opera *Fra Diavolo* (1830) by Jeanie MacPherson. Sound by James Greene. Musical direction by LeRoy Shield.

With Dennis King, Thelma Todd, James Finlayson, Henry Armetta.

In 18th-century Italy, Stanlio and Ollio encounter the charming-but-deadly singing bandit, Fra Diavolo (King). He appoints them as manservants to "The Marquis de San Marco." This phony title is the guise Diavolo uses at the Tavern del Cucu, where he attempts to romance Lady Pamela Rocburg when her wealthy, doddering husband isn't looking. Not coincidentally, Diavolo also tries to filch the 500,000 francs which are sewn inside her petticoat. Through the boys' bungling, the Marquis' true identity is revealed.

Ever since Laurel and Hardy had supported opera star Lawrence Tibbett in *The Rogue Song*, Hal Roach intended to someday put his most popular comedians into a comic opera. Almost immediately after *Pack Up Your Troubles* had been completed, preparations for an L&H musical began in earnest. It was an unusual idea; so unusual that the comedians themselves may have been apprehensive about it.

While talking to a reporter in London on July 25, 1932, Babe was quoted as saying, "In Hollywood, they want to dress us up for our next film, but we're not having any — no highbrow stuff for us." However, both Stan and Babe came to regard this as one of their favorite films.

No film comedian had attempted to use an opera's plot line since Chaplin parodied *Carmen* in 1915. Opera was not considered sure-fire at the box office by any means, and not many operas lent themselves to slapstick comedy. However, in *Fra Diavolo*, an obscure 100-year-old opera, there were two characters named Giacomo and Beppo, which could be altered for Laurel and Hardy. Further, the story was lighthearted and playful, so that the team's physical comedy could be inserted without turning it into a travesty.

By early December 1932, Jeanie MacPherson — who had written and starred in one-reel dramas on which Roach worked as an assistant director in 1913 — had started work on a screen adaptation of Daniel Auber's opera. The two preceding L&H features had been episodic, lacking a strong, unifying plot. By using a story adapted from an opera, the team would be freed of having to carry the plot, and could concentrate their energy on the comedy scenes.

Roach obviously intended this to be the film which would permanently establish Laurel and Hardy as feature-film stars and himself as a feature producer. The trend toward double-bills showed no sign of abating, and it was slowly eroding the market for short subjects. The period costumes and sets would make this an expensive production — an increasing rarity at the Roach

Clowning on the lot with a visitor.

lot, because Henry Ginsberg had been effecting economy measures which more and more closely affected Stan and Babe.

In the last months of 1932, Ginsberg modified both men's contracts, so that their salaries were reduced for one year. And, as longtime Roach film editor Richard Currier told it, Ginsberg still didn't feel they were earning their pay.

"Ginsberg called me over to the office one day and said, 'You go down on the sets, don't you, Dick?' I said, 'Yeah.' He said, 'Well, there's something that I want you to do for me. I think that Laurel and Hardy and that gang down there are wasting a hell of a lot of time just fooling around. I wish you'd go down there and keep track of everything they do for a half hour or so, and then come back and report to me.' I said, 'You must be kidding.' He said, 'No, I'm not.' I said, 'Well, you are as far as I'm concerned.'

"I said, 'I'm not gonna be watching people for you, just so you can jump on 'em about wasting a little time. And I don't know how long you've been in the picture business — ' He said, 'That don't make any difference.' I said, 'It does to me; if you were a picture man, you'd never ask me to do a thing like that. These fellows and everybody on this lot are friends of mine, and I'm not going around spying on them. You'll have to get somebody else.' And I walked out of the office.

"Well, the end of that week, I got my walking papers. And Hal didn't know about any of this; he was back East or in Europe or something when Ginsberg fired me. But in the meantime, I'd gone down to the set and put Laurel and Hardy wise to what happened." Currier had been in Roach's employ since 1920. His abrupt expulsion was a sign that conditions were changing around the Lot of Fun.

MGM made an agreement with Roach on December 28 to release the forthcoming feature; less than a month later, Roach had signed Dennis King to

Loew's STATE *Starts*

BY PUBLIC DEMAND! *Laurel and Hardy in another full-length feature comedy!*

A riotously funny feature by the boys who told the world to "Pack Up Your Troubles!" ...and you did! Here they are, funnier than ever, in a new kind of picture ...filled with heart-warming romance, grand songs and mighty thrills!

THE DEVIL'S BROTHER

From the famous comic opera "Fra Diavolo" by Auber

STAN **LAUREL**

OLIVER **HARDY**

with
DENNIS KING
and beautiful
THELMA TODD

Produced by Hal Roach
A Metro-Goldwyn-Mayer Picture

This picture will NEVER be shown in any other theatre in this city!

play the singing bandit Diavolo. King had been starring in stage operettas since 1924, with *Rose Marie, The Vagabond King* and *The Three Musketeers* to his credit.

Shooting began in February. Hal Roach personally directed the musical and dramatic sequences, with Hap Depew behind the camera and William Terhune handling the editing. The comedy scenes were nominally directed by Charley Rogers, with Art Lloyd and Bert Jordan taking their places as the "official" L&H cameraman and editor.

James Finlayson and Thelma Todd — who had shown her comedic abilities in the Marx Brothers' *Monkey Business* and *Horse Feathers* since her last appearance with Stan and Ollie — figured prominently in the dramatic scenes, ensuring that these would also have a lively tone. Dennis King worked well in his moments with Stan and Ollie, although he confided to a reporter that it was "hard to be secured" in light of the team's continual ad-libbing.

The sequences handled by the Rogers-Laurel and Hardy unit were so good that the film was virtually a guaranteed success. Each of the team's scenes is a self-contained, beautifully structured little masterpiece.

Shooting wrapped the first week of March, and on March 22 the picture was previewed at the Criterion in Santa Monica. *Variety* was not impressed:

> This 11-reeler has sufficient Laurel and Hardy and connecting story to cut down to six spools and get an entertaining L&H feature, thus eliminating the slow and old-fashioned opera that has been recorded probably in the manner of its initial presentation in 1830.
>
> ...Too much of the original music is retained and too little of the lyrics are heard....Nothing is done with camera or crowd manipulation to improve the original...

As a result of the preview, 27 minutes of the Roach-directed "plot" footage was cut from the film. Judging from an early outline, the deleted scenes included some Dennis King musical interludes, and much of the subplot with young lovers Lorenzo and Zerlina. "The original cut was good, but it was very long — *very* long," said editor Bert Jordan. "We had to cut a lot out of that one."

While the film was being modified, so was its title. On April 3, Roach announced that *Fra Diavolo* was being anglicized into *The Devil's Brother.* Recently, Roach explained, "We sent the film to New York, and the sales organization there for Metro said, 'What the hell is *Fra Diavolo*? It means nothing! We've gotta get a new title for this thing.' So they called it *The Devil's Brother* in the United States, but it hurt us because the people who would have appreciated the music never knew what the hell *The Devil's Brother* was."

By any name, the film garnered some of the team's best reviews. John S. Cohen, Jr., writing for the *New York Sun*, commented, "For the reason that its 18th Century grand operatic plot is played so seriously, the antics of Laurel and Hardy stand out in high relief in *The Devil's Brother* ...It is the first instance that this department has laughed whole-heartedly with them. Maybe, indeed, it is the first time that this [reporter] has understood the subtleties of their comic mysteries."

Mordaunt Hall of the *New York Times* found the comics' material "too obvious, blunt and rowdy," and sniffed, "Much less of their antics and more of Mr. King's fine baritone voice would have made this shadow version of an opera far more entertaining."

Conversely, Pare Lorentz in *Vanity Fair* found that the Roach-directed musical sequences were "so poorly done that they seem oddly unrelated to the antics of the leading men, Laurel and Hardy.... The director failed to show any selective judgment.... His sets, his groups, his costumes, his sound — everything connected with the singing, in other words — is poor, and seems to have no connection with Laurel and Hardy, or the well-worn but still entertaining plot."

In Europe, the film succeeded spectacularly. In Brussels, a French-dubbed version had run for nine weeks when a reporter noted, "and the end not in sight." Hal Roach recalled, "I saw the picture in France, and when every song came on, the whole damn audience joined in." In Paris, it was held over during a revival in August 1935, and Stan and Babe saw an Italian-dubbed version in Genova during a 1950 reissue.

Hal Roach was already in London when the film was first released there in May 1933; he was joined by Dennis King, Thelma Todd and James Finlayson, who made personal appearances in connection with the film at the Empire Theatre. Finlayson decided to stay on, making features for Gaumont-British until March 1935. Todd and King, perhaps emulating their film roles, were reported as "billing and cooing in London." In another case of life imitating art, while Todd was staying at the Dorchester Hotel, someone stole $500 from her room.

She should have sewn it inside her petticoat.

ME AND MY PAL

Production history: Script written mid-March 1933. Shot mid-late March. Released April 22. Copyrighted May 10, 1933 by MGM (LP 3867). Two reels.

Produced by Hal Roach. Directed by Charles Rogers and Lloyd French. Photographed by Art Lloyd. Edited by Bert Jordan. Sound by James Greene.

With James Finlayson, Eddie Dunn, Bobby Dunn, Frank Terry, James C. Morton.

Hardy, a successful businessman, is to marry the daughter of well-known oil magnate Peter Cucumber. Stan is the best man, and he arrives at the Hardy abode with a wedding present — a jigsaw puzzle. While waiting for the taxi, Stan and Ollie become absorbed in putting the puzzle together — and so do the taxi driver, Ollie's butler, a policeman, and a telegram delivery boy. By afternoon's end, Mr. Hardy's marriage, career, fortune and puzzle are in a shambles.

This film began life under the title of *The Best Man*, but this ironic comment on Stan's "help" with his friend's wedding plans was annulled. The final title was a play on Raoul Walsh's then-current hit with Spencer Tracy and Joan Bennett, *Me and My Gal*.

Me and My Pal's co-directors: Lloyd French and Charley Rogers.

The script was longer than usual this time around, and very little was changed from the transition to the screen. A couple of the supporting characters were different in the original outline. A tramp was supposed to come to the Hardy doorstep, begging for food; the butler brings out a sumptious platter of roast chicken for the poor, emaciated fellow, but by this time he too has become so absorbed in the puzzle that he shoves the platter away without noticing it.

In the script, one of the puzzle participants is a mailman who wants Ollie to sign for a registered letter; this role was changed to that of a telegram boy, nicely played by diminutive Bobby Dunn (no relation to tall, lanky Eddie Dunn, who plays the taxi driver). This change prompted the film's wrap-up gag — not in the script — which has Ollie finally reading the telegram and discovering that if he calls his broker now, he can sell his stock for a $2,000,000 profit. Before he can pick up the phone, a radio bulletin announces that the very same stock has crashed.

The voice of that radio announcer and the role of Ollie's butler were both filled by Frank Terry (aka Nat Clifford), an English comic and gag writer who would contribute to the team's scripts throughout the mid-'30s. (Terry handed Harold Lloyd the bomb that turned out not to be a prop during a near-fatal photo session in 1919 — in which Lloyd lost two fingers and was blinded in one eye.)

Charley Rogers and Lloyd French shared the direction credit, the only time that two directors were credited on an L&H short. French had been the assistant director on most of the team's films since 1927, and had just signed a two-year Roach contract as a writer-director.

Me and My Pal is hardly the team's greatest film; the jigsaw puzzle gag is cute, and it builds nicely, but it just doesn't have anything to build *to*. The climactic battle, in which all of the puzzle assemblers come to blows because they can't find the last piece, seems forced.

There was little time for anyone to come up with a better finale, though. The production of *The Devil's Brother* had kept the team from meeting their short-subject schedule, and so *Me and My Pal* was rushed through post-production to meet a release date of April 22, about a month after the shooting finished. Furthermore, Stan was still working on the editing of the feature film during the production of this short.

The studio closed in mid-April for its annual one-month hiatus, and Roach went to England with Charley Chase and Bob McGowan. The producer hoped to make a Laurel and Hardy feature and an all-star picture called *The Roach Revue* for a British company, but couldn't obtain a satisfactory deal.

Stan was traveling, too; he hoped to save his faltering marriage by taking a four-week motoring vacation with Lois to Victoria, British Columbia. Unfortunately, the couple's problems were not resolved, and Lois filed for divorce on May 25.

"The tragedy in Laurel's life was that his first wife, Lois, got a divorce," Hal Roach recounted. "She handled him beautifully; she was also his agent. When I made a financial deal with Laurel, I made the deal with her, not with Stan. If there was anything at the studio that was wrong, she was the one who came to me. I tried to talk her out of the divorce, but she said, 'Hal, it's not worth it.' So that was that.

"I think Stan's career was terrifically affected. He was very much in love with Lois, and he never dreamed she would really get the divorce. After that, Stan married all those other dames, and it cost him a lot of money."

Unfortunately, Stan's marital problems were far more weighty than a jigsaw puzzle.

THE MIDNIGHT PATROL

Production history: Script written early-mid June 1933. Shot circa June 24-July 6. Released August 3. Copyrighted August 3, 1933 by MGM (LP 4075). Two reels.

Produced by Hal Roach. Directed by Lloyd French. Photographed by Art Lloyd. Edited by Bert Jordan. Sound by James Greene.

With Frank Terry, Frank Brownlee, Eddie Dunn.

Officers L&H spend an exciting evening in their patrol car. They are called to investigate a man sneaking into a house, and after nearly interminable delays with a lost address and an irritable safecracker, the novice policemen break into the house and capture their suspect. Unfortunately, he turns out to be Chief Brassbottom, who has merely been locked out of his home. At the station, the boys apologize for their mistake — but the Chief aims, fires, and tells his sergeant to send for the coroner.

This picture is a reworking of *Night Owls* in reverse: here, Stan and Ollie are on the right side of the law, and they don't know they're breaking into the chief's house. Trying to get inside a building was a virtually inexhaustible source of gags for the team; the situation crops up from 1929's *Bacon Grabbers*

Promotional items for *Midnight Patrol.*

to 1937's *Way Out West*, with a half-dozen others in between. No one else has ever been so thoroughly frustrated by a locked door.

Stan and the gag men — including a new addition, Sidney Rauh — began a script on June 6. A week later the studio announced that Laurel and Hardy would soon film a short called *Tickets For Two*, relating "the trials and tribulations of a couple of prize fight enthusiasts." That idea was KO'ed, and replaced with a new story tentatively titled *Calling All Cars*.

A number of gags expired en route to the screen. One scripted routine has the boys eating lunch in their car, and reprising the salt-shaker gag from *You're Darn Tootin'*. While Ollie munches on his sandwich — which is too salty (and peppery) because Stan doesn't know how to screw the top back on the shakers — the following dialogue ensues:

STAN: Do you like riddles?
OLLIE: What?
STAN: I just made one up out of my own head.
OLLIE: What is it?
STAN: What is it that people eat, covered with skin and filled with meat, and whistles like a skylark soft and sweet? (*Ollie thinks for a moment, looks at his sandwich, and, very puzzled, looks at Stan.*)

OLLIE: Whistles like a skylark? *(Stan nods affirmatively.)*
STAN: Do you give up?
OLLIE: *(A little ashamed)* Yes.
STAN: A hot dog!
OLLIE: *(taking it)* A hot dog doesn't whistle like a skylark!
STAN: I know it doesn't. I just said that to make it hard.

Another gem from the mouth of Stan comes when Ollie has forgotten that the prowler is at 24 Walnut Avenue. Stan reminds him, "It's 24 Prowler Street. There's a man trying to steal some walnuts."

During a sequence where the intrepid officers are in the house's cellar and are about to break inside, the script suggests a subplot with the owner's black maid and butler. The butler is proposing marriage, but the maid can't make up her mind. The butler will unmake his mind by blowing out his brains if she doesn't say yes. The maid laughs and says, "Why, you haven't got the nerve!" The butler sits on the cellar doors. "Oh, I haven't got the nerve, eh?," he says, dramatically whipping out his gun.

Cut to the cellar. Stan tells Ollie to blow the lock off. Just as the butler puts the gun to his head, Ollie shoots off the lock — but that's not all he hits. The butler runs madly away, screaming all the while.

As Stan walks up the cellar steps, he carelessly drops one of the doors, so that Ollie's head is stuck between them. Stan tugs on the Hardy head, but it doesn't do much good — perhaps because Laurel is standing on the cellar door. When Stan lets go of Hardy's cranium, it snaps back through the doors. (This gag was later used in *Way Out West*.)

From here on, script and film are one until the script suggests a strange wrap-up gag: The boys are heaving the unconscious "prowler" into their police car; as they leave, the butler runs up to the front door and meets the maid, who asks what all the fuss is about. The butler — "in a high falsetto voice," according to the script — says, "I don't know what happened, honey; I've got troubles of my own." The implication here is that Mr. Hardy's gunshot did not exactly hit the butler's posterior region. "The girl does a double takem and looks at him wonderingly," says the script — but she doesn't wonder half as much as we do. These scenes were filmed but scrapped; Louise Beavers played the maid.

Rumors have circulated that British prints of *The Midnight Patrol* feature a different ending, with the boys being chased out of the Police Chief's house by what they think is a ghost (or possibly *becoming* ghosts themselves). However, neither the first script nor a supplementary "New Business" script mention any such scene, and Glenn Mitchell of the British Film Institute reports that surviving prints are identical to their American counterparts.

The resonant voice of the boys' patrol car was provided by Billy Bletcher, a comic whose tiny stature contrasted with his deep, authoritative voice. Bletcher had worked with Babe Hardy at the Vim Studios in Jacksonville, Florida back in 1916. His widow Arline recalled, "Every time Stan would see Billy on the set, he'd say, 'Billy! Come and tell me about Babe in Jacksonville!' And Billy would keep him entertained, and have him laughing. Stan used to get the biggest kick out of that, because Billy would tell him all of the things he and Babe did together, and the funny tricks they played on each other."

Both comedians were probably grateful to spend as much time at the studio as they could while this film was in production; their private lives were in a state of turmoil. A month after Lois Laurel filed for divorce from Stan, Babe Hardy sued for a divorce from his wife of 12 years, Myrtle Lee Reeves Hardy, and charged mental cruelty. Myrtle's alcoholism had caused well-publicized rifts in 1929 and 1931; there would be more to come.

The Midnight Patrol was the last L&H comedy of the 1932-33 season. Lloyd French got his first solo directorial credit since 1929's *That's My Wife* with Laurel and Hardy on this film; Jack Roach took over as assistant director.

Hal Roach had scheduled six shorts and two features starring the team for the coming season. As *The Midnight Patrol* finished shooting, Roach signed writer-actor Frank Craven to work on the screenplay for the team's next full-length picture. The feature films which had started almost accidentally with *Pardon Us* were now given more attention than the shorts. Stan and Babe still favored the two-reelers, but economics dictated that the comedians' favorite forum for their art would soon be denied them.

BUSY BODIES

Production history: Script written mid-July 1933. Shot circa July 15-25. Copyrighted September 16, 1933 by MGM (LP 4129). Released October 7. Two reels.

Produced by Hal Roach. Directed by Lloyd French. Photographed by Art Lloyd. Edited by Bert Jordan. Sound by James Greene.

With Charlie Hall, Tiny Sandford.

The boys are working at a sawmill, where they busy themselves primarily by cleaning up their own messes: Stan accidentally strips away the seat of Ollie's trousers with a plane, and has to glue it back; then he sticks a glue-filled paintbrush to Ollie's chin, and has to shave it off. After Ollie is caught in a sawdust flue and ejected onto a shed — which he smashes — the foreman chases the boys to their car. In their haste, they drive into a bandsaw, which cuts their Ford neatly in twain.

Busy Bodies has virtually no story; it's basically Laurel and Hardy playing with props and devising some inspired gags out of them for 20 minutes. This is the team at their best — unhurried, unencumbered by too much plot or too many supporting characters, milking all the laughs they can out of a simple situation. And this is precisely the type of thing which they would be unable to do in their features. Twenty minutes was just the right length for an L&H film; stretch it to an hour or more, and the extra time would have to be filled with subplots and musical numbers.

The team's comedy would change, too. Instead of extended milkings of one situation, they would rely more upon set pieces — brief, self-contained routines that could be sandwiched between the plot sequences. The surroundings which suited Laurel and Hardy best — like those in *Busy Bodies* — unfortunately didn't suit features very well.

This story was tentatively titled *Fifty-Fifty* for a reason not evident in the film or the script. The written outline doesn't suggest new routines, just slight variations on the ones which exist in the film. For example:

Visitors disrupt the *Busy Bodies* set.

In the film, Stan is planing a piece of wood, and when Ollie inadvertently bends over it, Stan "planes off" the seat of his pants. However, the script suggests that Stan accidentally tear away the seat of his underwear as well. When Stan glues everything back, we cut to Ollie's backside and see that Stan has glued the fabric on backwards, so that a big strip of underwear is plainly visible. Stan gets some paint and covers it up.

The script then proposes that Ollie should retaliate by having Stan bend over and get the same treatment. Once Ollie has planed away the seat of Stan's overalls and undies, he applies the sticky glue directly to Stan's backside, "ending up with a violent dig with the brush into Stan's fanny," before reapplying the material. This may have been considered a little too risque; in any event, Ollie gets his revenge in the film by simply giving Stan a sharp snap on the head with a saw.

The final sequence was also a bit different as scripted. Ollie is ejected from what the script calls a "sawdust-and-shavings suction pipe" into a pile of sawdust — despite Mr. Laurel's attempt to catch his partner. Ollie gets out of that mess, and immediately trips into a trough filled with lime. Stan asks if he can do anything to help. Enraged, Ollie chases him toward the bandsaw.

Stan jumps over the moving conveyor belt, but Ollie lands on it, and is carried toward the deadly saw. As he runs on the belt, he pleads for Stan's help, so Laurel throws the gears into reverse while Ollie is still running; this sends him flying out of the scene. The script then again shows us how much Laurel and Hardy's ad-libbing abilities were relied upon: "There is another gag here, then go into our last routine of cutting the Ford in two. The end."

A lot of ad-libbing went on, too, because many of the film's best gags aren't in the written outline. There's none of the business where the boys keep walking into a plank carried by two passing workmen (an old gag, but beauti-

Stand-in Hamilton Kinsey gives Ollie double trouble.

fully executed here); nor does Stan drive a nail into a wall (and a water pipe) so he can hang up his coat; nor does Ollie get contorted this way and that when his hands are locked into a window sash. Neither pesky irritable co-worker Charlie Hall nor burly irritable foreman Tiny Sandford are mentioned in the script.

Writer Charles Barr, in his 1968 book about the team, stated that the final gag, with Stan and Ollie driving their Model T through a bandsaw, "is said to have gone wrong and nearly killed them on the set." But special-effects wizard Roy Seawright asserted, "That gag was a collaboration between Fred Knoth's mechanical department and my photographic department. It was done with a traveling matte; a traveling split-screen. We had one half go through first, and then we introduced the other half. So, ultimately, it was accomplished on an optical printer."

WILD POSES

Production history: Written and shot in August 1933. Copyrighted October 20, 1933, by MGM (LP 4187). Released October 28. Two reels.

Produced by Robert F. McGowan for Hal Roach. Directed by Robert F. McGowan. Photographed by Francis Corby. Edited by William Terhune.

With Our Gang, Franklin Pangborn, Emerson Treacy, Gay Seabrook.

Spanky and his parents spend a difficult day trying to have a family portrait taken by prissy photographer Otto Phocus.

This is another cameo appearance for Laurel and Hardy. A door-to-door salesman tells a mother that she has the two most photogenic children he's ever seen. Cut to the two children — Stan and Ollie in nightgowns and bonnets. Stan is seated in a huge chair, left over from *Brats*. The boys smile and wave at the camera, then fight over an equally huge milk bottle, and finally Stan pokes Ollie in the eye. This 20-second guest spot is accompanied by a sort of Italian Baroque version of "Coo-Coo," lifted from the soundtrack of *The Devil's Brother*.

This gag was Hal Roach's idea; not only were these cameos amusing, they were also confirmation of the fact that Stan and Babe were the big stars on the lot. (The team did brief walk-ons in Our Gang, Todd and Pitts, and Charley Chase shorts, but there would have been no point in those stars reciprocating.)

DIRTY WORK

Production history: Script written late July-early August 1933. Filmed circa August 7-19. Copyrighted October 24, 1933 by MGM (LP 4206). Released November 25. Two reels.

Produced by Hal Roach. Directed by Lloyd French. Photographed by Kenneth Peach. Edited by Bert Jordan. Sound by William B. Delaplain.

With Lucien Littlefield, Sam Adams, Jiggs.

Two chimney sweeps come calling to the abode of mad scientist Professor Noodle. As they go about their business — wrecking the chimney and decorating the living room with soot in the process — the professor perfects his rejuvenation formula. He proudly demonstrates this to the boys, turning a duckling back into an egg. As he scurries off to find his butler for a human demonstration, the two sweeps decide to try the formula on a fish. But Stan accidentally tips Ollie into the formula-filled tank, and when Hardy emerges, he strikingly resembles his monkey forebears.

This film differs very little from the script. One intriguing note is that the roles of Professor Noodle and his butler, Jessup, were originally slated for Richard Carle — who had played a similar role in *Habeas Corpus* — and Frank Austin, the malevolent butler in *The Laurel-Hardy Murder Case*. Instead, the roles were filled by Lucien Littlefield and Sam Adams.

A brief deleted sequence exists in the script when the intrepid chimney sweeps are nailing some sackcloth over the fireplace mantle. As Stan hammers a nail into the mantle, the corner of the sackcloth drops away. Ollie takes the hammer from him, and spitefully tries to hit Stan's fingers while his hand is resting on the mantle shelf. Stan is too quick for Ollie, and dares him to try again. Ollie keeps trying to hit Stan's fingers with the hammer, until Stan puts his hand in front of a vase — he quickly pulls it away, and Mr. Hardy inadvertently smashes the ornament.

The most extensive departure from the film is a scripted scene which occurs after the professor has shown the boys his rejuvenation formula. Ollie thinks that the whole thing is a fake, so the professor dramatically climbs into the tank himself and evaporates — he's in some sort of chemical never-never land, from whence he will return as a younger man when the boys put in 30 drops of the solution. But Stan, being Stan, drops the glass container on the floor, and so the professor's disembodied voice has to give him the directions for making a new batch.

Ollie tries to reach a bottle of "Multi Boni Bevi," which is on a shelf over the tank; he falls backwards into the solution-filled tank, and the bottle conks Stan on the noggin, knocking him out. When Stan awakens, he finds *two* disembodied voices coming from somewhere beyond the tank. Stan asks Ollie — or what's left of him — "What did you go in there for?" Laurel and his invisible friend begin to argue, but finally Stan fixes a new batch of the formula. He climbs up the steps to the tank and crouches over it, with an eye dropper and the pitcher of rejuvenation formula poised at the ready. But the steps slide out from under him and Stan tumbles into the tank.

After water and foam spray all over creation, three monkeys clamber out of the tank. One is wearing Ollie's derby; another is scratching his head, and a third is wearing the professor's glasses. "We fade out on the funniest action the monks might happen to do," shrugs the script.

The filmed ending is much simpler — and it makes effective use of a running gag that's been spotted throughout the picture. When a chimpanzee Hardy climbs out of the tank and looks accusingly at Laurel, Stan cries, "Won't you speak to me?" Ollie replies as he has throughout the film: "I have *nothing* to say!"

Just before the shooting began on *Dirty Work*, Stan announced to the press that he and wife Lois had become reconciled, and added that "the Hardys are doing the same thing." The attorneys for Babe and Myrtle were surprised at this, since they were in the process of working out a property settlement. But indeed, it wasn't long before Babe and Myrtle, too, had reconciled — for a time.

With things running more smoothly in their personal lives, Stan and Babe prepared to make a comedy that, ironically, would center on their characters' struggles with "the wives." It was another feature, one which would help to establish them as more than "just two-reel comics."

SONS OF THE DESERT

Production history: Script written July 7 to mid-September 1933. Shot October 2-23. Previewed circa November 10. Copyrighted December 27, 1933 by MGM (LP 4380). Released December 29. 68 minutes.

Produced by Hal Roach. Directed by William A. Seiter. Assistant director, Lloyd French. Photographed by Kenneth Peach. Edited by Bert Jordan. Sound by Harry Baker. Story by Frank Craven. Continuity by Byron Morgan. Dance direction by Dave Bennett. Song, "Honolulu Baby," by Marvin Hatley.

With Mae Busch, Dorothy Christie, Charley Chase, Lucien Littlefield.

Ollie's wife won't let him go to Chicago for the annual convention of the Sons of the Desert, a high-spirited fraternity to which he and Stan belong. He feigns illness, for which the "cure" is an ocean voyage. Mrs. Hardy can't stand the ocean, and suggests Stan accompany Ollie. The pair have a grand time at the convention — meeting Ollie's brother-in-law (Chase) by coincidence — but return to find the ship on which they supposedly traveled has sunk. Ollie's elaborate fib of "ship-hiking" to safety earns him a pummeling with his wife's crockery; Stan's tearful apology entitles him to a comfy evening.

Sons of the Desert is a film about contradictions, but it is all of a piece. It's beautifully constructed, and the story is strong enough so there's no need for padding or subplots. (The one musical number, a charming rendition of "Honolulu Baby" sung by a Dick Powell look-alike at the convention, reminds the boys, and us, of the prank they've pulled on the wives.)

The seamlessness of the story was achieved over two months of preparation, with the help of some new collaborators. Stan was no doubt concerned that this new feature should be free of the patchiness which had marred *Pardon Us* and *Pack Up Your Troubles*.

Frank Craven wrote the original story treatment in July 1933, while Stan and Babe were filming *Busy Bodies*. By late August, Frank Terry was writing additional dialogue. (He also wrote the preposterous anthem of the Sons, the tune of which is a medley of "Give My Regards to Broadway," "Yankee Doodle Dandy" and "Tramp, Tramp, Tramp, the Boys are Marching," among others.)

Writing gags while filming the convention sequence. Clockwise: Stan, Babe, Charley Chase, director William Seiter, and gag man Glenn Tryon.

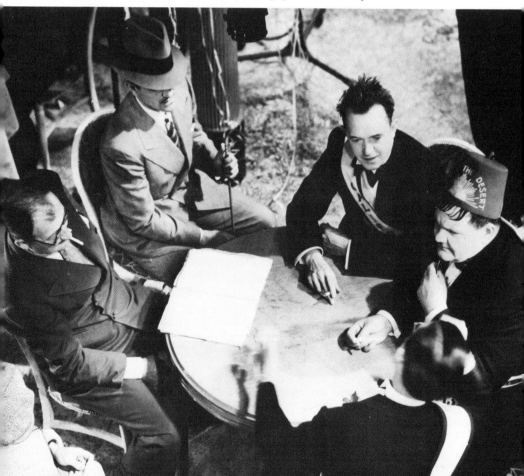

The last week of August saw Byron Morgan working on "continuity"; William Seiter, a close friend of Roach and Laurel, was signed to direct. While Craven, Terry and Morgan got the basic story together, Laurel, Seiter and former comedian Glenn Tryon worked on additional material for a month before shooting began.

All this preparation did not preclude a couple of scripted scenes from being eliminated before filming began. One such scene was an elaborate parade of the Sons through the streets of Chicago, with the members riding on bicycles. Predictably, Stan and Ollie turn the event into a shambles when they ride into a long banner and thus ensnare most of the other bicyclists, some of whom skid and tumble into a large fountain. Another deleted sequence had the boys turning the convention into a wild fracas and being thrown into jail.

Patsy Kelly was originally cast as Stan's wife, but Roach had loaned her to MGM for Bing Crosby's *Going Hollywood*, which ran over schedule. Her replacement was Dorothy Christie, who joined the cast four days into production.

On the Roach backlot, shooting the parade scene. Babe, Kenneth Peach (foreground on the camera platform), Bill Seiter, Stan, and English comic Billy Nelson.

Filming began October 2, 1933, under the guidance of William A. Seiter, who'd been directing dramas and romantic comedies at RKO. Hal Roach commented that "Bill Seiter had more control, I think, than anybody else of their directors." Certainly, Seiter knew how to allow the boys enough time for their comedy, and keep the story moving at the same time. In the team's previous features, the plots had been virtually independent from the comedy; here, everything is integrated.

Seiter obviously worked well with the comics, and one can assume that there were few disagreements about direction, owing to Seiter's friendship with Stan. (The two had gone on a yachting trip during the spring of 1933, which resulted in Stan meeting Virginia Ruth Rogers. Ruth was a frequent visitor to the *Sons* set, which buoyed Stan's spirits; his marriage to Lois came to an end on October 11, while the picture was in production.)

The picture was again shot mostly in continuity; the opening scene with the boys swearing to attend the Chicago convention was filmed first, with 20 members of the Hollywood American Legion Post among the 60 extras employed as fellow Sons.

Charley Chase does an outstanding turn in this film as Ollie's boisterous brother-in-law. Chase in later years reportedly professed to hate this role, because it was diametrically opposed to his usual charming screen character; however, Chase later portrayed a similarly obnoxious fellow in one of his best two-reelers, *The Heckler*. In any event, Charley, Stan and Babe have a wonderful chemistry in their scenes together.

Equally memorable is the tune "Honolulu Baby," which has proved one of the late Marvin Hatley's more enduring compositions. "Song will accompany a line of hula dancers in a cabaret scene and studio feels it will be a hit," noted *The Hollywood Reporter* during production.

More than 50 years later, Hatley found himself playing and singing the tune for a real club called the Sons of the Desert, established to perpetuate the team's work and memory. "The tune was composed in 20 minutes," Hatley said. "Fortunately, it came to me without hard effort." The number was recorded by an eight-piece band on the set, with Hatley playing his inimitable piano; the vocal was handled by crooner Ty Parvis, one-time dancing partner of Betty Grable.

One of the last sequences to be filmed was the "newsreel," wherein Stan and Ollie cavort in the Sons parade. The studio set a record for the number of extras used on any one film at one time during this scene, when 500 men — including the drill team of the American Legion's Glendale post — marched with the boys. The scene was shot on the backlot's New York Street, which Roach modernized for this film.

Sometime during production the ending sequence was reworked. A number of stills of the original ending exist, which show the boys hiding from their wives on the roof of their duplex, and later confessing to them. The scenes take place in early morning, with Stan and Ollie attired in their usual suits. In the final film, all of this takes place at night in a driving rainstorm, and the boys are clad in pajamas.

When the picture was previewed in early November, *The Hollywood Reporter* gave its nod of approval. "It is as good as any of the Laurel-Hardy comedies with the exception, of course, of *The Devil's Brother*," the paper remarked. "It has nothing at all to do with the desert, but plenty to do with real genuine laughter."

Upon its release, the film garnered good reviews, with the exception of *Variety*, which just plain didn't like Laurel and Hardy: "The story is thin to the point of attenuation. It's still a two-reeler that runs three times that long. It will get laughs, but no new business."

Conversely, Andre Sennwald of the *New York Times* was happily surprised that the film "has achieved feature length without benefit of the usual distressing formulae of padding and stretching. It is funny all the way through."

Richard Watts Jr. of the *New York Herald-Tribune* noted that the Rialto theater was "crowded with ecstatic delegates who showed every sign of regarding themselves as being in an ideal world where there were two Chaplins working in one film."

The movie did well enough at the box-office to merit designation among the 10 top-grossing films of 1934, according to *Film Daily* and *The Motion Picture Herald*. It did excellent business overseas, too. In Paris, during a heat wave that killed most of the theater business, the film was reported as "still going great in its 10th week at the Madeline."

Roach was undoubtedly pleased that his starring team had turned out

The boys with Mae Busch and Dorothy Christie in an early version of the ending, later reworked.

YOU'LL BE INITIATED

into a thousand new laughs in Laurel and Hardy's newest full-length feature picture!

HAL ROACH
presents

SONS OF THE DESERT

starring the screen's greatest comedy team

Stan **LAUREL**

Oliver **HARDY**

with **CHARLEY CHASE**
MAE BUSCH • DOROTHY CHRISTY • LUCIEN LITTLEFIELD
Directed by WILLIAM A. SEITER
A Metro-Goldwyn-Mayer Picture

• Just a couple of hen-pecked husbands on the loose, they sneak away from their wives to a grand convention of "the boys." But when their irate spouses find out, be prepared for the most hilarious moments of your picture-going days!

another successful feature; he wasn't too involved with the production, however, due to his preoccupation with starting the Southern California Turf Club, and raising the funds to build the Santa Anita Race Track. Babe Hardy was one of the original investors. "Hardy lost his shirt playing over there," recalled Roach. "Finally, he sold his stock; he knew nothing about horses, and he just — put up his money and lost it. But I was the president, and I put up my money and lost it too. I never won at the damn place."

If Roach was making the transition from short-subject producer to feature film producer, his studio still retained its comfortable, familial atmosphere. But the team's next film was a product of a big, impersonal movie factory — and the production would be a grueling experience for all concerned. Well, almost all.

HOLLYWOOD PARTY

Production history: Written and filmed March 1933 — late March 1934 (see below). Copyrighted May 14, 1934 by MGM (LP 4716). Released June 1. 68 minutes.

Produced by Harry Rapf and Howard Dietz. No director credited (see below). Photographed by James Wong Howe. Edited by George Boemier. Screenplay by Howard Dietz and Arthur Kober (see below). Music and lyrics by Rodgers and Hart, Donaldson and Kahn, Brown and Freed.

With Jimmy Durante, Lupe Velez, Charles Butterworth, Tom Kennedy, Eddie Quillan.

Schnarzan, once-popular star of jungle films (Durante), hopes to win back his following by battling some ferocious lions; he intends to buy them from Baron Munchausen, who is entertaining an offer from his rival. Schnarzan throws a big Hollywood party in the Baron's honor. Former lion owners L&H are uninvited guests who have been trying unsuccessfully to cash the Baron's phony check. They get involved in a tit-for-tat egg-breaking skirmish with haughty Lupe Velez before the lions escape and cause havoc.

Studios like Metro-Goldwyn-Mayer once prided themselves on running like factories — each department did its job to deliver a satisfactory product quickly and efficiently. *Hollywood Party* is an instance of the factory machinery breaking down.

This fiasco began in June 1932, when MGM planned an all-star comedy with comics from its own and other studios. Nothing more was heard until February 1933, when trade papers announced that MGM would film *Gland Hotel*, a Buster Keaton spoof of the all-star drama *Grand Hotel*.

Keaton, who proposed the idea to Irving Thalberg (under the title *Grand Mills Hotel*), recalled in later years: "In our version, Oliver Hardy would be a manufacturer of front collar buttons who is trying to arrange a merger with Stan Laurel, a manufacturer of back collar buttons." The idea remained just that.

In late March, the studio announced that it would produce *The Hollywood Revue of 1933*, a companion piece to its successful feature of 1929. Production began in April; from the start, every aspect of the picture ran into trouble.

The grueling, year-long history of *Hollywood Party* almost warrants a book in itself. The production was so chaotic that it become a sort of running joke in the industry trade papers. (One wag remarked that the picture "has been under three Presidents.")

Stars were announced with great fanfare, then quietly omitted from the cast. Clark Gable, Lawrence Tibbett, Joan Crawford, Marie Dressler, Wallace Beery, Jean Harlow and Johnny Weissmuller were but a few of the luminaries invited to the *Party* who didn't attend.

Rodgers and Hart wrote an entire score for the picture, including a specialty song for Jean Harlow, whose vocal range — according to the trade papers — was all of six notes. But Harlow was dropped from the film, which eased Rodgers and Hart's minds until they learned that most of their score had been dropped, too.

The writing of the film caused hardened veterans of the script-revision wars to gnash their teeth. Edgar Allan Woolf wrote an original story, which was rewritten by Howard Dietz and Edmund Goulding; final credit was given to Dietz and Arthur Kober. In addition, there was uncredited assistance from Herbert Fields, who wrote dialogue; Richy Craig Jr., who wrote *comedy* dialogue; and Henry Myers, who provided "additions." As late as October, production was being "delayed every other day to rearrange the numbers and to make revisions on the script," according to *The Hollywood Reporter*.

Directors came and went. Alexander Leftwich was set to direct, then Edmund Goulding, but both of them were booted before they guided even so much as one frame. Russell Mack was then given the megaphone and actually got to film a few scenes, starting on July 24th. Three days later, he had an argument over a chorus-line number with producer Harry Rapf, and quit. Things stood still until mid-August, when Richard Boleslawski became captain of the sinking ship.

In mid-September, MGM borrowed George Stevens from RKO "to direct the comedy sequences." Allan Dwan took over in January 1934, and when *he* gave up, Charles Riesner directed the remaining scenes in March. Roy Rowland is also rumored to have directed a few segments. "I think we had every director on the lot," said actor Eddie Quillan. "And when it was finished, nobody wanted the credit!"

Laurel and Hardy entered into this fray on September 21. Under the sympathetic direction of their former cameraman, George Stevens, they improvised a few sequences, including the beautifully timed egg-breaking battle with Lupe Velez. After four days, they politely tipped their derbies and sauntered back home to the Roach lot, where they went back to work preparing *Sons of the Desert*.

And, as if to show the big MGM movie factory that the small, personal, let's-kick-gags-around-for-a-while method employed by Roach could be more efficient than the regimented procedures used by Metro, *Sons of the Desert* was filmed and released and making all sorts of money while *Hollywood Party* was struggling to completion.

To add insult to injury, *The Hollywood Reporter* headlined its review like this when the picture was previewed in Glendale on March 28:

LAUREL & HARDY STEAL MGM'S "HOLLYWOOD PARTY":
COMICS HIGHLIGHT DULL MUSICAL

The *Victoria*

SCOOPS THE CITY!

First showing of this blue streak of musical fun shows! It starts TODAY . . . And what a honey of a picture it is!

LAUREL & HARDY

Jimmy Durante, Chas. Butterworth, Polly Moran, Lupe Velez, Jack Pearl, Ted Healy and Stooges, Mickey Mouse Himself, and more, more, more!

"HOLLYWOOD PARTY"

Hal Roach's comics emerged as the stars of MGM's extravaganza.

The review noted, "One of the funniest sequences seen in pictures in many a day is to be found...with Oliver Hardy, Stan Laurel and Lupe Velez furnishing the laughs. It had last night's preview audience rolling in the aisles and actually sobbing with laughter. That sequence is worth the price of admission, and is the highlight in an otherwise dull musical...The picture hardly rates the time and money that MGM has expended." The review concluded by calling the L&H sequence "the greatest and longest bellylaugh scene for a long time."

The team's scenes, and the Walt Disney "Red Hot Chocolate Soldiers" sequence, were the only items singled out for praise in most critiques.

Which goes to show that Laurel and Hardy, ad-libbing a few scenes on a four-day loan-out, accomplished more than all of mighty MGM's resources in an entire year.

There's a lesson in that somewhere.

OLIVER THE EIGHTH

Production history: Script written early December 1933. Filmed December 15-20, January 8—mid-January, 1934. Copyrighted February 13, 1934 by MGM (LP 4494). Released circa February 13. Three reels.

Produced by Hal Roach. Directed by Lloyd French. Photographed by Art Lloyd. Edited by Bert Jordan. Sound by William B. Delaplain.

With Mae Busch, Jack Barty.

Barber shop owners L&H both answer an ad from a wealthy widow, object matrimony. Ollie receives an affirmative reply and leaves Stan, preparing for a life of well-heeled bliss. Stan intrudes upon the scene, having found his letter — which Ollie hid — and demands his cut. The nutty butler confides to the boys that Ollie's going to get his cut, too — his throat, that is. The widow was once jilted by a man named Oliver; in revenge she's since murdered several Olivers. Before he can become her next victim, Mr. Hardy wakes up — it's all been a bad dream.

The Roach studio celebrated its 20th anniversary on December 7, as work began on the script for this film. A special dinner was held, with former Roach employees Will Rogers, Harold Lloyd, Jean Harlow and Janet Gaynor in attendance. NBC broadcast a half-hour radio show commemorating the event, and Stan and Babe made one of their infrequent forays into the medium. Charley Chase, Todd and Kelly and Louis B. Mayer were also featured on the show, which was probably a lot more fun than anything in *Oliver the Eighth*.

The script for this film was not much more inventive than the end result. A weird gag introduces the eccentric widow and Jitters, the butler: she realizes there's a hole in the toe of her stocking, and Jitters notes that she must have put the stocking on inside out. He attends to it by scissoring off the whole stocking toe. "That's much better," coos the widow.

One bit — involving diminutive dynamo Charlie Hall — was filmed but cut. Ollie leaves Stan for his new life of luxury, and tells Laurel he must look after himself from now on. Laundryman Hall then passes by, and Stan decides to give him some dirty towels. As Stan begins to count them, he finds his letter to the widow (hidden by Ollie) in the pile of linen. Stan opens the letter, finds

At the Roach Studios' 20th Anniversary party, with Thelma Todd, Hal Roach, and Patsy Kelly (partially hidden).

his picture, gets confused, and asks Hall whose picture it is. Hall snaps, "Why, it's you!" Stan asks, "Well, how did it get there?" Hall spits, "*I* don't know!"

The script has Stan an even worse businessman than he is in the film. All he gets when he sells the barber shop is a highly dubious gold brick — at least in the film he also gets some nuts.

Filming began on December 15, with Phyllis Barry cast as the malevolent widow. Two days later, Stan's brother Everett ("Teddy") went to have some teeth extracted; after receiving the anesthetic, he died of heart failure. He was 33. Production was suspended while Stan attended to funeral arrangements, and then for the holidays. By the time filming resumed in January, Phyllis Barry had been replaced by Mae Busch. Jack Barty, who had been brought over from England to play in Roach's All-Star series, resumed work in the role of the nutty butler.

It's ironic that Stan's brother died in a dentist's chair while the team was filming a story about Ollie falling asleep in a barber's chair and dreaming about being killed. Despite his loss, Stan's performance in this film is outstanding as usual, as is Babe's. Perhaps one notices the boys' performances more in a weak film such as this, since there's not much else to hold our attention. Their facial expressions, dainty gestures and reactions to each other are a joy, and they make even a lesser entry such as *Oliver the Eighth* a pleasure to watch.

Trouble in Toyland

By the fall of 1933, Laurel and Hardy were masters of the two-reel comedy. Although they had starred in four features for Hal Roach, their hearts belonged to the short comedies. They were the biggest draw in the short-subject field, and were often billed on theater marquees over the feature attraction.

Unfortunately, the death knell was about to sound for the comedy short. The Depression was killing the market for short films; the public had precious little money to spend on luxuries like movies, and exhibitors had begun to entice the customers with the new double-feature policy. Instead of giving you a cartoon, a newsreel, a short comedy and a feature for your quarter, the theater managers now gave you an "A" feature with the day's brightest stars, supported by a "B" feature with considerably dimmer stars.

As a producer who created virtually nothing but short subjects, Hal Roach knew he would either have to start making features or go out of business. Thus, despite the preference of just about everybody at the Roach lot for short films — including Stan Laurel, who wished they'd never gone into full-length films at all — Roach was forced to increase the number and importance of features made at his studio.

In November 1933, Roach bought the rights to Victor Herbert's 1903 operetta, *Babes in Toyland*. It seemed to have all the elements for a successful, prestigious feature. First off, there was Herbert's charming music. Second, there were fantastic, exciting characters that would be sure to captivate the kiddies: the Evil Spider, the Moth Queen, the Brown Bear, Bo-Peep the careless shepherdess, and the Master Toymaker. *Babes in Toyland* was sure to be a hit. It had exciting characters. It had great music. It had no story.

As produced on the stage, *Babes in Toyland* was a three-act musical

The beloved vagabonds almost *didn't* appear in *Babes in Toyland*.

extravaganza, a plotless revue. There was nothing to unify the musical numbers. But Roach knew how to fix that — he would write his own story. He was on a train en route to Los Angeles, having concluded negotiations with RKO executives in New York, who sold him the rights to *Babes in Toyland* after they realized there wasn't any story. Roach was determined to have a complete, original plot finished by the time the train pulled into Los Angeles.

"I worked like a sucker on that thing," declared Roach in a 1981 interview, "and I had what I thought was a hell of a story. Hardy was supposed to be the Pieman, and Stan Laurel was Simple Simon. You remember, 'Simple Simon met the Pieman going to the fair...' the Pieman says, 'Where's your penny?,' and Simple Simon says, 'I haven't any.' Well, now it's with Laurel and Hardy. Stan gets a pie and he eats it, and Babe says, 'Where's your penny?' Stan says, 'I don't have a penny.' Babe says, 'All right, then you push the cart until you *earn* the penny.' So now, they're teamed together. And the song about 'put down six and carry two,' would have been a perfect thing for them to sing.

"The finish was that the heavy, who was a spider turned into a man, wants to destroy Toyland and puts hate into the wooden soldiers. The wooden soldiers come out to destroy Toyland, but Laurel and Hardy find out that they're put together with glue, and water kills glue, and by putting water on the wooden soldiers they save Toyland at the end," said Roach.

"To get the hate to put into the soldiers, the heavy was to get great big drums full of love and happiness. He puts them through a machine, and out comes a little bit of hate. When he gets the hate, the heavy says to the soldiers, 'Destroy love and happiness with this.' The soldiers go out, each one with a big container of hate on his back, and if anybody argues with them they give him a shot of hate. Laurel can't resist putting his finger in the hate and tasting it — and right away he punches Hardy in the nose. Now Laurel and Hardy give everybody a shot of love and happiness, but they screw it up, and finally they fall in love with each other."

Roach began looking for a name star, one who could sing, to play the lead role of Alan. He tried to get former romantic idol Ramon Novarro, singer Donald Novis or Rudy Vallee, but couldn't come to terms with any of them.

Several actresses were tested for the leading lady's role, Little Miss Muffet, among them Anita Louise and Patricia Ellis. Charlotte Henry, who had just appeared in another fantasy film, Paramount's *Alice in Wonderland*, had the inside track for the part, though.

Each new publicity release from the Roach studio confirmed that big things were expected of *Babes in Toyland*. The film would have special stop-action animation sequences. It would be guided by four directors — one for the dramatic scenes, one for the musical numbers, one for the special effects scenes, and one for comedy. Eddie Prinz, a respected choreographer, was hired to direct the dances, and Ray Harris, a writer formerly at Paramount and RKO, was signed to polish up the script.

Toyland would be Roach's first real "All-Star Comedy." Laurel and Hardy's co-stars would include Charley Chase, Patsy Kelly, Spanky McFarland and other stellar personalities from the Roach lot. Production was scheduled to start in early March 1934, so the film could have a summer release.

There was only one problem with all of this. Stan didn't like Roach's story. "I thought Stan was going to go nuts about it," recalled Hal Roach. "I gave Stan the story when I got back, and he said, 'Oh, we can't do this.' I said, 'Why?' He said, 'We can't work without the derby hats. They are our trademark.' I said, 'In the first place, the derby was Chaplin's trademark. You can put a bandana handkerchief on your head and you'll still be Laurel and Hardy.' We argued for about two weeks. *Babes in Toyland* was a big property, and I was paying real dough for it. I had worked so hard on this thing, and I was so disgusted in light of his opposition, that I just said, 'Enough. I'm out of the thing completely. Go make the picture.'"

Frankly, Roach's statement is a bit curious. For one thing, L&H had already appeared in several films minus their derbies, and they don't wear their usual headgear at all in the completed version of *Babes in Toyland*. It's hard to imagine Stan turning down the story for the reason Roach states; it's more probable that he just didn't like it. Laurel had a lot of experience with this type of fairy-tale story, too; English Christmas pantomimes, similar to *Toyland*, had attracted him to the theater as a child.

Normally, it wouldn't have been important if Roach and Laurel disagreed over a story idea. It was generally accepted, thanks to Roach's generosity, that Stan would have the final say over the stories that he and Babe would make. However, it was one thing to disagree over an inexpensive two-reeler, but quite another to haggle over a big feature — especially when the boss had written the story.

Before Stan and Roach could resolve their differences, outside forces threatened to put an end to Roach's most ambitious film — and to the Laurel and Hardy team as well. *The Hollywood Reporter* of February 12, 1934 noted:

ALIMONY HEADACHE CHASES LAUREL AWAY

Hal Roach has the biggest headache in town today, with Stan Laurel definitely making plans to leave the country the end of the month, due to alimony trouble, and splitting the comedy team of Laurel and Hardy, which has been a big box-office winner for the producer for some time.

Laurel has offers to make personal appearances in London and other European cities, which he plans to accept. Roach, it is reported, will try to build up a new comedy team with Babe Hardy and Patsy Kelly.

Stan's plan to leave for England was actually just a ploy to keep his ex-wife, Lois, and her lawyers at bay. She had been awarded a divorce the preceding October, and Stan's lawyer, Ben Shipman, felt that her attorneys might attempt to tap his salary to get her settlement and their legal fees.

Roach stopped all work on the *Toyland* script in late February, reluctantly deciding to shelve the picture until Stan's tangled finances could be sorted out.

Laurel and Hardy were away from the cameras from February through May 1934. During this cessation, Stan's private affairs were put in order, so he didn't have to flee to England. Instead, he went to Mexico — where he got married again.

The new Mrs. Laurel was 29-year-old Virginia Ruth Rogers. Since Stan's divorce from Lois wouldn't be final until October 1934, his Mexican marriage to Ruth on April 2 was not legal in California. Stan told reporters there would be no legal complications, because he and Ruth would not live together until his divorce from Lois was final.

The newspapers gave a lot of publicity to what they termed Stan's "halfway marriage." Hal Roach was not happy about the headlines. He felt they jeopardized his image as a producer of wholesome family films.

Meanwhile, Babe Hardy's private life was a shambles. His marriage to Myrtle Lee Reeves Hardy, which had gone through numerous ruptures and reconciliations, was rapidly deteriorating. Myrtle's drinking had increased alarmingly, and by early 1934 Babe had placed her in the Rosemead Lodge Sanitarium.

Privately, Babe wished he could be free of Myrtle and the constant stress she induced. He spent a lot of time with a lady named Viola Morse, and felt much more comfortable in her company. But paradoxically, his sense of loyalty kept him from divorcing Myrtle. When there was a break in filming — such as the one that held up *Babes in Toyland* — Babe was usually at the racetrack, or at the Lakeside Country Club, where he could at least try to relax by playing his beloved golf.

The team didn't get back to the studio until mid-May, by which time Roach had left for a month's vacation in Alaska. The *Babes in Toyland* script was left to gather dust on the shelf, and no one was sure when — or if — it would go before the cameras.

GOING BYE-BYE!

Production history: Script written circa May 15-20, 1934. FIlmed circa May 21-26. Copyrighted June 20, 1934 by MGM (LP 4785). Released June 23. Two reels.

Produced by Hal Roach. Directed by Charles Rogers. Photographed by Francis Corby. Edited by Bert Jordan. Sound by Harry Baker.

With Walter Long, Mae Busch, Harry Dunkinson, Sam Lufkin.

Laurel and Hardy's courtroom testimony helps convict a notorious criminal, Butch (Walter) Long — who vows that he'll soon break out of prison and get revenge. Stan and Ollie decide to leave town, and place an ad for a third party to share expenses. A personable young lady responds, and asks if her boyfriend — who has somehow gotten locked in a trunk — can accompany them. Her beau, natch, is Long, who's already escaped from the slammer. When Stan and Ollie free him from the trunk, Long recognizes them, and exacts his revenge.

After the lengthy delays caused by the on again-off again *Babes in Toyland*, Stan and Babe needed to finish the final two shorts on the 1933-34 program quickly.

In mid-May, Charley Rogers and Frank Terry huddled with Stan and came up with a story based on the then-current John Dillinger manhunt. They called it *Public Enemies*; the script was reportedly retitled *On Their Way Out* before it was finally christened *Going Bye-Bye!*

By any title it was a fairly complex story, despite the brief time Stan and his cohorts spent writing it. Accordingly, the differences between script and film are minor. An example: the scripted version of the courtroom scene has Stan defying the bloodthirsty Walter Long with, "You buttered your bread, now lay on it!"

BEL-AIR PRISON

HAL ROACH, WARDEN

Record of: OLIVER HARDY

(Address)

RIGHT THUMB PRINT

LEFT THUMB PRINT

Date of arrest April 24, 1934
Charge Golf addict
Disposition of case Solitary confinement
Residence
Place of birth Russia
Nationality Asiatic
Criminal specialty Carrying concealed golf balls.
Age   Build Stocky
Height   Comp. Fair   Hair Dark
Weight 220   Eyes Brown
Scars and marks
Two toenails missing from left foot
Tattoo picture of 'Madame Kelly'
of Front Street, Colon, Panama
on left shoulder. A tough egg.

CRIMINAL HISTORY

Just before the filming of *Going Bye-Bye*, Roach gave a party and took mug shots of the guests.

Both script and film have a lengthy scene in which Stan and Ollie pack their belongings and receive a telephone call from Long's girlfriend, Mae. Stan absently hands Ollie a can of condensed milk instead of the receiver; at this point, the script has Ollie saying, "Excuse me, I'll be with you as soon as I get a towel. My ear's full of milk." But on film, Ollie has magically transformed this into one of the great Laurel and Hardy lines of all time — "Excuse me, please — my ear is full of milk." Such small modifications make all the difference in comedy. Hardy's version flows much more smoothly — as does the milk.

At this point, the script suggests that Ollie wipe his face with a cloth given to him by Stan; unfortunately, Stan doesn't realize Ollie has used it to polish his shoes. And Stan was originally supposed to hold the opened can of milk upside down, so that it pours all over Ollie's newly-cleaned shoes as he speaks to Mae.

Most of the variances in the script come while the boys are trying to extricate Butch from the trunk. The script suggests an elaborate scene in which Stan and Ollie have to carry the trunk downstairs (it tumbles over Ollie, naturally) and across town to a newstand run by Long's buddy, Jerry. In the tumble downstairs, Long's feet have smashed through the bottom of the trunk. Thus, as Stan and Ollie carry the trunk, it seems to be walking itself across the street.

As they arrive at Jerry's newsstand, newsboys are screaming about Butch Long's escape. Some suspicious cops drive up and wonder just whose legs are jutting out of that trunk. Mae takes it on the lam, and so does the trunk. But Ollie tackles it and explains that a friend of theirs is locked inside. The cop shoots the lock off, Long is discovered, and the script suggests "we go for a wow finish and fade out." The gag men never bothered to write those wow finishes.

And the script says nothing about Long's means of revenge — breaking off Stan and Ollie's legs and tying them around their necks. It's uncertain just who dreamed up such a bizarre gag, but my money's on Stan; he had a fondness for these freak-ending gags, and they would continue to show up in subsequent films.

This film marked Charley Rogers' first solo directing credit. The team's previous director, Lloyd French, had had his contract terminated in April, and had gone to New York to make comedies for Vitaphone. Now that Rogers was seated in the canvas chair, it was virtually certain that Stan's "suggestions" on the shooting of a given scene would show up in the completed film.

THEM THAR HILLS

Production history: Script written late May-early June 1934. Filmed June 11-20. Copyrighted July 18, 1934 by MGM (LP 4849). Released July 21. Two reels.

Produced by Hal Roach. Directed by Charles Rogers. Photographed by Art Lloyd. Edited by Bert Jordan. Sound by James Greene.

With Mae Busch, Charlie Hall, Billy Gilbert.

Ollie has the gout, and is ordered by his doctor to take a trip into the mountains and drink plenty of water. The boys rent a trailer and park next to a charming old well. Unbeknownst to them, a retreating gang of bootleggers has just dumped their product in it. The boys are visited by Mr. and Mrs. Hall, who need to borrow some gasoline. Mr. Hall goes to fill his car with gas, and returns to find the boys — and his wife — gloriously inebriated. He is not amused, and another reciprocal-destruction skirmish ensues.

One doesn't find L&H comedies much better than *Them Thar Hills*. It's a well-nigh perfect little film, with enough story to avoid unnecessary padding, yet enough room for the team to do several routines independent of the plot's demands. While the basic story was filmed as written, most of the film's best scenes were the result of on-the-set improvisation.

An examination of the script shows how Stan and Babe could wring humor out of unlikely sources. When the boys decide to have lunch, the script suggests the following dialogue:

OLLIE: How about a nice plate of beans, health bread and a pot of
               coffee?
STAN: That's swell.

There's nothing terribly funny about this bit, nor does there seem to be much potential for anything humorous to develop from it. But the boys' ad-libbing turns this into one of the most memorable exchanges in the film:

OLLIE: How about a plate of beans and a pot of steaming hot coffee?
STAN: Swell. You sure know how to plan a meal!

Likewise, most of the sublime sequence where Laurel and Hardy prevent each other from preparing lunch was ad-libbed. The script simply proposes that Ollie slice bread, make the coffee and open the can of beans while Stan busies himself with woodchopping. In the film, they turn this into a graceful

little ballet of maladroitness: Stan butters the edge of the loaf of bread, *then* cuts off a slice. Ollie asks him for a can opener, and Stan hands him an egg-beater. Stan moves some cans around on the counter, so that when Ollie intends to slice open the can of beans, he ruins a decorative coffee container instead.

All of this is punctuated with Ollie lustily humming "The Old Spinning Wheel," while Stan adds a countermelody at the end of each phrase: "Pum pum!" Stan's musical improvisations grow jazzier until Ollie smacks him on the head and intones, "*I'm* singing this song!" The script all but dismisses this extended sequence: "They go into the singing routine, with interruptions."

Conversely, the script suggests a few bits which aren't in the film. One gag has Stan unable to work the mechanism that draws the bucket from the well. Ollie takes charge, but the boys' combined ineptitude dampens Mr. Hardy's person and his ego.

Another scripted but unfilmed gag: After Stan has lit the wood stove, he blows out the match; Ollie, who has just bent over, is in close proximity. Stan's alcoholic breath causes a huge flame to shoot out from the match, starting a conflagration on the Hardy posterior.

Most of the gags in the final tit-for-tat battle were left up to Stan and Babe's improvisational abilities, though the gag with Hall being sprayed by a bellows filled with coffee, and the one where he's tarred and feathered with molasses and an old pillow, are present in the script. One unfilmed gag had Hall setting the motor of Laurel and Hardy's car on fire; the boys kick a hole in the radiator of Hall's car, water sprays out, and the fire stops.

When filming began on June 11, Stan and Babe were joined by their old cohort Billy Gilbert, who played the doctor; Gilbert's contract with Roach had been terminated the previous March, but he came back on a one-picture deal. Someone who probably wasn't on the set much was Hal Roach, who returned on June 4 from a month-long hunting trip in Alaska, and left a week later for meetings with MGM executives in New York and Chicago.

Them Thar Hills was supposed to be shot in six days, but it dragged all the way out to nine. The company (including new assistant director Don Sandstrom, who usually served as head prop man) was shooting on location in Santa Ynez Canyon; everything was going fine until heavy fog rolled in and they could hardly see anything, much less put it on film. So the whole company climbed in their vehicles, crawled down the canyon roads, returned to the studio and duplicated the entire outdoor location on a sound stage.

BABES IN TOYLAND

Production history: Original story written by Hal Roach, December 1933. Sets and stop-action sequences prepared, January 1934. Shooting scheduled to start February 15. Production suspended February 26; no filming (except screen tests). New story and screenplay, June 1934; final script completed July 28. Filmed August 6-August 16, September 24-October 17. Edited during late October; previewed November 9. Copyrighted November 28, 1934 by MGM (LP 5161). Released November 30. 79 minutes.

Produced by Hal Roach. Directed by Charles Rogers and Gus Meins. Photographed by Art Lloyd and Francis Corby. Edited by William Terhune and

Alice Moore, Charley Rogers, gag man Frank Terry and Henry Brandon play cards, while Charlotte Henry and Felix Knight look on.

Bert Jordan. Screenplay by Nick Grinde and Frank Butler. Adapted from the musical comedy by Victor Herbert and Glen MacDonough. Sound by Elmer Raguse. Music direction by Harry Jackson.

With Charlotte Henry, Felix Knight, Henry Brandon, Florence Roberts, William Burress.

Ollie Dee and Stannie Dum, employees at Toyland's toy factory, try to thwart the plans of evil Silas Barnaby, who holds a mortgage against the giant shoe in which the boys live with Mother Peep. Barnaby threatens to evict the old widow unless she can pay up — or unless her lovely daughter, Little Bo-Peep, agrees to marry him. When Dee and Dum trick Barnaby out of the mortgage and his potential bride, the old curmudgeon attempts to destroy Toyland with his army of Bogeymen. But the boys activate their own army — a squadron of six-foot-tall wooden soldiers — and all ends happily.

After being suspended since late February 1934, *Babes in Toyland* was finally resuscitated in late June. The Roach-Laurel impasse over the story was resolved; Frank Butler, the head of the scenario department, hired writer Nick Grinde to work with director Ray McCarey on a new screenplay.

Stan and Babe's roles were changed to Ollie Dee and Stannie Dum. They threw out Alan and the villainous spider and relegated Little Miss Muffet to a bit part. The idea of using all the stars on the lot also went out the window.

With director Gus Meins, Henry Brandon, Florence Roberts and Charlotte Henry.

While the script was being rewritten, Hal Roach was away in New York discussing next season's product with MGM executives. When he returned, he signed a young singer named Felix Knight for the leading man's role of Tom-Tom the Piper's Son. Roach also signed Henry Kleinbach — now known as Henry Brandon — to play the new villain, Silas Barnaby.

"I was playing the villain in a melodrama called *The Drunkard* at the Theater Mart in Los Angeles," recalled Brandon. "We were the first show where you could have a glass of beer and hiss and boo and cheer and make a fool of yourself. Everybody in Hollywood went. We'd peek through the hole in the curtain and say, 'My God, Cecil B. De Mille's out front!' That became a running gag. But one night somebody said, 'Hal Roach is out front!' And sure enough, he was.

"Mr. Roach called the next day, and asked me to come see him. Now, I played an old man in the play, and I was 21 years old. I walked into his office, and I'll never forget the look on his face. He said, 'You're not the old son of a bitch I saw in the play last night?!' I said, 'Yes I am, Mr. Roach.' He said, 'How are we gonna make you up to look like an old man?'

"He hired and fired about three make-up men," said Brandon. "Finally, he found a wonderful old guy who had been head of make-up at Paramount, Jim Collins. Jim used all sorts of primitive methods, but he turned my young face into an old face.

"Mr. Roach liked what I was doing in *The Drunkard*, and he wanted that same kind of overacting. This was for kids, and it had to be larger than life.

Several of the old character men told me they were mad because Roach gave the part to a young man. I didn't have the courage to tell them that the part would have killed them — because they ran me ragged! An old man couldn't have played it!"

Shortly after Henry Brandon was signed, Charlotte Henry was borrowed from Paramount to play Bo-Peep. Roach then hired hundreds of extra carpenters and painters who worked around the clock for weeks to build the mythical city of Toyland on two sound stages. They built the Old Woman's Shoe, the Toymaker's Factory, three houses for the Three Little Pigs and evil Barnaby's underground lair. The sets were in bright colors, like illustrations in children's books. Stan Laurel later voiced his regrets that the film wasn't made in color.

Trade papers made a big fuss over the film, reporting that Roach was "ready to shoot the works on this one." John Swallow, an NBC radio executive, and Harry Jackson were signed to oversee the scoring of the film, while director Ray McCarey began discussions with the actors. This preparation was far more painstaking than usual — but *Babes in Toyland* was intended to be more than the usual L&H film.

Unfortunately, there were continued disagreements between Roach and Stan over the story. This disharmony was compounded by Ray McCarey's attempts to write Laurel and Hardy material.

"Suddenly one day, Ray was off the picture," stated Henry Brandon. "He was in Roach's office, and Stan was there. Ray was explaining a scene, and he had his hand up in the air. Then he noticed the door was open; Charley Rogers had walked in. Rogers was standing behind Ray and holding his nose, going, 'Nyeeehhhh...' So Ray's hand just described an arc and hit Rogers in the face. Roach wasn't watching — he had his head down, he was thinking — and he said, 'What's going on here?' Nobody said a thing."

The next day, McCarey was notified that he would no longer be the sole director. When he learned Charley Rogers would now be doing all of the comedy scenes, McCarey lost his temper and walked out. He told Henry Brandon, "If I weren't a crazy Irishman, I could've just held out and they would've had to pay me off. I lost $12,000 by walking out!"

McCarey, whose first feature directing assignment this was, "wanted the story framed to suit him," according to the studio — which replaced him with Gus Meins. McCarey promptly went to Columbia, where he promptly directed the Three Stooges short *Men in Black* — which was promptly nominated for an Academy Award.

With Gus Meins now set to handle all the scenes which didn't involve Laurel and Hardy, and Charley Rogers set to direct all scenes which did, *Babes in Toyland* finally got started on August 6, 1934. It was shot simultaneously by the two units.

Roach was footing a tremendous bill for the film, although by now his original story was only a memory. But all the arguing over the story really didn't matter anyway, because the boys were back to their old habit of throwing away the script as soon as they got on the set.

"It was a beautiful script!" remembered Brandon. "It was really a fairy tale. But they did it their way, and who's to say they were wrong? It's a beautiful movie!

"I had never worked with comedians before. My first day I was pretty

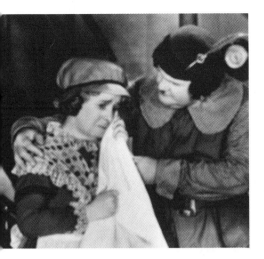

The first Mother Peep was Margaret Seddon; after Stan's recovery, Florence Roberts played the part.

scared; we had a very long scene to do, about eight pages. They all sat down, and there was quite an entourage — mostly Stan's. Babe had no entourage at all, but Stannie had a lot of friends, a lot of co-workers and seconds and gofers, and they sat around and told jokes for about half an hour. Then they said, 'All right, let's look at the script.' So they got out the script, which was very well written — and they said, 'Well, let's throw that out, let's throw this out.'

"Then, Stan turned to Babe and the other actors and said, 'Now you say that, and Henry, you say that, and then I'll do that, and Babe'll do that, and you'll do that...' That went on for about 10 minutes, and then Stannie got up and said, 'All right, let's shoot it!'

"Then," recalled Brandon, "I made the mistake that I will never make again in my life. I said, 'Aren't we going to rehearse?' And Stannie turned to me and said, 'Do you want to *spoil* it?'

"The only things they rehearsed were physical stunts. They never rehearsed the dialogue. They would sort of say what they were going to do, but they wouldn't get up and do it physically until the camera was rolling; they wanted to capture the magic of the first time."

After all the trouble of preparing *Babes in Toyland* — writing the script, testing actors, signing a director, devising special effects — then starting all over with new directors, massive sets and a new script which wasn't much adhered to, the film was finally in production. It was all smooth sailing from there on — for an entire week.

On August 14, Stan was shooting a scene with Babe and Henry Brandon. He was supposed to run in as the scene began. As Rogers yelled "Action!," Stan tripped and fell from a raised platform, and tore some ligaments in his right leg. He was rushed to Culver City Emergency Hospital, where his leg was put in a cast.

Meins and Rogers shot around Stan for a couple of days, filming scenes in which he wasn't needed. Then they decided to put the whole thing off, and try it again in two weeks. And then everyone else began having accidents.

Henry Brandon, who was still playing in "The Drunkard" at night, realized that he'd have two weeks to catch up on his sleep. He decided to celebrate. After the show that night he went with three pals to a Hollywood Boulevard bar called The Brass Rail, got drunk, and ended up in a fight with a group of waiters. One of the waiters hurled a sugar bowl across the room, and hit Brandon smack on the nose. The young actor was quickly escorted to Lincoln Heights jail, where he stayed for about a week, to the accompaniment of screaming headlines.

"The papers had pictures of me as the old villain in the play," noted Brandon. "The captions said, 'Everyone wanted to beat up on this old bastard, and finally last night they did.'" On the morning that Brandon returned to the studio, everybody came out of their offices and cheered him. Everybody, that is, except Hal Roach, who walked up and said, "Not funny. No more barroom brawls."

Laurel and Brandon were not the only casualties on *Babes in Toyland*. The day after Stan tore ligaments in his right leg, assistant director Gordon Douglas slid 15 feet from the top of the Old Woman's Shoe, and tore ligaments in his *left* leg. And Kewpie Morgan, a fat, jolly actor who played fat, jolly Old King Cole, had to laugh continuously for two whole days, until he ruptured his stomach muscles and had to be taken to the hospital. Babe Hardy entered St. Vincent's Hospital the day after the film wrapped and had his tonsils removed. Hal Roach might have been concerned about all this, but he was busy recovering from an appendicitis operation.

It was late September before everyone recovered. Despite all the pressure caused by delays, illnesses and other tribulations, Gus Meins directed his portion of the film with his usual air of serenity. Felix Knight remembered him as "a wonderful, fatherly kind of man, and very calm — very easy to work with. No temperament, no high pressure, and he always got what he wanted in the end, without any big fuss." Meins' easygoing attitude served him well when he directed many of Our Gang's best shorts.

When Meins was at the helm, his cast (which usually didn't include Laurel and Hardy) stuck completely to the script. But when Charley Rogers took the director's chair, it was every man for himself.

"Every man for himself" also describes the relationship between Stan and Hal Roach during the filming. Roach later said that while Laurel and Hardy were making *Babes in Toyland*, he "never paid a bloody bit of attention to what they did." But Felix Knight recalled, "He would come on the set almost every day. He had a lot of suggestions for the comedy part of it. He didn't interfere too much with the musical sequences, but I would see him huddling quite often with Stan and Ollie, and with Charley Rogers."

Henry Brandon was more explicit: "Roach and Laurel were arguing constantly through the making of it. Roach would tell Laurel his suggestions on the comedy scenes, then they'd go into Roach's office and yell at each other. It was a real battle of egos. But Laurel got to do things his way."

Aside from the Roach-Laurel friction, the production went pretty smoothly once it finally commenced, with Stan and Babe having as much fun as possible in the process. The set had a large "ducking pond," where Toyland troublemakers were immersed as punishment. Stan took every advantage to hurl an unsuspecting fellow actor into its depths.

"He never threw me in the pool," said Brandon, "because he knew it'd take an hour to get me back in shape with the make-up. But he did push a lot of people into the pool. There was enormous laughter all the time on the set. Comics need to be kept in that kind of mood. They were having a good time, and that transmitted itself to the screen."

Stan threw one too many actors into that ducking pond. A 19-year-old extra named John D. Wood sued Stan and his double, Ham Kinsey, for $40,500, claiming that his back was "seriously and permanently injured" after they gave him the old heave-ho. Stan settled with him out of court in June 1936.

Babes in Toyland shows none of the friction that marked its production. It isn't the funniest film L&H ever made, but it is the most charming. Its fairy-tale characters and elaborate storybook sets place Stan and Ollie, for once, in a setting that is as innocent and optimistic as they are.

The hackneyed stock-in-trade melodrama plot, which took the place of Hal Roach's original story, works well because it's easy for kids to understand. The film's climax — with Barnaby and his Bogeymen emerging from their subterranean lair to destroy Toyland — is just as spectacular as one could wish for, filled with vivid images of the hairy monsters swarming all over the place and stealing children from their beds.

The 6-foot-tall wooden soldiers activated by Stan and Ollie march smartly in precision through the miracle of stop-action animation. The actual soldiers used for this sequence were really one foot high, and made out of lead. Cinematographer Art Lloyd and special effects director Roy Seawright shot the scenes frame by frame on the Roach studio squash court.

Many reviewers thought the final scenes were too frightening for children. The original ending, however, was far more horrific. According to Henry Brandon, the filmmakers were going to have Laurel and Hardy put Barnaby in a cannon and shoot it off; the bits and pieces of his body were supposed to spell out "The End." Four different endings were ultimately shot. "They couldn't come up with one they thought would be conclusive," said Felix Knight, "and make the boys the heroes — and still be funny at the same time."

Babes in Toyland earned the team the best reviews of their career. In fact, it won unanimous raves. Andre Sennwald of the *New York Times* wrote, "Every youngster in New York ought to find a ticket for *Babes in Toyland* in his Christmas stocking." Even *Variety*, notorious for panning anything with the names Laurel and Hardy attached to it, had to admit, "Hal Roach...has succeeded in a measure beyond others who have sought to enter this realm. He has made a film of excellence for children.... It is a gorgeous fairy tale which gives everything to Laurel and Hardy and to which, in return, they give their happiest best."

The movie did excellent business in its initial release. While it is still shown on television and in theatrical revivals during the holidays, what today's audiences usually see is a reissue version called *March of the Wooden Soldiers*, which is nine minutes shorter than the original. Walt Disney remade the film in 1961, with Gene Sheldon and Henry Calvin in the L&H roles, but he couldn't top the hilarity and honest charm of the 1934 version.

Babes in Toyland was an almost miraculous accomplishment for a little studio like Roach's. Stan Laurel thought it had the fewest imperfections and the greatest entertainment value of all his films. Babe Hardy, who especially liked the films with "production," also counted it among his favorites.

Everybody liked *Babes in Toyland* — except Hal Roach. It was undeniably a success, but it had nothing to do with the film he had envisioned. Furthermore, Roach's pride in his original story, his disappointment over Laurel's rejection of it and the resulting battles for control had a permanent effect on the Roach-Laurel relationship.

In an interview for *Films in Review*, Roach made these comments about the film: "Because I wrote it, Laurel said, 'Oh, this is no good. It's not funny.' And we argued — and all the time they're getting paid! ...Anyway, I finally gave up; they went out and made a very bad picture, in my humble opinion... Laurel just couldn't take it that somebody else was writing the story... and Laurel in story construction was just impossible. His things were — hell, a 10-year-old kid could have written better."

In a February 1981 interview, Roach echoed those comments: "The film was a flop. It didn't even get the cost back. And I know the story that I had written would've gone very well, could've been one of the biggest pictures in the business... I knew that after *Babes in Toyland*, I was through making Laurel and Hardy pictures. At that time it got to the point where it was no longer any fun, or anything else to me."

From here on, Laurel's association with Roach became strictly business, riddled with ever-increasing disagreements over the next five years. As far as their relationship was concerned, *Babes in Toyland* cost a lot more than money.

THE LIVE GHOST

Production history: Script written late October-early November 1934. Filmed circa November 8-14. Released December 8. Copyrighted December 11, 1934 by MGM (LP 5220). Two reels.

Produced by Hal Roach. Directed by Charles Rogers. Photographed by Art Lloyd. Edited by Louis MacManus. Sound by Elmer Raguse.

With Walter Long, Arthur Housman, Mae Busch, Charlie Hall.

Stan and Ollie are persuaded to help shanghai some men for a burly captain's crew. Unfortunately, the boys themselves are shanghaied onto the ship. The craft is rumored to be populated by ghosts, but the incensed captain warns that if he ever hears the word "ghost," he'll turn the speaker's head so that "when he's walkin' north, he'll be lookin' south!" When their perpetually drunken bunkmate (Housman) — whom the boys think they've accidentally shot — turns up after having fallen in a trough of whitewash, L&H are sure they've seen a ghost, and the captain administers his unusual punishment.

Perhaps the best of the L&H horror-comedies, *The Live Ghost* underwent quite a transformation in its trip from paper to film. The written outline was even more morbid than the film: as the movie opens, the boys are fishing on the dock on their day off; in the script, they were there to commit suicide.

They stand at the edge of the dock. Stan is tying a large rock to the center of a piece of rope; with one end, he ties a slip knot around Ollie's neck. Ollie reacts and growls, "Not so tight! Do you want to kill me?" Stan picks up the rock and swings it back and forth, about to throw it in the water. As he counts, "One — two — ," Ollie stops him.

In a nautical mood at Catalina with wives Myrtle and Ruth.

OLLIE: Wait a minute! How can I be sure you're coming in with me?
STAN: Do I have to commit suicide too?
OLLIE: Of course you do! Wasn't that the agreement? I'd never rest in my watery grave if I knew you were running around without me to look after you!
STAN: *(Taking a look at the water)* Well then, couldn't we go someplace where it's not so deep?

Ollie gives him a dirty look, then ties the other end of the rope around Stan's neck. He picks up the rock and starts swinging it back and forth again, but this time Stan stops him. Ollie sets the rock down; Stan reaches out to shake his hand.

STAN: Goodbye, Ollie.
OLLIE: Goodbye, Stan...Whaddya mean, goodbye? We're not going to separate, are we?
STAN: Well, after we're drowned, we can't be sure we're going to the same place, and...I don't know where you're going.
OLLIE: Pick up that rock! Wait. We'll throw it in together. Close your eyes — it's just as well you don't look on this ghastly deed.

The would-be suicides close their eyes, reach down, and pick up the rock — only it's another rock that's been placed conveniently nearby. The captain enters, and watches as the boys throw the rock into the water. All three are drenched with a mighty splash. The captain convinces Stan and Ollie that instead of taking a trip to the great beyond, they should take a trip on his ship — along with a crew he'll pay them to recruit. Stan loosens the rope from his neck, and takes off his coat — revealing a life preserver around his waist.

The script is more notable for what it doesn't contain; as with the script for *Going Bye-Bye!*, there's no mention of the strange contortions which captain Walter Long inflicts upons his adversaries. And Mae Busch, who appears briefly in the film as a floozie, graces not a page of the script. One of the film's best lines appears to have been an ad-lib. When Stan and Ollie think they've shot whiskey-soaked Arthur Housman and are about to bury his "remains" at sea, Stan asks, "Do you think he's gone to heaven?" "I'm afraid not," Ollie replies, "probably the *other* place."

With Charley Rogers directing and Chet Brandenburg assisting, *The Live Ghost* was shot in one week. The trade paper *Boxoffice* reviewed the film when it was released on December 8, 1934, barely a month after shooting began. "Laurel and Hardy fans, and they are legion, will find plenty of good old-fashioned slapstick in this Hal Roach film. The laughs come fast and often during the scenes aboard a haunted ship...A-1 comedy."

Unfortunately, thanks to the double-feature policy implemented by many theaters, short subjects themselves were becoming old-fashioned.

TIT FOR TAT

Production history: Script written early December 1934. Filmed December 10-20, 1934. Released January 5, 1935. Copyrighted January 29, 1935 by MGM (LP 5304). Two reels.

Produced by Hal Roach. Directed by Charles Rogers. Photographed by Art Lloyd. Edited by Bert Jordan. Sound by William Randall.

With Charlie Hall, Mae Busch, James C. Morton, Bobby Dunn.

Stan and Ollie open their new electrical supply store, and almost immediately run into trouble with their next-door neighbor, grocery store owner Hall. The boys recall their run-in with him during a trip to the mountains, and offer to let bygones be bygones. But the memory of indignities past is too strong for Charlie, and he wants each party to mind his own business. When Hall accuses Ollie of a "clandestine meeting" with his wife, the neighbors heap mutual embarrassments upon each other for the rest of the afternoon.

If ever there was a film where Laurel and Hardy threw away the script and just shot off the cuff, *Tit For Tat* is it. Stan Laurel and many of his co-workers often remarked that when the team got on the set, the props would suggest better gags than the ones they'd planned. *Tit For Tat* is a film just loaded with such props.

The script is primarily a succession of mechanical, violent gags, which don't seem particularly suited to Laurel and Hardy's personalities. There's not much motivation for the battle, either, which starts when Stan's electric fan sprays Mr. Hall with the rubbish he's just swept up from in front of his store. The idea of this film being a sequel to *Them Thar Hills*, explicitly stated in the

Spanky McFarland visits the set.

film's dialogue, is only suggested in the written outline: "A retrospect shot may be used here, showing that Babe and Stan seem to recall Hall's voice and then remember having had trouble with him on their trailer trip."

Here's a sample of some of the gags which exist only in the script: Ollie is atop a ladder, putting light bulbs in an electric sign; the ladder is resting on a sidewalk elevator. Stan, in the cellar of the boys' store, presses the elevator button, which causes the ladder to lose its balance, and sends Babe crashing through the awning over the entrance to Hall's grocery store. Mr. Hall, unfortunately, has been directly underneath the awning, setting out a case of marshmallows. As Ollie gets up, Charlie's head emerges through a tear in the awning; a marshmallow is lodged in each of his eyes. Stan tries to remove them, but they just stretch out elastically and snap back.

Mr. Hall does a little snapping back of his own when Stan and Ollie are demonstrating an electric range to a lady customer. While their backs are turned, Hall throws some limburger cheese into the range's oven and turns on the heat, before slinking away. The woman takes a whiff, and exits in a huff.

A great deal of none-too-inventive slapstick follows, with the boys applying a curling iron to Hall's tongue; Mae putting a light bulb in Stan's trousers and kicking him in the fanny; Hall balancing a basket of eggs over his front door and ending up the victim of his own gag; Stan and Ollie using pepper and an electric fan to give the Halls an uncontrollable sneezing fit; Stan giving Charlie a reverse Mohawk haircut by running some electric clippers down the center of his head — and on and on.

The script proposes that this should all end with the Halls pelting Stan and Ollie with eggs, while the boys shield themselves with a washing machine and throw light bulbs at the Halls. The boys start to argue, and the washing machine rolls away. Stan runs into the store and brings out an electric steambath cabinet. Says the script, "Babe and Stan both try to get inside it for protection, but Babe's head gets stuck outside through the hole in the top. He gets socked with plenty of eggs. Finally a couple of cocoanuts bounce against his head, and we fade out."

What a sorry mess this script is. No motivation, no resolution, no characteristic L&H material, nothing. Doubtless Stan and Babe realized this, because when they got on the set they ignored the script and, as if by instinct, ad-libbed until they had a comedy that was a model of first-class construction.

First, they established the adversarial relationship between Laurel and Hardy and Charlie Hall by making a specific reference to *Them Thar Hills*. (Actually, it's Mae who recalls the skirmish in the earlier film by humming a bit of "The Old Spinning Wheel," which brings a "Pum pum" from Stan.)

Next, they provided a specific reason for the current contretemps by having Hall accuse Ollie of romancing his wife. Through a Laurel-caused accident, Mr. Hardy is propelled onto the Halls' second story window ledge; he comes downstairs through the courtesy of Mrs. Hall, and as the two giggle, Ollie exclaims, "I've never been in a position like that before!" (One wonders how that line got past the censor — it's quite a daring double-entendre for an L&H film.)

The individual gags which the boys ad-libbed on the set are much more graceful and characteristic than those in the script; they emphasize injury to one's dignity rather than one's person.

Tit For Tat has a distinctive appearance, a more streamlined and stylish look. Much of this is due to the unusual set, a rare instance for Laurel and Hardy of an "outdoor" location being reproduced indoors on the sound stage. As an economy move, location shooting was being done less frequently at the Roach studio; all of the series were becoming increasingly sound-stage bound.

A reviewer for *Box Office* didn't think much of the film. "A good deal of obvious slapstick and just a thread of a story turns this into only moderate comedy," wrote the critic. However, the Academy of Motion Picture Arts and Sciences disagreed, and in January 1936 nominated the film for the Best Short Subject-Comedy award. When the awards were given out in March, *Tit For Tat* placed second, losing to Robert Benchley's *How to Sleep*.

Hal Roach was busy making the transition to feature film production. He signed Sam Taylor to supervise and direct three musical comedies. And he promised a series of "two yearly Laurel and Hardy full-length comedies," but nothing was said about the continuance of the short subjects.

The days of the great L&H two-reelers were nearly over, and not even an Oscar could have saved them.

At the Academy Awards in March 1936: Babe, Myrtle, unknown, Gus Meins, James Parrott and his wife Ruby.

A December 1934 hunting trip, with Douglas Dumbrille and Guy Kibbee.

THE FIXER-UPPERS

Production history: Script written early January 1935. Filmed circa January 11-19. Released February 9, 1935. Copyrighted February 26, 1935 by MGM (LP 5371). Two reels.

Produced by Hal Roach. Directed by Charles Rogers. Photographed by Art Lloyd. Edited by Bert Jordan. Sound by James Greene.

With Mae Busch, Charles Middleton, Arthur Housman, Noah Young.

Door-to-door Christmas-card salesmen L&H come upon a woman who is distraught because her artist-husband, Pierre Gustave, neglects her. When Stan tells of a similar case in which a third party was hired to make the husband jealous and realize his neglect, Mrs. Gustave offers Ollie $50 if he'll provide this service. Unfortunately, the plan works too well, and Pierre orders Ollie to return at midnight for a duel to the death. The duel isn't fatal, but when the artist vows to cut up Ollie's body in little pieces, the boys scamper away.

A reworking of 1927's *Slipping Wives*, this is a fairly pedestrian little picture. It's notable for its locale, which may or may not be Paris. The sets and costumes have a Gallic look, yet other aspects of the film are decidedly American. (One of the Christmas card verses Ollie recites refers to the Civil War.)

The pacing of the film is a bit slow, but there are a number of amusing bits. The dialogue is quite entertaining too; in another "Tell me that again" bit, Stan gives a garbled recounting of a romantic triangle. And he utters a priceless line when the boys call the artist to tell him they're not showing up for the duel: "If you had a face like mine, you'd punch me right in the nose — and I'm just the fella that can do it!"

Mae Busch offers another sympathetic portrayal (echoing those in *Them Thar Hills* and *Tit for Tat*), although she does kick Stan in the backside when his suggested "romantic triangle" plan backfires. And the histrionics of Charles Middleton — making his first appearance with the team in over two years — do much to enliven the proceedings. Noah Young, who had been a perennial nemesis in the boys' earliest silents, has a brief bit as a bartender; his thick, vaguely-accented speech provides a clue as to why he wasn't used as extensively in the talkies.

During the filming, a fire broke out in one of the studio's cutting rooms, destroying that room, various editing equipment, and a small amount of footage. The loss totaled about $10,000; fortunately, the three editors on duty escaped without injury.

Although this film was the second entry in the team's 1935 series, trade papers noted that the "total number they will make is not definitely set." As events happened, this picture came close to being Laurel and Hardy's last.

BONNIE SCOTLAND

Production history: Initial script written late January 1935. Rewritten, April 4-May 1. Filmed May 1-June 15. Previewed July 21, July 27; retakes shot late July. Copyrighted August 20, 1935 by MGM (LP 5753). Released August 23. 80 minutes.

Produced by Hal Roach. Directed by James Wesley Horne. Photographed by Art Lloyd, Walter Lundin. Edited by Bert Jordan. Screenplay by Frank Butler and Jeff Moffitt. Sound by Elmer R. Raguse.

With June Lang, William Janney, Anne Grey, James Finlayson, David Torrence, Daphne Pollard.

Escaped convicts McLaurel and Hardy go to Scotland to claim an inheritance. The hapless pair are soon without money or lodging, and Ollie is without pants. When the boys try to accept a tailor shop's offer of a free suit, they unwittingly end up in the army. Their regiment is sent to India. Alan Douglas, a clerk, quits his job and joins the regiment, to be near his sweetheart, Lorna McLaurel. Stan and Ollie foil the evil plans of Khan Mir Jutra, whose dreams of conquering the Scottish fort vanish as the boys accidentally upset several beehives and send the natives into a frenzy.

The original story for this film, *Kilts*, was written by Roach scenario department head Frank Butler. When Jefferson Moffitt joined the project, the Indian locale entered the story, which was re-christened *Laurel and Hardy of India* (or *In India*). Butler was loaned to Goldwyn in early March 1935 to work on scripts for Eddie Cantor; his story became re-re-christened *McLaurel and McHardy*.

By March 16, it looked as though the picture wasn't going to be made under any title. Reported *Variety*:

> Claiming he was fired, Stan Laurel left the Hal Roach employ yesterday, thus splitting the team of Laurel and Hardy... Studio and actor disagree on statements as to the cause of the splitting. Roach official explanation is that the inability to get together with Laurel on stories was the reason for the contract cancellation.
>
> According to Laurel, he was called into Henry Ginsberg's office yesterday and notified that his contract was terminated as of yesterday, although having until May 7 to run...
>
> Back of the trouble between the actor and the studio is said to be a refusal of Laurel to sign a new long-term contract with the company under the terms suggested by the studio...
>
> Studio intention, it was announced, is to replace the Laurel and Hardy comedies with a new series called *The Hardy Family*, in which Hardy, Patsy Kelly and Spanky McFarland will be featured.

Stan told the press that the rescinding of his contract was a complete surprise. "We were working on the story, and although there had been difficulties, these were all ironed out and settled. I was amazed when I was notified the picture had been called off and my contract terminated."

Babe was mystified, too. A *Los Angeles Times* reporter caught up with him on the Del Monte golf course, where he declared, "We've not broken up. We're the best of friends. [Stan] and I have been together longer than seven years and our team must not be broken up... I think the difficulty is between him and the studio. His contract expires in May and mine in November."

Asked about this episode in 1981, Hal Roach was certain that money was

The distinguished Angus Ian McLaurel.

not the issue: "There never was any time that either Laurel or Hardy ever said, "We're getting underpaid," or that the financial thing was wrong. So, that I guarantee. And if Laurel walked out, it seems impossible that I wouldn't remember it. I forget what the fight was with Laurel, but a contract was not up. Laurel's big problems were family problems that had nothing to do with the studio; the only thing that Laurel and I had arguments about was the construction of the story."

In any event, the Roach studio maintained that the new *Hardy Family* shorts would start production on March 25, beginning with *Their Night Out* under James Horne's direction. This was certainly just a studio ploy to get Stan to come to terms; Roach had used the same device during the *Babes in Toyland* hiatus. Furthermore, by making such a series, Roach would have been eviscerating two others by removing Spanky McFarland from *Our Gang* and separating Patsy Kelly from partner Thelma Todd.

Claude Bostock, Stan's longtime friend and sometime manager, came from New York to discuss the problem with Hal Roach and Henry Ginsberg. *The Hollywood Reporter* noted, "Both Laurel and Hardy are anxious to preserve their professional combination. Should the studio refuse to restore the team, Bostock will discuss a settlement of Laurel's current contract.... Laurel maintains he was fired without his contractual 60 days notice, on pretext of insubordination, but that the real difficulty was his failure to agree with the studio on terms of renewing his contract."

Stan and Babe made a rare appearance together at the Ambassador Hotel's Cocoanut Grove on the evening of March 27. They strolled in, arm in arm, to the surprise of fans and fellow actors. "Resplendent in dinner jackets and broad grins, they denied by their appearance together that there had been a rift," noted *Variety*.

The *Hardy Family* series was "postponed" for a month or so while Bostock began negotiations. After all, Roach needed Laurel and Hardy to spearhead his move into feature-film production. On April 8, all was settled. Stan signed an agreement "for one short and one feature, then one year — six four-reel pictures."

Commencing with the four-reelers, Stan would be paid in four installments per picture, the fourth installment payable upon satisfactory preview and "completion" — meaning that Roach would have to be happy with the film. In fact, Stan's new contract stipulated that Laurel's services would be "under personal supervision of Hal E. Roach, President." This confirmed in writing what had always been their working relationship; with Laurel's marital and financial problems possibly jeopardizing the studio's future, Roach felt he had to formalize the understanding.

With that all settled, Stan settled down with Charley Rogers, Jeff Moffitt, James Horne, and a couple of new Roach staffers to polish the script. The newcomers were Wilson Collison and Albert Austin; the latter had appeared in Chaplin's Mutual comedies. (He's the poor fellow who stands dumbfounded as Charlie destroys his alarm clock in *The Pawnshop*.) Their script contained a lot of material which should have remained in the movie.

One lengthy sequence had some crusty old Scottish soldiers convincing Ollie that mirages exist. Taking the boys to an imaginary race track, the soldiers run an imaginary race with imaginary horses, but not before Stan and Ollie make a bet with real money. Stan wants to bet on the same horse as Ollie, because "There's no use tiring out *two* horses." As the race progresses, Stan follows the action, craning his neck from left to right. Ollie shoves him and yells, "They're going the *other* way!"

One imaginative scripted scene has the boys encountering a Hindu magician, who makes a rope uncoil by itself and stretch up into the sky. The magician's boy assistant scrambles up the rope and disappears into some unknown plane of existence. Stan is unimpressed, but Ollie is determined to show him that disappearing is easily done if one believes in mirages. With Stan's help he also climbs up the rope and vanishes. The magician casually packs up his rope and strolls away.

Stan warns Ollie, "Don't come down the rope, because it isn't there." Ollie scoffs, "Of course it's there! You just can't see it!" He proves this by coming down — but a little faster than expected. Stan pulls Ollie out of the massive hole in the ground he has just created. The magician's assistant also crawls out of the hole, gives Ollie a dirty look and asks, "What did you do *that* for?"

One of the film's best scenes has the boys picking up litter while the regiment's band rehearses; gradually, the infectious rhythm sends the boys into a charming dance routine. In the script, the scene has a more elaborate finish, with soldiers, horses and everyone in the fort joining in a Highland fling. When Sergeant Finlayson orders a halt to the dancing, everyone stops in whatever position they happen to be in. Stan is frozen two feet off the ground, in the midst of a high kick. He explains that it's another mirage — and Finlayson stalks off.

The wrap-up chase at Mir Jutra's palace was different in the script, with Stan and Ollie unleashing a herd of goats and keeping the Indian natives busy until the Scot soldiers capture the palace. Roy Seawright's cartoon bees were evidently considered funnier — and less expensive — than the goats.

The film just fades out at this point, without bothering to wrap up the romantic subplot. In the script, Alan is promoted to Lieutenant — and he wins Lorna's hand. Stan and Ollie are commended for their valor, and given their discharge from the army.

Before they can return to the States, the boys are confronted by a mysterious character in a dark suit and derby hat, a detective who has been after Laurel and Hardy ever since they escaped from jail. (The role was intended for Fred Kelsey, the ultimate hammy detective type.) The script proposes a final gag where Stan, Ollie and the detective are trudging through the vast Indian desert; a camel train strides up beside them, and Stan tries to thumb a ride, to no avail.

As the script neared completion on April 19, James Finlayson returned to Los Angeles from Britain, where'd been appearing in films and plays for the past two years. June Lang was borrowed from Fox to play opposite Barry Norton, the juvenile lead. One day after shooting began, Norton was replaced by 26-year-old actor William Janney.

"The poor guy was very conscientious," said Janney. "Norton studied the whole script real hard, learned it word for word. And he didn't know how Laurel and Hardy worked — they made it up as they went along! Well, Norton could never unlearn those old lines, you see.

"Usually, a director wants you to come on the set already knowing your lines. But in this instance, it was different — the boys thought the gags up right then and there, and the dialogue was secondary. I think the shooting took six weeks; they threw out the first couple of days' work and started over again when I came on."

Lunch on location, with Ruth Laurel and William Janney.

Janney recalled one incident that happened during the location shooting of one of the film's best-remembered scenes. "We were shooting the marching sequence, where Stan's out of step, and he gets everybody else out of step. Well, I got so hot, because it was in the summertime, and the heat was pouring down. I was trying to be very gung-ho; the boys had fake guns made out of balsa wood, and I wouldn't use that. I insisted upon a heavy rifle!

"Babe was marching right in front of me, and when we broke for a little rest, his valet came over with a canteen for him. I said, 'Oh, boy — I'm so thirsty — could I have a drink?' Well, I was so hot, and I took a drink of this stuff and it almost took the top of my head off. Babe thought it was very funny, and it was — it was straight gin!

"Jimmy Finlayson was a wonderful person. Finlayson wisecracked a lot, and he would ham it up when we'd go out someplace. He'd turn and give people that look, you know, where he'd squint one eye. But he wasn't trying to show off; it was all done in a very nice way."

As Alan Douglas, Janney was called upon to do little but weep and sniffle. "I couldn't believe I was doing a Laurel and Hardy picture," he said. "I had three days at the start of shooting where I cried, all the time! My girl was leaving me, and I was crying to my boss, to let me go, and so on — ohhh, God!" Indeed, the script outlines at least six major scenes wherein Alan agonizes over Lorna.

The story problems that had formed at least part of the disagreement between Roach and Laurel were still plaguing the picture, even after its first

A clean-shaven James Finlayson visits the *Bonnie Scotland* company.

preview. "The trouble with the film was that it had two stories," said Janney. "When they had a preview of it in Glendale, why, I had the whole picture, and Laurel and Hardy were the comedy relief. And of course, you couldn't do that, because it was supposed to be a Laurel and Hardy picture." *The Hollywood Reporter* agreed in its review of the preview:

> There is a commanding position open on the screen for Laurel and Hardy features, for they are surely two of the funniest men alive. But they are absurdly wasted when the plot does not make them the central figures of their own starring comedy. In this instance, fully half of the footage is devoted to a sorry tale of love of a poor but honest lad for an heiress who, because his letters are being withheld from her, is about to marry another man... The story continually pops up to throw grand comedy for a loss.

After the preview, Roach and Laurel decided to cut out much of the plot footage. When *Thicker Than Water*, the team's next two-reeler, had been completed, Stan and Babe re-shot about 10 minutes' worth of material to cover for the deletions. The final product was not entirely satisfying, mainly because what "story" footage was left didn't seem to make much sense.

As Janney quite rightly exclaimed, "Stan cut so much out of it that when you'd see one scene, the scene before it was missing, so you'd wonder, 'What in the hell are they doing *that* for?' It would have been a much better picture if they had started out having Laurel and Hardy as the stars, and making my part a secondary part. I had many, many scenes in which they didn't appear at all, and most of those were cut out."

When the picture was released, 20 minutes shorter than its preview length, it garnered middling reviews. *Boxoffice* found it "packed with the Laurel and Hardy hokum and good for plenty of laughs," while *Variety* thought it was only "fair fun." *Movie Mirror*, a fan magazine, was the most perceptive: "This has marvelous gags but the picture doesn't quite come off because it is composed of two distinct plots which don't merge."

The picture was nevertheless very successful overseas. In Barcelona it did well, re-titled *Two Riflemen Without Bullets*; in Lisbon it broke box office records despite stormy weather, and in Mexico City it did record business at its premiere theater and at eight other houses.

Bonnie Scotland's schizophrenic plot only demonstrates how difficult it was to write a good feature-length story for L&H. The team had to carry most of the footage, but not all of the plot. They had to be on screen enough to satisfy their fans, but not so continuously that they wore out their welcome. The story had to be strong enough so that the film didn't disintegrate into a series of episodes.

It was a conflict that would cause future disagreements between Laurel and Roach, although their relationship would remain fairly stable for the next year or so. If *Babes in Toyland* marked the first major rift between star and producer, *Bonnie Scotland* signaled a distance between them that would mark their relationship from here on.

THICKER THAN WATER

Production history: Script written mid-June 1935. Filmed circa July 1-8. Copyrighted August 6, 1935 by MGM (LP 5709). Released circa August 6. Two reels.

Produced by Hal Roach. Directed by James W. Horne. Photographed by Art Lloyd. Edited by Ray Snyder.

With Daphne Pollard, James Finlayson, Charlie Hall, Bess Flowers.

After Ollie has an argument with the wife over a tardy furniture payment, Stan convinces him to draw out the family savings and buy the furniture. The boys are lured into an auction, where they end up squandering most of the Hardy fortune on a grandfather clock. They attempt to carry it home, only to have it smashed by a truck. Mrs. Hardy's resulting wrath sends Ollie to the hospital. Stan is enlisted as a transfusion donor, but the pair's blood gets mixed up; Stan inherits Ollie's look and mannerisms and vice versa.

Thanks to the economics of the movie industry, Laurel and Hardy were about to make their last starring two-reeler.

Stan was clearly unhappy about the demise of the short subjects. Roach was reluctant to scrap them, too, but had little choice in light of the diminishing market. He attempted a compromise; general manager Henry Ginsberg announced in late June that the team would make at least three 40-minute comedies, the first one to be called *The Honesty Racket*. But nothing came of the idea.

While Roach began planning more features, Stan and the writers knocked some story ideas around. Stan wrote an incomplete script wherein the boys decide to draw out Ollie's savings and bet the works on a horse named Molly-O. (Stan and Ollie continually refer to the horse's winning ways with the phrase, "Right on the nose." This provides some clue to the story's probable ending, which more than likely had Mrs. Molly Hardy inflicting injury to her hubby's proboscis.)

Stan's script had an opening sequence with the Hardys sharing breakfast with their boarder, Mr. Laurel; after an argument about family finances, Mrs. Hardy orders them to wash the dishes. This led into a routine where Stan keeps putting the clean dishes back into the pile of dirty ones, much to Ollie's exasperation. All of this was retained.

One gag which existed in the final script — but not in the film — had the boys carrying their bulky clock aboard a bus, which passes the homes of some Hollywood stars on the way to the boys' home. "There's the home of Miss Bennett," cries the bus driver. "Joan?" asks Stan. "No, Constance!" comes the reply. And when the driver exclaims that the next home belongs to Mr. Chaplin, Ollie asks, "Charlie?" The driver answers, "No — Sydney!"

With James Horne continuing as director, the picture got underway on July 1, bearing the working title of *Saturday Afternoon*. As usual, it appears to have been shot in sequence; Bess Flowers, Allen Cavan and Grace Goodall, who appear in the climactic hospital scenes, were signed to appear near the end of shooting, on July 6.

Thicker Than Water boasts an unusually cinematic gag for L&H: whenever the boys are about to move from one setting to another, one of them reaches over to the very end of the frame and "pulls" the next scene into view. This is another example of Roy Seawright's optical-effects ingenuity combining with Laurel and Hardy's humor to create an inventive gag. It also shows that the film was not just quickly churned out, even though it was the team's last short.

The final gag of the team's final short combines two of their favorite motifs: the duplicate-identity gimmick, and the freak ending. After the blood transfusion, the pair are seen strolling out of the hospital. As the nurse bids them goodbye, a mustachioed, spit-curled Stan twiddles his tie, while a clean-shaven Ollie scratches his head and cries. As the Ollie-like Stan registers exasperation, the Laurelish Hardy pulls the end title onto the screen.

The short-subject field lost a lot of prestige when the L&H two-reelers came to an end. And even though they would have great success in feature films, Laurel and Hardy lost something, too.

THE BOHEMIAN GIRL

Production history: Planned July 1934, abandoned January 1935. Script written mid-August—late September 1935. Filmed October 9-circa November 30. Previewed December 11. Retakes shot December 31-circa January 6, 1936. Copyrighted February 12, 1936 by MGM (LP 6453). Released February 14. 70 minutes.

Produced by Hal Roach. Directed by James W. Horne and Charles Rogers. Photographed by Art Lloyd and Francis Corby. Edited by Bert Jordan and Louis

McManus. Based on the opera by Michael W. Balfe. Sound by Elmer R. Raguse. Musical direction by Nathaniel Shilkret.

With Mae Busch, Antonio Moreno, Jacqueline Wells, Darla Hood, James Finlayson, Thelma Todd.

The boys are gypsies who have camped near the palace of the gypsy-hating Count Arnheim. After Arnheim orders Mrs. Hardy's beau — the dashing Devilshoof — flogged for trespassing, she abducts Arnheim's daughter and tells Ollie it's his child. She then runs off with Devilshoof. Years later, the gypsies again camp near Arnheim's domain, and Ollie's "daughter" is arrested for trespassing. The Count eventually recognizes her — but not before Stan and Ollie pay a visit to the torture chamber for trying to save her. Result: an elongated Ollie and a shortened Stan.

By 1936, there appeared to be a rule of thumb around the Roach lot: When you can't think of a good feature-length story for Laurel and Hardy, make another comic opera. This third excursion into operetta was actually planned in July 1934, before *Babes in Toyland* had been completed. That film's profitability ensured that this one would eventually be made.

Frank Butler was scheduled to write a screenplay based on Michael Balfe's 1843 opera in November 1934, but by the following January the project had been shelved.

Although a four-reel comedy based on the adventures of FBI agents entitled *The Honesty Racket* had been planned for the team in July 1935, by late August Charley Rogers, James Parrott and Charlie Hall (yes, *the* Charlie Hall) were writing a treatment based on the Balfe opera. Stan joined them as the writing continued through late September. They wrote so much material, they could have made *Bohemian Girl II*.

The major differences in the script occur in the second half of the story, when Arline has grown into a young woman. A breakfast scene begins when Ollie chastises Stan for not washing behind his ears. Arline then checks Ollie's ears and tells Stan he'll have company at the wash basin.

After breakfast Ollie tells Stan to put new shoes on their horse. Predictably, a confused Stan returns with a horse wearing four brogans. Ollie disgustedly snaps, "I meant for you to take him out and have his shod!" Teary-eyed, Stan ties a blindfold around the horse's eyes, and sorrowfully aims a blunderbuss at his equine friend.

"I said shod, not shot!" yells Ollie. "Shod-da!" When he asks Stan how they'll raise the money to buy another horse, Stan suggests they raffle off their old one. "You don't have to tell them that he's dead," he explains.

A number of the boys' gypsy neighbors take part, with Mr. Finlayson emerging the winner. He is overjoyed — until he sees what he's won. While the boys are congratulating themselves on their ingenuity, Finlayson demands his money back. The other gypsies are incensed when they learn they've wagered on a dead horse, and chase Stan and Ollie into their caravan. The wagon dislodges and rolls down a treacherous mountain road, the gypsies chasing it until it crashes near Count Arnheim's palace.

A gala banquet is about to take place, honoring the Duke of Camembert and the Marchioness of Gorgonzola. As the royal visitors wait in an anteroom,

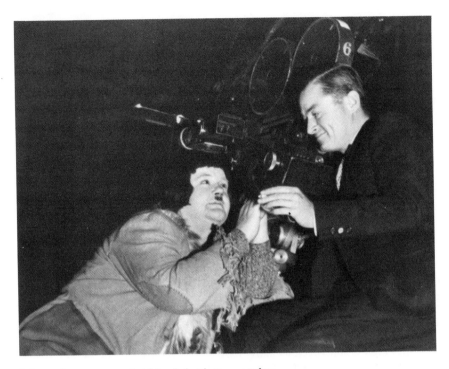

Babe and cameraman Art Lloyd chat between takes.

Stan and Ollie hide behind a nearby screen. When the two guests are announced, they look strikingly like Ollie in a nobleman's clothes and Stan in a dress and wig.

Officers and noblemen ask the charming "lady" to sweeten their glasses of wine by tasting them. Stan is thoroughly intoxicated before long. A foppish nobleman — whom the boys had robbed earlier — flirts with the Marchioness. Ollie recognizes him, and from behind a column, he pantomimes to Stan, "That's the fellow we robbed!" Stan thinks Ollie wants him to rob the fop, and tells the nobleman, "Your eyes are the windows of your soul, and to know all, I must touch them." The fop tries to remember where he's heard that before.

Before Ollie can spirit Stan away, another nobleman asks "her" to dance. They waltz toward a table sagging with desserts. Stan keeps twirling his partner around, so he can grab another more of the goodies. At one point, Stan pilfers a piece of birthday cake and swallows a lit candle. He reacts with alarm as smoke billows out of his ears.

Count Arnheim announces to the assembled throng that a gypsy girl, caught prowling the grounds, will immediately be lashed. The boys realize it's Arline, but their attempts to save her are hampered by some suspicious guards. The guards follow the pair up a stairway — where they're met by the real Duke and Marchioness.

Meanwhile, the Count has discovered that Arline is his long-lost daughter; he orders that she be spared, with the two other gypsies taking her place. Arline

Discussing a forthcoming sequence with director James Horne.

pleads for their release from the torture chamber, and the Count finally relents. As the guests gape in astonishment, Stan escorts a 10-foot-tall Ollie out the palace gates.

It's a pity that none of this scripted material was used in the film. Unlike the previous two comic operettas, the "straight" plot and musical footage has all the entertainment value of a wet dishrag. When Laurel and Hardy leave the screen, we have to endure poorly-photographed shots of purported gypsies lip-syncing to a pre-recorded chorus. Arline sings an interminable rendition of "I Dreamt I Dwelt in Marble Halls."

The best-remembered scene in *The Bohemian Girl* has Stan trying to bottle some wine, and sucking on a tube from the wine barrel to start the flow; before long, he is filled with wine from the barrel *and* the bottles. The film is wonderfully alive during the comedy scenes; when the operetta lurches back into view, the film dies.

In late September 1935, just before shooting began, Hal Roach and sound engineer Elmer Raguse left for New York, to supervise the recording of the background music. The score was recorded under the supervision of Nat Shilkret, a producer for the Victor record company, and the vocals added later in Culver City.

Hal Roach was announced as "personally directing the dramatic sequences," with James Horne taking charge of the comedy scenes. However, Roach's ambitious plans to construct two new sound stages and increase feature-film production left him little time to direct. When Stan was sent home because of influenza on October 15, Roach suspended the comedy-scene unit. When Stan returned a week later Horne was the primary director, with Charley Rogers assisting as co-director.

Filming resumed October 23 and continued until November 5, when Stan caught the flu again. This time, Horne suspended all shooting, having already shot all scenes not requiring Stan. Production resumed on the 13th, and surged forward until the end of November, when everything was finally photographed.

Babe Hardy reported the production problems in a letter to his estranged wife, Myrtle, who was in the hospital recovering from a bout with alcohol. "Have been working awfully hard," Babe wrote. "There has been so much illness on this picture. Stan was laid up for 2-1/2 weeks, Mae Busch for 4 weeks. It seems we have been on it for a year."

On December 11 the picture was previewed. *The Hollywood Reporter* found the musical comedy "a swell number, and sure box-office up and down the line," and hinted at some sequences in the first cut that no longer exist in the film:

> The Laurel & Hardy fun-making rises from a medium low at the beginning to uproarious heights in succeeding episodes, with tops reached by Laurel in a solo pantomime of a man bottling a cask of wine and producing a set of musical bottles. It sounds foolish and it is, but aided by tricky sound-track ingenuities, it is ten minutes of robustious laughter....
>
> Supporting the comedians is an excellent company of players....Thelma Todd is the beautiful queen of the gypsies, and she looks it and is it. Mae Busch plays the virago wife of Hardy with convincing virulence. Antonio Moreno is the handsome Gypsy villain and he too proves that he can sing.

On December 16, 1935, five days after the preview, Thelma Todd was found slumped behind the steering wheel of her car. Her body was discovered in the Santa Monica garage of her companion, former film director Roland West. An autopsy revealed carbon monoxide poisoning. The county autopsy surgeon maintained that she had breathed the fumes accidentally, and stated that blood on her face probably stemmed from wounds she received when her head struck the steering wheel.

However, other events clouded the issue. Miss Todd's chauffeur told police that the comedienne ordered him to drive home at breakneck speed from the Saturday evening party where she was last seen; she had received extortion notes threatening to blow up her seaside cafe, and had feared she might be kidnapped or slain by gangsters. An actor testified that Todd's demeanor changed violently during the party; she had been happy and vivacious early in the evening, but after a conversation with Sid Grauman, "she was terribly depressed." This lead to a suicide theory. The only certainty was that a talented and popular comedienne had died much too soon. Thelma Todd was only 30 years old.

"Nobody will ever convince me that Thelma Todd committed suicide, ever," said Anita Garvin. "She had everything going for her. She had looks, she had talent, she had everything. She was murdered."

Thelma Todd and Antonio Moreno in a scene cut from the film.

Hal Roach, her employer for seven years, told reporters Todd was "joyous and happy and seemed thoroughly to enjoy her work. She was a favorite with everyone on the lot from the lowliest employee to the highest."

Roach and Laurel agreed that to prevent any notoriety from surrounding *The Bohemian Girl*, most of Thelma's scenes should be cut from the picture. Her romantic scenes with Antonio Moreno were reworked so that Mae Busch now became his love interest. The Gypsy Queen, which Thelma had portrayed as a vivacious young vixen, now became an elderly matriarch played by Zeffie Tilbury. Felix Knight was called in to warble "Then You'll Remember Me." (It appears that Antonio Moreno may have sung this to Miss Todd in the original cut.)

"The person who had sung the tune just didn't come off," recalled Knight, "so they called me in at the last moment to do that one scene. They were trying to put the film together, and found that this particular sequence was not working, and they wanted it re-done with a different character." Judging from existing production material, it doesn't appear that any of the Laurel and Hardy scenes were changed as a result of Thelma's death.

What with the virtual rewriting of the script, the illness during production and the hasty rearranging and refilming of the "plot" footage following Todd's death, one might expect *The Bohemian Girl* to be a chaotic mess. Actually, the plot is quite cohesive — it's just not very entertaining. Fortunately, the Laurel and Hardy scenes are among the their best (easily better than anything in

A British advertisement promotes the team's newest feature.

Bonnie Scotland), and they have enough footage to make the film one of their funniest.

When it was released in February 1936, the picture garnered mixed reviews. Frank S. Nugent of the *New York Times* enjoyed the team's antics: "unseemly their conduct may be, but it's guaranteed to get a laugh — in fact, several of them," he wrote. "Against the antic lunacies of the screen's popular dimwits, Mr. Balfe's score hasn't much chance. Mr. Balfe probably wouldn't approve what Laurel and Hardy have done to his *Bohemian Girl*. Then again, being Irish, perhaps he would."

But *Variety's* reviewer was downright hostile. He called the picture "A comedy with little or no comedy" and lambasted the filmmakers for "inept direction" and "dreadful camera angles." He summed it up with, "There is not a good performance in the production."

The film did acceptable business in the States, but it was a sensation in Europe. A three-day convention of the Laurel and Hardy Clubs of France was held in August 1936 at the Paris Town Hall; the members, primarily children, arrived in buses festooned with the team's likenesses. When *The Bohemian Girl* debuted at the Olympia Theater in connection with the convention, it broke the theater's records for a single day's receipts. (In Germany, the Nazis disapproved of the gypsy element and banned the picture.)

Stan wanted to take a more active part in guiding the team's future. The contract problems during *Bonnie Scotland* had shown Stan that Roach could break up the team if he wanted to. And although Stan had a free hand in writing the comedy sequences and assisting in the direction and editing, it was still Roach who was determining the types of stories.

It was Roach's idea to do the comic operas and *Bonnie Scotland*; all had been enjoyable, but all had the common problem of trying to shoehorn Laurel and Hardy into plots that existed independently of the team. Stan felt that an L&H picture should at least have a story carried by Laurel and Hardy.

OUR RELATIONS

Production history: Script written circa February 4-March 6, 1936. Filmed circa March 16-May 4. (Working title: *The Money Box*). Previewed July 10. Copyrighted September 29, 1936 by MGM (LP 6695). Released October 30. 74 minutes.

A Stan Laurel Production for Hal Roach Studios, Inc. Directed by Harry Lachman. Photographed by Rudolph Maté. Photographic effects by Roy Seawright. Edited by Bert Jordan. Screenplay by Richard Connell and Felix Adler. Adaptation by Charles Rogers and Jack Jevne. Suggested by "The Money Box," a short story by William Wymark Jacobs. Sound by William Randall. Musical score by LeRoy Shield.

With Daphne Pollard, Betty Healy, James Finlayson, Alan Hale, Sidney Toler, Iris Adrian, Lona Andre.

Stan and Ollie's community is visited by their long-lost twin brothers — Bert Hardy and Alfie Laurel — who are sailors on shore leave. The gobs are entrusted by their captain with a pearl ring, which causes grief for both sets of

Laurels and Hardys, who are continually being mistaken for their twins. Two gangsters, trying to get the ring, cast Stan and Ollie's feet in cement and set them teetering at the dock's edge. The Captain eventually gets his ring back, and Bert and Alf recognize their twin brothers and save them from a watery grave.

The Hal Roach Studio was changing dramatically as 1936 began. The old free and easy atmosphere was disappearing as Roach concentrated his energies on the production of prestigious features. The *New York Times* mourned the good old days:

> The double-feature mania which has gripped the nation has killed one of the cinema's most flourishing institutions, the slapstick comedy factory... Hal Roach, however, has adapted himself to the times by renouncing the two-reelers for the more respected multiple-reel films. The man who once said that there is nothing as funny as a custard pie in the face still clings to his theory — with certain amendments. The pie must be composed of sterner stuff than was used ten years ago and it must be tossed a little more artfully...
>
> With the studio devoted to features, the lot has taken on a more serious aspect... Stan Laurel may get Babe Hardy to jump into a pen of pigs just for a laugh but the making of comedies has become a more somber business. It's all right to joke when you are making pictures costing $60,000 but when they get into the $150,000 to $200,000 class, they must be treated with a degree of respect.

Not only was the Roach studio becoming more somber and regimented; there was an abrupt reorganization of the executive board. Henry Ginsberg, the cost-cutting general manager, resigned on January 16, 1936. With the new lavishness applied to features — and the appointment of Roach's friend David Loew as vice-president in charge of finances — Ginsberg saw his power eroding.

Loew became the new general manager; Matt O'Brien was appointed construction and lot manager; Lawrence Tarver became Roach's assistant on production activities; Joe Rivkin was picked to handle all matters relating to talent, directors and writers; and L.A. French, one-time assistant production manager, became sole production manager of the L&H unit.

Stan Laurel was given a new title, too. The opening credits for *Our Relations* bill the film as "A Stan Laurel Production." However, it's doubtful that Stan was really functioning as a producer, considering French's new role; furthermore, Stan was still working under his contract of April 8, 1935 — which specified that his services would be under Roach's personal supervision. (The contract had been extended for one year, commencing July 22, 1935.)

Hal Roach's close associate, film historian Richard W. Bann, offers this view: "Roach generously gave this special credit to Laurel in order to salve his bouts of temperament. This was really a meaningless concession, and it allowed Laurel to save face." Indeed, the credit makes it appear as though Laurel emerged from the *Bonnie Scotland* contract squabbles with more creative control.

Bann continues: "The *Our Relations* press book, in its official credits section, says, 'Producer: Hal Roach.' So does the press book for *Way Out West,* which was likewise billed as 'A Stan Laurel Production.' Neither film was registered, assigned or renewed by or to Stan Laurel Productions."

And yet it seems clear that by 1936 Stan aspired to become his own producer. For one thing, the disagreements over stories between Laurel and Roach were becoming more frequent. Roach offered his view on the subject: "I would have been delighted if Laurel could've written the stories. But he would come up with ideas, and I'd have to say, 'Stan, that's just childish. It's just not going to play.' And then he would pout. That was the great weakness Laurel had, and if he would have only admitted it and forgotten about that part of it, because it was not important to his career, I would have continued with them."

In Stan's view, however, it was vitally important that he and Babe appear in films with suitable stories — and Laurel felt he was a better judge of the team's material than Roach.

Another source of conflict was that Stan wanted Laurel and Hardy to be put under a joint contract. Under Stan's current contract, the studio was not obligated to co-star or team Laurel with any particular person, although the contract would have been suspended had Babe become disabled for a time.

When asked in January 1981 why Laurel and Hardy never shared a contract, Hal Roach replied, "It was much better not having them under contract as a team — for Hal Roach. The advantage I had was that they could not leave me as a team, because I always had one of them under contract. So, when I made a new contract with Stan, I was at an advantage because Babe was already under contract."

Furthermore, Stan and Babe were working for flat salaries, and had no ownership whatsoever in the pictures. Stan wanted to retain ownership of their films, as Chaplin did. The important difference between Laurel and Chaplin, however, is that Chaplin also financed his films with his own money. Laurel and Hardy were not in Chaplin's league financially, and despite the team's immense popularity, no one considered them artistically or financially astute enough to back them in an independent production. So, in early 1936, Stan had to be satisfied with his current Roach contract.

Roach, however, did give Stan a great measure of creative control. The only Roach-Laurel contract available for scrutiny is one drafted by the studio, dated October 22, 1936 — which neither party signed. Although this would have been a later pact than the one in effect during *Our Relations,* we can assume some similarities.

Stan was employed as an "actor and writer," and had story and director approval; he was responsible for the preparation of the story and other elements needed for the film's production. The studio owned any material written by Laurel for the films, and kept the rights to make "adaptations, changes, novelizations, dramatizations, musical versions of, interpolate in, transpose, add to and subtract from said work or works."

Translation: Stan had story approval, but the studio still had the right to change that story after he'd approved it. The studio retained all title and copyright to Laurel's work, but after two years, Stan could use the routines for stage and radio appearances. He received no percentage of the profits, working for $75,000 per feature. (Stan made $135,000 in 1936. Babe made $88,600 that year; while Stan was paid on a picture-by-picture basis, Babe remained on a weekly salary.)

Cameraman Rudolph Maté films the boys and Arthur Housman.

The first "Stan Laurel Production" drew upon new sources in all areas. This was the first Laurel and Hardy feature other than the comic operas to be based on an outside source: a short story by William Wymark Jacobs, a prolific writer of stories and novels about the sea, which usually featured eccentric British characters. Given Stan's love of the ocean and of English-style humor, it was a logical choice of material.

New writers Harrington Reynolds and Clarence Hennecke were the first to work on the adaptation; they were followed by Mauri Grashin and the reliable Felix Adler, who divided his life with the twin careers of gag man and circus clown. Jack Jevne was brought in next, and Richard Connell, who had written the famous short story *The Most Dangerous Game* and had just finished Harold Lloyd's *The Milky Way*, was signed last. Stan and Charley Rogers worked on the script as well, although they didn't receive credit.

There was a new director at the helm, too — one who had never worked at Roach. Harry Lachman was a post-Impressionist painter of great renown who gave up his oils in 1928, at age 42, to direct films. *Dante's Inferno* (1935), his best-known film to date, was a Spencer Tracy vehicle with a visually imaginative sequence taking place in Hell — which was accomplished in collaboration with his cameraman, Rudolph Maté.

For *Our Relations*, Maté took over the position usually held by Art Lloyd, at Lachman's behest. The cinematographer had had a very distinguished career in Europe, bringing his flair for sophisticated lighting and inventive camera angles to Carl Dreyer's *The Passion of Joan of Arc* and Fritz Lang's *Liliom*.

In addition to James Finlayson, Tiny Sandford (in his last film with the boys) and Daphne Pollard (who'd recently toured in a vaudeville act based on her previous L&H movies), burly Irishman Alan Hale played waiter Joe Groagan, Sidney Toler (later the star of Monogram's *Charlie Chan* series) was cast as the wiry Captain, and bubbly Betty Healy — former wife of the Three Stooges' mentor Ted Healy — played Mrs. Laurel.

Director Harry Lachman had asked to join the project because he was a Laurel and Hardy fan, according to his widow, Tai. Unfortunately, liking Laurel and Hardy was not the only requirement needed to be a good director for them, and there were some differences between Lachman and Laurel during the shooting. Recalled Roy Seawright, "Lachman was a great director, but he wasn't the director for these guys. Stan would always correct him. Lachman would say, 'No, I want you to do this — " and Stan would say, 'No. We do it *this* way.' And that was it. But they got along fine."

Rudolph Maté, too, had to be taught that L&H comedies required a unique style of photography. "Stan insisted that the lighting be very flat. And Art Lloyd put light all around, so it gave their faces that comical, blank look," recounted Seawright. "But Rudy Maté was a dramatic cameraman. And they had a hell of a time — Stan would not accept the first week's worth of dailies; Maté had lit it too dramatically, with shadows on their faces, under their chins, and so forth. And Stan did not want the artistic, theatrical type of lighting they were employing in those days."

Maté found a way to compromise with Stan; the lighting in *Our Relations* is markedly different from Art Lloyd's, with subtle textures and a more polished look overall — yet Stan and Ollie still retain their blank, childlike visages.

Once Lachman and Maté became accustomed to Laurel and Hardy's working methods, the filming seems to have progressed smoothly. It appears that the picture was shot in sequence: Noel Madison and Ralf Harolde, who play the gangsters in the film's climactic scenes, were added to the cast not long before the picture wrapped.

Iris Adrian, who appeared as Alice, a beer garden good-time girl, offered an amusing sidelight on Babe Hardy's off-screen life. Babe was separated from his wife, Myrtle, and was dating occasionally. "Hardy said, 'Have dinner with me tonight?' I said, 'All right.' Then later he called me and said, 'You don't want to go out with me. I'm an old fat fellow,'" recalled Adrian. "I didn't think he was so bad — but he got home, got tired, had a couple of drinks — he said, 'I'm too fat, you wouldn't like me.'"

LeRoy Shield, who had written many of the breezy scores used for the early talkie shorts, took a leave from his job as NBC's music director to compose the film's score. Shield's tunes for this feature were also tacked onto new prints of *Perfect Day*, *Blotto* and *Brats*, which were reissued in 1936 and '37. (There was still some demand for L&H shorts, which the studio filled by putting some of the earliest talkies back into release, with new music tracks.)

The feature was previewed in early July. *The Hollywood Reporter*, usually sympathetic to the team, was not impressed:

> *Our Relations* turns out to be a weak sister for Laurel and Hardy...
> story and direction sends the boys floundering through a morass of

"Bert" and "Alf" had trouble shaving in a deleted scene.

unfunny incident. The only laughs in the feature are obtained from pieces of business seemingly adlibbed in the typically Laurel and Hardy style... The screenplay is cumbersome and wordy, direction rather deliberate. The whole thing lacks spontaneity. A major job of cutting is called for, as sequences run far past the point of laughter....

Existing stills indicate that at least two sequences were cut from the film before its final release. One had Stan and Ollie and their wives out on a motoring trip and encountering a massive traffic jam — possibly an updating of the classic scene from *Two Tars*. Another deleted bit had Bert and Alf trying to shave in their cramped quarters on the S.S. Periwinkle, causing much grief for Bert.

The recutting of the picture must have helped it enormously, because the final cut moves along at a much more rapid tempo than usual for Laurel and Hardy. The whole production looks far more lavish than any of the previous features, with Maté's unusual compositions adding extra visual interest. The special-effects sequences showing two sets of Laurels and Hardys are held to a minimum, but they are seamlessly accomplished by Roy Seawright.

In sum, *Our Relations* is a well-crafted and consistently amusing comedy. The film's major flaw: there's so much story that the boys don't have time to just stop for a while and be funny. Even though there are twice as many Laurels and Hardys in this picture, one leaves it feeling unsated.

Still, the film earned Stan and Babe some of their best reviews. *Variety*, which usually hated the team, gave the picture lavish praise — but for the wrong reason: "Stan Laurel has done himself proud on his first fling as a producer....For one thing, both Laurel and Hardy get plenty of chances to talk and the dialog handed them is considerably above par."

Other reviews were likewise enthusiastic, without denigrating the largely mute brand of comedy that was generally Laurel and Hardy's trademark. "Laurel and Hardy time their laughs like a [Max] Schmeling punch and earn the right to be known as the laugh champ team of filmdom," exulted *Box Office.*

Only Frank S. Nugent of the *New York Times* was a party pooper. He whined that the team "should know when to stop — and that is after the third reel"; he also griped that the guy who sat next to him kept exploding in mirth and digging into Nugent's side with his elbow. It's a sorry day when comedians earn a critic's scorn for being too funny.

In mid-October, King Edward VIII of Great Britain requested a command performance screening of *Our Relations* at Balmoral Castle, even before the film was released. When the film opened at the Rialto in New York, it drew a packed house, though it hadn't yet been advertised in newspapers. The picture was screened for President Roosevelt just before he sailed for a goodwill tour of South America.

ON THE WRONG TREK

Production history: Written and filmed mid-late April 1936. Released circa mid-June. Copyrighted June 11, 1936 by MGM (LP 6425). Two reels.

Produced by Hal Roach. Directed by Charles Parrott and Harold Law. With Charley Chase, Rosina Lawrence.

Stan and Babe did a cameo in this Chase two-reeler, as two of many hitch-hikers encountered by the family during their motor trip. The mother-in-law suggests Charley pull over and give a lift to those two fellows with "kind faces." Cut to the roadside, and we see Stan and Ollie thumbing it — with their thumbs pointing in opposite directions. Ollie realizes Stan is undermining their efforts, and tries to correct him as the Chase auto passes by. Growls Charley, "They look like a couple of horse thieves to me!" He expresses his disgust by aping Stan's grin and head-scratching gesture.

This was Chase's next-to-last film for Hal Roach, owing to movie exhibitors' preference for double features. When the producer reluctantly let Chase go in late May 1936, the comedian took out a full-page advertisement in the trades: "Thank you, Hal Roach, for a wonderful engagement that lasted over 17 years. I knew I shouldn't have cleaned up that dressing room!"

With Chase's dismissal, two-reelers were a thing of the past at the Roach studio. The Todd-Kelly series had ended with Thelma's death, and Laurel and Hardy were making features exclusively. Only the *Our Gang* comedies remained, at Louis B. Mayer's insistence, and those had been halved to one reel. The Lot of Fun, which had poured out so many classic short comedies so effortlessly, was now becoming a feature-film plant, attempting to compete with the major studios. And more changes were soon to come.

WAY OUT WEST

Production history: Script written circa mid-May—mid-August 1936. Filmed August 27-early November. Previewed December 16. Copyrighted April 9, 1937 by MGM (LP 7051). Released April 16. 65 minutes.

A Stan Laurel Production for Hal Roach Studios. Directed by James W. Horne. Photographed by Art Lloyd and Walter Lundin. Photographic effects by Roy Seawright. Edited by Bert Jordan. Story by Jack Jevne and Charles Rogers. Screenplay by Charles Rogers, Felix Adler, and James Parrott. Musical score and direction by Marvin Hatley. Edited by Bert Jordan. Sound by William Randall. Art direction by Arthur Royce.

With James Finlayson, Rosina Lawrence, Sharon Lynne, Stanley Fields, Vivien Oakland.

Laurel and Hardy travel to Brushwood Gulch, where they are to deliver the deed to a gold mine to Mary Roberts, daughter of a belated friend. They've never seen Mary, and when they ask unscrupulous saloon owner Mickey Finn where they might find her — to give her the valuable deed — Finn passes off his girlfriend, singer Lola Marcel, as Mary. Soon the boys discover that the real Mary is a trusting innocent who works as a slavey for Finn. They spend that evening in a none-too-stealthy attempt to regain the deed from Finn's safe, and eventually succeed.

Just after *Our Relations* finished filming, in mid-May 1936, Roach announced that Laurel and Hardy would soon make a new feature entitled *You'd Be Surprised.* But Roach himself was surprised, because the title was already owned by another studio. The picture became *Tonight's the Night* just before filming commenced, but yet another studio had claim to that title. By mid-September the latest L&H opus was called *In the Money*, but somebody was already using *that* title. It wasn't until the film was halfway completed that it got its lasting name.

While Roach was wrestling with titles, a group of writers were grappling with gags and structure. Felix Adler was first to work on the story, beginning in May; he was joined quickly by Charley Rogers and newcomer Arthur Vernon Jones. Jack Jevne, the new head of the editorial department, supervised the development of the script. By late July, James Parrott returned to the Laurel and Hardy fold (for the first time since November 1932) to add gags to the script. A few days later, James Horne was signed as "a staff writer" according to trade papers, and on August 20 he was asked to direct as well. Art Lloyd was again behind the camera.

Stan's wife, Ruth, reportedly suggested that the boys should do a comedy western. Indeed, it was an angle fertile with comic possibilities; hardly anyone had done such a picture since Buster Keaton decided to *Go West* in 1925. (After Laurel and Hardy's success with this film, it seemed as though everyone wanted to make a comedy western.)

As usual, the script contained a number of funny routines which never made it to the screen. An early scene in the script has the boys tramping along with their mule in the middle of nowhere, trying to find Brushwood Gulch. A signpost points the way, but it keeps shifting direction with the wind. Stan argues that the town is in one direction, while Ollie maintains that the other direction is "the right way."

As the pair trudge off in the "right" direction (Stan's), a burly sheriff gallops along and tells them that they're definitely going in the wrong one if they want to get to Brushwood Gulch. Ollie snaps at Stan for being so dumb; for once Stan is fed up with his partner's pompousness, and draws his gun. Ollie covers his ears and yells, "Don't you dare shoot me!" Stan fires his gun in the air as Ollie braces himself, eyes shut. When Ollie hears the gunshot, he falls to the ground, decrying the fact that his bosom pal has killed him.

Then the sheriff yells from offscreen — Stan has shot a hole through his hat. Ollie recovers from death immediately, and gets up to explain everything to the sheriff — but the lawman replies with a kick to Ollie's rear. Then the mule gives the sheriff a swift kick which sends him flying; he lands sprawled in a bed of cactus. The boys make a mad dash for Brushwood Gulch.

The two tenderheels tie their mule to a hitching post just outside Mickey Finn's Palace. Inside the saloon, Ollie throws a silver dollar on the bar, and a stocky bartender barks, "Name your poison." Ollie requests "a nice gin fizz — with an egg." The bartender pours him a straight whiskey. When Stan asks for "a nice mint julep, with a mint," the bartender pours Laurel a slug from the same bottle. "Pardon me — haven't you made a slight mistake?" says Ollie. The bartender switches their glasses. Stan takes a sip from his new glass and remarks, "That's much better!"

A number of script changes occur during the scene in which Laurel and Hardy tell "Mary" (Lola) that her father has died and left her a fortune. Intones Ollie, "Your father made us a very solemn promise before he — he — went away." "He didn't go anyplace, he died!" says Stan, with his usual understanding of nuance. "I was only trying to find a tender way of telling her that her father is deceased," replies Ollie. Trying to cover for his faux pas, Stan tenderly tells Lola, "Yes. He was so deceased that he died."

Lola begins to play a sentimental tune on the piano, just as her "daddy" used to do. Ollie begins to sob, and tears roll down his cheeks. Stan moves a potted plant over so that Ollie's cascading tears will water it. All three wail in sorrow as Lola plays, and when she turns a page of the sheet music and starts playing in a higher key, they all wail in a higher key as well. This is out of Stan's vocal range, so he wipes his teary eyes and turns back the page — and all three change their sobbing to a more comfortable pitch.

The script deviates radically from the film when Laurel and Hardy go back upstairs to reclaim the deed from Lola and Finn, realizing they've been duped. Stan takes aim at Lola with his pistol after she locks the deed in the strongbox. He shoots her high-heeled shoes off; she loses her balance, stumbles into the bathroom and falls in the tub.

Next Stan and Ollie shoot it out with Finlayson. Stan takes cover behind a table. Finn shoots at Stan and hits a bottle of ketchup, which dribbles on Stan's forehead; he thinks he's been shot, and lays down to die. Babe shoots down a deer head trophy, which falls to the floor; the antlers poke Finn in the rear. Stray bullets repeatedly strike the Victrola, a final bullet "killing" the record.

Stan and Ollie have forced a bottle of seltzer water into Finn's mouth and are apparently trying to drown him when the sheriff — having heard the commotion from the bar downstairs — enters and rescues him. He then tells

Filming the "At the Ball, That's All" soft-shoe number in front of a process screen.

the boys to get out of town. The script makes no mention of one of the film's highlights: the scene with Lola tickling Stan, and the laughing routine which follows.

The proposed finale was also markedly different. The script has Stan and Ollie are resting under a tree — following the sheriff's ultimatum — when a band of Indians take them to their camp and do a dance of welcome. When the chief shows them knives of various sizes, they think he is asking them to choose weapons; he is merely offering them for sale. The boys then join the Indians in a ceremonial dance, brandishing the knives.

Stan and Ollie sneak back to town disguised as cigar store Indians. They have stolen blankets and headdresses to facilitate the ruse; the Indians come to town looking for revenge, and chase the boys through Finn's establishment. At one point, Finn thinks an Indian is trying to scalp him; to save him the trouble, he takes off his toupee and hands it to the Indian.

The boys reclaim the deed and alert Mary Roberts. They escape Finn — and the Indians — by hiding in a player piano. The piano runs down the street on their legs, with the Indians shooting arrows at it. Cut to a small cliff on the edge of a stream. Unable to see where they are going, the trio runs over the cliff. The piano lands upside down in the water. Three pairs of legs continue "running"; the piano floats downstream as we fade out.

Preparation for the shooting began in late August. Originally, the role of Mary was to go to Jacqueline Wells (Arline in *The Bohemian Girl*). Before long the part was reassigned to Rosina Lawrence, who was kept busy at Roach in her role as Miss Jones, the school teacher of Our Gang. Sharon Lynne, a Texas-born beauty who'd been working in films and Hollywood nightclubs, was cast as Lola. And Stanley J. "Tiny" Sandford was tabbed for a prominent role as the burly, menacing sheriff.

A cute gag which opens and ends the film has the boys and their mule crossing a creek, with Ollie repeatedly falling into a huge pothole. The scene was shot in Sherwood Forest, about 40 miles north of Los Angeles. The picturesque area which Stan wanted to use for the gag had no lake, so the Roach studios rented a steam shovel, dug out a river bed, and poured 25,000 gallons of water from a nearby lake into the man-made one.

Music played a large part in this picture. Roach had signed the Avalon Boys quartet — Walter Trask, Art Green, Don Brookins and a young Chill Wills — on May 26. Originally, the foursome were just going to provide a musical number by themselves in the picture, but they ended up accompanying a Laurel and Hardy dance routine. The scene does not appear in the script, and was apparently dreamt up during pre-production.

In one of the most endearing sequences the team ever did, Stan and Ollie begin to tap their feet as the Avalon Boys sing "At the Ball, That's All," a hit song of 1905. Gradually, they dance some tentative steps by themselves, and eventually join for some unison dancing that's outrageously funny and poignant at the same time.

Another musical interlude added sometime after the script had been completed is the charming duet by Stan and Ollie, singing "The Trail of the Lonesome Pine." The song was performed live, with the exception of the final chorus, where Stan's voice changes to a deep bass and finally — after a clunk on the head — into a high falsetto. The trick voices were provided by Chill Wills and Rosina Lawrence. (In 1975, a record of the duet was issued in

Tiny Sandford played the sheriff, before he was replaced by Stanley Fields.

England, and hit the Number Two slot on the charts.)

These musical scenes may or may not have been devised on the set, but one of the film's funniest gags was. When Ollie asks Stan for a match, Stan strikes his thumb against his curled fingers as if his hand were a cigarette lighter, and produces a flame. The editor of the film, Bert Jordan, recalled, "One of the gag men on the set was trying to light a cigarette one day, and it wouldn't light. It gave Stan an idea, and that's how they got that gag."

There were tricks going on behind the scenes, as well. "Stan's double was Hamilton Kinsey — a tall, lanky kid from the South, very nice kid," said Roy Seawright. "Stan usually expressed humor and warmth, but — I hate to say this — there were times when he could be cruel. Ham would do anything because he needed the work; it was steady work, and he got a good payroll check, plus a bonus from Stan. But Stan would make him do the damnedest things — he'd make him wear a piece of pie on his shoulder, or make him walk around wearing a big red nose.

"One day, they were wiring up the set for a gag where the donkey was going to go flying on the pulley," said Seawright, recalling the scene where the boys use a block and tackle to climb up to the second story window of Finn's saloon. "Well, instead of the donkey, they put Ham on there! They put the wire belt around him and hooked him up to the thing. And instead of just pulling Ham up to the balcony that held the donkey, they kept pulling until Ham was up at the top of the soundstage. Then Stan said, 'Okay, gang — let's go to lunch!' They tied off the rope, walked off the stage and closed the stage doors — and left Ham tied on the rope, 30 feet in the air.

"Well, Ham is up there, yelling and screaming. And Stan and the crew are outside, laughing like hell — you could hear him screaming through the stage door. Finally, one of the grips got Ham down. And the poor guy was so upset that they took him in the dressing room, and called a doctor in. Apparently, he hadn't been able to breathe, and damn near suffocated up there. And then, of course, Stan couldn't do enough for him; he kept apologizing. He just didn't realize the embarrassment that Ham went through, so Stan could have everyone on the stage laughing and happy. It made Stan look good, but Ham took the brunt of it."

Midway through the filming, on September 17, 1936, *The Hollywood Reporter* told of yet another conflict between Laurel and Roach:

> The tempestuous career of Stan Laurel at Roach's reached a new climax with the comedian threatening to end his relations with Oliver Hardy and the studio. Laurel signs only single picture contracts, while Hardy is on a term deal with Hal Roach. Laurel may go off on his own and seek a contract with another lot.

The next day, the *Reporter* printed Stan's view of the situation:

> Commenting on reports of trouble between himself and Hal Roach, Stan Laurel yesterday stated that everything is harmony on the picture he is now making, and that his friendship with Roach has not been disturbed.
>
> Laurel states he will take a long rest at the end of the picture, which completes his three-picture deal, and that he has assured Roach that he will have the first call on his services when he returns.

Translation: time for Stan's contract to be renewed. Since Roach had long worked Stan and Babe's separate contracts to his own advantage, Stan tried as best he could to work the situation to his favor. If Roach could always lure Stan back to the fold because he already had Hardy under contract, then Stan could hold out for a better deal from Roach because Hal obviously needed both members of the team working for him.

During October 1936, with *Way Out West* still in production, Stan's advisors — attorney Ben Shipman and manager-agents Claude and Gordon Bostock — hammered out a new contract with Roach's legal people. Shipman had resigned as Roach's legal counsel to join Laurel in April 1935, during the *Bonnie Scotland* contract dispute.

A tentative pact, dated October 22 and ultimately unsigned, called for Stan to deliver four features during the contract's two years. Roach was always very concerned about his studio's image; he'd made his name by producing films for the whole family, and didn't want to see his reputation tarnished. Stan's contract therefore contained the following clause: "Second party [Stan] agrees to conduct himself with due regard to public conventions and morals, and agrees that he will not do or commit any act or thing which will tend to degrade him in society, or bring him into public hatred... or prejudice the producer or the motion-picture industry in general."

Meanwhile, there were more changes in the executive board at Roach's, prompted by the death of Hal's father, who was secretary-treasurer. Matt O'Brien took over that job, and Roach's cousin Sidney S. Van Keuren was promoted from head of the construction department to production manager.

As *Way Out West* neared completion, Stan had his usual case of the flu and held up shooting for a couple of days. When he returned, the unit shot a newly-written sequence, to be inserted early in the film: the scene in which Stan and Ollie share a stagecoach ride with matronly Vivien Oakland, and incur her wrath — and that of her husband, the burly sheriff.

At this point, all of the scenes featuring Tiny Sandford as the sheriff were re-shot, for reasons unknown. Gravelly-voiced Stanley Fields — perhaps best remembered as the crime boss in *Little Caesar* — replaced him. (Some of Sandford's footage exists in *That's That*, the bizarre reel of out-takes given to Stan as a present by editor Bert Jordan.)

By early November 1936, the picture had been shot and edited. All that remained was for the studio's musical director, Marvin Hatley, to compose and record the score. Van Keuren was taking full advantage of his new position as production manager, which didn't make Hatley's job any easier.

"Sid would say, 'Now look, Hatley. I want this out Tuesday night, 7 o'clock.' He didn't ever say, 'Would you be ready?' He *told* me when he was gonna be ready," recalled Hatley. "And I *had* to be *ready*, I'm telling you! So, I'd go home, and the nervous sweats would be popping out all over my face, and my hands would be shaking, and I'd say, 'Oh, God, what do I do for an idea?'

"When I started to compose, I didn't go to bed for about two weeks. I'd just work day and night. There are no words to describe the terrifying pressure. I wasn't a big guy in the movies, I was just a little guy. Composers like Alfred Newman, they can take all the time in the world; they're making $2,000 a week, and they can hire a bunch of arrangers and do all kinds of things.

"The most I ever made at Roach's was $200 a week," said Hatley. "We were just a little studio; you had to do everything as fast and as cheaply as possible. I'd be in my studio at the piano, just nervous and sweating like hell, wondering if I was ever gonna get the score done. I always managed to get it done on time.

"For *Way Out West*, I wrote tunes that sounded like the Gay '90s; different periods have different harmonic styles. There's a scene where Stan has to eat Hardy's hat after losing a bet; Stan suggested that we put in a tune called 'Where Did You Get That Hat?' I don't think anyone gets the connection today, since the tune was popular around 1915.

"One day, I was in the projection room when they were running the dailies. So they ran that scene where Stan Laurel's walking down the road with the jackass, and Babe Hardy's riding, before they came to that puddle of water, where Babe fell in. I had some 6/8 music there, keeping in step with them, and it had a lot of eccentric orchestration in it. And Mr. Roach was sitting next to the director, Jimmy Horne — and Roach turned to me and said, 'Cute music! Cute music!' And that's the only word he said to me while I worked at that studio!"

It's amazing that *Way Out West* is so cohesive and effortlessly funny, because it was made at a time when Stan and Babe's private lives were in terrific turmoil. On September 2, 1936, a week after shooting started, Stan and his wife Ruth separated; she sued Stan for separate maintenance.

Meanwhile, Stan's ex-vaudeville partner, Mae Laurel, returned from Aus-

On and off-camera nemeses. Left: actor Rychard Cramer, whose scenes were deleted. Right: Mae Laurel, who resurfaced during filming.

tralia and sued Stan for $1,000 a month separate maintenance. She asserted that she and Stan had entered into a common-law marriage in 1919 in New York and that Stan had deserted her on January 11, 1925. (In fact, Mae had agreed to return to Australia in 1925 under terms specified by Stan's producer, Joe Rock.)

Then in November 1936, Babe's estranged wife, Myrtle Lee Reeves Hardy, sued him for separate maintenance of $2,500 a month. Babe cried at the hearing, which prompted callous reporters to write things like, "A fat tear rolled down comedian Oliver Hardy's chubby cheeks." Babe filed an affidavit in opposition to Myrtle's suit, and testified about Myrtle's heavy drinking, her confinement to sanitariums, and her frequent escapes from those institutions. Interestingly, Myrtle's attorney was the same as Ruth Laurel's: Roger Marchetti.

The final days of November brought new anguish: Babe's first wife, Madelyn Saloshin Hardy, whom he'd married in 1913, was now destitute in New York. She claimed that after their 1921 divorce, Babe had agreed to pay her $30 a week in alimony. "The written agreement was destroyed by fire, but I have witnesses," she said, asking for 15 years' worth of back alimony.

The team's marital turmoils were, eventually, settled. On December 24, 1936, Ruth Laurel won a divorce from Stan by default. She also won the home on Glenbarr Street, two cars, a bank account of $17,000, and 5% of Stan's future gross earnings until her remarriage or death. Mae Laurel's suit dragged on for over a year, until she finally agreed to make no more claims to being Stan's wife in exchange for a cash settlement.

Babe and Myrtle Hardy made a new agreement for the distribution of

THEY HIT THE WILD AND WOOZY WEST... *and it'll never be the same!*

Stan and Ollie are panning for gold now . . . and what pans they have! But real surprises pop out of the fun bag when they sing! and dance! their way in—and out—of trouble! It's FULL-LENGTH Hilarity that'll put you in laughing stitches!

HAL ROACH STUDIOS
Present

STAN **LAUREL** OLIVER **HARDY**
in
Way Out West

A
STAN LAUREL
PRODUCTION
Directed by
JAMES W. HORNE
Screen play by Charles Rogers,
Felix Adler and James Parrott

A
Metro-
Goldwyn-
Mayer
PICTURE

THEATRE

HAL ROACH STUDIOS *Present* stan **LAUREL** oliver **HARDY**

IN THEIR BIGGEST AND MERRIEST FULL-LENGTH FEATURE SHOW!

A panic of joy—6 reels of fun —with Stan and Ollie as gold-seekers with hearts of gold. A fortune in laughs for their millions of fans!

Way Out West

THEATRE

A *Metro-Goldwyn-Mayer* PICTURE

A STAN LAUREL Production   Directed by JAMES W. HORNE

their community property on April 14, 1937, and on May 18 Babe was granted a divorce from Myrtle.

The judge commended Babe for "trying to keep his marital difficulties to himself." It had been a wrenching experience; Babe had tried to reconcile with Myrtle many times, but he just couldn't take any more. On May 20, he sent her a telegram:

ALWAYS KEEP IN YOUR MIND THAT THERE IS ONLY ONE THING IN ANY LIFE AND THAT IS YOU AND YOUR WELFARE THIS MOVE IS BEST FOR BOTH ALWAYS YOUR HONEY — OLIVER.

The Madelyn Hardy case disappeared from newspapers without a trace; the matter was was settled out of court.

Hal Roach was not happy with the headlines his starring comedians attracted. Fortunately, *Way Out West* received excellent notices upon its release in April 1937. *The Hollywood Reporter* found it "quite a few degrees funnier than the more recent L&H features," and praised the team's singing and "over-emphasized hoofing." *Boxoffice* termed the picture "a hilarious comedy, probably the best the [team] has made, one sure to be a money-grabber in all markets...at no time does the picture drag, despite its necessarily simple story."

Variety demonstrated once again that not all criticism is justified: "Latest Laurel-Hardy opus just about extinguishes the good results achieved in previous effort... There's too much driving home of gags... the ponderous way in which they are put over washes out their expected effect... Stan Laurel is given partial credit for being producer, which probably proves that he is best as a comic."

British film critic Basil Wright had an emphatic answer to those who disliked the team when he wrote his review for *World Film News*: "Maybe you don't find them funny? Then you are my enemy, and I hope you will many times be forced to sit through a Laurel and Hardy feature film, tortured by the unceasing laughter of an audience of ordinary people who realize, if only subconsciously, that they are looking at a film which sums up more simply than any philosophical treatise the need for laughter, and supplies it in the form of a thin, diffident Cockney and a fat man from the southern states."

Marvin Hatley was nominated for an Academy Award for the Best Musical Score of 1937. This was quite an accomplishment considering that L&H films were regarded as little more than filler by most people in the film industry. The "terrible pressure" that Hatley underwent while writing and recording the score is nowhere to be found in his music. It is wonderfully easygoing and lyrical, and is vitally important in establishing the mood of the film.

Stan, Babe, and just about everyone else regarded *Way Out West* as being one of the team's finest films. That the boys could have made such a perfect comedy while embroiled in personal traumas was a miracle. And miracles, unfortunately, don't happen very often.

STAN LAUREL-OLIVER HARDY

I DET VILDE VESTEN

EN METRO-GOLDWYN-MAYER FARCE

The team's Western spoof was popular even in Finland.

PICK A STAR

Production history: Script written summer 1936. Filmed November 16, 1936-early January 1937. Previewed April 14. Copyrighted May 18, 1937 by MGM (LP 7164). Released May 21. 70 minutes.

Produced by Hal Roach. Directed by Edward Sedgwick. Photographed by Norbert Brodine and Art Lloyd. Photographic effects by Roy Seawright. Edited by William Terhune. Screenplay by Richard Flournoy, Arthur Vernon Jones, and Thomas J. Dugan. Sound by William Randall. Musical score by Arthur Morton and Marvin Hatley. Songs by Johnny Lange and Fred Stryker, R. Alexander Anderson, and Marvin Hatley.

With Patsy Kelly, Jack Haley, Rosina Lawrence, Lyda Roberti and Mischa Auer.

Small-town girl singer Cecilia Moore flies to Hollywood, accompanied by her wisecracking sister Nellie, to try her luck in the movies.

As *Way Out West* was shooting, Hal Roach was making preparations for a whole series of musicals. The *New York Times* noted, "The producer of comedy shorts... will become an entrepreneur, a publisher of feature-length musicals, before the year is out. The last citadel has fallen."

Pick a Star seems closer to the Busby Berkeley-Warner Bros. musicals of the early '30s than to anything previously produced by the Roach studio. It features scene after scene of high-kicking chorines and somersaulting chorus boys, aided and abetted by intriguing camera angles and flashy montage sequences. (The final sequence, a tour de force of optical effects, is one of Roy Seawright's more notable accomplishments.)

Laurel and Hardy were billed last, and appeared in two scenes, each lasting about five minutes. In the first, Nellie (Patsy Kelly) watches the boys — who are playing bandits — film a scene in a Mexican cantina, under the guidance of director James Finlayson. At the bar, they get into a battle with tough-guy Walter Long, using bottles for ammunition and each other's craniums as the targets.

When the filming stops, the boys explain to Nellie that the bottles are breakaway props, and invite her to try smashing one of them over their heads. Of course, the bottle Nellie uses turns out to be no prop. (The boys seem to relax their on-screen characters a bit in this "off-camera" scene, affording us a glimpse of their true personalities — but only a glimpse.)

In the second scene, Stan and Ollie are relaxing on an adjacent set. Stan amuses himself by playing some rather discordant melodies on a toy horn; Ollie shows off *his* musical prowess with the tiniest of harmonicas, rendering a perfunctory performance of "Listen to the Mocking Bird." When Ollie accidentally swallows the harmonica and Stan discovers he can get different notes by pressing different areas of Ollie's ample stomach, they collaborate on "Pop Goes the Weasel." These scenes were shot on November 18, 1936, in the midst of production on *Way Out West*.

Roach put the boys into this musical extravaganza as box-office insurance; even though Roach was devoting more time to a series of musicals and less to

L&H, the team's films were easily more popular at this time. Still, Roach went ahead with his ambitious plans. In late December 1936, he embarked upon a $200,000 expansion program, including a new sound stage, a new machine shop and new transportation facilities.

Impasse

As 1937 began, it was uncertain whether Laurel and Hardy would be able to celebrate their 10th anniversary as a team. Stan's contract of 1935 had run out, and neither Roach nor Stan seemed to be in a rush to be working together again.

Indeed, on January 21, the Roach studio issued a press release which stated, "For the first time since Stan Laurel and Oliver Hardy became established as a team, one of the comedians is to do a solo job. Hardy, minus Laurel, will go into Roach's *Road Show*, which Norman McLeod is to direct." (This story of an escaped lunatic joining a traveling carnival was finally filmed in 1941, with Adolphe Menjou.)

Events were just as uncertain with Stan. In early February, newspapers reported that he had reconciled with wife Ruth — and that the couple had taken a train to New York. The reconciliation only lasted until May, when Ruth decided to let the interlocutory decree of divorce stand. While in New York, Stan formed a union that lasted slightly longer. *The Hollywood Reporter* of March 2 explained:

> Stan Laurel is staging a one-man sit-down strike on Hal Roach. His new contract is waiting his signature at the studio, but the comic continues to remain in New York, and has written to friends here that he will not return to that studio.
>
> His holdout took on further significance yesterday when Laurel, through his attorneys, filed incorporation articles at Sacramento for his own company, Stan Laurel Productions, with capitalization at $100,000 "for general theater amusement enterprises."...
>
> Oliver Hardy, Laurel's partner, is under contract with Roach for two years more, and unless Laurel can be persuaded from his sit-down position, the famous team of comics will be separated. Hal Roach, who admits the holdout, says the new incorporation is all Greek to him.

Another article noted that Stan would "spend $500,000 a film, and bracket himself with top comics."

Why did Stan form his own corporation? One reason may be that Roach was not taking Stan's demands of production control and $100,000 per feature very seriously, and Stan wanted to show Roach that he aspired to be an independent producer. Stan may have entertained the idea of doing solo films or finding another partner, but he knew his best work would be done with Babe, and that the public only wanted them as a team, not as single comics. Stan may have felt that he could do a feature or two as a single until Babe's contract with Roach expired, and then they could make films together on their own terms.

Author Fred Guiles has alleged that Stan Laurel Productions was designed to consume Laurel's earnings, so he could deprive ex-wife Ruth of the 5% of Stan's gross earnings due her as a result of the divorce settlement. The corporation was more than just what Guiles termed "a shadow organization," however.

In early 1937, Stan made an agreement with producer Jed Buell to make low-budget westerns starring singing cowboy Fred Scott. Three of them were released by Spectrum Pictures (*Knight of the Plains*, *The Ranger's Round-Up* and *Songs and Bullets*) before Buell left to produce an all-midget western, *The Terror of Tiny Town*, and was replaced with L.A. French, former production manager of the L&H unit at Roach.

While Stan had commitments to produce nine more Scott films, he left the series behind after doing these three. One wonders what Laurel actually contributed to these films; it is true that a companion of his, Alice Ardell, played the heroine in *Songs and Bullets*, and a shot from *Way Out West* was used in one of the films.

Although Stan wanted to become a producer, it is, frankly, doubtful that he would have succeeded at running his own corporation and studio. His great gifts were in the creative end of filmmaking — writing, directing, acting, editing. He was not a businessman (as evidenced by the disordered state of his finances, even when he was commanding up to $3,500 a week). Nor was he a tough negotiator. It simply wasn't in Laurel's nature to make demands and stick to them — which he would have had to do as a producer.

(Babe's widow Lucille recalled that the one time her husband was irritated with Stan was during one of the contract disputes in the late '30s. Laurel wanted to have the team under a joint contract, and Hardy agreed to meet with Laurel and Roach, so that the two comics could put up a united front. As soon as Roach began listing the various points of the comedians' new, *separate* contracts, Stan melted and meekly responded, "Whatever you say, Hal, whatever you say.")

The basic problem in the Roach-Laurel relationship was this: Stan Laurel was an artist, and Hal Roach was a businessman, although one who had a great sense of what made a good comedy. The troubles arose when Stan, a salaried employee, tried to assume more control over films Roach was financing — and when Roach disagreed with Stan, who was under contract as a writer as well an actor, over what constituted a good story for Laurel and Hardy.

During the impasse with Stan, Hal Roach was making production deals too. By September 16, Roach was a partner in an Italian production deal with Vittorio Mussolini, son of the Italian premier.

According to Roach, "I went to Europe so I could do the little things that you would do with your family; I had no intention of making any deal whatsoever. Three top men in Mussolini's group, and his son, came to see me in my hotel. The first thing I said was, 'The motion picture business is a Jewish business. If you have sanctions against the Jews, forget this talk, because I want no part of it.' Mussolini was not anti-Semitic at that time."

The Italian premier was an L&H fan and had long admired Roach's films. Soon, he and Roach had an agreement to produce motion-picture operas with Italian actors and American technicians. The new Italian-American corporation was to be called RAM — ("Roach And Mussolini") — and would feature a ram's head in its logo, similar to MGM's lion.

Roach didn't forsee the controversy that would erupt as a result of his association with Il Duce. In September 1937, Mussolini's eldest son, Vittorio, accompanied the producer to Hollywood, where Roach gave a lavish party to welcome him and celebrate his 21st birthday. Roach's guest was not exactly received with open arms by the Hollywood community — or by Roach's own employees.

"We had an actor on the Roach lot named Sammy Brooks, a little man about 3 feet 6 inches tall," said Roy Seawright. "I was in the still department one day talking to Stax Graves' wife, Googie; I didn't know much about politics in those days and I said something about what a great guy Vittorio must be. And all at once, the door burst open, and Sammy Brooks started to tear me apart verbally. He said, 'How can you condone a man who just dropped bombs on all those black people in Ethiopia? What kind of an American are you?!' And he stormed out of there and slammed the door."

The Mussolini-Roach partnership came at a time when Roach was trying to expand and become a major feature-film producer in the ranks of Goldwyn and Selznick. Like those independent producers, Roach had to secure distribution through one of the eight major studios, which owned the theater chains. The studios were controlled by Jewish businessmen who did not approve of Roach's partnership. The Hollywood community had been critical of Roach for welcoming Nazi propagandist filmmaker Leni Riefenstahl sometime earlier; the Mussolini deal further tarnished the producer's reputation.

"The industry as a whole let Roach know, but fast, that they weren't happy about it," said Roy Seawright. "But Roach could be stubborn; he used to be a truck driver, and he ran his business the way he did a truck. He saw a road to take, and he was going to go down that road come hell or high water. He got out of the deal gracefully, but I have a feeling that he suffered by it."

While Stan was making headlines for reconciliations and separations from ex-wife Ruth, and Roach was being criticized for his financial partnerships, Babe Hardy was also in the news. His friend, golfer John "Mysterious" Montague, had been jailed on a robbery charge; Babe offered to pay Montague's $10,000 bail, and proclaimed him to be "one of the finest fellows that ever lived."

Although Laurel, Hardy, and Roach seemingly got publicity — most of it unfavorable — for everything but making films, the team's popularity was unaffected. *Way Out West* did excellent business in the spring of 1937, and Roach undoubtedly wanted Laurel to re-join Hardy. (Babe remained on salary during the contract impasse.) By June 30, Stan had dropped his old agents, Claude and Gordon Bostock, and engaged agent Charles Feldman to sort out the mess.

Laurel wrote his ex-wife Ruth, "I will win out. It is tough sledding now but it won't be long. If Roach wants me, he will pay my price, if not, that's that. I have waited long enough and intend to go to work elsewhere, so you will soon be receiving your five percent." But alimony, legal fees and commissions to agents were rapidly devouring Stan's savings.

Laurel and Roach needed to settle their dispute and go back to work together, whether they wanted to or not.

SWISS MISS

Production history: Script written October-November 1937. Filmed December 28, 1937-February 26, 1938. First preview held March 29. Added scenes shot April 1. Second preview held April 18. Retake shot April 21. Press preview held May 3. Copyrighted May 3, 1938 by Loew's, Incorporated (LP 8025). Released May 20 by MGM. 72 minutes.

Produced by Hal Roach. Associate Producer, S.S. Van Keuren. Directed by John G. Blystone. Photographed by Norbert Brodine and Art Lloyd. Photographic effects by Roy Seawright. Edited by Bert Jordan. Story by Jean Negulesco and Charles Rogers. Screenplay by James Parrott, Felix Adler and Charles Melson. Sound by William Randall. Musical direction by Marvin Hatley. Music arranged by Arthur Morton. Songs by Phil Charig and Arthur Quenzer.

With Walter Woolf King, Della Lind, Eric Blore, Charles Judels, Ludovico Tomarchio, Charles Gemora.

Two mousetrap salesmen travel to Switzerland, where they sell their entire stock to a cheesemaker for 5,000 Bovanian francs. They realize there is no such country only after consuming a large meal at a posh hotel. The boys become handymen to pay off their debt. Ollie soon falls in love with the hotel "chambermaid," Anna Hoepfel Albert, who turns out to be a a famous opera singer. Her composer husband, Victor, has secluded himself at the hotel to write his greatest work, which he hopes will cause the public to notice his talents instead of his wife's.

On October 8, 1937, Roach made a deal for four pictures with Stan Laurel Productions. (Many eyebrows were raised in the film industry because Roach's pact was with the corporation, and not with Stan personally — a unique arrangement at the time. Under the terms of the new contract, the Laurel corporation could make any number of films away from the Roach studio, with or without Stan.)

Employed by Roach as "actor-performer-writer-director," Laurel signed for $2,500 per week, plus $25,000 per picture under the two-year pact. Stan returned to the Roach lot in mid-October for the first time in nearly ten months.

Roach presented his star comic with an undeveloped story idea of his called *Swiss Cheese* when Stan came back to the fold. "What I was trying to do," Roach recalled, "is make musicals where a second plot carried on, so that Laurel and Hardy didn't have to be on all the time. And Laurel, because he didn't understand those kinds of things, was not very cooperative in making those kinds of films."

Indeed, Stan didn't much care for Roach's projected story line. Laurel later explained, "I thought it lacked very much. Hal Roach and I differed a great deal on story ideas, and gags and what have you, and we didn't get along too well on that picture; disagreed very much. When Roach told the other writers to write this or that, they wrote it that way, although they disagreed with the way it was being handled. And they were all for my version of it, but we just couldn't sell it to Roach."

Stan had many conversations about the story with Milton Bren, the supervisor of production and studio management. Laurel told Bren that the story was very weak, and needed alterations. "On certain changes, I agreed with him," Bren later recalled. "I went to Mr. Roach with many suggestions — not necessarily those which Mr. Laurel had made, but some which I had made. Some suggestions that Laurel had, in my own opinion, would have been costly, and not good."

Stan was finding it more difficult than before to inject his own ideas into the films. The team was becoming a victim of its own success. Their popularity enabled Roach to spend more money on this film and thus enhance his own reputation as a feature-film producer, but Stan's control dwindled as the budget increased. The budget of the picture was set at $700,000, more money than had ever been spent before on a L&H feature.

Roach told film historian William K. Everson in 1969 that Laurel "had no overall story sense at all; the only time we ever fought was when he'd come up with a story line that I just knew wouldn't work. So we'd fight and we'd both give in a little, and of course the compromise wasn't good for the picture. *Swiss Miss* is an example.

"Stan suffered from what I'd call the curse of Charlie Chaplin," said Roach. "Chaplin was great and could do everything himself — star, direct, write the story, make up the gags. From then on every comic thought he had to do the same; Stan Laurel, Harry Langdon. It never worked."

As we've seen, the people who worked closely with Stan spoke of his talent in guiding the creative aspects of filmmaking. Unfortunately, his employer did not always share that same high regard.

Unlike the two previous L&H features, *Swiss Miss* was not billed as "A Stan Laurel Production." A new associate producer was assigned to the picture, and his name filled the screen at the end of the credits so that everyone would know it: Hal Roach's cousin, Sidney Van Keuren.

"He was general manager," recalled Roach, "and we had to put someone's name on it as an associate producer, so we put his name on it." However, Van Keuren himself claimed he was on the set "every day of shooting, and had conversations with Stan Laurel about the picture, always about the production."

Van Keuren was not an especially popular man with some of his co-workers. "He was intensely disliked, and it wasn't because he was Roach's cousin, because everybody loved Roach," says one former studio associate. "The spirit of the whole studio just went down when Van moved in," said Roy Seawright. "L.A. French, a wonderful man who had been head of production, was just fired on the spot."

Although Stan was no longer receiving a producer credit, he did approve the selection of the film's director. John G. Blystone had piloted a number of unremarkable comedies and a few adventure films since leaving an acting career to write and direct in 1923; his most notable effort was *Our Hospitality*, for which he shared directing credit with Buster Keaton.

Like most of Roach's other current productions, *Swiss Miss* was planned as a very musical comedy. The "second story" that Roach proposed was going to have just as much importance as the supposed "first story" featuring Laurel and Hardy. Accordingly, Roach and Van Keuren needed experienced singers to fill the roles of the composer and his wife. The role of Anna was won by Della Lind, a Viennese musical comedy star who had been brought to Hollywood by Paramount and then virtually forgotten.

Miss Lind helped decide the casting of her co-star. "Sid Van Keuren gave me the choice between two leading men," she explained. "I made a test with Walter Woolf King first, and then Ray Middleton — and I refused him, because he was a little flirt! So I said, 'I'd rather have Walter Woolf King.' He was my type."

King, who began his career in vaudeville, is best remembered as the evil

Walter Woolf King and Hal Roach Jr. (extreme right) watch Stan and Marvin Hatley play a duet.

tenor Lasparri in the Marx Brothers' *A Night at the Opera.* "I knew the casting director and I knew Mr. Roach," recalled King. "They'd heard me sing before; I had a nice easy quality that was good for that kind of film."

A musical comedy needed songs, so Van Keuren hired songwriter Phil Charig; Arthur Quenzer, a budding writer and former saxophonist with the recently-disbanded Ben Bernie orchestra, signed on as lyricist.

"The producers asked me to write some lyrics," said Quenzer; "They didn't tell me the plot of the picture, but they said it was set in Switzerland. So, I came up with 'I Can't Get Over the Alps.' I worked with Phil Charig, who wrote the melody, and Sid Van Keuren was pretty enthused about the song. So, I got the job. As a result, the other songs were written to fit the story line. Van Keuren was the man who was in between us and the studio heads; Hal Roach, I don't think I met but once.

"We knew what the general story was, but I don't think I ever saw the script. There was very little that we had to do with Laurel and Hardy; Walter Woolf King and Della Lind were the stars of the picture. We used to go down on the sets and watch them; we would get the background for the song which was going to follow, so we could come up with lyrics that might be more apropos. Laurel and Hardy had nothing to do with the songs, although I was hoping that maybe Stan Laurel would get to do some yodeling on a song called 'Yo Ho De O Lay Hee.'"

The shooting was supposed to have begun on December 28, 1937, according to studio files. If it did, the company apparently worked around L&H, because Stan was otherwise occupied.

On December 31, the same day Stan received a final decree of divorce from Ruth, he told friends he would be married again — the next day. Stan celebrated New Year's Day, 1938, by driving to Yuma, Arizona, where he married Vera Illiana Shuvalova, a vivacious Russian singer. Papers reported that Stan had met her "when he gave her a try-out five weeks ago as a prima donna," conceivably for the role of Anna.

The new marriage was clouded immediately when Ruth, claiming that the final divorce was not legal, drove to Yuma, battered Stan's hotel room door and threatened to have him arrested as a bigamist. Stan had to show the Yuma County Clerk that he had obtained his final divorce from Ruth before the ex-Mrs. Laurel would leave.

When Stan returned to work on *Swiss Miss* a few days later, he filed suit against Ruth to prevent her from "annoying and harassing" him. With that settled, Illiana began having "nervous breakdowns," two of them in as many weeks — but she still seemed healthy enough to allow news photographers into her hospital room. And the parade of the screaming headlines marched on. Somehow, with all this turmoil in his private life, Stan managed to get a film made. (He looks quite tired throughout the film, and no wonder.)

John Blystone had never worked with the team before, but he fit the mold of previous L&H directors; he knew who the real comedy director was on this film, just as he undoubtedly did on Keaton's *Our Hospitality*. "He was a very easygoing man," recalled Walter Woolf King. "Very easy to get along with, and very easy to please. I guess the people he had in the picture knew their jobs."

Evidently, some of the first shooting days were spent in making some color test footage. Della Lind has asserted that "it was originally a color film"; Stan's first wife, Lois, who was probably on the set when the Laurels' daughter worked as an extra, recently recalled that the film was envisioned in color, but that Roach decided it would be too expensive, midway through the first week of shooting.

One day, director Blystone found himself suffering from laryngitis. Rather than hold up the production, Hal Roach turned director for a day, guiding King, Lind and Eric Blore in a scene where Anna tells her composer husband that she's just gotten a job as a chambermaid. However, according to studio vice president Milton Bren, "The part Mr. Roach directed was not in the picture. We might have used one or two scenes, but in the course of cutting the picture down, it was not used."

Hal Roach Jr. worked on the film as an assistant to the assistant director. (Roach's daughter Margaret, alias Diane Rochelle, appeared as an extra.) Stan always liked Hal Jr. — despite occasional differences with his father — and the two often had long talks during production. "Stan told me he thought he was the man to write, produce, direct and cut the Laurel and Hardy pictures," said the younger Roach in a 1938 deposition. "I agreed that he had a fine comedy mind."

Although Stan may have wanted more control over the films, he was losing ground. The contract battles and the incessant headlines about Stan's hectic personal life had not set well with Roach. The appointment of Van Keuren as associate producer, and Stan's inability to sell his own reworking of the plot to Roach, did not bode well for Laurel.

Swiss Miss— the most schizophrenic L&H feature since *Bonnie Scotland* — looks as though it was shot by two separate units. "It was really like a vaudeville show," said Walter Woolf King. "First Laurel and Hardy, then Della

The team's doubles (Charlie Phillips and Ham Kinsey) with the crew at Lake Arrowhead. Script clerk Ellen Corby is seated in the foreground.

Lind and me. It had a little story going through it, but it was pretty corny."

Owing to the film's setting, most of the supporting cast was new to L&H films. People like Charles Judels and Adia Kuznetzoff were playing the type of roles formerly essayed by Charlie Hall and James Finlayson. One performer was making a welcome return to the boys' pictures, after an absence of seven years: Anita Garvin, who was cast as an irate hausfrau.

"I was supposed to have a nice part in that," recalled Anita. "Eddie Kane [her on-screen husband] and I were to do more in the picture; kind of a running gag, where at various spots, you'd see me walking through with an angry expression and carrying a frying pan! But it ended up being nothing, because after the third day, I got sick. I was developing a thyroid condition..."

In addition to the Garvin-Kane scenes that went unfilmed, another gag that was planned but finally omitted had Stan giving Ollie a shave, and accidentally slicing off Ollie's nose and his big toe. Mr. Hardy's discomfort is compounded when Stan tries to replace the bodily parts and reverses their rightful positions. Fortunately, this turns out to be another one of Ollie's nightmares.

The saddest omission from the film was a lengthy musical number in which Stan and Ollie describe their mousetraps to cheese-shop owner Charles Judels. The last couple of verses are retained in the film, providing a tantalizing glimpse of what the original sequence was like. Arthur Quenzer, who wrote the lyrics for the other songs, claimed he had nothing to do with the mousetrap

Star-crossed lovers: Stan and Illiana.

cantata; Marvin Hatley only vaguely recalled it, though he remembered writing the charming background music for the film — for which he didn't receive credit.

Most of the comedy scenes in the film have an unusual surreal quality. One in particular — which Roach didn't care for — had Stan and Ollie moving a piano to a hilltop hideaway across a narrow suspension bridge. When a gorilla meets the boys halfway across and decides to play with Ollie's hat, a mad scramble ensues; the ape and the piano end up in the river below.

Most of this scene was filmed on a sound stage, where the mountain bluffs, the front of the chalet and the suspension bridge were all constructed, about eight feet from the ground. The long shots were photographed through a piece of glass, on which artist Jack Shaw painted the bottom of the chasm. The river bed was painted on canvas, with pinholes allowing light to shine through, simulating the sun on the rippling water.

The bridge on which Stan, Ollie and the gorilla twisted and turned was actually a miniature replica, designed by Fred Knoth. "I suggested we could do a miniature," Knoth said. "Roy Seawright said that Roach didn't believe it could be done. I got up a couple of hundred bucks and did a test, and it was convincing. That sequence was the start of big special effects at the Hal Roach studio." Seawright remembered that Laurel was particularly concerned about this scene. "Stan was in charge. Whether the director was actually there or not, Stan was supervising the bridge sequence."

Indeed, the scene — while being a bit less plausible than most Laurel and Hardy routines — is one of the team's most celebrated. Its success is a tribute not only to the skill of Seawright, Knoth and Shaw — but to Charles Gemora, who donned his ape suit to cavort with Stan and Babe for the first time since *The Chimp* (1932).

What used to be "comedies" were now "Big Lavish Musical Superfeatures."

Another gag which depended on Seawright's special effects had Stan and Babe cleaning a stairway, near a large pipe organ. The boys' bucket of soapy water accidentally empties into one of the pipes, so that when Walter Woolf King depresses the keys, bubbles issue forth; as the bubbles break, we hear the notes that were trapped inside them. Seawright accomplished this remarkable gag by rotoscoping small cut-outs of bubbles — photographing them one frame at a time on an animation table.

"I had worked all day, photographing the paths of the various bubbles, until 10 or 11 o'clock at night," Seawright recalled. "I stopped right in the middle of the scene; just couldn't go any farther. Next day, I worked all day, had a sandwich brought in for lunch, no dinner; I was working on it at 10 o'clock at night again. For some reason, I forgot to turn on the red 'Do Not Enter' light outside my animation room. And I had the window open; it was a hot night. I heard a key enter the lock, and a janitor opened the door — a draft came through, and my bubbles went flying all over the room. I damn near died, because it meant I had to start all over again. And the janitor couldn't figure out what was wrong — he said, 'What's wrong with you?'"

If the usually family-like cameraderie prevailed on the set, two people who did not feel very comfortable with each other during the final stages of production were Hal Roach and Stan Laurel. In December 1938, several months after the film had been completed, Roach stated in a deposition that he was constantly speaking with Stan about his "refusal to accept instructions."

"I would criticize him for not being to work," Roach said at the time, "and not giving the full attention of his time to the picture, and changing the ideas of the picture, and [his] failure to cooperate with other people who were working on the picture. Stan would say usually that it would not happen again, that he would try to follow all the things I had desired."

341

Marital discord was making Stan's personal life unpleasant, and as a result his work was affected — just at a time when he needed to prove himself a capable and efficient filmmaker if he was to retain control of his films. In Roach's view, Stan's private life and professional ability were deteriorating, and since Roach was spending more money on the films, it was only proper that *he* assume more of the creative control.

This extended into the process of cutting the picture. According to Roach, Stan was consulted during the editing "by myself, by [production supervisor] Milton Bren, the cutters and the director" — but there was one instance where Roach re-cut a scene after Stan had finished it.

"We had this sequence of taking the piano across the swaying bridge," Stan recalled years later. "The chef in the hotel, it was plain that he hated music. Music just drove him crazy. So this composer came to the hotel, and all night he would be composing, and this chef couldn't stand this music... So he decided to put a bomb in this piano, so when the composer struck a note, it would blow the piano to pieces, you know, and the chef would hope that the other guy wouldn't be too badly off!

"Anyway, I suggested this bomb idea to make the scene on the bridge — give it more *power*. Because here we are on this swinging bridge, God knows how high up, and we just kept missing this one note in the handling of the piano — it had a lot of suspense. But Roach said, 'No, I don't want the bomb.' We shot it all, and then he took out the scene where the guy put the bomb in the piano. So all our business of messing around over the keys seemed to be nothing in the film. There was no reason for it. I'll never know why he did that."

Some of the editing was planned at Stan's new home in Canoga Park, which he dubbed Fort Laurel — so named, he said, because it was his refuge from blondes, ex-wives and reporters. The current blonde in Stan's life was still within Fort Laurel's gates, however, and she didn't make the editing any easier. "Illiana always wanted to sing for me," said film editor Bert Jordan. "She used to play a record of her own voice and sing a duet with it. It was murder. We used to get rid of her, so we could work."

The first cut was assembled on March 4, and the picture was reworked until the 29th, when it was previewed at the United Artists Theater in Long Beach. On April 1, the studio shot a retake of the last scene — in which the gorilla, bandaged and hobbling from his fall, throws a crutch at the fleeing Laurel and Hardy.

The reviews were wildly mixed when the film was released. Predictably, *Variety* found it "just a filler-in and not a very good one," concluding, "*Swiss Miss* misses by a mile and a furlong." *Boxoffice* wasn't much more enthused: "Heavy-handed Laurel and Hardy comedy, in which the team's typical gag situations — some good, but many of ancient vintage — are completely lost in the maze of a wandering story... below the standards of previous Laurel and Hardy efforts."

B.R. Crisler of the *New York Times*, however, found the picture "a bargain excursion in slapstick: a regular ski train, out of season, to the indefensible heights of fantasy... There is too much operetta, on the whole, but the Laurel and Hardy episodes are so delightful that the film even takes Walter Woolf King in its stride." The critic declared, "with enthusiasm and pride," that he was a "a recent Laurel and Hardy convert — as recent as yesterday."

The wildly divided reaction to the film continues today. The team's scenes

— particularly the suspension bridge gag and the sequence in which Stan outwits a St. Bernard for his keg of brandy — are universally acclaimed, but the "second story" about the bickering composer and his prima donna wife is less than vastly entertaining. As is, *Swiss Miss* is enjoyable but seriously flawed. One can only speculate what it might have been like if Stan could have sold his version to Roach.

BLOCK-HEADS

Production history: Script written May 23-June 7, 1938. Filmed June 1-July 1. First cut completed July 6. First preview held July 22. Added scenes shot July 27 and 28. Second preview held August 1. Final cut completed August 2. Press preview held August 12. Copyrighted August 17, 1938 by Loew's (LP 8463). Released August 19 by MGM. 58 minutes.

Produced by Hal Roach. Associate Producer, Hal Roach, Jr. Directed by John G. Blystone. Photographed by Art Lloyd. Photographic effects by Roy Seawright. Edited by Bert Jordan. Original story and screenplay by James Parrott, Charles Rogers, Felix Adler, Harry Langdon, Arnold Belgard. Sound by Hal Bumbaugh. Musical direction by Marvin Hatley.

With Minna Gombell, Patricia Ellis, Billy Gilbert, James Finlayson.

When Ollie hears about a soldier found in the trenches 20 years after World War I has ended, he can't imagine anyone being that dumb — until he realizes it's his old pal Stan. When Hardy brings Laurel home to meet the missus, Mrs. Hardy storms out. They try to fix dinner themselves with disastrous results. Next-door neighbor Mrs. Gilbert offers to help clean up, only to have Ollie spill a bowl of punch on her. She is forced to wear Mr. Hardy's pajamas while her dress dries; neither Mrs. Hardy nor Mr. Gilbert — a big game hunter — are very understanding.

Block-Heads is generally regarded today as one of the best L&H features. There are no unnecessary subplots or musical numbers; there's just enough story to sustain the film through its running time, and the gags flow unceasingly. It's such a serene, easygoing little movie, it's hard to believe the production was surrounded by utter chaos.

In early May 1938, Stan and the writers were working on a story which had the boys in a swashbuckling adventure on Devil's Island. The idea had been hatched four years earlier, about the time of *The Live Ghost*. Laurel wanted to film the picture quickly, so he and Babe could make personal appearances in Europe that September. He also wanted his wife Illiana to play the feminine lead in the film, and vice-president of production Milton Bren agreed to give her a screen test.

Laurel and the writers had some difficulty trying to merge the original two-reel story with a dramatic script Bren had recently commissioned. The two-reeler's script took place entirely on the island, while the dramatic story was confined to a ship. By May 19, Roach told Laurel that if the story was going to take a long time to develop, it had better be scuttled. Roach needed a loan, and he couldn't get the money from the Bank of America unless a picture was already shooting; he told Stan he wanted to make a short, cheap film, and it had to start filming a week from the following Monday. After he got the camera running, Stan could stop if necessary.

Stan suggested they do a reworking of the team's first talkie, *Unaccustomed As We Are*. It was nine years old, so it probably wouldn't be remembered by most audiences; better yet, it had all taken place on one inexpensive set. Roach thought this a fine idea, and told Laurel to rush it into production.

Part of the reason Roach needed that loan quickly may be that on May 16, he secured a new distribution agreement with United Artists, abruptly severing his 11-year association with Metro-Goldwyn-Mayer. The reason for the break remains unclear; Metro had given little publicity to Roach's screwball comedy *Topper*, and some felt they had intentionally sabotaged the picture, possibly as retribution for Roach's attempted deal with Mussolini. (A lawyer later decided that MGM owed Roach $2 million, and a lawsuit ensued; Roach settled for $200,000.)

In any event, Roach had one last picture to deliver under his old Metro deal, and the new L&H feature would be it. Between May 23 and June 7, Stan and the writers whipped up a new script, which as usual bore little resemblance to the final product.

Ollie's wife is referred to as Mae in the script, which leads one to conclude that Mae Busch was slated for the part played by Minna Gombell. By any name, Mrs. Hardy is even more of a witch on paper than on film; she's constantly throwing vases and chairs at Ollie, just to ensure that he gets her point.

Most of the unused scripted gags occur in the apartment sequence. For example, while they're walking up the stairs to Ollie's thirteenth-floor home, the boys encounter a drunk who speaks unintelligibly. They discover that if they shake him, he'll speak with perfect diction. When they find the drunk is having trouble with his bathroom plumbing, Stan and Ollie offer their assistance.

Ollie notices a trickle of water spraying from the keyhole of the bathroom door. He sneaks up on the door, than flings it open — which prompts a torrent of water to send the boys cascading down 13 flights of stairs, through the lobby and out into the street — where they are narrowly missed by sadistic motorists.

The script had a scene in which the two ex-soldiers contrive to prepare dinner. Since the wife has stalked out and Mr. Hardy can't cook, Ollie proposes that they dine on a can of beans and a bottle of wine. After a complex gag in which Stan slices Ollie's tie while opening the can of beans, the boys adjourn to the dining room and consume some wine. They start to reminisce, and get misty-eyed.

Stan finds a tune of World War I vintage on the radio and asks Ollie if he remembers it. Ollie doesn't, so Stan absently says, "It goes like this — ," and hums it; Stan begins to dance as he hums, and soon Ollie joins him, culminating in another full-fledged flight of terpsichory.

From here, the script resembles the film fairly closely, except that it's a more literal remake of *Unaccustomed As We Are*. Mr. Gilbert goes to the Hardy apartment to patch up the couple's quarrel, realizes the boys have hidden a girl in a trunk (although he doesn't know that she's his wife), tells them they should be discreet about their dalliances like *he* is when he's in Borneo, moves the trunk to his own room, and catches hell from his wife. Mr. Gilbert marches back to the Hardy apartment with murder in his eye and an elephant gun in his hand.

Gilbert chases the boys out of the building and into an alley, where his

Filming on location near the Veteran's Administration Hospital on Sawtelle Blvd., Los Angeles.

shotgun blast and cry of "I'll teach you to fool around with my wife" is met with hundreds of windows flinging open, and pantsless philanderers running off into the horizon. (This bit was borrowed from 1928's *We Faw Down.*)

Stan's original concept of the ending was a coda to this gag: In the Gilbert apartment, Billy is proudly detailing the capture of each of his new trophies. The camera pans over, and we see the latest additions to the trophy wall — Laurel and Hardy's heads are mounted on plaques, with Stan's face frozen in a weepy grimace as Ollie glowers at him. (Hal Roach never cared for the occasional freak endings that Stan employed; while he tolerated them in the past, he ordered this one deleted.)

This script has more plot and dialogue than the film; in the movie, the plot is simpler, and many, many gags have been added. Most of the best gags appear to have been invented on the set — Stan smoking his fist like a pipe; Stan finding a glass of water in one pocket and ice in the other; Ollie being unable to free his key chain from the front door lock and having to strip to his undies; the argument scene in the Hardy bedroom where Stan is continually prodded by a cantankerous bedspring.

One of the writers was new to L&H films, but he was no stranger to film comedy. Harry Langdon had been hailed as the new Chaplin in the late '20s, before he fired director Frank Capra and attempted to write and direct his own pictures. By 1929, Langdon was struggling in talkie two-reelers for Roach, in a series which barely lasted a year. Laurel greatly admired Langdon; some of the early scenes in *Block-Heads* echo Langdon's *Soldier Man*.

Laurel and Hardy's new feature bore the titles of *Meet the Missus* and *Just a Jiffy* while in production. Shooting started June 1, six days before the first script was completed. According to statements given by Roach studio executives in December 1938, the picture was troubled from the beginning.

Hal Roach and his son both stated that on several days during the filming, Stan failed to come to the studio; the elder Roach later chastised Stan for not showing up. Roach, however, admitted that Laurel was generous enough to suggest that Hal Jr. receive credit as associate producer — although the younger Roach was simply following Stan's orders.

"There are certain capacities that all pictures have, when you put the names on a picture... to make it look like a picture that has importance," Roach Sr. said at the time. "And if you had everything on the picture that Laurel does, his name would be on there about 10 times... Hal Jr. never gave directions to Laurel... how could he give instructions to Laurel when Laurel was the head man?"

Roach asserted much time was lost due to Laurel's absences — and because of alleged drinking on the set. Roach said he could tell Stan was drunk during the filming "by looking at him and seeing some of his work on the screen and scenes we had to cut out of the picture" — but admitted to Stan's attorney that he never complained to Laurel about this.

When asked if he ever actually saw Stan drinking, Roach said he'd visited Stan for five-minute periods about two or three times during the filming. "I never saw him actually take the bottle up to his lips," said Roach. "He was drinking beer and the beer was there in a half-consumed bottle. That was the drinking that I saw."

Roach *père* added that he would often call Stan into his office; Stan would promise he wasn't going to drink anymore, and he'd work hard and fast to make up for lost time. "He was always very pleasant when he wasn't drinking," Roach said. Roach *fils* told of a few occasions when Stan would "rehearse for an hour and would then leave the stage"; he felt Stan was morose about something.

The root of the whole problem seemed to be Stan's stormy marriage to Illiana. "I would read in the paper certain cracks about Laurel being in a certain cafe with his wife, and that there was a disturbance," Roach Sr. said at the time. "The police of Beverly Hills from time to time would tell me that they were called over to Laurel's house because of fights, or neighbors complaining about noise, and they seemed to think I should be kept informed of those things. This happened all during the course of the picture."

Block-Heads wrapped only a month after it had started, on July 1 — but Roach maintained that "it could have been done much faster because that picture had no production in it at all." Yet Roach conceded that the film had been brought in well under schedule.

On July 2, according to Roach Jr., Stan was supervising the cutting. He wanted to retake an insert shot of a French aviator; Hal Jr. wanted some retakes on scenes showing Stan in the trenches guarding the post, and Stan agreed. There was already some disagreement about the film's ending; the younger Roach recalled Stan telling him, "We will wait to change the ending until after the first preview."

On July 9, Stan left Los Angeles. Hal Jr. and Matt O'Brien, the studio's

Signing autographs for young admirers while on location.

secretary-treasurer, both tried unsuccessfully to contact Laurel. Ernie Murphy, Stan's secretary, told them Stan had gone but didn't know where. Two days later, O'Brien again told Murphy the studio needed Stan until the final cutting and preview, and that no one had given him any right to leave.

Roach's secretary, Ruth Burch, finally called Stan's attorney, Ben Shipman, who admitted Stan was out of town and was "very much upset emotionally and hardly his usual self." Shipman attributed Stan's strange conduct to this "mental condition," and added that Stan had called him on the 18th — at 1:30 in the morning — for advice on his marital problems.

Meanwhile, the studio treasurer gave Ernie Murphy a check for Stan, for the two days he'd spent working on the cutting, and told him that Stan was off the Roach payroll as of July 12.

The first preview was held July 22 at the Tower Theater in Compton. Hal Roach and his son talked with Jimmy Parrott afterwards about Stan's absence, and Hal Sr. decided then that "The finish was no good. We had to make the finish over."

The next day, both Roaches and the quartet of writers met in a projection room to discuss retakes and additional scenes. Charley Rogers told Hal Jr. he'd received a telegram from Stan, with an Atlantic City postmark. Stan wanted to know how the preview had gone.

In the meantime, Parrott, Rogers, Felix Adler and Harry Langdon went back to work on the Devil's Island story — but they made little progress without Stan. The writers were laid off July 25.

By July 27, another cut of *Block-Heads* had been assembled, screened and deemed unsatisfactory. The company shot some newly-written scenes that day with Babe and the other cast members, including the scene with Ollie meeting Mrs. Gilbert and her jealous husband in the apartment hallway.

The next day, retakes were made of the street fight between Ollie and Jimmy Finlayson; the sequence was lengthened a bit. The company also did a retake of the final gag, with Billy Gilbert's double (Ben Heidelman), chasing Stan and Babe's doubles (Ham Kinsey and Charlie Phillips) — and 25 half-dressed extras jumping out of apartment windows at the sound of a rifle blast.

Stan returned home, just as mysteriously as he'd left, on July 30. Two days later, a second preview of the film was held at the United Artists Theater in Inglewood. Stan and Roach had a brief conversation afterwards. Stan failed to come to the studio the next day; he wouldn't return until they paid him — his salary had been docked during his absence.

On August 5, the Roach studio received a telegram from Stan Laurel Productions, saying Stan was "most desirous and is able, ready and willing to perform any and all services" under his contract of October 8, 1937, especially for the completion of *Block-Heads* and the preparation of the new story.

The telegram stated that weekly salary checks and story payments for *Block-Heads* had not been paid to Stan. It also assured the studio of Stan's "ever-continuing desire and willingness to perform the obligations imposed upon him under the contract..."

During all of this, a final cut of *Block-Heads* was completed by Bert Jordan. On August 6, the film's 45-year-old director, John G. Blystone, died of a heart attack.

Stan, Illiana and her sister, "Countess Sonia," at Sardi's in New York during the disputed vacation.

On August 9, Stan's attorney, Ben Shipman, met with Roach and his attorney, Victor Collins. "The gist of the conversation," said Roach in December 1938, "was that we had gone as far as we possibly could go with Laurel breaching the terms of the contract, and it was just impossible for us to continue... Mr. Shipman tried to convince me if we would give him another chance, he would straighten himself out and would live up to the contract..."

Roach's reasons for wanting to cancel the contract were "general insubordination, and that the man's brain was to some extent affected by worry over different wives, and over drinking and over late hours, and he was unable to coordinate as well as he had in the past." Roach told Shipman he made the decision "with great regret... but it was just a hopeless task as far as the studio was concerned to continue with a man with the attitude of mind that he had."

On Friday, August 12, the Roach studio notified Stan Laurel Productions that Stan's contract had been terminated. The press preview for *Block-Heads* was held that night at the Fairfax Theater.

News of the firing hit the papers on August 17. Stan maintained he had obtained permission to leave town with Illiana, and that he had not been told to remain for retakes. The studio felt that Stan had violated the contract by being unavailable. Rumors prevailed that Harry Langdon would substitute for Stan on the "two remaining pictures" on the contract.

The following day, the Associated Press reported that Roach had signed Langdon "to replace Stan Laurel in a series of films opposite Oliver Hardy... The studio said the Hardy-Langdon film series would differ sharply from the broad slapstick of the Laurel-Hardy comedies and would be based on important novels."

Block-Heads was released on August 19. The reviews were generally enthusiastic, although *Variety*, as usual, found the film "an awful letdown" — a strange criticism, since the paper hadn't liked many of the team's previous releases. The *New York Herald Tribune* was brazen enough to assert that the film was "a comic tour de force" only because Harry Langdon, "who in his heyday was undoubtedly a greater comedian than either the sad-faced man or the fat fellow ever could be," was one of the five credited authors.

Frank S. Nugent's *New York Times* review, by contrast, was almost a eulogy. "There are vague and distressing rumors that Laurel and Hardy are about to dissolve their screen partnership," he wrote. "'T'would be a pity, as almost any one will admit... Masters of the delayed and double takems, the slow burn, the dead pan, the withering (or vacuous) looks, the tailspin and asthmatic wheeze, Laurel and Hardy seem equally at ease with or without plot material.... *Block-Heads*, in a sentence, is a chip off the old slapstick."

The Academy of Motion Picture Arts and Sciences recognized the lyrical beauty of Marvin Hatley's music for this picture by nominating it for the Best Original Score of 1938. (His contribution to Roach's *There Goes My Heart* was nominated the same year for Best Score; neither won.)

Even though it looked like Laurel and Hardy would be a team no more, Stan told *Los Angeles Times* reporter Read Kendall that he wasn't worried at all. "Laurel disclosed that he is going to let his lawyer do all the fretting," Kendall wrote, and added that Stan wasn't concerned about the proposed Langdon and Hardy partnership.

Stan may have been confident that L&H would get back together, but at the time he seemed to be the only person holding this opinion. Babe still had several months left on his contract, and with the most serious disagreement yet between Roach and Laurel clouding the future, it looked very much like Mr. Hardy would be working with a new partner from now on.

Trouble, Folks, Right Here in Culver City

Laurel and Hardy's personal and professional lives were chaotic during and after the production of *Block-Heads*, but from the summer of 1938 to the spring of 1939, Stan had Trouble with a capital T.

First, there were the difficulties between Laurel and Hal Roach. Soon after *Block-Heads* was released, Ben Shipman, attorney for Stan Laurel Productions, received a letter from Roach studio production manager Milton Bren and studio attorney Victor Collins. It read in part: "You are quite right in your assumption that the publicity relating to Mr. Laurel's marital difficulties tends to invoke some contentions on our part... As a matter of fact, it is our distinct contention that Mr. Laurel breached the terms of his contract by placing himself in a position to have such adverse publicity."

Thus, the studio made it clear that Stan had been fired for something other than just being unavailable for retakes. His contract was apparently terminated largely because of Ruth and Illiana's misadventures.

As summer turned to fall, the prospect of Laurel, Hardy and Roach working together again seemed increasingly remote. On September 11, 1938, Mack Sennett announced that he had signed Stan as the star of a series of films for the newly-formed Sennett Pictures Corporation. The first project on the slate: *Problem Child*, about the full-sized son of midget parents. Jed Buell, who had produced the all-midget western *The Terror of Tiny Town*, was named as associate producer.

It's unlikely that this project was ever intended to be produced. It appears that Stan and Ben Shipman put some readily available elements together (Buell had been associate producer for Stan's westerns starring Fred Scott) and made the announcement to hasten a deal with the Roach studio. Stan knew, as he wrote ex-wife Ruth, that "Laurel is no good without Hardy and vice versa."

If Stan was threatening to work with Roach's old rival, Sennett, it was a pretty hollow threat. By 1938, there was no comparison between the comedy producers. Roach had adapted to current trends, and was making features which bore little resemblance to his old slapstick comedies; Sennett hadn't even adapted well to talkies, and had been semi-retired for five years.

While Roach kept making plans for ambitious new features, Stan wasn't doing much of anything — except getting more unfavorable headlines. On September 28, there was an altercation in Laurel's home. He maintained that Illiana had quarreled with him, pushed his arm through a window, threatened to hit him with a skillet, and tossed sand in his eyes. An alternate version of the story was that a thug broke into the house, pushed Stan around, ordered him to open the safe, and ran out with $10,000.

In any event, Stan was arrested for driving at 55 miles per hour on the wrong side of Reseda Boulevard. When two patrol officers caught up with Laurel after chasing him for seven blocks, he admitted he'd been drinking. Stan was booked for driving under the influence and spent the night in jail; the next day, he was released on $250 bail.

A trial was set for October 24. Ben Shipman told the jury he would prove

Personally and professionally, Stan's life was troubled late in 1938.

that Stan was not drunk, but upset over Illiana's antics. The jury deliberated for six hours and was dismissed after being deadlocked 8 to 4 for acquittal. Stan was ordered to return to court for a retrial on December 5, but was cleared on this date of misdemeanor drunk-driving charges.

With that cleared up, Laurel got involved in another court case two days later. On December 7, he sued the Hal Roach Studios for $700,000, charging breach of contract. Stan told a *Los Angeles Times* reporter he felt he was being boycotted from the film industry; the proposed deal with Sennett was off, because the producer couldn't find a studio interested in releasing *Problem Child*.

Meanwhile, Hardy was busy. Roach had bought the rights to a short story by H. C. Bunner entitled *Zenobia's Infidelity* some time before the contract problems with Stan. Roach originally planned to star Roland Young, of *Topper* fame, as a country doctor who unties a knot in the tail of a carnival barker's elephant, and unwittingly becomes the object of the pachyderm's affections. With Stan gone, the story became a vehicle for Babe — with Harry Langdon cast as the elephant's jilted owner.

As the picture was written and produced, it bore a plethora of working titles. It was finally released as *Zenobia*, but it was not a terribly funny or cohesive movie by any name. Babe gave a fine, understated performance that let his genial warmth shine through, but he didn't have much in the way of material. His widow Lucille remembered that Babe felt somewhat uncomfortable during the filming; he'd become so accustomed to the give-and-take with Stan that it felt strange to be carrying a picture by himself.

And he truly carried the picture too, because for all of the ballyhoo about a Hardy and Langdon team, the two comics shared very few scenes. There were amusing scenes with Langdon and others, but the strange story of a fickle pachyderm seemed awkward when juxtaposed with the romantic subplot, Babe's semi-dramatic scenes, and the lush Old South settings.

"*Zenobia* was a disaster from the very start to the finish. It was a louse," Hal Roach said flatly. "I signed Marc Connelly up for a lot of dough to write the story. He was so important he couldn't work at the studio, he had to work at the Beverly-Wilshire Hotel. It turned out to be the worst script I'd ever seen. In one scene, the elephant walked into a bank, and nobody knew the elephant was there.

"Then, the worst producer we ever had produced the picture — Eddie Sutherland. He started out as an actor with Sennett, and then he became sort of a boy-about-town; if you needed an extra man, socially, you invited him. He knew everybody in the business, but had very little ability, actually."

The production seemed to be doomed from the start. Even before the cameras began rolling, an article in *Boxoffice* noted that the United Artists sales force had been advised "not to sell the two Hardy-Langdon feature length comedies until each one is completed," which was not exactly a vote of confidence in the new "team."

As *Zenobia* was being filmed and released, Stan endured more private woes. In late December 1938, Illiana sued him for $1,500 monthly alimony. On January 1, 1939, she began serving a five-day jail sentence for crashing into two parked cars the previous April. (When Stan came to the jail to take Illiana home, the newspapers ran a pithy photo caption: "They're together again — but not for long.") The Laurels reportedly reconciled in early February, but on March 5, Illiana sued again for alimony.

At the alimony hearing on April 13, Illiana testified that Stan had dug a grave for her in the back yard of their home, and invited her to step in to be buried alive. She also maintained that Laurel had invited his first wife, Lois, along on a honeymoon cruise; that second wife Ruth had sent her a telegram stating that Stan was mentally unbalanced; and that Stan routinely administered severe beatings.

As this colorful testimony leaked from court proceedings and spilled across the headlines, Stan could see his image as a purveyor of wholesome family comedy being ripped to shreds. He made an out-of-court settlement on the 15th. On the 25th, *Stan* filed for divorce, protesting that he'd tried to be a devoted husband while Illiana frequently left on merry sprees for days at a time without notifying him. On May 17, Stan obtained a divorce by default. The tempestuous story of Stan's life with Illiana was over — for a time.

Stan's relations with the Roach studio had been chilly while *Zenobia* was being filmed. On February 4, 1939, the studio issued a reply to Laurel's breach of contract suit. Completely abandoning its earlier defense that Stan had been fired for leaving town during editing and retakes, the studio charged that Laurel had been terminated for violating the morals clause of his contract. According to the studio, Stan "drank while at work; sometimes arrived late for work, and again left the studio before the proper time."

The studio then tried to justify this charge by commenting upon Laurel's problems *after* the cancellation of the contract — a dubious defense, indeed. The Roach studio charged that Laurel "on numerous occasions has been

Langdon and Hardy seem to like their first script.

intoxicated in public and has participated in public disturbances which have brought about police interference and has caused his arrest... Laurel has also taken part in public quarrels and reconciliations with his wife Illiana and with his former wives... all of which have caused him much adverse publicity and have brought on him the ridicule and contempt of the public."

As *Zenobia* laid an elephant-sized egg, however, the Roach studio became somewhat more receptive to the possibility of Stan rejoining its ranks. On April 8, 1939, attorneys representing Roach and Laurel appeared before Superior Judge Thomas C. Gould and signed an agreement to drop the legal action.

Under the terms of the out-of-court settlement, Stan would return to work as a member of the L&H team and would receive an undisclosed amount of money — which would be held in trust, pending the outcome of Illiana's concurrent alimony suit. Stan had always wanted the team to have a joint contract with Roach; the producer compromised by putting Stan and Babe under separate — but concurrent — contracts. Both comedians signed one-year pacts with Roach on April 8, 1939.

Finally, there was a semblance of peace. Stan had unshackled himself from his tempersome wife, he'd settled his dispute with Roach, and he was set to re-join his old teammate.

Meanwhile, another producer expressed interest in the reunited team's services. Boris Morros, a former musical director, wanted to use Stan and Babe in his first film as an independent producer. On the same day of the settlement, Roach agreed to loan Laurel and Hardy to Morros for a remake of a French comedy, *Les Aviateurs*. The film was slated to start filming on July 1, with Edward Sutherland — the producer of *Zenobia* — in the director's chair.

But first the boys had to complete a new film for Roach, the first of a series of what the producer termed "streamliners." Henceforth, L&H were to make a quartet of four-reel comedies for Roach, their first in this format since *Beau Hunks* in 1931. This would eliminate padding and unneeded subplots, and would be attractive to exhibitors who were getting complaints about overly-long double-feature bills.

A CHUMP AT OXFORD

Production history: Script written mid-April-May 15, 1939. Filmed June 1939. Final cut completed by August 31 (42 minute version). New material written and filmed September 1939. New cut completed by October 4 (63 minute version). Copyrighted January 19, 1940 by Roach (LP 9377). Short version released in the United States February 16, 1940 by United Artists. Long version released overseas simultaneously; released in U.S., early 1941.

Produced by Hal Roach. Associate Producer, Hal Roach, Jr. Directed by Alfred Goulding. Photographed by Art Lloyd. Photographic effects by Roy Seawright. Edited by Bert Jordan. Story and screenplay by Charles Rogers, Felix Adler and Harry Langdon. Sound by William Randall. Musical score by Marvin Hatley.

With Forrester Harvey, Wilfred Lucas, Forbes Murray, Eddie Borden, Peter Cushing, Charlie Hall.

Street sweepers Stan and Ollie foil a bank robbery, and are rewarded with the finest education money can buy, at Oxford. The boys are somewhat confound-

ed by the pranks played on them by fellow students. When Stan gets hit on the head by a window sash, he reverts to his "true" personality, Lord Paddington — the haughty but brilliant athlete and scholar who wandered away from Oxford years before. Ollie is reduced to being Paddington's valet, and endures many humiliations before the faulty window smacks Paddington and restores his alter ego.

In April 1939, Stan got together with his writers for the first time since the previous July. Harry Langdon was once more employed as a gag man, in the company of Felix Adler and Charley Rogers.

Conspicuous by his absence from the crew was James Parrott, who died on May 10, as the script was nearing completion. The official cause of death was heart disease, but according to former associates, Parrott's drinking had led to a drug problem. "Jimmy got to the point where he knew he couldn't quit," said one Roach employee. "Nobody would hire him. He was broke — he needed money desperately, and his brother Charley Chase said, 'I can't give him money, because he'll just use it for more dope, and we've got to put a stop to it.' Jimmy committed suicide as a result; Charley never got over it."

The details of Parrott's death remain clouded, except for the fact that he died much too young. Parrott was 42. Tragically, his brother died just a year later, on June 30, 1940, from a heart attack brought on by *his* drinking problem. Charley Chase was 46.

Rogers, Adler and Langdon came up with an intriguing idea which placed Laurel and Hardy in the dignified environs of Oxford University. Assisting them on the script was Alfred Goulding — the ex-vaudevillian who had brought about Laurel's introduction to Roach in 1918, after seeing Stan's act and suggesting that Roach sign the comic for five one-reelers. Although Laurel and Goulding were quite friendly, *Chump* was the first time Goulding directed the team; the director had recently moved back to the States from England when he became involved with the new L&H picture.

The director's widow, Betty Goulding, offered this perspective on her late husband's working relationship with the team: "Stan always respected Alf's judgment, and respected him as an artist. But when Alf was doing a picture, he was in command. He wouldn't be told. If Stan suggested something, if he said, 'What do you think if I did so-and-so' — if Alf thought it was good, he would say so. If he didn't think it was right, he would stick by his guns and they would understand.

"There's a scene in the film where Stan and Ollie get lost in a maze of hedges. Alf told me he had a little difficulty in selling that to Stan. Stan wasn't quite sure how that would go — and apparently Alf must have explained it and shown him why it would be funny.

"Stan and Babe were both very sensitive. I remember Alf saying to me, 'You have to handle Stan very carefully. You have to handle him with kid gloves.' If you had an idea for a gag, and Stan didn't see it, you didn't say, 'Well, we're doing it and that's it.' You had to explain it to him, and then he'd see it.

"I'm sure they had a lot of fun working together, because Alf was a great practical joker. He always used to say, 'I like a happy set.' But he didn't like intrusive joking. Alf was absolutely a professional on the set; with Stan, they wouldn't be playing around while they were working. But when they were finished shooting, then they would have fun."

Fun and games with Charley Rogers, Harry Langdon and director Alf Goulding.

The filming must have been like a trip back home for Stan; not only were fellow Britons Charley Rogers, Alf Goulding and Charlie Hall on the set — they were joined by English character actor Forrester Harvey (who lent a great deal of charm to his role as Meredith, the boys' valet) and a number of young English actors portraying some prankish students. Among them was Peter Cushing, more than a decade away from fame in horror movies. Cushing was a bit awestruck by the legendary comics, and even in later years considered this a highlight of his career.

One of the film's best gags — the scene where the hapless duo attempt to get out of the outdoor maze — was largely dependent on special effects. Two-thirds of the maze was actually a matte painting; the remaining section was constructed on a sound stage. As with the bridge suspension gag for *Swiss Miss*, this gag was created through the joint efforts of Fred Knoth's prop department and Roy Seawright's optical effects unit.

The most dazzling aspect of the film is Stan's acting. *A Chump at Oxford* provides our only clue as to how Laurel would have essayed a straightforward dramatic role. As Lord Paddington, he's the absolute opposite of his familiar screen self; he's haughty, self-important, and persists in belittling Ollie, his valet (whom he refers to as "Fatty"). He delivers his insults in an accent that's the epitome of upper-crust.

The resolution of the story, provided through the courtesy of the faulty window sash, is a bit abrupt, but Ollie's shouts of joy as he embraces his returned buddy are particulary poignant. It's the brief moments like this that set Laurel and Hardy so strongly apart from other, more superficial, comedy teams.

June 16, 1939: Stan receives a birthday serenade, courtesy of Western Union.

After Stan and Babe completed the four-reel version of this film, they left to make *The Flying Deuces* for Boris Morros. During the team's absence from the Roach lot, Roach decided to expand *A Chump at Oxford* for the European market, where Laurel and Hardy were looked upon with much greater regard and were invariably the top attraction on the bill.

In September 1939, the team returned to Roach's and, in effect, shot their first two-reeler since 1935's *Thicker Than Water*. The new scenes seem like a self-contained film. Stan and Ollie go to an employment agency and overhear that an opening is available for a butler and a maid. Before you can say "Fade out," butler Ollie and maid Stan are at the ornate door of Mr. and Mrs. Van-devere. From here, it's a reworking of *From Soup to Nuts*, with several new gags thrown in. Adding to the homey atmosphere of these scenes are the familiar faces — Vivien Oakland as the receptionist, Harry Bernard as a cop, Sam Lufkin as a street-sweeper driver, and in particularly welcome returns, Anita Garvin and James Finlayson as the Vandeveres.

A Chump at Oxford benefits from another serene, lyrical score by Marvin Hatley. Although Hatley had been in the studio's employ since 1930 and had garnered three Oscar nominations, his talents were not fully appreciated by Frank Ross, a new executive hired by Roach to oversee the running of the studio.

One day, Ross was watching Hatley record the score for a concurrently-produced Roach swashbuckler called *Captain Fury*. In one section, the melody was supposed to be played by trombones and cellos, but the arranger had copied it for the cellos only. When Hatley asked his copyist to put the melodic line in the trombone parts, Ross calculated the cost of 65 musicians waiting 15 minutes while being paid $10 an hour.

"Frank Ross didn't know anything about all the years I'd put in there, all the instruments I could play — he knew nothing about those things," said Hatley. "He was just interested in showing Mr. Roach how efficient he could be — so he told the executives how inefficient Hatley was. I don't know what happened to Mr. Ross [afterwards], but he ended Marvin Hatley's career in movies." Tired of the "terrifying pressure" of composing for the movies, Hatley spent the next 20 years as a pianist in cocktail lounges — and earned more than he had at the Roach studio.

Hal Roach's "hands-off" philosophy — hiring talented people and letting them alone — generally worked well with his creative employees and benefited the studio enormously. But the policy sometimes backfired when applied to the executive board.

A Chump at Oxford got excellent reviews upon its initial release. Bosley Crowther of the *New York Times* found it a "priceless burlesque," and termed the film "as silly and unintelligent as a lecture in double-talk, and also about as funny as clowns can be these days."

Graham Greene observed in *The Spectator* that it "ranks with their best pictures—which to one heretic are more agreeable than Chaplin's; their clowning is purer; they aren't out to better an unbetterable world; they've never wanted to play Hamlet."

Even grouchy old *Variety* allowed that it was "mildly comical without offending." However, the paper adhered to its usual bias against visual comedy, remarking, "They have more witty dialog than usual and it seems to help overcome the necessity of so much old-fashioned hoke panto." Oddly, most of the reviews gave the picture's running time as 63 minutes, indicating that the longer version may have been shown in some regions of the United States at the same time as the four-reel edition.

After making a film for Hal Roach with virtually no conflicts for the first time in years, Stan and Babe were now set to make one feature for another independent producer. It would be the only film made away from Roach's where the team would have the same measure of control over the final result — and consequently, the only one that approached the quality of the Roach features.

THE FLYING DEUCES

Production history: Story outline written by Alfred Schiller, mid-April—mid-May 1939. Revised script by Ralph Spence, Charles Rogers, Harry Langdon and (uncredited) Stan Laurel written mid-June—early July. Filmed July 22—mid-August. Editing and retakes, late August. Previewed in Los Angeles and New Rochelle, New York, September 1939. Released by RKO-Radio Pictures, October 20. Copyrighted November 3, 1939 by Boris Morros Productions, Inc. (LP 9209). 69 minutes.

Produced by Boris Morros. Directed by A. Edward Sutherland. Second unit direction, Robert Stillman. Photographed by Art Lloyd. Aerial photography, Elmer Dyer. Edited by Jack Dennis. Original story and screen play by Ralph Spence, Alfred Schiller, Charles Rogers and Harry Langdon. Sound, William Wilmarth. Musical direction by Edward Paul.

With Jean Parker, Reginald Gardiner, Charles Middleton, James Finlayson.

While on a Paris holiday, Ollie falls in love with innkeeper's daughter Georgette, unaware that she's already married to Francois, a Foreign Legion officer. After she gently turns Ollie down, he attempts to drown himself — taking Stan with him. But Francois stops their suicide attempt and suggests the boys join the Legion. L&H prove less than efficient soldiers and are soon arrested for desertion. They escape a firing squad by stealing an airplane, but the plane crashes and Ollie is killed. Happily, Stan soon meets his pal again — reincarnated as a horse.

The saga of *The Flying Deuces*, you'll recall, began on April 8, 1939, immediately after Stan had settled his contract dispute with Hal Roach. Boris Morros, a one-time Broadway producer who went on to write movie scores, had decided to become an independent producer; he took advantage of Laurel and Hardy's reunion by arranging a loan-out deal with Roach. Morros set up a Hollywood office, and hired Alfred Schiller to write a story outline, based loosely on a French comedy film called *Les Aviateurs*.

Laurel and Hardy would learn very quickly that writers who had never worked with them before, like Schiller, could not be trusted to deliver a satisfactory script. Schiller apparently never saw an L&H movie, judging from the woefully ill-fitting material he wrote for the team. An examination of his original story outline is intriguing, because it shows just how much work Laurel, Rogers and Langdon had to do to turn Schiller's treatment into a suitable script. *The Flying Deuces* would be the only story by an outside writer which Stan would be allowed to rewrite.

In Schiller's original story, Laurel and Hardy are on vacation in Paris with an American Legion convention. They are having great luck in a crap game when Ollie suggests they go pick up some real money in Monte Carlo. Their luck at roulette is dismal, but a mysterious stranger loans them money and fixes them up in a posh hotel — after they sign two receipts. Upon awakening, they learn they've actually signed up for the Foreign Legion.

Hustled aboard a train for Roix, they are both smitten with another passenger, Georgette Jabin, the new schoolteacher in Roix. The boys do not adapt well to military life, nor to their jobs as mechanic's assistants at a military aviation center. They sneak away to the schoolhouse to visit Georgette, and insult her boyfriend, Francois — who turns out to be their new commanding officer.

Francois assigns the pair to all sorts of impossible tasks; when they're not busy bungling these jobs, Stan and Ollie attempt to outwit each other in making time with Georgette but are thrown in the guardhouse for their efforts. (Their attempts at romance are not half so feeble as Alfred Schiller's attempts at writing comedy material.)

After the boys have served their detentions, they try to win Georgette's affections by becoming brave aviators like Francois. They sneak aboard a plane to see how it works. Unbeknownst to them, this aircraft has been readied for two other aviators who plan to break an endurance record. Stan and Ollie accidentally set the plane in motion and before long their craft is airborne. They find some wine in the cockpit and get wildly drunk, as the flight stretches through the night, and into the next day. At long last, they somehow make a perfect landing, and are dubbed national heroes for breaking the endurance record.

Director Eddie Sutherland would've preferred to have lunch with a tarantula.

Their commander offers the pair a reward for this heroic deed, and they ask for a release from the aviation corps. Mischievously, the commander reassigns them to duty in the vast desert wasteland. In our last view of the boys we see them astride two camels, while Ollie points out the huge expanse of sand and growls to Stan, "You see this, sucker?"

(A better wrap-up line could have been employed here, maybe something to do with a nice mess. Evidently Mr. Schiller wasn't familiar with that particular phrase.)

Obviously, this story is less than suitable. L&H are depicted as snappy wise-acres who keep trying to outwit each other, and insult anyone within earshot. When they meet Francois for the first time, they yell, "Go on, beat it, Frog! And mind your own business! Who are you to tell us what to do?"

Schiller also suggests that while on board a train for Roix, Ollie "snarl" at the guards with, "For Pete's sake, when is this rattletrap going to get us to Roix?" And when Stan emerges from the plane's cockpit at the end of their flight, he sees the cheering throng and berates Ollie: "Well, wise guy, what do you say now? Look at them! Even Lindbergh didn't get a reception like this!"

Nobody in Schiller's script is remotely likable, certainly not Laurel and Hardy. Other characters enter the story, try to look important, then disappear. The complex plot doesn't make sense (the attempted romance with Georgette is never resolved) and the purported comedy scenes split the team, giving them little to do together.

Rogers, Hardy, Langdon and Laurel, between takes on the final scene.

Another fault of the script is that we're requested to sympathize with Francois and the other "serious" characters. We're asked to laugh along with the tough guys while they kick around these two dopes — as if we weren't *supposed* to like Laurel and Hardy.

Stan's hopes for the film must have plummeted when he read this script. Obviously, it was going to take a lot of work to get *The Flying Deuces* airborne.

Since Stan was involved with *A Chump at Oxford* during much of the time while the *Deuces* script was being whipped into shape, it's uncertain how much he contributed to the final version. Stan was obviously consulted in some measure, because the story has been changed into a fairly literal reworking of 1931's *Beau Hunks*, and a sequence where the boys almost commit suicide was taken from an unused portion of the script for *The Live Ghost*.

The final script, completed early in July, is much more detailed than the scripts used for the Roach films. Morros was working on a tight budget and shooting schedule; he evidently wanted the team to do most of their ad-libbing on paper, so they could shoot the comedy scenes quickly without the usual process of working everything out on the set.

Despite this restriction, Morros gave Laurel a great deal of control. A copy of the final script — a virtual twin to the finished film — still exists with Stan's additions and notations to director Eddie Sutherland. This script provides us with a concrete example of Stan's meticulous attention to details.

A joke suggested by Stan but unused in the film: In the script, Ollie asks

Stan, "Can you keep a secret?" and Stan answers, "Sure." Laurel has changed this line to read, "I'll tell the world!"

Stan was acutely aware of nuances. In a sequence between the boys and Georgette at the inn, the original dialogue reads:

BABE:	*(to Georgette)* My friend and I would like to have a nice bottle of wine. Bring three glasses.
GEORGETTE:	Three glasses? *(A little surprised)*

Laurel has revised the dialogue to read:

BABE:	*(slightly nervous)* We'd like to have a nice bottle of wine — and — er — three glasses.
GEORGETTE:	Three glasses? *(A little surprised)*
BABE:	*(With a nervous giggle)* Er — we thought maybe you might like to join us.

The revision conveys Ollie's coyness and shyness much more effectively.

This script retains the gag of the plane flying for three days and breaking the endurance record; the scenes with the boys getting drunk on wine have been excised, though. The plane flies wildly, doing all sorts of unintended acrobatics. People of various nationalities watch the aircraft as it hovers over their respective homelands. Then a French newsboy yells that the plane is again over Paris.

A radio announcer takes up the story, gushing, "Here it is, folks! The two American bad boys have just broken the world's endurance record! The crowd is going wild here! Listen to that cheering!" Whenever this golly-gee dialogue shows up, Stan has crossed it out and written in the script's margin, "*OUT. OUT. OUT.*"

After the boys' plane crashes and dust fills the screen, the script proposes that "then we superimpose..." — then ends without telling us what to superimpose. Either the writers wanted to keep the reincarnation gag a surprise, or they hadn't yet thought of it.

Boris Morros signed the cast and crew at minimal salaries, with a guaranteed percentage of the profits. Eddie Sutherland, under contract to Hal Roach, was loaned to Morros to direct. Rudolph Maté, who shot *Our Relations*, lent his expertise in things Gallic as a production adviser. Stan insisted upon Charley Rogers and Harry Langdon as part of the writing staff.

Roach also loaned out the team's perennial cameraman, Art Lloyd. Stan admired Lloyd's work so much that he persuaded the photographer to take part in a pending project overseas. Venice Lloyd recalled, "We were going to go to Europe for a three-year deal with Stan and Babe — they were going to make films at the Elstree studio in England; they were also going to make stage appearances there and in France. Art was going to be with them the whole time.

"We waited around for a whole year — in fact, Artie didn't make any pictures that year — he was set to do some work at Universal, and he had to break it because he was loyal to Stan. But then the war came along, and that put an end to the deal."

RKO RADIO PICTURES

cordially invites you to attend a Special

PRESS PREVIEW

of

LAUREL AND HARDY in

"THE FLYING DEUCES"

at the

Hollywood Pantages Theatre

Thursday, October 5th at 8:30 P. M.

A pre-release program.

Filming began on July 22 at the General Studios in Hollywood. A new member of the production crew was the script clerk, Virginia Lucille Jones. She had worked with Sol Lesser for three years and had recently begun freelancing. "One day I got a call through the guild, from Boris Morros, and they wanted me to work on a Laurel and Hardy picture," she recalled. "Well, I had never done comedy and I was frightened by it. But it sounded like a challenge. They gave me a script to read over the weekend, and the following Monday I went to work and met Stan and Babe for the first time. I never worked on any other pictures but theirs from then on; I went back to Roach with them and was there until they left.

"On my first encounter with Babe, after the master shot had been taken and we were going in for the close shot, I saw that Babe's hat was in the wrong hand; his cane, his gloves, his stance — nothing was right. So I walked over to him and said, 'Mr. Hardy, in the last shot your cane and your hat — ' He said, 'It's all right, my dear, I know how it was.' I thought, 'Oh, this is really going to be a chore! I'm not going to have any fun on *this* picture!' I found out how wrong I was, because the minute they were ready to shoot, everything went back the way it should have been. And he was always that way; he was a great study."

Although Lucille stated that she "wasn't aware of any problem with Eddie Sutherland and Stan," the director recalled a great deal of friction between himself and Laurel. In 1972, Sutherland claimed he was forced into directing *The Flying Deuces*. "I didn't want to do it, I didn't like doing it and I hated the finished film," he said.

Sutherland was a first-time L&H director on a film made away from Roach under a tight schedule and budget — and Stan no doubt wanted to maintain as much control as possible. But Sutherland felt it was "just chemistry" that he and Laurel did not get along. "Stan was very creative, like Chaplin," he acknowledged, but called the making of the film "a painful experience." Summing up his relationship with Laurel, he added, "I'd rather have worked with a tarantula."

On Monday, August 21, Stan watched an early cut of the film; he evidently was not going to able to work with editor Jack Dennis as closely as he worked with Bert Jordan at the Roach lot, but he did submit five pages of "Cutting notes," suggesting how the film could be tightened and improved. As with his detailed notes on the script, these provide a striking example of Stan's concern over details, and his skill as a filmmaker. The following sample gives an idea:

> Main titles should be over plates of Paris, then go right to the artist at the sidewalk cafe. At finish of cafe scene, dissolve on CU of Babe to a new insert of picture of Babe. Picture should be closer and clearer, letting the frame fill the screen — and stay on it long enough to read the note. Then dissolve to present scene of picture on table, and dolly back for scene.
>
> Go to scene upstairs. Start it in LS, then go to two-shot and play through to showing Stan the ring. Need insert of ring to intercut here. Then back to LS and then to two-shot, and follow Stan over to wall for bump.
>
> The proposal scene: Babe orders wine and three glasses. Take Georgette out in two-shot. Cut to waitresses watching and laughing. Back to Babe and Stan. Babe says feels as fidgety as a jitterbug, this is the first time he's ever been married. Cut to waitresses watching and laughing. Then bring Georgette into table. When Georgette sets bowl of nuts on table, need insert bowl of nuts.
>
> In scene of Stan and Babe getting tangled up with soldiers drilling, perhaps can use part of 204-B camera. Put in #207 from outtakes of Stan and Babe coming through line of soldiers to Lieutenant Blair in f.g. Use closer shot from outtakes of Babe yelling, 'Hey! Where you gonna have dinner?' Then back to longer shot of Lieutenant and sergeant, taking them on into office. Also put back last take in outtakes of Francois' reactions to above.
>
> In jail scene, put in CU of Babe as Stan is picking the bedsprings. Need insert Stan's hands picking first couple of notes. Put in another CU of Babe as Stan is taking springs off bed. At finish of number, as Stan draws foot across springs, hold for his smile at Babe, then go outside to the jailer. Put in more sound effects of harp when tangled up in bedsprings.

As these brief excerpts from Stan's copious notes show, he had a very definite preconception of how he wanted each scene to look, and was rightly concerned about the pacing and shot selection of each sequence. These notes show Stan doing the actual editing *on paper* — which is all he could do, under the circumstances.

The press preview for *The Flying Deuces* was held on October 5 at the Pantages Theater in Hollywood. The reviews were generally favorable; Laurel and Hardy had been away from the screen since the summer of 1938 (*A Chump at Oxford*, although completed in its four-reel version, was still on the shelf), and critics welcomed the team back.

Bosley Crowther in the *New York Times* remarked, "The happy reunion of Stan Laurel and Oliver Hardy after a characteristic interlude of reproachful squabbling may not be as handsomely celebrated by *The Flying Deuces* as it might be, but their new picture at the Rialto is reason enough for a glad hand and a bit of hatchet-burying all around." (Crowther, and others, seemed to think the conflict of the previous year was between Stan and Babe, not Stan and Hal Roach. This misconception would haunt the team to the end.)

Immediately after finishing *The Flying Deuces*, Stan and Babe returned to the Roach lot, where they shot the two reels of additional footage for *A Chump at Oxford* and then embarked upon a script for a new feature. It would be their last time at The Lot of Fun.

SAPS AT SEA

Production history: Script written mid-September—October 20, 1939. Shot November-early December. Copyrighted April 26, 1940 by Roach (LP 9591). Released May 3 by MGM. 57 minutes.

Produced by Hal Roach. Directed by Gordon Douglas. Original Story and Screenplay by Charles Rogers, Felix Adler, Gil Pratt and Harry Langdon. Photographed by Art Lloyd. Photographic effects by Roy Seawright. Edited by William Ziegler. Art Director, Charles D. Hall. Sound by W.B. Delaplain. Musical score by Marvin Hatley.

With James Finlayson, Rychard Cramer, Eddie Conrad, Robert McKenzie, Harry Bernard.

L&H work in a horn factory, where Ollie goes beserk. Dr. Finlayson diagnoses his condition as hornophobia, and prescribes an ocean voyage. Stan suggests renting a boat and keeping it tied to the dock. After the boys settle in, escaped criminal Nick Grainger evades the cops by hiding on the boys' boat; worse, their goat chews away the mooring rope. The duo try to incapacitate their unwanted guest by serving him a meal of inedible look-alikes, but he makes them eat it instead. Stan thwarts the criminal by playing his trombone and prompting Ollie's rage, but the pair end up in a jail cell — with Nick.

During various stages of production, this film bore the working titles of *Two's Company*, *Jitterbugs* and *Crackpots* before its final appellation was decided upon. The completed picture is a free-wheeling little effort; since most of the story concerns either "Laurel and Hardy in their apartment" or "Laurel and Hardy on the high seas," the film looks like a couple of short subjects stuck together — but the material is good enough to overcome any deficiencies in construction.

After doing the added scenes for *A Chump at Oxford*, Stan and Babe were obligated to deliver three more four-reel pictures under their April 1939 contract. Stan began script conferences with Charley Rogers, Harry Langdon, Felix Adler and Gilbert W. Pratt, a veteran of comedy films whose association with

366 Laurel and Hardy

Hal Roach dated back to 1917. They put together a detailed script, which differed — as usual — from the resulting film.

One gag evidently dreamed up on the set involved the apartment's mixed-up plumbing and wiring. Ollie prepares for a relaxing bath and is unexpectedly soaked when water gushes out of the shower. Stan tries to light the gas stove, can't get the proper burner to ignite, and blows up the kitchen.

Indignantly, Ollie calls the apartment's plumber and tells him that everything is all mixed up. Cut to a close-up of the plumber: it's cross-eyed Ben Turpin, who logically says, "It looked all right to me!" (This affectionate cameo was Turpin's last screen appearance; he died July 1, 1940.)

The ending proposed by the script is substantially different from the filmed finale. As Ollie is being chased around the drifting boat by Nick Grainger, Stan hits upon the idea of blowing a horn to ignite Ollie's wrath. Laurel blows into a fish-horn, but Ollie has cotton in his ears because of his affliction, and can't hear. Stan removes the cotton — but as he reaches for the horn, it's knocked into the briny depths.

Stan joins in the fracas. As he puts up his dukes, Nick wallops him, sending him head over heels to the other end of the boat. Stan crashes into an old ratchet-type foghorn. It bellows loudly, and the sound triggers Ollie's hornophobia. He gets fighting mad, and gives the criminal a terrific beating until the Harbor Patrol comes to the rescue. (As filmed, this sequence is not as elaborate, but funnier.)

The script proposes an entirely different wrap-up after Nick is captured:

An impromptu concert with actor Eddie Conrad (seated), Marvin Hatley on cornet and propman Bob Saunders (extreme right).

The boys are seen parading with a marching band. Stan plays his trombone; his rotund friend, now fully cured of his debilitating aversion to brass instruments, plays a sousaphone.

Stan and Babe stepped before the cameras in early November, under the direction of 30-year-old Gordon Douglas, who had worked at the Roach lot since his late teens, playing small roles on both sides of the camera. Douglas had guided Babe Hardy through *Zenobia*, but this marked his first time as the team's director.

While Douglas has stated that Stan tore the script to shreds on the first day of shooting — and then conferred with the writers each day to determine what they'd do next — his recollections are a slight exaggeration. Babe Hardy's widow, Lucille, worked as the script clerk on this picture; she did not remember anything like the total improvisation Douglas described, although she said the boys' ability to anticipate each others' actions resulted in a lot of ad-libbing while the cameras were rolling.

Stan had liked Lucille's work on *The Flying Deuces*, and asked her to join the crew for the *Chump at Oxford* additions and *Saps at Sea*. She replaced their former script girl, Ellen Corby (later the star of TV's *The Waltons*). Lucille sat in on the writing sessions for this film, and spent mornings at the studio trying to organize the gagmen's ramblings of the previous day into a cohesive outline. Babe would come to chat and bring her a cup of coffee as she worked.

One day during production, Lucille tripped and fell on a rolled-up carpet, hit her head against one of the cameras and landed in a hospital. Babe sent

On tour in *The Laurel and Hardy Revue*, with James C. Morton.

her a box of roses, along with a courtly note wishing her a speedy recovery. Lucille soon realized her relationship with Babe was becoming more than just a professional association. Babe proposed to her at the studio one morning; although they'd never even been on a date, she accepted, and Babe and Lucille were married on March 7, 1940.

Stan was involved in quite a different marital matter. On November 8, Illiana filed an affidavit to set aside the divorce Stan had won the previous May. (If *she* divorced Stan, she could claim more of his estate.) Illiana testified that she hadn't contested Stan's divorce because his violent actions had frightened her into silence.

Judge Joseph W. Vickers accused Illiana of perjury and sent the case to the District Attorney's office. Stan's divorce was upheld. Illiana received $6,500 as a complete settlement and agreed not to capitalize in any way on their stormy marriage. She told reporters she planned to resume her singing career. "I don't even want to use his name," she sneered. "I don't need it." Although her settlement was a pittance compared to the sums Lois and Ruth had received, Illiana had done so much damage to Stan's reputation that she was by far the most expensive of his wives.

If Stan sometimes seemed to have little control over events in his private life, he at least retained the guiding hand on this film. As Laurel preferred, *Saps at Sea* was shot in sequence. One of the later scenes, where the boys rent the leaky "Prickly Heat" from boat owner Robert McKenzie, was filmed at the San Pedro harbor. Thomas Benton Roberts, the former Roach prop man who had appeared in *Two Tars*, had since gone into business supplying boats of every conceivable variety to the studios; he furnished the boys' disreputable little craft.

The sequence in which the boys hope to incapacitate their captor by serving him a synthetic meal (string substituting for spaghetti, sponge for meatballs, red paint for tomato sauce) was a memorable one for Stan — unfortunately. "It was the first time I gagged, literally, on a gag," he recounted to studio publicists. "I was doing all right until I started swallowing a piece of string. It was about two feet long, and as I kept drawing it into my mouth, it started tickling me, and then choking me. Before I finished, I would have been happy if it had hanged me."

Saps at Sea is very much a "gag" comedy. In this, it more closely resembles the old two-reelers than the later Roach features. The cast is comprised of familiar faces, which adds to the nostalgic feel. James Finlayson has an extended turn as Hardy's physician; Charlie Hall, as the apartment desk clerk, participates in a wonderful running gag of non sequiturs.

Rychard Cramer, so menacing as the judge in 1932's *Scram!*, played the most sadistic L&H heavy of all time in the role of Nick Grainger. (By comparison, Walter Long is the soul of jocularity.) Diminutive Harry Bernard, the perennial cop, played the bemused little Harbor Patrol captain.

Even though his employment with the Roach studio had been abruptly terminated, Marvin Hatley came back to write another outstanding musical score for *Saps at Sea* at Stan Laurel's request. It was Hatley's last work for the Roach studio. (According to Jack Roach, the studio had to hire several new men to perform all of Hatley's former duties.)

As it turned out, this film was also L&H's last at the Lot of Fun. Just as the filming began, on October 25, 1939, articles of incorporation were filed in

Lucille and Babe in 1942.

Sacramento for Laurel and Hardy Feature Productions. Stan, Babe and Ben Shipman were the corporation's directors. When their Roach contract expired, the team planned to become independent producers themselves; in this way, they would have complete artistic control, and would retain the rights to their films — or so they hoped.

On February 5, 1940, *The Hollywood Reporter* ran an article headlined, "Laurel and Hardy to Roll Their Own" — the first public announcement of the team's pending break from Hal Roach. The article noted that the team had been signed for a quartet of four-reelers in April 1939, but had instead delivered two full-length features. "It is doubtful whether the contract will be carried out," said the article, "because of a clause which specifies the deal is to be completed early in April. No stories are now in preparation. The new company... will make a series of full-length features, and, through its legal advisor, Benjamin Shipman, is considering several major studio release offers."

On April 5, 1940, the team's contract expired, and Laurel and Hardy ended their association with Roach. As an independent producer, Stan felt he would finally be able to control the team's films. There would be no more battles over stories, no more scenes cut out by the producer after Stan had edited them, no more prolonged contract fights.

While the team searched for backing for their own films, they were asked to perform at a benefit for the Red Cross. On August 22, 1940, they appeared at the Golden Gate International Exposition on Treasure Island in San Francisco Bay. The boys did a 15-minute sketch of Stan's entitled "How to Get a Driver's License."

The team had been planning to produce a stage revival of Victor Herbert's musical comedy *The Red Mill*, with Stan rewriting the dialogue to fit their film roles. As a result of the response to the "Driver's License" routine, they instead took the sketch on tour in the company of "Thirty Madcap Merrymakers" as the stars of *The Laurel and Hardy Revue*.

The 12-city tour began September 27 in Omaha, and ended in Buffalo in mid-December. The early part of the tour followed the same itinerary as presidential candidate Wendell Willkie, purely by coincidence; when Stan and Babe were given to key to the city by officials at Omaha's Union Station, the officials took the key back to give to Willkie later that evening.

The reviews and the audiences were favorable and enthusiastic. The team played to packed houses at every engagement, and appeared at civic events when they weren't giving interviews. Other movie stars occasionally made brief personal appearance tours, but rarely to such acclaim. The reception accorded Laurel and Hardy certified their standing as genuine folk heroes.

Stan and Babe returned to Hollywood, secure in the knowledge that thousands of fans still loved them. Now they were finally masters of their own destiny. They hoped to obtain backing for their independent productions, under which they would have full artistic control — and secure a distribution agreement with a major studio. The future, as far as Stan and Babe could see, had never looked brighter.

The Later Films

Those Fox People

The Golden Age of American Film Comedy that began with Chaplin's Keystone comedies in 1914, and flourished in the 1920s and '30s, ground to a dead halt in 1940. For varied reasons, all of the mythic, other-worldly clowns who had gladdened the globe for over 25 years suddenly departed, or were relegated to a status demeaning to their talent.

Chaplin made his last "Little Tramp" film, *The Great Dictator*, in 1940. Harold Lloyd had retired in 1938, and was occasionally producing films. Buster Keaton and Harry Langdon were appearing in inferior low-budget Columbia two-reelers that bore no resemblance to their great work of the '20s.

W.C. Fields made a genuine classic in 1940, *The Bank Dick*; with one exception, there were only sporadic guest appearances in other peoples' films after that. Our Gang, which had flourished for 16 years at the Roach studio, was now a sickeningly wholesome and unfunny series at MGM — a studio which was singularly inept at comedy. This was also proven in that studio's mis-handling of the Marx Brothers, who retired from the screen in 1941 as a result of three dismal MGM features.

Although the Roach lot had outlasted its other comedy-studio rivals — Sennett, Christie and Educational — its outlook was not encouraging. The period of ambitious expansion which brought about *Of Mice and Men*, *Captain Fury* and *One Million B.C.* had ended. Roach was instead producing low-budget featurettes starring character actors.

The old guard of film comedy had suddenly disappeared, it seemed; the old clowns were being replaced with slicker, brasher, more verbal comics who were somehow more "realistic" than their predecessors. Bob Hope, Danny Kaye and (in his early films) Red Skelton were definitely *of* this world, not apart from it; they weren't outlandish, and they always got the girl.

In defiance of this trend, however, the newest sensations of comedy films were purveyors of hoary, low comedy straight from burlesque. Bud Abbott and Lou Costello, unlike their contemporaries, could never be the romantic interest in their pictures, but they displayed the same type of slick, brash, cynical humor that marked comedies of the '40s — humor which had little of the humanity and the warmth displayed by Laurel and Hardy. In the year after *Saps at Sea* was released, Abbott and Costello became a sensation in their army comedy, *Buck Privates*; before 1941 was over, they had four starring features in release.

Stan remarried Ruth in January 1941; they separated on May 31.

Despite changing tastes in comedy, Stan was sure that L&H still had a bright future, still had yet to do their best work. Their popularity was intact; the tremendous response to *The Laurel and Hardy Revue* proved that. If they needed proof of their continued high esteem in other countries, they got it in mid-April 1941, when they appeared to great acclaim at the Mexico City Motion Picture Industry Festival, as guests of President Avila Camacho.

Unfortunately, Ben Shipman was not able to convince the heads of major studios to produce new L&H films — not under Stan's terms, anyway. The executives of big movie factories were reluctant to provide the financial backing for films that would be written, produced and essentially directed by a comic — especially one who had participated in well-publicized battles with his former employer. The only comic who could make films entirely on his own terms, release them through a major studio and retain all rights, was Chaplin — and he financed his films with his own money.

Stan and Babe spent their money in other ways. Babe and Lucille purchased a three-acre estate on Magnolia Boulevard in Van Nuys for $20,000 in March 1940, and were busy furnishing it. The Hardy acreage boasted a swimming pool, guest houses, horse stables and before long, a theater which Babe dubbed "Laurel and Hardy's Fun Factory."

On January 11, 1941, Stan remarried Ruth in Las Vegas. Despite the couple's earlier divorce, some affection obviously remained. "It happened suddenly, like heart failure," Stan told reporters. "Making love to an ex-wife isn't like starting in from scratch. You've already been over the preliminaries, so everything goes faster."

Unfortunately, Stan's income was going faster too. According to one report, he owed over $7,000 in back taxes for 1937 and 1939, and more than $16,000 in alimony for Lois and child support. Commissions and destitute vaudeville friends also swallowed much of Stan's earnings.

Babe had financial problems as well. In April 1941 ex-wife Myrtle sued for $21,625 in back alimony — a complaint she lodged on several occasions over the next 15 years, without success. Simultaneously, the Tax Appeals Board ruled that Babe had to pay $75,755 in added tax on his income from 1934 to 1937. With interest, the tax bill came to $110,000 before the case was finally settled in 1951.

With Ben Shipman managing their careers, things were at a standstill. At one point, Stan was set to produce an independently financed L&H version of *Don Quixote*, to be filmed in Mexico. Then, Shipman almost closed a deal for a series of Spanish-language comedies (for Latin-American distribution only), which would begin production at Mexico City's Azteca Studios in the summer of 1941. Neither project was realized.

Shipman was a humble man, and Stan treasured his friendship — but he simply was not an aggressive negotiator. He was a lawyer, not a businessman, and wasn't qualified by training or temperament to be an effective agent for the team.

In April 1941, executives of 20th Century-Fox contacted Shipman about signing L&H. Stan and Babe never talked directly to the Fox executives, allowing Shipman to handle all negotiations.

"Stan told Shipman that he wanted to have some say over the script," said Lucille Hardy. "I don't know if Stan went into the fact that he wanted his say on the set — but apparently, Ben Shipman led them to believe that everything was just going to be okay, that they weren't going to have any problems."

On April 23, 20th Century-Fox made an non-exclusive agreement with Laurel and Hardy Feature Productions. Stan and Babe would make one feature for Fox (which the studio had already decided would be an army comedy called *Forward March*); afterwards, the team had an option to make nine more films for Fox over the next five years. Fox would pay Stan and Babe's corporation $50,000 per picture. The comedians were free to make films for other companies, and to appear on stage and radio.

Laurel was elated with the Fox contract. The Roach lot was a small studio with restrictive budgets; now, Stan assumed he'd have all the resources of a major studio at his command.

However, there were differences between the studios which Stan overlooked. In its glory days of the late '20s and early '30s, the Roach studio was filled with technicians who, in the words of film editor Richard Currier, "knew comedy A to Z and backwards." Stan was the guiding hand behind the team's films, but he was working with people who understood the subtleties and mysteries of film comedy.

Fox, however, was hardly a comedy studio. It specialized in slick musicals, biographical dramas and mysteries. The only out-and-out comedies the studio had made in recent years were the Ritz Brothers pictures, and even the Ritzes hadn't been too pleased with the studio's treatment of them. (When the team was demoted from the "A" pictures supervised by Darryl Zanuck to the "B" unit under control of Sol Wurtzel, Harry Ritz remarked, "Things have gone from bad to Wurtzel!")

Fox owned its own distribution network and a chain of over 500 theaters. It kept those houses full by churning out about 30 films every year. Roach had owned no theaters; he had to distribute his films through major studio channels. At the peak of production in the late '30s, he made only five or six features a year; consequently, his fortunes rested solely with the quality of his product. Although his films were inexpensive, Roach lavished time and care on each one to ensure its quality. Conversely, some of Fox's "B" pictures were shot in as little as 12 days.

As with other major studios, Fox contract employees were compartmentalized. Writers, directors, cameramen, editors and other technicians took charge of their individual jobs and nothing else. (This was due more to studio management than the rise of labor unions; the Roach studio had to respect unions, too, but the employees were given much more flexibility.) For someone like Stan, whose talents crossed over all the boundaries, the rigid division of labor would be a major hindrance — as he soon found out.

Laurel and Hardy cannot be blamed for the poor quality of the Fox films, because they were prevented by the studio system from making any creative contributions. However, Stan and Babe were, unfortunately, responsible for agreeing to a contract which put them in this position — and for continuing with Fox after completing their first picture for the studio.

"I can't tell you how much it hurt me to do those pictures, and how ashamed I am of them," Stan told biographer John McCabe in recalling the years at Fox. "I didn't always see eye to eye with Roach, but for the most part he left us alone... But those Fox people! You can give it to *them* good."

Unfortunately, from 1941 to 1945, those Fox people were giving it to Stan and Babe, and the results did no one any good.

GREAT GUNS

Production history: Story treatment completed by Lou Breslow, May 24, 1941. Filmed July 11-early August. Copyrighted October 10, 1941 by 20th Century-Fox Film Corporation (LP 10769). Released October 10. 74 minutes.

Produced by Sol M. Wurtzel. Directed by Monty Banks. Original screenplay by Lou Breslow. Photographed by Glen MacWilliams. Edited by Al de Gaetano. Sound by W.D. Flick and Harry M. Leonard. Musical direction by Emil Newman.

With Dick Nelson, Sheila Ryan, Edmund MacDonald, Russell Hicks, Ludwig Stossel.

Dan Forrester is a wealthy but frail young man who would love to serve his country, but is prevented by his multitude of illnesses. Dan is drafted and pronounced perfectly fit by the army doctor. Fearful that life in the service will kill him, his two valets, Stan and Ollie, enlist so they can protect him. During war-games maneuvers, Stan and Ollie are "captured" and have to help build a bridge for the enemy. But Dan, aided by Stan's pet crow, Penelope, discovers the "enemy" camp's whereabouts, and wins the "war" for the boys' side.

It was appropriate that Laurel and Hardy's first film for 20th Century-Fox was an army comedy. As soon as they stepped on the lot, Stan and Babe realized Fox was giving the orders.

The executive producer of Fox's low-budget "B" movies was Sol M. Wurtzel, who had joined the company as a stenographer in 1914 and was elevated to the role of producer in 1933. While he was occasionally associated with a prestigious film, he usually turned out action pictures and mysteries that could be produced quickly and cheaply. Some of his better-remembered efforts are entries in the *Charlie Chan* and *Mr. Moto* series.

"Wurtzel was a hard taskmaster in a way, but if you knew how to handle him, you'd be okay," asserted Lou Breslow, a writer of Fox "B" pictures dating back to the early '30s. "There was one key to working with him: if you just exorcised fear from your mind, you'd get along great with him. I never let him intimidate me — I just laughed at him."

Cameraman Glen MacWilliams, whose association with the Fox studio began with the silent era, concurred: "He was a Simon Legree. He was rarely complimentary to any member of the crew, because it might cost him a buck in a raise, you know, if he complimented you."

Like the proverbial bride, as soon as the Fox studio got the men it wanted, it began changing them. A Fox press release, dated September 22, 1941, illustrates vividly the studio's control over the team:

> There is a subtle but nevertheless revolutionary change in the comedy of Stan Laurel and Oliver Hardy, as presented in their first 20th Century-Fox picture, *Great Guns*.
>
> They remain, as always, slapstick pantomimists, but the comedy of the new Laurel and Hardy is much less broad than it has been... In a word, their work has been streamlined.
>
> In the first place, their appearance has been revised. Stan Laurel has always worn a special light makeup, a modification of the "dead white" worn by the circus clown. This tended, it was believed, to accentuate the amusing ineffectuality of his screen personality. In *Great Guns*, his makeup is the usual greasepaint worn by blond actors.
>
> Their clothes, too, have been modified a bit....In the early scenes of the picture, in which they are dressed as civilians, there is just the slightest suggestion that Ollie finds difficulty in covering himself, while his partner's trouble is the reverse....
>
> These changes are the result of long and terribly serious conferences between Stan, Ollie, director Monty Banks and other 20th Century-Fox officials. It was felt that the public taste has changed somewhat and that the unbelievable antics of Laurel and Hardy would be more amusing if they themselves were more believable characters. That is, in *Great Guns* they will be a funny and oddly-assorted pair, but not completely beyond what a person might find in real life...
>
> Stan and Ollie believe revisions in their style will hold their millions of old friends and find them many new ones. This opinion is backed by every experienced showman at 20th Century-Fox.

The Fox studio not only did away with the unique characteristics and techniques that made Laurel and Hardy so special, it trumpeted this new look as an improvement. Stan and Babe were definitely not in favor of these "revisions in their style;" unfortunately, there wasn't much they could do about them.

Stan was prevented from making story suggestions from the outset. On May 5, 1941, a young writer named Manning O'Connor submitted a report entitled "Research Material For Laurel and Hardy Story." O'Connor had visited Camp Roberts, near San Miguel, California, and asked some of the soldiers for anecdotes about their days in training camp. None of the material had the slightest resemblance to anything done by Laurel and Hardy. O'Connor might have spent his time more profitably had he simply asked Stan for some ideas, but no one in the Fox organization appears to have consulted Laurel.

The job of writing the story and screenplay was given to Lou Breslow, who had an unavoidable liability in that he was only one man. Stan knew that comedy scripts almost always benefited when two or more writers shared inspirations; so did Hal Roach — which is why a group of writers usually collaborated with Stan on the Roach feature film scripts.

Breslow at least had the good sense to talk to Stan and Babe while he was writing the script — but he was still the man in charge. Before, Stan had been in authority, and had chosen the writers' ideas which appealed to him, embellishing them with his own material. Now, someone else was doing the bulk of the writing, and occasionally asking Stan and Babe for suggestions.

"In those days," Breslow said, "we'd get an assignment and knock it out in about three or four weeks, and be shooting in the fifth week. And I always talked to the boys and got their reactions. If there was something they objected to, I'd fix it. We'd sit down together — it was a very cooperative thing.

"But Stan was very quiet. He was a very peaceful, sweet little guy. So was Babe, but Babe was a little bit more involved in story discussions. He'd involve himself, where Stan had other things on his mind. And Stan was the kind of a guy who left things to others, you know, 'They'll take care of me.'"

The fact that Babe was more involved in story discussions than Stan, who was uncharacteristically "very quiet," seems to indicate that Stan already felt he'd been beaten by the Fox system, even as their first film was being written.

Breslow's story outline is quite different from the finished film. The main change is that Breslow has added a love interest for L&H in the character of Noodles Hunnicut, a role intended for the slapstick comedienne Joan Davis. She works as a waitress and entertainer with the heroine, Sis Hammond, at the fort's social center, a club called the Rendezvous. Unfortunately for the boys, their top sergeant, Hippo Howard, also has developed a taste for Noodles, and tells them to lay offa his goil. Daniel, enjoying freedom from his sickbed, discovers that he likes girls when he meets Sis.

Says Breslow's outline: "The story from here on concerns itself with the further trials and tribulations of the boys — their attempts to outsmart each other in winning Noodles, and their final reckoning with Sergeant Howard." Alfred Schiller had introduced an equally unsuitable element in his story for *The Flying Deuces*. Since when do Laurel and Hardy try to outwit each other, especially over a girl?

One problem with this idea is that it splits the team up so that they can't cause each other trouble — which is the source of most of their comedy. Another problem: the scene implies that Stan regards Ollie as a dope who is easily deceived. Problem three: while Ollie often falls in love, Stan is incapable of erotic interest — he's too much a child for that. As Beanie Walker so aptly put it, "Mr. Hardy is at last conscious of the grand passion — Mr. Laurel isn't even conscious of the Grand Canyon." (In the film, the Noodles character was

With the man responsible for the script: Lou Breslow.

omitted, and the sergeant became Daniel's rival for Ms. Hammond — re-named Ginger.)

Three days after he'd finished his story outline, Breslow completed a treatment on May 24. Certain sections of it are quite telling. Someone familiar with Laurel and Hardy's previous work could have immediately spotted the script's flaws, its denigration of the team's characterizations.

The story is really about Daniel, not Laurel and Hardy, and all they get to do is cluck their tongues in dismay at his new-found red-bloodedness. They don't even need to *be* in this picture. One could call them the comedy relief — if they had something funny to do.

Another section of Breslow's treatment shows a marked change of attitude toward the Stan and Ollie characters. At Roach's, the team had always been the good guys in their movies, the ones who carried the audience's sympathy. Breslow describes them in one scene as "a rather sorry looking pair of dopes," and throughout the subsequent Fox scripts the boys are referred to as "jerks," "dopes," "half-wits," and other contemptuous names.

This shows how the Fox writers perceived Laurel and Hardy as two idiots who get in the way of the real hero — the romantic lead. Our sympathies are supposed to go toward the "normal" characters for having to put up with Stan and Ollie's stupidity — the exact opposite of the philosophy in the Roach films.

Breslow wrote a full-length script for *Forward March* in early June (the title wasn't changed to *Great Guns* until shooting began in July), chock full of gags which just don't work for Laurel and Hardy. Two examples will suffice:

1) In the breakfast line at the mess hall, the boys plot to get more food. Stan stands behind Ollie, making it look like Ollie has four arms. Ollie tells the cook, "Tragic, isn't it — just one of nature's little pranks." The cook tops this witticism with a riposte of his own: "Hey, what are you — a centipede?"

2) About to be issued uniforms, Stan asks the sergeant, "May we pick any color we want?" The sergeant cracks, "Sure, just so's it's O.D. or blue denim!" Ollie quips, "Blue denim — sounds like a Strauss waltz!"

These might be good jokes for the Three Stooges or the Bowery Boys — but they just don't jibe with the true L&H characters. Laurel and Hardy got their laughs from human situations, not bad one-liners.

One gag which went unused in the film tells us where the Fox executives got the idea to put Laurel and Hardy in an army comedy. When Lou Breslow was asked if Fox tried to capitalize on the success of Abbott and Costello's *Buck Privates* by placing Stan and Ollie in an army setting, he asserted that it was "just a coincidence." But the script reveals otherwise:

> Picking up the basin of water, Stan prepares to heave it out the door.
> OLLIE: Wait —
> STAN: What's the matter?
> OLLIE: Don't throw that water out there!
> STAN: Why not?
> OLLIE: The sergeant is just liable to come walking in!
> STAN: What's the matter with that?
> OLLIE: Don't you remember? They did that in *Buck Privates*!

Curiously, there are a couple of scenes that are perfectly in keeping with the boys' characters in Breslow's script. One which survived into the film is a gag with Stan unscrewing a light bulb and bringing it over to his shaving quarters; miraculously, the bulb stays lit.

Another similarly magical gag was cut before filming: Stan rolls an imaginary sheet of paper into an imaginary typewriter, and starts tapping away. When the "typewriter" bell rings, Ollie asks, "What are you doing?" Stan replies that he's writing a letter. Intrigued, Ollie gets up and watches over Stan's shoulder as he fastidiously erases a mistake. When Ollie tries to read whatever Stan is writing, Stan covers up the "paper" and loftily says it's personal. When Ollie asks Stan who he's writing to, Stan replies, "To myself" — prompting a delayed take from Ollie. Finally, Ollie's curiosity gets the better of him, and he implores, "You can trust me. What does it say?" Pulling the paper out of the machine (with a full compliment of sound effects), Stan says, "I don't know — I won't get it until tomorrow." Ollie raises his arms in exasperation.

This brief scene has the ring of authentic L&H material, in the midst of a script that's totally foreign to their previous work. One can only speculate that either Stan wrote the bit and gave it to Breslow, or that for one brief shining moment Breslow caught the essence of their comedy. But for naught.

Before filming began on July 11, the studio held several preparatory meetings. Cameraman Glen MacWilliams explained, "You'd have a production meeting. Represented at that meeting is the director, the writer, the producer, the assistant director, the cinematographer, the special effects man, wardrobe, art director, the greenery man, the property man, the standby painter, every part of the crew. You'd go through the whole script and break it down.

"Now, Stan and Babe would *not* be at this production meeting. The writer, Breslow, would be there, but not Stan and Babe. It's not that they weren't interested, but that we couldn't talk freely if they were there, see what I mean? The production meeting is for the guys that have got to *make* the picture. Stan and Babe would never be actually in the studio until we were ready to shoot. They had nothing to do with the production of the picture except for early meetings with the guy who was writing it."

MacWilliams' remark about the inability to "talk freely" implies that Fox, far from asking for Stan's suggestions, hoped to make the picture with as little interference from him as possible.

Glen MacWilliams asserted that he was hired for *Great Guns* at the special request of Babe Hardy. They had worked together on a 1923 Howard Hawks production called *Quicksands*; Babe was employed as a gag man. Now, 18 years later, MacWilliams had returned to the United States after five years in England, and found it impossible to get re-established.

MacWilliams later recalled, "I will always feel obligated to Babe, because here I was in Hollywood, trying to get back to where I'd been, and I couldn't; you don't realize the politics that goes on. But Babe gave me the opportunity to make two pictures with them, and that got me to where I could make *Lifeboat*... You don't think I love Babe? He got me re-established."

It's interesting that Babe could have chosen the cameraman on this film, given the frustration encountered by the team at Fox. But MacWilliams had worked for Fox earlier, so he still had some reputation with the studio.

The film's Italian-born director, however, was not nearly as congenial a collaborator. Monty Banks had starred in silent comedies and directed some of them; in 1928, he went to England and married the most popular entertainer in the British Isles, comedienne Gracie Fields. When war broke out, the couple moved to Hollywood — where Gracie starred in Fox films. *Great Guns* was Banks' first and only directorial assignment after his return to the States. The reminiscences of his co-workers help explain why.

"There are probably a hundred other directors that would have been better on this picture than Monty Banks," Glen MacWilliams exclaimed. "The boys weren't happy with him, I know that. *I* wasn't happy with him. He simply didn't know his business, didn't know the mechanics of making a motion picture.

"In my opinion, Banks was a very, very poor director. And he was very aggressive, very vulgar. He yelled a lot; he wanted a whipping boy around him all the time. Stan and Babe held their ground, though. And Banks respected them enough to know that he couldn't roust them around. The best I can say for Monty Banks is that he's well forgotten."

Lou Breslow concurs. "Monty was lucky to get a job. I remember a scene where the leading man, Dick Nelson, had to leave the boys' quarters, and his exit line was, 'Well, so long, fellows.' I was on the set with him, and thought of a better line; I told Nelson, 'Why don't you say, "I'm going to mess, fellows."' Then they shot it, and Banks came over and said, 'Jesus, that was a marvelous touch.' I said, 'What touch?' He said, 'You know, that Catholic bit, "I'm going to Mass."' Now, me being Jewish, where would I get that? Monty was no Hitchcock as far as I was concerned."

As the director of photography on *Great Guns*, Glen MacWilliams was closely involved with many phases of the production. His comments provide a vivid picture of how the Fox method of moviemaking differed from the old free-and-easy Hal Roach approach.

"I met Stan and Babe before the shooting started, where we discussed makeup. They had been wearing this white makeup; it was very light. I explained to them that I had to balance them with the rest of the cast, and that it wasn't necessary to wash out their facial features, which were so important. Stan might have been a little squeamish about it — he may have been concerned about wrinkles or something like that. And I can understand it; he wanted to look more like a clown. We let the first day's work stand as a test. And they were very happy with the results.

"You see, at Fox we were thinking of the whole picture; Stan and Babe were backed up with all that production. At Roach's, they would have a free hand to do anything they wanted. There was just a general flat light all over the set; they weren't in for pretty photography. But that was a different type of production altogether. At Fox, you didn't see any pratfalls or anything like that from the rest of the cast. On these pictures, they were surrounded with reality. And with the makeup, we wanted Stan and Babe to look more like a couple of human beings. When you've got a cast working with them that are normal people, not comedians, you have to hit a happy medium."

The irony of the whole makeup situation is that Laurel and Hardy (like mimes and clowns) wore the light makeup precisely to emphasize their facial features. Despite MacWilliams' good intentions, Stan and Babe's expressions are not nearly as noticeable with the new makeups. Worse, the boys look as though they've suddenly aged 10 years. Their innocent, boyish look is gone; now they simply look like foolish old men.

Stan soon found that he would have to adhere to studio policy in all phases of production. For one thing, there would be no more shooting in sequence. "The only place I could do that was at Roach's," Stan said in a 1957 interview. "Anywhere else, they wouldn't go for that. And many times, it just ruined the prospects for the picture.

"We had, with Roach, more freedom," Stan said. "We could do what we wanted, make it how we wanted; and with the other places like Metro and 20th Century-Fox, the story was written cut and dried and it had to be shot by script... So it was a disgusting affair to us all the way through."

Much of the gag creation at Roach came during the actual shooting, whereas at Fox, just about everything had to be written directly into the script, for technical reasons. This did not exactly engender the spontaneity that was so vital to an L&H comedy.

At Roach, Laurel and Hardy had rarely rehearsed before shooting a scene, because they wanted to capture the spontaneity of the first run-through on film. Now, however, there were rehearsals for dialogue, positioning, camera placement and lighting before every take. Because Fox cinematographers did not use "a general flat light all over the set," Laurel and Hardy now had to be very conscious about hitting their marks, so they would remain properly lit.

Said MacWilliams, "If they started adding things and didn't hit their positions, the director would cut, and say, 'What the hell's the matter with you, Stan? Where are you?' 'Oh,' Stan would say, 'gee, I'm sorry,' and he'd be very apologetic about it.

"An actor has to be conscious of his position, his timing, his cues — he's got to come in just right," MacWilliams continued. "With Stan and Babe, if either one of them would miss a cue, it would throw them a curve, and they would stop right there — they wouldn't go any farther."

Ironically, a Fox press release makes it look like *Great Guns* was filmed using the same methods the team had employed at the Roach lot:

> Stan Laurel and Oliver Hardy enjoy a special privilege in the making of *Great Guns*, that has been accorded to no other star in all the history of 20th Century-Fox.
>
> They alone can end a scene of the picture. The camera must run until they call, "Cut!"
>
> The reason for this is that the boys, while doing a scene, occasionally come forth with a spontaneous bit of business which isn't in the script at all. They have learned that if they don't catch it the first time, it's not worth trying again.
>
> To make sure that there would be no misunderstanding over the point, Laurel and Hardy had it included in their contract with 20th Century-Fox.

Amazingly, the Fox publicity department understood that Laurel and Hardy needed the freedom to improvise, while the people actually in charge of making the films failed to grasp this.

When Glen MacWilliams read the foregoing account, he exploded. "Pure hogwash," he exclaimed. "Nonsense! They had to follow a certain routine. They had to follow a script; they couldn't go in there and ad-lib all over the bloody place. They *did* have a perfect right to stop a scene and say, 'Wait a minute. This is lousy.' But if you had them calling 'Cut,' well, you'd never finish the picture.

"If the director wanted Stan to do something, and he didn't feel it, Stan would say, 'I can't do that — it's not me. I'd rather do it *this* way.' In both of the pictures I did with them, they had *bad* directors. It was a bad break for the boys. Someone in the front office just had a director under contract, and put him on the picture."

MacWilliams advanced the interesting theory that Stan and Babe might have had more control over the pictures — or at least had better directors — if they hadn't been so stoic, and complained to the Fox executives.

"You couldn't have two more humble people in the world than Stan and Babe," he said. "If they were unhappy, it didn't show on the screen. The front office would never have thought of asking them, 'Look, are you unhappy, do you want a new director?' All I ever saw from Stan and Babe was complete cooperation."

According to both Lou Breslow and Glen MacWilliams, it was Fox policy to sneak preview the pictures and make the necessary changes before the actual release. But while many of the team's co-workers at Fox speak of their ad-libbing abilities, and of the preview system that was employed, the final scripts of all of the Fox films are virtual twins to be finished pictures — which means that Stan and Babe had very little opportunity to improvise.

Lou Breslow describes the kid of ad-libbing the team got away with on the Fox pictures. "In *Great Guns*, there's a scene where the boys come out of the barracks in their uniforms for the first time. At that time, the cavalry wore boots and riding breeches, which were wide at the top. Naturally, Stan's were three times as wide as normal. And they lined up with the other soldiers. While the cameras were going, Stan looked over at me, and he just took the widest part of the breeches and stretched them out. He did it so cute and funny; it was so impulsive, so natural. I damn near spoiled the shot, and the crew wondered what I was laughing at. But Stan knew — because he looked right at me when he did it."

When one realizes how Stan concerned himself with every detail of the editing process (as is evident in his notes for *The Flying Deuces*), it's a disgrace that he wasn't allowed to provide suggestions for the cutting of the Fox features. But at Fox, Stan was merely another contract player. The powers that be at Fox would no more have let Stan edit *Great Guns* than they would have let Betty Grable edit *Mother Wore Tights*.

Great Guns hardly seems like a Laurel and Hardy movie at all. The boys don't much resemble their former selves, and their familiar traits have vanished. The boys are no longer charmingly naive; they're exasperatingly stupid. One example: During the war games at the end of this picture, Stan and Ollie are driving in a jeep when Ollie is hit by a "bomb" — actually a sack of flour. The old Stan would have tried to clean up Ollie, and gotten him even messier in the process. Here, Stan turns to Ollie and cracks, "You look like a biscuit," and then howls in contemptuous laughter at Ollie's misfortune.

The film suffers from the conspicuous lack of talented supporting players. Fox's idea of "surrounding them with reality" means that instead of Jimmy Finlayson and Charlie Hall, we get colorless performers like Dick Nelson. And there are long, tedious stretches that could have been brightened by Marvin Hatley's background music. (The absence of his music in the Fox films convinces us just how valuable it was.)

When *Great Guns* was released, it got greatly mixed reviews. In an astonishing turnabout, *Variety* — which had panned most of the team's previous releases — proclaimed this one a minor masterpiece: "As good as any Laurel and Hardy have made, which is plenty good.... The gags run riot, and the characteristic Laurel and Hardy antic has a lot of elbow room for a hilarious workout.... Brilliant is the gag, pure fantastic panto, where Stan keeps marching past the amazed Oliver during a bridge-building sequence in pairs, as if he were twins. Numerous other inventions are tops in creative comedy." (The aforementioned gag is one of the few authentic L&H routines in the picture, having been lifted from the silent short *The Finishing Touch*.)

The one review which perfectly summed up Laurel and Hardy's dilemma at Fox was Thomas M. Pryor's in the *New York Times*:

> They say a change does a man good. Maybe, but it hasn't helped the team of Laurel and Hardy. The boys have changed studios quite frequently these past few seasons without any noticeable improvement in their pictures. In fact, their present offering, *Great Guns*, produced by 20th Century-Fox and deposited yesterday at the Globe, is the weakest thing they've been mixed up in yet. Not that the boys are slipping; but alas!, how desperately do they need a script writer with an understanding and appreciation for their particular style of fun-making.

The real "nitwitz" were in the executive offices at Fox.

January 1942: On tour again.

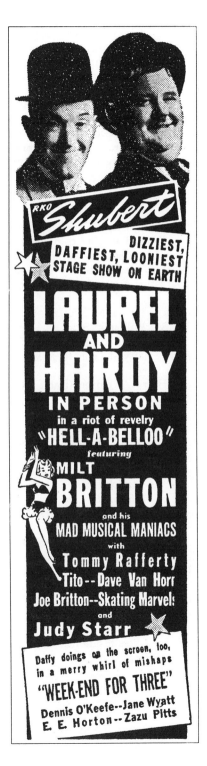

Lou Breslow obviously isn't that fellow, for *Great Guns* is a haphaz-ardly contrived comedy about the Army which makes preposterous demands upon the comedians. The few laughs the picture has to offer can be credited solely to the Messrs. Laurel and Hardy.

The Fox studio's insistence on efficiency meant, in sum, that it quickly and economically produced a film which was, so far, the worst of the team's career. This, in retrospect, does not seem like a cost-effective procedure, but the Laurel and Hardy names guaranteed enough business so that the films were assured of making a profit even though they were terrible.

A-HAUNTING WE WILL GO

Production history: Original outline completed by Stanley Rauh November 29, 1941. Revised outline completed by Lou Breslow January 20, 1942. Original screenplay, first draft, completed by Breslow January 27. Revised final draft of screenplay completed by Breslow March 18. Filmed March 15-early April. Copyrighted August 7, 1942 by Fox (LP 11773). Released August 7. 67 minutes.

Produced by Sol M. Wurtzel. Directed by Alfred L. Werker. Photographed by Glen MacWilliams. Story by Lou Breslow and Stanley Rauh; screenplay by Breslow. Art direction by Richard Day and Lewis Creber. Sound by Arthur von Kirbach, Harry M. Leonard. Musical direction by Emil Newman.

With Harry A. Jansen (Dante the Magician), John Shelton, Sheila Ryan, Don Costello, Elisha Cook Jr.

Vagrants L&H have 24 hours to leave town; a newspaper ad offers a free train trip to Dayton. However, the boys must accompany a coffin. Unbeknownst to them, the "corpse" is Darby Mason, a live fugitive on the lam. Stan and Ollie are fleeced en route by two con men, who sell them a money-making machine. Dante the Magician, who is traveling with his troupe, takes pity on the boys and pays for their meals; they end up as his assistants. Meanwhile, the coffin has gotten mixed up with a prop used in Dante's act.

It's a dreary experience to spend 67 minutes of one's life in the company of this wretched excuse for a movie — especially when one could spend the same 67 minutes watching *Way Out West*. Laurel and Hardy wander into this Grade-Z gangster melodrama at odd moments and try to inject some of the old gracefulness into material that is entirely humorless. Watching the team trying to insert their familiar characteristics into routines that would be woefully unfunny for *any* comedian is heartbreaking. Darby Mason may be the character who's inside that coffin, but the death knell sounds for Stan and Ollie in *A-Haunting We Will Go*.

Before the comedians got ensnared in this supremely annoying picture, they had been once again appearing before live audiences. On November 2, 1941, Stan and Babe flew to San Juan, Puerto Rico with several other stars, on the first stop of the *Flying Showboat* tour. The troupe traveled in three B-18s, and over two weeks visited defense bases in Antigua, Saint Lucia, Trinidad and British Guyana.

Then, in January 1942, the team embarked on a second personal appearance tour, once again performing the "Driver's License" sketch. The *Hell-a-Belloo* tour played Chicago, Detroit, Fort Wayne, Cleveland and Pittsburgh before arriving for a Boston engagement; there, on February 20, Babe was stricken with acute laryngitis, and the balance of the tour was cancelled.

As the team returned to Hollywood, Fox writers Stanley Rauh and Lou Breslow had nearly completed the script for Laurel and Hardy's second Fox feature. It's significant that this script had been written while the boys were away on tour, and it illustrates just how little say Stan had in the writing and production of the Fox pictures.

Ironically enough, Stan and Babe in effect gave the Fox studio the permission to treat them this way. *Great Guns* had been made under a one-picture contract which gave Laurel and Hardy the option to continue with Fox. Evidently, Stan felt that he could eventually regain some of his old control over the pictures; "I kept thinking that sooner or later they would let us do the pictures in our own way, but it just got worse," he recalled.

The melancholy history of *A-Haunting We Will Go* began in November 1941, when Stanley Rauh concocted a story outline entitled *Pitfalls of a Big City*. The outline conveys as much humor as the title. It is incredibly morbid, with murders and beatings galore. There are more plots in this story than in a

Touring Caribbean Army bases in November 1941, with Jane Pickens, John Garfield (extreme right), and in the foreground, Ray Bolger and Chico Marx.

cemetery, and the overall mood is just as grim. (If Stan and Babe had written a script about working for Fox, they could have called it *Pitfalls of a Big Studio*.)

The few gags that Rauh wrote for L&H make the mistake of having Stan as the aggressive, take-charge member of the team. (The general public grasped the essence of the Stan and Ollie characters more readily than did the Fox writers.) One gag will suffice as evidence of Rauh's misdirection:

As comic magicians, the boys have to entertain the audience — Dante is recovering in his dressing room after being knocked unconscious by a thug. Stan announces that he will saw Ollie in half. Ollie is quite nervous about this, but Stan is all confidence, assuring his partner, "It's a cinch!" Ollie gets inside a box, and Stan starts sawing away. Momentarily, Ollie emits an anguished scream. Stan, in a gag that might have been more suitable for Harry Ritz, runs to the footlights and yells, "Calling Doctor Kildare!" That's Stan, all right. A wisecrack for every occasion.

Rauh's outline ran 59 pages — more than twice the length of a usual outline — which barely accommodated all those characters. The project was handed over to Lou Breslow, to eliminate some of the *dramatis personae* and hack through the thicket of subplots. He also wrote some L&H routines, hardly any of which fit the boys' characters.

Breslow kept confusing Oliver Hardy with Groucho Marx. A line which survives in the film occurs when the pair have to decide whether to accompany the body to Dayton; Ollie turns to Stan and quips, "It's better to spend one night with a corpse than 60 days with the cops!" In a scripted backstage scene, Ollie finds a gangster named Dixie Draper, who's been hiding from the cops by disguising himself as a mummy. Ollie looks at the thug's bandaged body, turns to the camera and, in a close-up, wisecracks, "You see? That's what comes from careless driving!"

The Fox scripts tend to give the team quick and unfunny dialogue exchanges, rather than allowing them the time to do pantomime routines. If Laurel and Hardy had made *Hog Wild* at Fox, they would have spent the whole film *talking* about putting up an aerial.

Breslow wrote an outline, a first draft of the screenplay, a temporary screenplay, a final draft, and a *revised* final draft. Stan was apparently not consulted at any point during the writing; he wasn't even in Hollywood until February 24, by which time a "final" script had been completed. Recalling his work on the multitude of scripts, Breslow said, "I got the idea from this magician that was working on Vine Street — Dante. I thought they'd be funny working with him, that's all. You know, you whip up a story and it's like a roll of the dice. It either comes out seven or snake eyes."

The assigned director was Alfred Louis Werker, who began his career in the mid-'20s and made a number of routine films in a variety of genres. Drama was definitely better suited to his talents than comedy.

"Werker was a bright guy," remarked Lou Breslow. "He did *The House of Rothschild* with George Arliss. And that's the kind of thing he should have done. He should never have been allowed even to *see* a Laurel and Hardy picture. Oh, no; he knew nothing about that kind of comedy."

Glen MacWilliams, who rejoined the team as the director of photography on this picture, put it more bluntly. "Alfred Werker — I don't think he ever smiled in his life! He was the last person in this world I would pick to direct Laurel and Hardy in a picture, because of his lack of humor. He was a miserable, grouchy person."

Werker's known comments about the film were brief; he said that Stan did not direct himself and Ollie in their routines, and that the team was given "very little" freedom to stray from the script. The working atmosphere was "very friendly and happy" according to Werker, who called the film "a very pleasant assignment."

A-Haunting We Will Go was the team's happiest experience on a Fox sound stage "simply because they enjoyed working with Dante," according to Bob Chatterton, a friend of Stan's in later years. But it was not an entirely happy experience.

"One of the things that Stan didn't like to do, throughout his whole career, was his business of scratching his head and crying," Chatterton related. "It became like a trademark, but he didn't really like to do it. He didn't want to *overdo* it. And in this film he was called upon to continue this crying to the point where it was painful to Stan. And you can see it, in the way he carries himself, and in his face, that it was painful. But these were the things he had to do, and this was why he hated those Fox movies." Indeed, during his last scenes in the film, Stan does virtually nothing *but* cry.

Veteran character actor Mantan Moreland — best remembered for his portrayal of Birmingham Brown, Charlie Chan's chauffeur — had a brief sequence as a waiter who is dismayed when the boys can't pay for their meal on the train. In a 1968 interview, he seemed to recall that the team tried to inject their own bits of business despite the restrictions imposed upon them by Fox.

"When they were working for Roach, he gave them everything they wanted," Moreland said. "If you asked Fox for a mansion, they'd give you a five-room house. If you had any ideas for comedy you'd have to cut it down to this five-room house. That's what made this picture bad.

"I remember that we were ad-libbing on that train... The script was there, all right, but we'd get ready to shoot a scene, and if they had something in the script that wasn't really funny, Stan would say, 'Wait a minute. Why don't you try this?,' see, and we'd try to get something out of it, you know?"

To some extent, Moreland's recollections are contradicted when one compares the film to the revised final script. There doesn't seem to have been much ad-libbing done by anybody; a line may be altered here or there, but the wholesale improvisation that marked many of the Roach films is nowhere to be found.

The boys are very subdued in the finished film. There is nothing magical, enchanting or funny about them. They have no comedy material through most of the film, and so the only humor comes from the way they move and react. The few gags offered by the script are stock routines that could be done by any comic.

This film may *look* more "professional" than the low-budget Roach releases, but that's no consolation when all of the warmth, humor and humanity has been squeezed out of the L&H characters.

One old gag — the bit from *Wrong Again* where the boys break a statue of a nude woman, then reassemble it with the midsection reversed — is repeated here. But not very well. Werker shot it from a bad angle, and didn't give the boys enough time to react, so the gag doesn't build. If one needs an example of how bad direction can turn a belly laugh into a throwaway, this is it.

This is such a depressing, disheartening movie that it's disturbing to read the glowing reviews it received upon release. *Variety*, so uncharitable to the

The Fox makeup and lighting techniques aged Stan's appearance, as evidenced by this portrait with Sheila Ryan.

team's earlier films, proclaimed this one "lively entertainment... a lot of fresh and novel gags, carried out neatly in [Lou] Breslow's script and smartly punctuated in Alfred Werker's direction." The review praised Werker for his "knowledge and skill in handling comedy values," and commended his "careful and sure craftsmanship."

The Hollywood Reporter thought the film "several notches better than any of the recent features Laurel and Hardy have made." But Theodore Strauss in the *New York Times* was on target when he huffed, "*A-Haunting We Will Go* is a veritable feast of cliché, a five-finger exercise in boredom."

Glen MacWilliams felt that Stan and Babe were "miscast" in both Fox films he made with them — this sort of carelessness had never occurred at the Roach studio, but being forced to perform unsuitable material churned out by writers who knew little about the team's comedy was becoming the order of the day.

Immediately after finishing *A-Haunting We Will Go*, Laurel and Hardy did their bit for the war effort by participating in the Hollywood Victory Caravan — a whistle-stop tour that featured the biggest names in show business.

Stan and Babe, who trotted out the ever-reliable "Driver's License" sketch, were always among the best-received acts on the bill. Comedian Frank McHugh recalled, "When the orchestra played Laurel and Hardy's sign music, you've never heard such an ovation." The tour began March 29, 1942 in Washington, D.C. (where the actors lunched with Eleanor Roosevelt at the White House), and traveled to 12 major cities in the East and Midwest before finishing in San Francisco in mid-May.

Meanwhile, back in Hollywood, the outlook for comedy films was not bright. Hal Roach commented on the situation in *The Motion Picture Herald*.

"There is not one-tenth as much comedy produced now as there was in the old days," he said. "There has been no new comedy talent, to speak of, developed in the past few years, because the young actor and actress look with disdain upon comedy acting. They all want to emote and become Clark Gables and Bette Davises.

"As a result," Roach concluded, "we must develop the kind of talent we can use and teach them the rudiments of comedy and timing." Before the producer could put his plans into action, however, he was called into the service as a lieutenant colonel. The Roach lot was leased to the U.S. Government, which made training films there with many of the old Roach staffers during the war years.

While Stan and Babe couldn't re-join the Roach studio even if they wanted to, they could work for studios other than Fox; their contract with that studio was non-exclusive. In mid-1942, Laurel and Hardy Feature Productions made a pact with Metro-Goldwyn-Mayer for two features.

AIR RAID WARDENS

Production history: Story treatment by Jack Jevne and Martin Rackin completed August 18, 1942. Screenplay written September. Filmed December 1-early January 1943. Copyrighted March 17, 1943 by Loew's Incorporated (LP 11931). Released by MGM circa April 4, 1943. 67 minutes.

Produced by B.F. Zeidman. Directed by Edward Sedgwick. Screenplay by Martin Rackin, Jack Jevne, Charles Rogers and Harry Crane. Photographed by Walter Lundin. Edited by Irvine Warburton. Musical score by Nat Shilkret. Sound by Douglas Shearer. Art direction by Cedric Gibbons, Harry McAfee.

With Edgar Kennedy, Jacqueline White, Horace McNally, Nella Walker, Howard Freeman, Donald Meek.

The boys are about to close their bicycle shop to enlist in the service, but return when they're rejected by all branches of the armed forces. They then become partners with Eustace Middling, who sells radios. Stan and Ollie's patriotic urge is satisfied by participating in Civil Defense safety drills, but their ineptitude gets them dismissed. L&H do their part for the war effort by discovering that Middling is actually a Nazi spy who plans to blow up the town's magnesium plant — and alerting Civil Defense workers just in time.

MGM excelled in romantic comedies such as the *Thin Man* series, but out-and-out visual slapstick was a major stumbling block for the studio. Metro's movies were glossy, glamorous entertainments that reinforced the status quo; slapstick, traditionally, has always been gritty, messy and subversive.

The studio's track record with comics might well have caused Stan and Babe to pause before signing their contracts. As has been well documented elsewhere, Buster Keaton and the Marx Brothers suffered mightily when MGM executives wouldn't allow the comedians to make their pictures in their own way.

It is likely that Stan tried to prevent a similar fate by getting Charley Rogers on the writing staff for the team's first MGM film. Rogers and a young

Some idea of the fun to be had in *Air Raid Wardens*.

writer named Harry Crane developed the screenplay along with Martin Rackin and Jack Jevne, who had previously written the story. Rackin would later become head of production at Paramount, but at this stage he was a 24-year-old novice writer. Although Jevne had worked on the scripts of several Roach features, including *Our Relations* and *Way Out West*, the story bore little resemblance to a typical L&H plot.

Jevne and Rackin's treatment has even more of the homespun wholesomeness that saturates the film. In their outline, the boys are called Stanley Smith and Oliver Jones — a way of typifying them as American Everymen.

The outline contains more plot and even less comedy than the finished film. There's a great deal of stuff about the Nazis blowing up a train which is carrying dynamite — in doing so at a strategic location, the Germans will also destroy a dam and wipe out the entire town. The handsome hero, a newspaper editor named Scoop, saves the day. There's also a gag with Stan and Ollie trying to beat the Nazis to the train by racing alongside it on a tandem bicycle.

Stan thought that the story had some potential. And, to be fair, Metro seemed to be trying harder to make a good L&H movie than Fox had. For one thing, there were four writers working on the script instead of the one at Fox, and Jevne and Rogers had worked with the team before. Cameraman Walter Lundin had photographed portions of *Bonnie Scotland* and *Way Out West*. Director Edward Sedgwick had guided the team through *Pick a Star*; he was also especially close to Buster Keaton during his struggles with MGM management, so he was sensitive to the needs of comics. (Sedgwick had been a comic himself in vaudeville and in films until 1921.)

Why, then, is *Air Raid Wardens* such a bland and unamusing movie? One answer lies in the fact that the filmmakers reportedly had to put up with a Civil

Edward Sedgwick directs an early scene; Stan doesn't look happy.

Defense official who would not stand for any kidding of the organization's procedures. The boys have several comedy scenes which couldn't possibly offend the Office of Civil Defense, but they simply don't work — probably because Stan wasn't able to assert his creativity behind the camera.

Even when the script exhibits promising material, the sequences are undercut by camera angles which don't accentuate the gags, and by editing that interrupts the flow of the film. This mishandling of the material is, in a roundabout way, a testament to Stan's importance as the "director's director" and the overseer of the editing.

For example, two encounters with Edgar Kennedy, which should have been as funny as similar episodes in *Bacon Grabbers*, don't work — partly because of the script, partly due to the direction. An L&H tit-for-tat sequence has to start out small and build, as minor indignities develop into major ones. The pace at first should be slow, with all participants acting as gracefully as if they were dancing a minuet. Gradually, the tempo increases — but not very much. The scene should be filmed in medium long shot, so we can see the surrounding environment of the combatants. Close-ups must be used sparingly, but are effective as reaction shots after one of the participants has been newly embarrassed.

The tit-for-tat sequence which takes place in Kennedy's kitchen has all the pace of a mixing machine with a short circuit. It starts out fast, then pauses, then rushes forth again. Sedgwick has framed it in tight three-shots, so the comedians have no room to move. There are no close-ups to heighten the reactions — everything is played in the same tight shot, and before Ollie has finished his reaction to one gag, Kennedy has already started in on the next one. The gags don't build — the last indignity is no more damaging than the first.

Poor scripting and direction gang up to kill another traditional L&H gag. Usually, when the boys have to sign their names on a document, Ollie does so first — beaming with pride and self-importance, he dips his pen nobly in the inkwell, describes some elegant and joyful curlicues with the pen in mid-air, then admires his handiwork as he inscribes his triple-barrelled name.

After Ollie ceremoniously hands the pen over to his friend, Stan dips the pen in the inkwell — and instantly obliterates everything written on the page. He tears out the page, with some chagrin, and starts over. (All of this is played in a two-shot, so that we can see Ollie's reactions to every new blunder.) Stan wants to write his name, but he can't get his arm into a comfortable position, and he begins moving paper, pen and himself in wild gyrations all over the desk. Finally, Stan has everything at the ready. He positions his pen, holds steady, and scrawls a large X.

In *Air Raid Wardens*, all opportunities for gags are immediately erased. Mr. Laurel is about to sign his name on a document *first*, so we're denied the joy of seeing Mr. Hardy inscribe his moniker. Then, the punchline gets killed right away, because Ollie has to say, "No X's. Sign your *name*." Next, there's no room for Stan to mess things up, because the surface he's writing on is too small. Pointless close-ups of the document interrupt the flow of his reactions. Then the camera laboriously dollies in on Stan; the camera movement distracts us, and cuts Ollie out of the shot, so we can't see his reactions. All we're left with is a close-up of Stan tearfully trying to write "Stan," with insert shots showing us how badly he's doing. It's like being asked to laugh at someone who's mentally retarded.

Among the movie's more appalling moments: the scene where the sadistic Nazi forces Stan to shoot Ollie; a poster-hanging bit that's utterly ruined through poor direction and cutting; and an encounter with a pompous banker that might be funny if it weren't wholly bereft of gags. The ending is terrifically bad, too: the boys capture the chief Nazi, but there's no comedy in their attempts to capture him. They just see him about to get into a car, walk over, and nab him — and that's it.

Stan must have seen some of the rushes; he certainly realized that MGM's editor was snipping all of the comedy out of the footage. Laurel called on Bert Jordan, who was working on those training films at Fort Roach. "When Laurel and Hardy went to MGM, there was a fellow there [Irvine Warburton] who was going to cut their shows for them," said Jordan. "They sent him down to the Roach studio to run the dailies with me, to give him ideas of what Stan liked.

"Stan really didn't care for the way they were treated there. He told me, 'We're not happy there. We go to work in the morning, we do what they tell us, and we go home. They don't care whether we're funny or whether we're not.'" Whatever advice Jordan gave to MGM editor Warburton, it apparently went unheeded.

Once again, the *Variety* reviewer seemed blind to the film's flaws: "*Air Raid Wardens* gives Laurel and Hardy a chance to shine in their best comedy style and boys pull all stops in hitting the laughs in their fast-moving topical farce... story was expertly fashioned to favorably display generous talents of Laurel and Hardy."

Unfortunately, the very problem with this movie was that *nothing* was fashioned to favorably display those talents. Whatever laughs the boys got were attained in spite of the ineptitude surrounding them.

Two Unproduced Scripts

While Stan and Babe were toiling at MGM, Sol Wurtzel assigned the next
L&H picture to a young writer named Paul A. Yawitz. Lou Breslow had gone on
to greener pastures, and Wurtzel seemed to think that a good way to train
fledgling writers was to let them try a relatively unimportant picture like a
Laurel and Hardy.

On September 18, 1942, Mr. Yawitz completed a story outline entitled *Me
and My Shadow*. In it, Laurel and Hardy run a Coney Island wax museum
which is bereft of customers. A photo gallery next door is run by Eric Miller, a
handsome young refugee from Germany. His heart-throb is Joan Williams, the
pretty cashier at the wax museum. It so happens that two Nazi agents, Kurt
Schleicher and Helmina Friederichs, have been entrusted to deliver some
important microfilm to another agent, Karl von Fritsch, in the States. The two
agents disguise themselves as a refugee couple, obtain a baby orphaned by the
blitzkrieg bombings, and hide the microfilm in the cloth belt of the child's
tunic.

In New York, they learn from Fritsch that the agent who handled microfilm
has been arrested; the only other man familiar with the developing and enlarg-
ing process is Eric Miller. (The Nazis know how to *make* the microfilm, they just
don't know how to develop and enlarge it.) Kurt and Helmina visit the photo
gallery to persuade Eric to help them, but are unexpectedly confronted by a
suspicious detective, Anthony Steele. In their haste to leave, they grab one of
Laurel and Hardy's wax dummies, mistaking it for the the baby bearing the
microfilm.

Stan and Ollie, meanwhile, are being interrogated by two gangsters, Big
Manny and Benny Blue Eyes. Manny works for a collection agency, and wants
the six months' rent the boys owe. When he sees the baby crawling around the
grimy museum, Manny's heart softens. He *loves* babies, so much so that he
gives the boys money to pay their rent, and warns them not to let the kid out of
their sight. Says Yawitz's outline, "When they attempt to notify the authorities
that they have a lost child, their actions are misunderstood, and they find themselves in a series of comedy situations, mostly at the end of Benny Blue Eyes'
gun."

Kurt and Helmina discover they've got a wax dummy instead of the child
with the precious microfilm. Fritsch decides to purchase and run the shooting
gallery across from L&H's wax museum. So — the Nazis are plotting to kidnap
the child, the two thugs are threatening Stan and Ollie to keep it from harm,
Detective Steele is suspicious, and Laurel and Hardy are afraid. "We have
these elements playing for hilarious comedy," says Yawitz's outline, without
bothering to mention what that comedy is.

In a chase, Stan leads the Nazis back to the midway. Stan and the baby
hide on a "Flying Circus" ride; the Nazis spot them and grab the controls. The
ride spins faster and faster. The outline tells us, "Stan is a very sick man. He
puts his head out again in attempt to heave."

This chase scene goes on for many pages, and Ollie is nowhere to be found
until Laurel and Hardy somehow get trapped in a hall of mirrors. That's the last
we hear of them. For the final nine pages, the gangsters, Nazis, cops and young
lovers finish up the chase and the story.

Me and My Shadow was so bad that even Sol Wurtzel refused to produce

At Stan's home, reading something far more worthy than the Fox scripts. (Note the portraits of James Horne, Babe, Hal Roach and Harry Langdon.)

it. Instead, he got two more young writers, Charles Roberts and Eugene Ling, to write another script. *Untitled Laurel and Hardy* was completed on December 8, 1942.

In this one, L&H are the proprietors of Alpshaven, a sanitarium located in a very remote region of the Swiss Alps — so remote, in fact, that the boys don't know World War II has been raging about them since late 1939. Nor do they know that: their two hypochondriacal patients, Mr. and Mrs. Schweiz, are really British Intelligence agents; two new arrivals, Greta and Anna, are trying to escape the Gestapo; two *other* visitors, Reinhard and Heinrich, are Gestapo agents who want to kill Anna because she's married to a Gestapo chieftain and knows too much; yet *another* new visitor, an inscrutable Monk, is actually another British agent trying to rescue Greta and Anna.

Despite the grimness of the plot, there are a few scenes which indicate that Roberts and Ling had a better grasp of the L&H characters than their Fox cohorts.

In one scene, the evil Heinrich discovers Ollie in a hallway, talking secretively to someone who's in a private room. That someone is Greta, whom the boys are trying to hide. When Heinrich asks Ollie just who he was talking to, Ollie alibis that he was speaking to the new upstairs maid. Guess who gets elected to play *that* role. Stan is made up as the new maid, Katrinka, and some scenes where Heinrich flirts with "her" are quite amusing, especially when the loaves of bread which comprise Stan's bosom keep slipping.

Stan and Ollie, independently of each other, discover there's a hidden passageway underneath the sanitarium. Mr. and Mrs. Schweiz and Greta hide there from the Nazis; so do Stan and Ollie, but neither knows the other is there.

While Ollie frantically looks for Stan, the Nazis blow up Alpshaven. A barrel of flour from the kitchen falls on Stan. When Ollie discovers Stan's "angel," he sobs at the death of his old friend. Before long, though, Ollie discovers that flour is the true source of Stan's new-found luminescence, and chases after Stan in a rage. (This gag is somewhat overdone, but it shows that Roberts and Ling understood Stan and Ollie's relationship.)

Finally, the boys escape with Mr. and Mrs. Schweiz and Greta in one of the Gestapo agents' cars. They flee into Occupied France, where they find a rusty old cable car that will cross the mountaintops from France into Spain. With the Nazis in hot pursuit, Stan and Ollie and their friends at last get the ancient machinery working. There's a hair-raising scene where Ollie falls out of his cable car and clings desperately to it, 6,000 feet above a treacherous chasm. However, there's a happy ending when the boys and their comrades escape the clutches of the Nazis and cross into Spain.

While this is a fairly grim story — and Laurel and Hardy seem to be supporting characters — the same is true of most of the Fox stories which *did* get filmed. Why this script was vetoed is not readily apparent; even if the story is grim, it's well constructed. (It's almost a comic version of Hitchcock's *The Lady Vanishes*.)

If the dialogue doesn't always sound exactly right for Laurel and Hardy, there's none of the infuriatingly *wrong* stuff that other writers put in their mouths. This script, all things considered, probably wouldn't have made a very good picture — but it might have been better than some of the films they eventually made.

Sol Wurtzel decided that if the young turks on the staff couldn't write an L&H story, then an old pro certainly could. Wurtzel was wrong.

JITTERBUGS

Production history: Story written by Scott Darling and Malcolm St. Clair, January 1943. Final screenplay completed by Darling February 2. Filmed February 15-late March. Copyrighted June 11, 1943 by Fox (LP 12220). Released June 11. 74 minutes.

Produced by Sol M. Wurtzel. Directed by Malcolm St. Clair. Photographed by Lucien Andriot. Special photographic effects by Fred Sersen. Screenplay by Scott Darling. Art direction by James Basevi, Chester Gore. Dances staged by Geneva Sawyer. Sound by E. Clayton Ward, Harry M. Leonard. Musical direction by Emil Newman. Lyrics and music by Charles Newman, Lew Pollack.

With Vivian Blaine, Robert Bailey, Douglas Fowley, Noel Madison, Lee Patrick, Anthony Caruso.

Proprietors of a mechanical "zoot-suit" band, the boys are stranded in the desert. Luckily, they are befriended by Chester Wright, a dapper young man who sells pills which purport to turn water into gasoline. They set up business at a carnival in Midvale, where Chester meets pretty Susan Cowan, whose mother has been swindled by con men. Chester cons the con men with an elaborate scheme that prompts Ollie to masquerade as Southern sheriff Wattison Bixby, and Stan to dress up as Susan's refined but fun-loving aunt.

Since fledgling authors had provided L&H scripts that were even more unsuitable than Lou Breslow's, Sol Wurtzel gave the next assignment to a comedy veteran, W. Scott Darling.

Darling had a long and not particularly distinguished career, and had written scripts for two-reelers produced by Al Christie in the early 1920s. Neal Burns, one of Christie's top comics, noted: "W. Scott Darling was a writer who had but one plot." During the '30s and '40s, most of Darling's assignments were mysteries; just before joining Fox, he'd scripted *Ghost of Frankenstein* at Universal. Whatever comedy skills Darling had seem to have evaporated by the time he was handed the L&H assignment.

A new director was at the helm, and, to Fox's credit, he appeared to be a good choice for the team. Malcolm St. Clair had worked with Mack Sennett and received credit for co-writing and co-directing two of Buster Keaton's best shorts; he'd also been likened to Ernst Lubitsch for his sophisticated comedy style. However, at the end of the '20s, his films suddenly and unaccountably deteriorated, and by the '30s he was directing B-picture comedies.

Darling and St. Clair collaborated on the original story for *Jitterbugs* at the start of 1943, and by early February, Darling had completed the final screenplay. The plot they ended up with is virtually incomprehensible; if Darling only had one plot, it was a complicated one.

To modern audiences, *Jitterbugs* might seem like an earlier version of the Paul Newman-Robert Redford film *The Sting*. Both pictures are about con men trying to out-con some of their more unscrupulous brethren. Unfortunately, *Jitterbugs* is hampered by a plethora of subplots and characters that waltz in for a few minutes and abruptly leave.

For example, the boys are introduced as the leaders of a mechanical big band; after providing an excuse for a musical number the band is never heard from again. (It's not a very good idea, anyway. As further evidence of the fact that the Fox writers just didn't know how to get laughs out of the team's characters, it's the musical gadgets which are supposed to provide the humor here. Stan and Ollie hardly have to appear in the sequence.)

What little pleasure there is to be gotten from this movie arrives in the scenes where the boys masquerade as other characters. Laurel and Hardy the actors don't get much of a chance to play Laurel and Hardy the characters in this picture, but it's diverting to see them sporting other characterizations. Stan is captivating as Aunt Emily, and Babe gets an opportunity to display his Southern heritage as the flirtatious Colonel Bixby.

What's disturbing is that Laurel and Hardy are so busy playing other roles and wading through the cumbersome plot, there's virtually no characteristic L&H comedy. Even when they're supposed to be "Stan and Ollie," they're given the unsuitable occupation of zoot-suited swing musicians. Ollie has to say lines like, "Come on, hep cats, we're going to spread a load of jam!"

Jitterbugs was a much more lavishly-mounted production than its Fox predecessors, primarily because the studio was using the film as a showcase for the up-and-coming Vivian Blaine. Her co-star, Bob Bailey, was a Chicago-based radio actor making his film debut; Blaine had a handful of movie credits, but this was her first major role.

Vivian Blaine had this to say about her work with the team: "They were perfect gentlemen, who made me feel wonderful; they were very relaxed. Stand-up comics drive me insane because they're always *on*. But Laurel and Hardy

"Just a couple of gut-bucket guys."

and I went to lunch one day, and I said to them, 'You're not being funny!' And they said, 'Well, we're just normal human beings.' And that's when I realized the artistry of these two men. They were dedicated to their work; they did their performing on camera only. And they didn't make fun of a newcomer, which I was at the time. I wish I could think of a funny story about them, but I can't because they were so sincere about what they were doing."

The comedians apparently got along well with St. Clair. Blaine speaks of them as being a clique, "a threesome, the likes of which I've never known." He remained the team's director for the rest of their days at Fox.

Lee Patrick, who had a brief but enjoyable turn as Dorcas — the gangster's moll who tries to ensnare "Colonel Bixby" into a shakedown with her Southern belle charms — said of her work with the boys: "It was unquestionably one of the most pleasant experiences I ever had in films. And I can't go along with today's Johnny-come-lately critics who go into ecstasies about their art of improvisation. Those boys worked hard at their craft. Everything they did in

"Aunt Emily" fixes her makeup between takes.

Jitterbugs — their timing, their finesse, their reactions — was as carefully worked out and rehearsed as a Fred Astaire dance routine."

A comparison of the film with the final script reveals that St. Clair allowed Stan and Babe to change lines and make them more suitable to their established characterizations — but there was no opportunity to suggest an entirely different scene, or to shoot "off the cuff," as they'd frequently done at the Roach lot. In other words, they could only try to inject their own improvisations on the Fox writers' discordant themes.

The most pronounced alteration, oddly enough, comes in the scene where Lee Patrick as Dorcas, the moll, is trying to seduce Stan, having mistaken him for the colonel. In Darling's script, Stan rather uncharacteristically falls under her spell; the dialogue doesn't sound right for him, either:

DORCAS: I still feel a little faint. Let me order some drinks — say, a couple of Sazeracs.

STAN: *(With a wave of his hand)* Madam, I do not drink.

DORCAS: You don't drink!

STAN: *(Feeling this is no way to make any progress)* Your lips are an intoxication in themselves, Madam.

DORCAS: Oh — yes? Well, anyway, hand me that bottle of brandy. I feel like a little snifter — I mean a little sip.

STAN: I will be your cup-bearer, Madam.

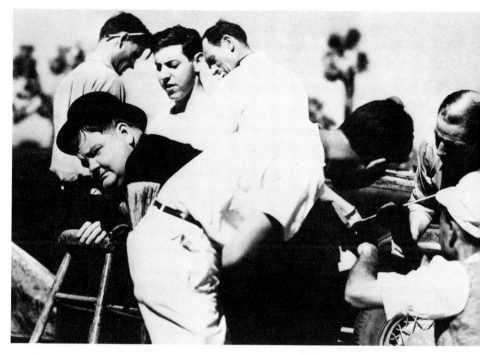

Prop men apply a "Ford" insignia to the trousers of the mortified Mr. Hardy.

> DORCAS: *(Having half-finished her drink)* See — I have sweetened
> it...one little sip.
> STAN: *(Affecting to weaken)* You tempt me, Madam. *(He drains
> he glass to the bottom)* Say! That was a bit of all right.

As Stan plays the scene in the film, the dialogue is more in line with his innocent, sexless character:

> DORCAS: Come sit here beside me.
> STAN: Why?
> DORCAS: Why, I still feel a little faint.
> STAN: I'll go get a doctor —
> DORCAS: Oh, let us have some drinks. Shall I order a couple of
> Sazeracs?
> STAN: I'm sorry, lady, but I don't drink.
> DORCAS: *(Losing her Southern accent)* You don't drink?! I mean —
> you-all don't drink?
> STAN: Uh uh.
> DORCAS: Oh, would you mind if I had a little snifter? I mean, a little
> sip.
> STAN: Certainly not. Help —
> DORCAS: Oh, would you mind pouring it for me? *(She takes the
> glass, sips)* See, I've sweetened it. One little sip.

STAN:	Uh uh.
DORCAS:	Just for poor little me?
STAN:	Just one little sip? *(Thinking it over)* Well, just one. *(He takes a tentative sip, does a double take, then tosses back the whole drink. He swallows, pauses, and his hat flies off his head.)* You know, that's a bit of all right.

In a 1951 interview with *Los Angeles Times* film critic Philip K. Scheuer, Stan and Babe commented on the constraints imposed on them by Fox. "The writers they brought in only wanted to write highbrow stuff; they couldn't be bothered with us," said Babe. "Our producer never read our scripts. 'You boys don't need a story,' he'd tell us. 'Your pictures are making money; what more do you want?'"

Stan told Scheuer, "We tried to tell them, 'If a bad one makes money, what would a good one do?'" Babe continued, "That's a pitiful thing, when they don't think you have to have a story or a cast. Then they'd give us a young girl or boy who had never been in pictures, so that we'd be busy teaching them to act and trying to be funny ourselves at the same time."

"Like Vivian Blaine, in *Jitterbugs*," Stan commented. "All those old movies you see on television were written and supervised by us," Laurel told Scheuer, the hurt and bitterness evident in his voice. "Naturally, it breaks your heart when they send you a script Friday night and say you're to start shooting Monday morning. We're not used to that kind of treatment."

Stan's copies of the Fox scripts indicate that his statement about getting the scripts almost immediately before shooting began was quite true. Stan wrote notations and comments on each of these 120-page scripts, but the notes stop at about page 35 of each one — he apparently had a very short amount of time in which to read the script before shooting began.

Jitterbugs was released on June 11, 1943 (with the ad copy billing Laurel and Hardy as "Just a couple of gut-bucket guys — beating it out eight laughs to the bar!"). The critics were not impressed. *Variety* called it "generally un-funny...Laurel and Hardy's usual tomfoolery much subdued, and comics given little comedy to display."

The Hollywood Reporter offered the most perceptive observation: "*Jitterbugs* hopes to entertain an audience by introducing a hodgepodge of ideas and developing none to a conclusion of hilarity. It is a start-stop, hit-miss affair that is not so very funny despite the labors of Laurel and Hardy to make it jell."

In recent years, the film has gotten quite a favorable reputation by being the most tolerable film of a very sorry lot. But comparing *Jitterbugs* to the other post-1940 L&H films is like comparing diarrhea to leprosy. One may be prefer-able, but neither is any fun.

THE TREE IN A TEST TUBE

Production history: Filmed circa February-March 1943. Released early 1943. No copyright registration exists for this film. One reel, color; silent with narration, music and sound effects.

Produced by the U.S. Department of Agriculture, Forest Service. Directed by

Charles McDonald. Photographed by A.H.C. Sintzenich. Edited by Boris Vermont. Sound by Reuben Ford. Music by Edward Craig.

Narration by Pete Smith, Lee Vickers.

Laurel and Hardy's only surviving theatrical color film appears to have been shot at 20th Century-Fox during the production of *Jitterbugs*. Reportedly, they made their appearance while on their lunch hour.

This 16mm film seeks to demonstrate the varied uses of wood products, which, we are told, contribute to the war effort and to life in general. Stan and Ollie improvise some comedy business with a suitcase filled with wood-derived props, to the accompaniment of Pete Smith's wiseguy narration. ("C'mon, boys," he exhorts, "let's see some more of yer junk — uh, I mean your nice things!")

After five minutes of these pleasantries, the film reverts to serious footage about new wood products — which, inadvertently, is even funnier than the Laurel and Hardy routine.

THE DANCING MASTERS

Production history: Original story written mid-April 1943. Screenplay completed May 4. Final script completed May 28. Filmed June 1-circa June 25. Released and copyrighted November 19, 1943 by Fox (LP 12453). 63 minutes.

Produced by Lee Marcus. Directed by Malcolm St. Clair. Photographed by Norbert Brodine. Special photographic effects by Fred Sersen. Edited by Norman Colbert. Screenplay by W. Scott Darling. Suggested by a story by George Bricker. Art direction by James Basevi, Chester Gore. Sound by Bernard Fredericks and Harry M. Leonard. Musical direction by Emil Newman. Music by Arthur Lange.

With Trudy Marshall, Bob Bailey, Margaret Dumont, Matt Briggs, Charles Rogers, Daphne Pollard.

Dance instructors Stan and Ollie are beset by creditors, and by extortionists who force them to buy an "insurance" policy. The one bright spot in their life is their favorite pupil, Trudy Harlan. Her boyfriend Grant Lawrence, an inventor, wants to demonstrate his new invisible ray machine for Trudy's father, a munitions manufacturer — but Mr. Harlan dislikes him, so Grant asks Stan to pose as a foreign inventor, with Ollie as his interpreter. The demonstration works well, until Stan forgets to turn off the machine and it blows up.

Laurel and Hardy's earlier movies for Fox failed because the team's unique characters had been ignored by the writers. *The Dancing Masters* was an attempt to rectify this by resurrecting several old L&H bits. Unfortunately, the careful build-up to these routines was eliminated, so they look like they've just been arbitrarily thrown in. Even the most brilliant routine will look silly if it's not placed in the proper context. In this film, *everything* is out of context.

Stan and Ollie run a dancing school, but after the first 10 minutes it's never heard from again. Two confidence men (one of whom is a young Robert

Mitchum) force the boys to buy an insurance policy. As soon as they buy the policy, the con men walk out and are immediately nabbed by police, neatly killing the point of the whole episode. Then there's a pointless remake of the auction scene from 1935's *Thicker Than Water*. Ollie's attempts to cause an accident for Stan echo *The Battle of the Century*, and a final hospital scene recalls *County Hospital*.

None of these scenes seems logical or necessary; they've just been stuck together with new, banal material. (Upon release of the film, *Photoplay*'s reviewer was asked to write what the movie was about. Instead he wrote, "Name something it isn't about.")

Lee Marcus was in charge of the production this time around. A producer of B-pictures since the mid-'30s, his few comedy credits included two of Wheeler and Woolsey's worst features. Marcus assigned the story to George Bricker, who'd been writing B-pictures with little distinction for almost a decade. Bricker's original story, *A Matter of Money*, is much better constructed than the final film; it's not terribly funny, but it at least makes a little sense.

In Bricker's story outline, L&H run a repair shop, which provides a more logical connection with the rest of the story than the dancing school. They can't repair even the simplest article, but their young assistant, Tommy, is a mechanical genius; he is also working on a secret invention.

Tommy has a girlfriend, Sylvia, but her wealthy parents want her to wed Lawrence, a well-heeled heel. Stan and Ollie arrange an elopement for Tommy and Sylvia, and in "a stealthy night comedy sequence" they clumsily get Sylvia out of her house and scurry away in a horse and buggy.

Tommy's secret invention is a rocket gun, for anti-tank warfare. Tommy, Sylvia and the boys go out to the country to test it; the gadget is a success — until Stan accidentally causes it to self-destruct.

All is woe until Ollie hears a radio commercial for Acme Finance Company, which lends money on anything. He plans to borrow $2,000 on Stan's year-old insurance policy by proving Stan is desperately ill, and give the money to Tommy.

The company manager, a mobster, lends the money — on the condition that Stan makes Acme the beneficiary of the $10,000 policy. When the racketeers suspect Stan is too healthy for his own good, they decide to kidnap and kill him; they'll make it look like an accident, so they can collect a double indemnity.

When both Stan and Ollie are kidnapped, Sylvia calls the cops and dashes off to tell Tommy, who is out in the mountains demonstrating his new rocket gun to a government representative. The cops can't locate the "impregnable mountain fortress" where the mobsters have hidden Laurel and Hardy, but a search-and-destroy gizmo on Tommy's gun does just that to the racketeers' hideout. So boy gets girl, government gets new invention, gangsters get a few years in the slammer, and L&H get to gaze with pride at the young lovers.

Bricker's story was given to Scott Darling, who turned this only mildly offensive story into a long-winded mishmash with several arbitrary "comedy" scenes which are either distasteful or downright stupid. Darling worked on the script throughout May 1943, writing and discarding a number of scenes before he ended up with his episodic final draft.

In the first draft, the heroine works in a defense plant, along with her beau and Stan and Ollie. L&H act as drill sergeants for a squadron of midget

Stan with "One-Take Marshall."

defense workers. Darling proposes such delights as the sight of Stan and Ollie building a bomber and "loading the midgets one by one into the interior of a wing, stuffing them in like sardines in a can." As if that isn't funny enough, Laurel and Hardy then *extract* the midgets. "If we can get enough of the little people," suggests Darling, "we can have a switch on the old Fatty Arbuckle taxicab gag, where we have a perfectly incredible number come out one after another."

Throughout the rest of this first-draft script, L&H have little to do but watch the young lovers do all the gags. Their only dialogue is unfunny exposition. After watching *The Dancing Masters*, one wonders how it could have possibly been worse. Scott Darling's early scripts show how.

The only flashes of true L&H humor in the movie are incidental bits the team has managed to squeeze in — for example, a brief "Tell me that again" routine filled with Stan's garbled words of wisdom. Although it lasts perhaps all of 30 seconds, it's the best moment in the film.

Trudy Marshall, a former model from New York, was cast as the lovely heroine, Trudy Harlan. "I just want to tell you how sweet those two men were," she said. "The very first day, the scene was in the dancing school; Stan has broken something, and we go running to see what's keeping Stan. And as we do the rehearsal, I have to run with Ollie. Then we're ready to start shooting, and Ollie says, 'Trudy, dear, come here. Now, look, darling. I'm an awfully big man. When we come around that corner, you make sure you stay beside me — don't get behind me, or they're not gonna see you on that screen!'

"One day, we were talking on the set, and I said, 'What I really want to do is comedies, like Irene Dunne.' They said, 'All right. We've never allowed any girl to do our routines with us. But we'll let you try one.' So, they let me try the routine where we're passing their derbies and dinner plates around. And we did it in one take. Stan looked at me and he said, 'Okay, you're a comedian. We're going to call you One-Take Marshall.' It was a great honor.

"When I met Stan and Ollie, they had been through so much, they were like a right hand and a left hand. They were quiet with one another, they were respectful of one another. Stan was extremely quiet," recalled Marshall. "I found them very serious, and very professional."

While a press release — as usual — implies that producer Lee Marcus gave the team carte blanche to write their own material, a comparison of Scott Darling's final screenplay with the finished film reveals otherwise. The differences between screenplay and film are only minor ones.

The only purpose served by propaganda like this is to put the blame on Laurel and Hardy for the weakness of the movie. If that was the intent of the Fox studio — and its unflagging *duplicity* department — it worked. Given the truth of the situation, it's almost heartbreaking to read reviews like this one from *The Hollywood Reporter*:

> Many Laurel and Hardy comedies, since the team said farewell to short subjects in favor of devoting themselves exclusively to features, have not been funny because the stories were not about Laurel and Hardy. Producer Lee Marcus circumvented such criticism of *The Dancing Masters* by making the stars the unquestioned central characters of the wacky yarn. That Stan and Babe fail to get the roars of laughter for which they bid is therefore their own fault, for most of their routines are unmistakably their own creation, and most of the business fails to pay off. It is sad to report that a pair of the screen's top comics are so far out of step with the times.

Many of the routines in *The Dancing Masters* were in fact the team's own creation. But when the gags were first filmed, years before, they had been given the proper setting — which made all the difference.

THE BIG NOISE

Production history: First draft screenplay completed by W. Scott Darling September 18, 1943; final draft completed December 3. Filmed April 1944. Copyrighted by Fox August 10, 1944 (LP 13060). Released September 1944. 74 minutes.

Produced by Sol M. Wurtzel. Directed by Malcolm St. Clair. Screenplay by W. Scott Darling. Photographed by Joe MacDonald, A.S.C. Art Direction by Lyle Wheeler, John Ewing. Edited by Norman Colbert. Special Photographic Effects, Fred Sersen. Sound by Bernard Fredericks, Harry Leonard. Music by Cyril J. Mockridge; Musical direction by Emil Newman.

With Arthur Space, Doris Merrick, Veda Ann Borg, Esther Howard, Robert Dudley, Bobby Blake.

One of the funnier scenes from *The Big Noise*, with Phil Van Zandt.

Amateur sleuths Stan and Ollie are hired by eccentric inventor Alva Hartley to guard his new super-bomb. At Hartley's home, the boys are confounded by other strange inventions; they also meet his bratty son Egbert and the much-married Aunt Sophie. The inventor gives L&H a phony bomb to take to Washington, to throw a gang of crooks off the trail; after a hectic train journey, the boys discover they have the real bomb. They elude the gangsters by hiding in an old airplane — which turns out to be a radio-controlled target for a gunnery crew's training.

It is so disheartening to watch this terrible film that one can scarcely imagine what agonies Stan and Babe must have endured while filming it. It's even harder to understand how Scott Darling could work on the screenplay for over three months and come up with nothing better.

While it's depressing to read the early versions of the script, a few scenes may serve to illustrate what Laurel and Hardy were faced with in trying to make something palatable out of Darling's palaver.

All of the incarnations of the script are entitled *Good Neighbors*, an ironic comment on the crooks who live next door to Professor Hartley. A discarded opening scene shows how misguided Darling was. Laurel and Hardy are vagrants who decide to rob a bank, which turns out to be a blood bank. Inexplicably, the boys then donate blood, which leads into a gory gag where we see blood going from Ollie's arm into a five-gallon bottle; unable to fill even a two-ounce container, Stan takes the tube from the big bottle and fills his own container with Ollie's blood.

This nauseating attempt at humor is followed by a scene in a park, where the two vagrants have an altercation with bratty Egbert. They chase the boy toward a lake; Egbert gets away, but Stan ends up in the lake head first, with only his feet protruding. A park attendant asks Ollie, "Why don't you rescue your pal?" Replies Hardy, "He's only in ankle-deep!" Darling's comic philosophy seems to be, if you have to violate the traits of the characters to get a quick, cheap laugh, go right ahead.

A number of episodes follow in the script, with the pair eventually being hired as detectives and moving into the Hartley house. The fluttery Aunt Sophie flirts with Ollie, prompting another batch of irritating dialogue. Sophie says, "Mr. Hardy, your face is so familiar to me. Have you ever been in the movies?" Ollie answers, "No, but I am often mistaken for a certain famous comedian."

He didn't get famous with dialogue like that. Not only has Darling obliterated L&H's characters, he makes them spout self-conscious jokes *about* those characters — as if we're just watching impostors, and the real Laurel and Hardy are somewhere else. Which is pretty close to the truth.

This gag survived all the way into the final script, followed by some pointless dialogue about Tyrone Power. This type of gag was far better suited to Hope and Crosby than Laurel and Hardy. Whenever Stan encountered a scene he knew was unworkable, he'd mark the offending passage by writing squiggles in the margins of his script. There are some big squiggles here.

The best scene in the film is a rehash of the *Berth Marks* gag where L&H try to get undressed and go to sleep in a crowded upper berth. Darling originally scripted it with them getting into a *lower* berth, missing a great opportunity for gags with the boys struggling to climb into the upper compartment. Worse, Darling has Stan *leaving* the berth to change his clothes, so there's no opportunity for him to get in Ollie's way.

There are more pointless episodes in Darling's script, but there's no need to go into them. Although I sometimes wonder just how those Chinese jugglers would have fared in the movie.

In an attempt to bolster his anemic screenplay, Darling evidently looked at a batch of vintage L&H two-reelers between the time he completed the first draft in mid-September and the final draft in December. The final script treats us to reprises of The Never-Ending Hat Routine; the gag from *Habeas Corpus* where Ollie clambers up the signpost to discover that it reads "Wet Paint"; the bit from *Wrong Again* where Ollie mimes that other people are "twisted" by flicking his wrist; and a misplaced reworking of *Oliver the Eighth*. All of these old routines are just arbitrarily inserted, much as gags from previous films had been thrown into *The Dancing Masters*.

Stan did not object entirely to the lifting of gags from earlier films — after all, the team had done it before at the Roach lot. What annoyed him was that the gags no longer had the proper context. Moreover, Fox writers and executives ignored his pleas to update and improve the gags. (Stan wanted to rework the *Berth Marks* routine in an airliner, but Fox executives told Laurel the gag would work just as well in its original setting.) Fox simply wanted to get the films made as quickly and cheaply as possible. They didn't want to take the time to experiment; Laurel did.

During production, Stan and Babe were able to inject an occasional bit, but the genuinely funny moments in *The Big Noise* add up to about two minutes' worth of the 74-minute running time. Many of the best moments are provided by Ollie's looks to the camera. (This essential trademark had vanished from the earlier Fox films, but here Ollie once again communicates his innermost thoughts by staring at the camera. Ironically, his disgusted glances at us seem to be more a commentary on the poor quality of the script than anything else.)

Some idea of the production values in this film can be had from the fact that the only location scenes were shot in rural Arcadia and Monrovia, near Pasadena, California; the latter locale doubled for a small airport near Washington, D.C. The whole film has a typical Sol Wurtzel low-budget look to it. Studio press releases tried to justify the film's cheapness by making it look like an act of patriotism — including a fabricated quote from Stan defending the team's "first non-destructive film."

"We cut out automobile chases and food-wasting gags when the war first started," Laurel supposedly said, "and with *The Big Noise* we decided to slash every gag that might conceivably have a bearing on wartime shortages and destruction."

It boggles the mind to read some of the reviews this picture received. *The Hollywood Reporter* noted, "It's a Laurel and Hardy well up to the standard of the better comedies offering the antics of this veteran team. It has been well-produced and excellently directed and should prove completely satisfactory to all L&H fans." *Variety* praised the film's "lively script" and "copious laughs," and called it "one of the better Laurel and Hardy offerings of recent time." One wonders if these two reviewers didn't skip the press screening and go to the race track — or maybe the saloon.

The saddest review — because it was so accurate — was provided by Bosley Crowther in the *New York Times*, who called the film "A groan...Even the most devoted patrons of Laurel and Hardy films will probably balk at the comics' latest cut-up... Once, long ago, it was funny to see them joust with wet paint and folding beds. But now it is dull and pathetic. And they don't even seem to care."

The film has continued to win the disdain of Laurel and Hardy fans — and non-fans — to this day. Few of the team's partisans are inclined to dispute its inclusion in the notorious book, *The Fifty Worst Films of All Time.*

The best critique of the film was given by Stan Laurel. In a 1962 letter to fan Richard Sloan, he wrote: "Note you saw *The Big Noise* film recently — 'NUFF SAID!'"

'Nuff said.

NOTHING BUT TROUBLE

Production history: Original story written circa June 1943. First draft script completed July 31, 1943; final draft completed September 10. Filmed circa October 1944. Previewed November 26. Copyrighted November 28, 1944 by Loew's (LP 13016). Released by MGM March 1945. 70 minutes.

Produced by B.F. Zeidman. Directed by Sam Taylor. Direction assistance by Bert Glazer. Photographed by Charles Salerno, Jr. Edited by Conrad Nervig. Original screenplay by Russell Rouse and Ray Golden. Art direction by Cedric Gibbons and Harry McAfee. Sound by Douglas Shearer and Thomas Edwards. Musical score by Nathaniel Shilkret.

Henry O'Neill (left) and Stan discuss a scene with director Sam Taylor.

With Henry O'Neill, Mary Boland, David Leland, Philip Merivale.

Stan and Ollie are hired as butler and chef by wealthy socialites Basil and Elvira Hawkley. When L&H mistake King Christopher of Orlandia — a boy-king in exile — for an orphan, they adopt him and hide him in the Hawkley home. The pair's ineptitude as servants costs them their jobs. Chris' nasty uncle, Prince Saul, hires the team for a reception — where he plans to slip Chris a poison capsule in his salad. Chris and the boys eventually escape — and Saul is the unwitting recipient of the poison capsule.

Nothing But Trouble has the same ineptitude and overwhelming bland-ness that characterized the team's previous effort at MGM, *Air Raid Wardens*. Like that film, this one has yet another story about foreign spies, and supremely distasteful "gags." The big laugh finish to this picture comes when Prince Saul eats a poisoned canape and dies.

The original story, entitled *The Home Front*, was written by Russell Rouse, who later co-wrote films as excellent as the film-noir thriller *D.O.A.* and as terrible as the trashy soaper *The Oscar*. In June 1943, however, he was a 27-year-old beginner, who had just graduated to the Metro writing department after a spell in Paramount's prop department.

Rouse was soon joined by Ray Golden, a young writer who had worked on scripts for several Ritz Brothers movies, and the Marx Brothers' final MGM

Sharp humor on the set of *Nothing But Trouble*.

effort, *The Big Store*. In 1986, Golden recalled the Laurel and Hardy assignment, admitting, "I wasn't crazy about them like everyone else."

Golden stated that neither he nor Rouse made any attempt to watch earlier L&H films before writing the screenplay. "There was no such thing as research back then," he said. "They were a comedy team, and I was an established comedy writer. That was all there was to it."

It seems never to have occurred to Fox or MGM executives that a comedy writer wasn't enough; they needed someone who was attuned to the unique characteristics of the comedians for whom he was writing.

As a result, the team's material here consisted of textbook stuff, timeworn gags that didn't particularly suit them — like going to a zoo to steal a steak from a hungry lion, or dangling on the ledge of a skyscraper. When Laurel and Hardy *were* given a situation more appropriate for their personalities, the gags made no use of those personalities.

When Stan and Ollie ruined dinner parties through their ineptitude in *From Soup to Nuts* and *A Chump at Oxford*, the gags focused on their lack of familiarity with the social conventions of the well-to-do: Stan munching on the hors d'oeuvres as he serves them. In *Nothing But Trouble*, though, we're treated to gags that show L&H merely as brainless dolts: unable to cut a tough steak, they bring in a huge hacksaw.

The dialogue, too, has little to do with the brand of humor peculiar to the team. When Ollie is trying to persuade Stan to enter the lion's cage and swipe the steak, he offers a fact about lions and adds, "I read it in a book." In the tradition of hundreds of other comics, Stan predictably responds, "Yes, but did the lion read that book?"

One would think that the script might have been better, given the number of writers who worked on it. After Rouse and Golden finished, the screenplay was turned over to a gaggle of gag men, including Robert Halff, Wilkie Mahoney, Harry Crane, and Buster Keaton; additional dialogue was later added by Bradford Ropes and Margaret Gruen. Of Keaton, Ray Golden said, "He wasn't well treated by the studio. He was always good for a bit of business, though."

It's a pity Keaton couldn't inject more of those bits into the screenplay — but at least he contributed something, which is more than Laurel and Hardy were able to do. "They were not involved in the script while I was working on it," said Golden. "They might have worked on it before I was assigned." (This is unlikely, since the team was at Fox filming *The Dancing Masters* while the original story was being written.)

The script lingered around for more than a year before filming began in the fall of 1944. The director was Sam Taylor, a comedy veteran who had directed and co-written some of Harold Lloyd's best films. Taylor then piloted several Mary Pickford films. (The Pickford-Fairbanks version of *The Taming of the Shrew* bore the infamous credit, "By William Shakespeare, with additional dialogue by Sam Taylor.")

Nothing But Trouble proves that even "established comedy writers" and a veteran comedy director could not ensure a good L&H comedy, without L&H themselves allowed to contribute some of their own unique comedy — which, from the looks of the film, they weren't allowed to do.

The reviews reflected the prevailing opinion among critics that Laurel and Hardy were relics from the prehistoric Mack Sennett-pie-throwing era. John T. McManus of *PM* gave them an affectionate review but a backhanded compliment, dubbing them "those last lingering practitioners of the ancient movie art of biff-bang custard-pie comedy." In the same vein, the *New York Times'* Bosley Crowther called them "those two old-time slapstick cut-ups."

When Laurel and Hardy used stock comedy situations in their classic films, they used those situations to show how *different* they were from other comedians. When they threw pies in *The Battle of the Century*, they did it politely and with logic; the epic battle became a *lampoon* of pie-throwing itself. Just because they had worked during the heyday of slapstick, they were now thought of as "biff-bang custard-pie" comics, by the critics and by their writers — which was something they had never been.

Given the fact that the comedians were unable to breathe life into the hackneyed script — before or after the cameras rolled — Howard Barnes was nothing short of perverse in the *New York Herald-Tribune*. Commenting on the comedy cliches which littered the story, he wrote, "These are good, solid ingredients for slapstick. They have been used on the screen any number of times before. In the case of the Rialto offering, they merely serve to demonstrate the comic deficiencies of the stars. Laurel and Hardy do not need a better script in their current show, bad as the script is. They need to polish up on their ability to make people laugh."

Stan and Babe were still masters at making people laugh. They were simply prevented from exercising that talent by studio executives, veteran directors, so-called comedy writers and assorted other technicians who may have known how to make an old-time biff-bang custard-pie slapstick comedy, but who had no idea how to make a Laurel and Hardy film.

THE BULLFIGHTERS

Production history: Story idea conceived June, 1944. Screenplay completed fall 1944. Filmed mid-November-December 16. Copyrighted April 20, 1945 by Fox (LP 13383). Released May 18. 69 minutes.

Produced by William Girard. Directed by Malcolm St. Clair. Direction assistance by Jasper Blystone. Original screenplay by W. Scott Darling. Photographed by Norbert Brodine. Special photographic effects by Fred Sersen. Edited by Stanley Rabjohn. Sound by Arthur von Kirbach and Harry M. Leonard. Musical direction by Emil Newman. Music by David Buttolph. Art direction by Lyle Wheeler and Chester Gore.

With Richard Lane, Ralph Sanford, Margo Woode, Carol Andrews, Diosa Costello, Edward Gargan.

Detectives L&H trail the infamous Larceny Nell to Mexico City, but they lose her after an egg-breaking skirmish. When famed matador Don Sebastian is unable to make an upcoming bullfight, promoter Hotshot Coleman persuades Stan — an exact double — to take Sebastian's place. Coleman's business partner is one Richard K. Muldoon, who threatens to skin the boys alive for wrongly identifying him as a criminal and sending him to prison. When the real Don Sebastian shows up in the bullring, a riot ensues. Stan and Ollie escape the stampeding bulls, but not Muldoon's knife.

While *The Bullfighters* isn't prime Laurel and Hardy, it isn't as bad as the preceding Fox films — at least not until the final reel.

We're finally rid of all those gangsters and enemy spies who cluttered the other post-1940 films. We don't have to endure the cooings of a young romantic couple. The reworkings of old gags fit into the story — they're not just thrown in. Most importantly, L&H are once again the innocent good guys menaced at every turn by people not nearly as good-hearted as they.

The Bullfighters is far from perfect, however. There is still considerable dialogue which is inappropriate for the boys' characters. Someone has done away with their eccentric hairstyles, so that Stan's fright wig and Ollie's spit-curls are slicked back for the first time since *Hats Off*.

The supporting cast is wildly uneven. Richard Lane is an excellent foil as the worldly-wise, fast-talking Hotshot Coleman. But Ralph Sanford, playing the type of part so well acted in earlier days by Walter Long and Rychard Cramer, has all the menace of cottage cheese. (His portrayal of Muldoon should inspire fear, but Sanford's puppy-dog jowls and wispy voice inspire only bewilderment at why anyone would cast him in the part.) Diosa Costello, a brassy Mexican bombshell, rates an off-the-scale reading on the Annoyance Meter. Her vulgar gyrations during a song-and-dance scene have no place in an L&H picture.

The whole film falls apart in the last 10 minutes. The bullfight sequence is a

Richard Lane added a much-needed kick to *The Bullfighters*.

mess: the editors patched together old newsreel footage, clips from *Blood and Sand* and new shots of Stan and Ollie running around in fear, resulting in a feeble and unconvincing finale.

The story idea was born during the filming of *The Big Noise*, when the studio announced that the team's next picture "would be filmed in Mexico, and feature the boys as bullfighters." It wasn't filmed in Mexico — except for some stock shots — but the plot was a way of acknowledging the team's huge popularity in Mexico and South America. A Fox press release noted that "El Flaco y El Gordo" were making the picture "in appreciation for the continued loyalty of these Spanish-speaking fans."

William Girard, the new producer in charge, doesn't seem to have given the team much more attention than Wurtzel did; his major contribution was in signing Diosa Costello for the film after seeing her at the Trocadero nightclub.

A script for *The Bullfighters* has yet to turn up, thereby making it difficult to determine why the picture is slightly better than its predecessors. Either Scott Darling finally learned how to write for the team, or uncredited co-author George O'Hara did an extensive rewrite — or Stan and Babe were given freer reign on the set by St. Clair.

Richard Lane's recollections of working with Stan and Babe indicate that the boys were given room to ad-lib. They also indicate that Stan's heart was not in his work, since he couldn't control the creative aspects of the production.

"By this time Ollie was more the leader of the two, because Stan was having his problems," observed Lane. "But it was quite an experience to work with them. They'd get an idea and talk it over; if it sounded like it fit in, they'd show it to the director, and if he liked it, he'd say, 'Let's shoot it.' Many times, he'd say, 'Let's rehearse it on film.' A lot of that, you couldn't rehearse; the more you rehearsed, the worse it would get.

"Remember the scene where they were breaking eggs?" said Lane, referring to the reprise of the egg-smashing encounter (originally done with Lupe Velez) from *Hollywood Party*. "You couldn't rehearse that. They just started playing with the girl's shoe, and the hats — and the director said, 'Let 'em roll, let 'em roll!'" (While marred by a hyperactive musical score and intrusive sound effects, this is perhaps the best scene in the film.)

"Malcolm St. Clair was wonderful, too," Lane continued. "He was very lenient, yet he wanted the story told. He wanted you to stay within the story idea. When we'd finish a scene and he'd cut it, he'd ask the script girl, 'How close did they come to it?' And she was going out of her mind, because they never did two scenes alike."

The critics were not amused when *The Bullfighters* stepped into their arena. "It may be a matter of timing and pointing, but whatever it is, Stan and Ollie get snickers and chuckles instead of loud guffaws," noted *Variety*.

The Hollywood Reporter was more damning: "The stock shots of the arena and the crowds are infinitely more entertaining than the comedians themselves... their work is too slow, the double-takes being extended beyond all reasonable proportions, and the gags suffering from too lengthy development." This review reflected the changing tastes in comedy: the team's work in this film isn't any slower or more deliberate than in their vintage comedies, but it probably seemed funereal when compared to the rapidly-paced antics of comics like Abbott and Costello.

The Bullfighters wrote *finito* to the team's association with Fox. "They didn't want to give us stories or casts, so we quit," they explained some years later. More accurately, the team's five-year contract had simply expired. Fortunately for us all, the boys only made six Fox films instead of the 10 called for under the pact.

Fox wanted to sign Stan and Babe to another contract, according to Lucille Hardy Price, but the comedians had had enough of "those Fox people" and called it quits, even though there were no film offers forthcoming.

Laurel and Hardy's career is an example of the film industry economics destroying first-rate talent. The creative freedom that made their short subjects such a great success began to diminish when Hal Roach was forced to put them into features. The resulting films were more expensive to produce, which caused Roach to exert more control over them.

This led to ever more frequent clashes between Laurel and the producer, which led Stan and Babe to move to larger studios — which unexpectedly barred Stan from working in any creative capacity, all in the name of economy. After appearing in efficiently-assembled garbage for five years, Laurel and Hardy found their reputations as reliable laughmakers tarnished by events which were out of their hands.

Unable to employ their unique filmmaking methods at the big studios, Laurel and Hardy were forced to retire from the screen. For the remaining decade of their career, the team performed solely on the stages of European theaters — with one unfortunate exception.

Exile

Very little was certain about the future of Laurel and Hardy's career in the spring of 1945, except that they couldn't take any more of the uncaring treatment they'd gotten from 20th Century-Fox and Metro-Goldwyn-Mayer.

The only headlines Laurel and Hardy made for most of 1946 were caused by their private lives. Myrtle Hardy launched yet another unsuccessful suit for more alimony, which was excuse enough for the Hearst papers to run a gaudy feature article entitled "Funny Mr. Hardy's Unfunny Alimony Troubles."

Stan's remarriage to Ruth had soured rapidly, with the couple separating May 31, 1941, little more than five months after their wedding. Ruth sued for separate maintenance in 1943 and again in 1945, finally obtaining a divorce on April 30, 1946. A week later in Yuma, Arizona, Stan married Ida Kitaeva Raphael, an opera singer born in China of White Russian parents. Stan had married a vivacious Russian singer in Yuma once before — but all resemblances to his disastrous union with Illiana ended there. Stan's marriage to Ida lasted until his death, providing a legitimate happy ending to his tumultuous private life.

Throughout 1946, Stan worked with writer Sam Locke on a film script which was never completed. In July, a major revival of L&H films played London theaters; this reawakened interest in the team, and late that year British theatrical impresario Bernard Delfont arranged for Stan and Babe to make a brief tour of England. The comedians were booked for two weeks at the Palladium in London, followed by a four-week tour of provincial theaters.

A Laurel and Hardy version of *Robin Hood* — to be filmed in England — was discussed, but never came to fruition. But the boys' live appearances were more successful than anyone could have anticipated when they arrived in Southampton on February 11, 1947.

The boys' ever-reliable *Drivers' License* sketch was so well received by the Palladium audiences that after the initial tour was over, they were booked into another major London theater, the Coliseum. The overwhelming affection shown by their fans was even more intense than it had been during the 1932 "vacation." Stan and Babe again found themselves mobbed wherever they went. It was not an easy life being folk heroes.

In September 1947, Delfont booked the team into the Tivoli Gardens, Copenhagen. This was followed by dates at Aarhus and Odense. From there, the comedians went to Sweden for shows at Stockholm, Gotenborg, and Malmo; then it was back to Copenhagen for a radio performance, and then to Paris for six weeks at the Lido nightclub. This stint was interrupted by a trip to London, where on November 3, 1947 Laurel and Hardy appeared in the Royal Command Performance at the Palladium. From Paris, the tour stopped in Belgium, for engagements in Brussels and other cities. The six-week tour stretched out to 11 months; Stan and Babe and their wives returned to the States in January 1948.

Laurel and Hardy were well received by foreign audiences, despite the fact that they only spoke English. But while they were hailed as great artists in Europe, their status hadn't changed much in America. Indeed, the boys seemed forgotten by Hollywood.

In 1949 Stan discovered he was suffering from diabetes, and concentrated his energies toward recovery that year. Babe appeared in a brief stage tour of

Left: Stan found lasting happiness with wife Ida. Right: Touring England in 1947, with Ida (left), Lucille Hardy (seated, right) and two trapeze artists.

At the Lido nightclub, Paris, with dancer Daisy Daix, in November 1947.

Babe rehearses at the Masquers Club with Maureen O'Hara, George O'Brien and Michael Ross.

What Price Glory?, sponsored by the Masquers Club and directed by John Ford. In the company of John Wayne and Maureen O'Hara, Babe performed in Oakland, San Francisco, San Jose, Long Beach and Pasadena.

Not long after completing the tour in March, Wayne asked Hardy to play his sidekick in Republic's upcoming film, *The Fighting Kentuckian*. Babe needed quite a bit of convincing — he was afraid a solo role would start rumors that he and Stan had quarreled. Once Stan assured him that he was delighted about the offer, Babe tore into the work with great zeal.

The Fighting Kentuckian shows what a fine actor Babe was; if he hadn't teamed with Stan, he could have easily carved a niche for himself as a genial character actor in the Edgar Buchanan mold. Hardy is subdued yet effective in the role of Willie Payne, and there are few similarities to the "Ollie" character; he appears to have made a deliberate — and successful — attempt to break away from his established screen personality.

Soon after he finished the John Wayne film, Babe was asked by his friends Bing Crosby and Frank Capra to appear in *Riding High*, a remake of Capra's 1933 racetrack yarn, *Broadway Bill*. Babe's brief scene was closer to the type of comedy with which he was usually associated. The gullible horse-player Babe portrayed was somewhat meeker than "Ollie," but otherwise a virtual twin — he even wore the derby hat.

Having been convinced to bet his last dollar on a nag named Doughboy — by sharpies William Demarest and Raymond Walburn — Hardy excitedly

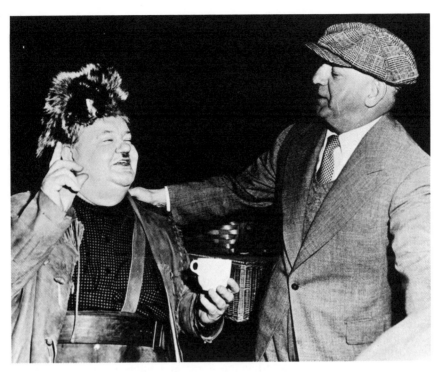

With Republic studio chief Herbert Yates on the *Fighting Kentuckian* set.

spreads the news about this can't-miss bet. Word heatedly circulates around the track until Walburn is taken in by his own story. The horse naturally loses the race, and we see Babe being hoisted and carried on the crowd's shoulders as he dazedly yells, "Doughboy! Doughboy!"

As 1950 approached, Stan felt well enough to work again; by that March he and Babe received an offer to star in a comedy to be filmed in France. The conditions seemed promising — and although Laurel and Hardy loved performing for live audiences, their hearts still belonged to movies. Plans were soon underway for the first L&H film to be produced in five years, and their first to be made overseas.

ATOLL K

Production history: Written March-June 1950. Filmed August 1950-March 1951. Released in France by Les Films Sirius on November 21, 1951. 98 minutes. Released in the United Kingdom (at 82 minutes) as *Robinson Crusoeland* by Franco-London Films in 1952; reissued in the UK by New Realm. Released in the United States as *Utopia* by Exploitation Productions, Incorporated, December 1954.

Produced by Raymond Eger for Franco London Films S.A., Films E.G.E., Films Sirius, and Fortezza Film. Directed by Leo Joannon. Screenplay by John Klorer, Frederick Kohner, Rene Wheeler and Pierro Tellini, based on an idea by Leo

Joannon. Director of Photography, Armand Thirard. Cameraman, Louis Nee. Art direction by Roland Quignon. Sound by Pierre Calvet. Editing by Raymond Isnardon. Original Music by Paul Misraki.

With Suzy Delair, Max Elloy, Adriano Rimoldi, Luigi Tosi.

L&H inherit a yacht and an island — tax-free. They sail for their new home, joined by a stateless deportee and a bricklayer. During a storm, the yacht is beached on an atoll. The beachcombers are joined by Cherie Lamour, a singer trying to forget a romance. Her ex-boyfriend discovers that the uncharted atoll is loaded with uranium. Ollie becomes president of the new country, Crusoe-land, but fortune-hunters soon overrun it and the atoll sinks. The boys finally arrive at their South Sea island — where their supplies are confiscated for failure to pay inheritance taxes.

Early in 1950, an American financier named George Bookbinder realized that Stan and Ollie were still idolized in Europe. Between 1947 and 1949 the 11 L&H films made since *Block-Heads* got their first release overseas, having been withheld during the war. Despite the poor quality of the post-1940 films, they were well received by a war-weary public.

The French, Italian and British governments were eager to get their film industries going again, and a picture starring Laurel and Hardy would be a sure-fire hit. Bookbinder contracted a producer named Deutchmeister who was affiliated with Universalia Produzione in Rome; meanwhile, two French production companies, Franco-London Films and Films E.G.E., joined forces and made distribution agreements with Les Films Sirius of of France, Fortezza Films of Italy and International of Great Britain.

Stan and Babe were intrigued by the unusual offer. Despite the uncertainty of working for a French and Italian coalition, the proposal was inviting — the money was good, and the film was to be shot in 12 weeks. And there would surely be none of the big-studio interference that had plagued the team in their last pictures.

Bookbinder, shopping for writers, contacted agent Paul Kohner, who specialized in handling projects with European interests. Kohner suggested his brother Frederick, who had written several screenplays with his partner Albert Mannheimer.

"Paul called and said, 'I have a job for you in Paris,'" remembered Frederick Kohner. "I said, 'Well, that's fantastic!' He said, 'Well, now, wait a moment — it's for Laurel and Hardy.' I said, 'Oh, God. How do I fit into that?'

"Paul said, 'It's a very sophisticated story. Something that I think you will enjoy.' And then he told me over the phone the story of *Atoll K*, which in its original form sounded very enticing — but like many other projects, they didn't tell you all of the other ramifications. Many ideas on two pages look wonderful, but when you start to analyze them, you see that there is not really much to go by."

The story idea was contributed by Leo Joannon, a French writer-director who had written short stories and a novel before embarking on a film career in 1930. Most of his films were routine melodramas; he had little experience with comedy.

The picture was to be entitled *Entente Cordiale* (although this was soon

With Max Elloy, Suzy Delair and Leo Joannon near the start of production.

changed to *Atoll*); the cast was to include French comedian Fernandel, Italian clown Toto, and French actress Simone Simon. Selected to direct was Tim Whelan, who had worked on the scripts of several silent Harold Lloyd features, and directed a variety of films in England and the United States.

Before Kohner and Mannheimer could sail for France to begin work on the script, Mannheimer accepted the plum assignment of adapting *Born Yesterday* for the screen. Babe suggested that his friend and golf partner, screenwriter John Klorer, could substitute for Mannheimer. "I had the feeling this was not the right match for me," said Kohner, "but I didn't want to lose the job."

Kohner had been told at the outset that he would have free reign in writing the script. Upon arrival in Paris he discovered — to his surprise — a French writer, Rene Wheeler, and an Italian, Pierro Tellini, who were to collaborate with the Americans.

The writers soon found that collaboration was impossible. "Klorer spoke English. Wheeler spoke only French. Tellini spoke a few words of French, and Italian. I didn't speak Italian," said Kohner, "but I spoke French. So we decided that each would write his own version, then we would see. I was dubious about the success of this, because I saw right away that the Italian wanted to make a social document, a statement. The Frenchman just wanted to write a pure farce. And we wanted something in between."

Kohner recalled that the working conditions were *too* ideal — producer Raymond Eger wanted to put him and Klorer in a quiet resort out in the country. "Klorer said to me, 'Tell the son of a bitch I'm not going to the country. I'm going to stay right here in Paris... I don't need inspiration.' I felt the same way as Klorer — but the producers were absolutely adamant. We *had* to go.

"So, we repaired to a place called Montfort la Marie, near Paris, and we lived in a beautiful old hotel, famous throughout France for the kitchen. But, of course, nothing was accomplished."

After four weeks, Kohner and Klorer returned to Paris. In the meantime, Wheeler and Tellini had started work on their scripts. Of his collaborators, Kohner said, "Pierro Tellini was a charming Italian. Rene Wheeler was a very smooth Frenchman. He needed a job, and he sold himself — but none of us, including me, had *any* concept of what they wanted!"

As the writers tried to create "something different" for Laurel and Hardy — with no idea what the difference would be — Stan and his wife Ida arrived in Paris the first week of April. Laurel was eager to work on the script, but learned from producer Eger that the story was not yet ready. All he could do was wait.

Since the writers failed to accomplish anything at one hotel, Eger sent them to another one in Deauville. Said Kohner, "The four of us had a whole floor in one of the most beautiful hotels in the world, and we were supposed to all work together there. But the others repaired at 5 o'clock to the casino, and stayed there until 1 o'clock in the morning, losing every penny they had."

The pennies were considerable, too. "This was not a shoestring production," Kohner pointed out. "This was a [French] government-subsidized project. I think they spent $2 million, which was a fantastic amount of money for that time. I got 35,000 francs every week, an enormous amount — and of course, everything was very cheap in France after the war."

Whether or not the producers got their money's worth is open to question. "I tried to build a story that made sense," said Kohner. "But it got worse every week; it was terrible. Very soon in the game, frankly, I gave up. I decided there was absolutely nothing I could do but enjoy myself while I was in Paris."

Kohner and his three confreres worked on the script for three months. An early draft of the script — which bears no writer credit — reveals the confusion which marked the writing sessions.

This unfilmed script is a bizarre story. Stan is swept away from his home in Florida by a typhoon which lands him on a Pacific atoll. There he finds several boxes filled with guns, grenades and gas masks — except for one crate, which contains a grand piano. The piano, in turn, contains Mr. Hardy, who emerges and greets Mr. Laurel. They sit down and play the theme from *Fra Diavolo*.

The hungry beach bums decide to cook a whale that has washed up on shore. Ollie gets in the piano crate and, using a board as an oar, sails off in search of matches. He is almost immediately shanghaied by a boatload of castaways and is not heard from again for most of the script.

British, French and American ships meanwhile discover the uncharted atoll, and determine that it is loaded with uranium. Each ship rushes to the islet to stake its country's claim, but the officers find Stan already occupying the territory. Stan explains that he's not a citizen of any country (although he had a home in Florida).

The commanders of each ship tell Stan that he's considered the owner of the atoll until the United Nations has made a decision. The UN eventually decides that the atoll can't remain in the possession of an individual, so Stan must decide which of the 65 UN member nations to adopt — the atoll will belong to the country of his choice.

Stan finally decides he'll award the atoll to the country that finds his old pal, Ollie. Hardy is still with the stateless passengers aboard the good ship Salvator — which docks at the atoll. But since Ollie has been discovered by a group of similarly stateless people, Stan still has to choose a country as the atoll's proprietor.

The UN decides that if Stan and Ollie leave the island, it will no longer be theirs. The British, French and American powers try to starve the boys, but the Russian delegation gives them all kinds of foodstuffs. Then the three Western powers unleash a swarm of mosquitoes, but L&H have conveniently concealed powerful insecticide guns about their persons. The governments then send some voluptuous lovelies to seduce Stan and Ollie into leaving, but the girls end up fighting amongst themselves.

Laurel and Hardy then alibi that there just happened to be a third person who landed with them at the same time, and possession of the atoll can't be determined until *he* shows up.

The atoll starts to sink. L&H sail away in the piano crate — which has somehow returned after Ollie's disastrous voyage in it. Fortuitously, they run aground on a *new* atoll. The boys wait for some country to seek their favor. Fifty years later, bearded and wearing tattered clothes, Laurel and Hardy are still waiting. But ship after ship passes them by, and the script explains why: "For quite a long time it has been definitely established that the island contains no mineral deposits of any kind."

When it appeared that the writers were as close to having a script as they ever would be, Babe and Lucille set sail for Paris on June 10, 1950, on the R.M.S. Caronia. They were greeted by Stan and a host of L&H fans wearing masks of Laurel's likeness at the Gare Saint-Lazare.

In a move characteristic of this confused production, the comedians were

Republic Pictures president Herbert Yates (second from left) and John Wayne visit the set during a Paris vacation.

immediately whisked away on a tour of Italy, to publicize a film they hadn't yet made. In Genova they saw a revival of *The Devil's Brother* dubbed in Italian; in Rome Stan was hoisted on the shoulders of a cheering throng at the new Stazione Termini depot.

"Laurel and Hardy were idolized in Europe — but not here in the States. Here, as is typical of Hollywood, no one bothered with them," said Frederick Kohner. "They were heroes, like Lindbergh. They walked down the Champs-Elysees, and people were just yelling; a woman came up, leaned down and kissed their hands."

One afternoon, Kohner and Klorer visited the comedians in their suite at the George V, Klorer nervously clutching a copy of the script, and Kohner feeling a sense of impending doom. "Well, I *knew* that they wouldn't like it," he said. "It was terrible! I mean, sometimes you write something and you know it's awful. What can you do?"

The meeting was brief and amicable enough. Stan asked how the authors liked their own script; Klorer explained that it needed a little more work. Stan jovially responded that *every* script needed a little more work, and promised to read it right away. The writers went back to their hotel for a sleepless night.

The next morning, Kohner and Klorer were summoned to the George V. Stan had had a sleepless night, too. His eyes were bloodshot after reading their script, and translations of the other two scripts. Kohner remembered Stan's voice cracking as he said, "Is this what you did all these months, boys? Did you really expect us to accept this rubbish?"

Klorer tried to convince Stan and Babe that this was something sophisticated and daring. The comedians tried to convince Klorer that they wanted something comprehensible and funny. "Klorer tried to talk them into it, but they had made up their mind that this script was not what they wanted," Kohner related. "Klorer stayed a few days longer in Paris, but I left. I'd had enough. We were on good terms — I simply felt that I'd done the best I could, and that was it."

By July 16, Stan and Babe were on the Cote d'Azur, on the southeast coast of France — with Stan still trying to make some sense of the script. He summoned Monty Collins, a veteran comic and gagman, to inject some gags into the screenplay. Tim Whelan showed up at some of the writing sessions, but had to return to England to straighten out some legal difficulties, and thus couldn't direct.

Fernandel and Toto, perhaps sensing that the production was poorly organized, declined the producers' offers. Fernandel was replaced by French comedian Max Elloy; the role slated for Toto was filled by actor Adriano Rimaldi after the film went into production. Suzy Delair, a sprightly French actress, was signed a few days before filming began.

Leo Joannon may have become the film's director by default when Whelan abruptly left, but he felt he was firmly in command once the filming began on August 8. This opinion was not shared by Stan and Babe. The crew spent six days filming at the port of Marseille, and then moved to a location on the island of Cap-Roux, between Cannes and St. Raphael. Joannon strutted around in a regulation Movie Director's uniform — he wore a pith helmet and puttees, and had a number of different megaphones, selecting them for various kinds of shots.

To say Joannon worked in an unhurried manner would be a supreme understatement. He spent three days getting shots of a lake because he thought it so photogenic. On the first day of shooting, the crew had spent three hours setting up the first shot, when Joannon said, "All right, let's rehearse it." Stan and Babe countered, "We know what we're supposed to do — let's take it." Joannon was doubtful, but humored the comedians by letting them have their way; he was amazed when they did everything perfectly on the first take.

The team's ability to ad-lib was severely hampered by the multilingual cast. One actor would speak his line in French, another would speak Italian, and Stan and Babe would have to answer in English, pretending they'd understood every word.

Atoll K was the exact opposite of the team's experience with 20th Century-Fox. At Fox, the studio had been firmly in control of every aspect. On *Atoll K*, however, no one was in control. Joannon's indecision and ineptitude was compounded by the lack of communication between cast and crew. Joannon did not understand much English; his American assistant spoke nothing but. The two cameramen spoke only French. A script girl was the only person in the entire crew who understood all three languages.

Whenever anyone disagreed over how a scene should be played, produc-

The less-than-happy crew of *Atoll K*. Note director Leo Joannon, kneeling in foreground, in pith helmet and puttees.

tion would stop and everyone would argue, each person yelling at someone else who didn't understand him. When everyone thought the dispute had been resolved, they'd start filming again — only to discover the agreement had been lost in translation.

On top of all of this, there was a debilitating heat wave. Everyone began the day's work feeling exhausted, and went downhill from there. Babe's health began to suffer. The heat and exhaustion caused an irregularity in his heartbeat, and he worried that he might not be able to finish the film.

The production was in chaos when Stan called his old friend Alfred Goulding in London and asked him to come over and help restore order. "Alf couldn't actually direct the film, because of the rule that a French production had to have a French director; the unions were very strong there," recalled Betty Goulding. "But Stan wanted Alf there to supervise, to make sure filming would go all right. Alf felt very frustrated, though. The French and Italian crew resented Alf being there. And Stan insisted, so that immediately started a conflict. The French director felt he was being undermined, but Stan and Alf didn't have a full command either," said Goulding's widow.

"Alf said to me, '*None* of them know what they're doing. That man Joannon doesn't know anything about comedy. And I can't do anything — they won't give me a free reign.'"

Havoc persisted off the set as well as on. "One day, Alf went and bought a suit, and Stan wanted to get one like it," Betty Goulding related. "But Stan said, 'I can't go out, Alf — the people always mob Babe and me.' Alf said, 'Why don't you put on a cap?' So Stan put a cap down over his eyes — like Popeye — and put a pipe in his mouth. Alf said, 'You look great.'

"They started walking down the street, and they were doing fine, until a little French kid came up and looked at Stan and said, 'Oh! Monsieur Laurel!' Well, the people just came from everywhere and mobbed poor Stan. There was a hat shop nearby, and Stan and Alf ran in. The owner said, 'Oh, please, monsieur, don't!,' and tried to push them out — but they got inside and locked themselves in. A woman in the crowd outside got her leg broken, another broke an arm. Stan and Alf had to get a police escort back to the hotel. That was the last time they went for a walk!"

Meanwhile, what little production organization there was began rapidly unraveling. On top of the language barrier and the disagreements, Stan found that a request for the smallest prop could cause massive delays. One day he got an idea for a gag with a pencil sharpener. Due to red tape, the company couldn't get the prop in nearby Cannes; they had to send the request to Paris, across the country.

Laurel had other ideas that went unused because the film was shot out of sequence. He bitterly recalled the experience years later. "They had the storm, the shipwreck, and then we're on the island," said Stan. "Well, they shot the island footage before they did the shipwreck. So it was awfully difficult, to try and figure out how you're going to look after a shipwreck. It stopped us from doing gags that I would have done. We were stymied — just handcuffed."

As if enough problems hadn't plagued the production, illness now threatened to put an end to it. Babe's heart fibrillation was still causing him concern. Stan, who had been a bit slimmer than usual even before filming began, started losing weight and developed prostate trouble. He was in terrific pain, but doctors were unable to help him.

Stan looks far better in this still than he does in the movie.

Stan was taken to the American Hospital in Paris, where a specialist determined the problem. Ida stayed at his bedside, translating his requests into French and changing his bandages. Stan remained at the hospital through mid-November, gradually improving but still not fully recovering.

Laurel felt obligated to finish the picture, and returned to the location at Cap-Roux. Goulding had to fulfill a directing commitment in London and was unable to remain. The production dragged on for months, with the company getting three or four set-ups shot each day and arguing in between.

Stan's health continued to cloud the production. He got dysentery from the food served on location, and his weight gradually dropped from 165 pounds to 114. A makeshift hospital was erected on the set. Stan would try to work for half an hour or so before his strength began to wane. Deep lines etched his face; he bore little resemblance to his "Stanley" character of the 1930s.

Finally, in the spring of 1951, the film completed production. Stan and Ida left for home on April 1; Babe and Lucille sailed for the States on the M.S. Washington on April 23. Back in California, Stan concentrated on recovering his health, and tried to forget the whole miserable experience.

Atoll K was released in France and Italy in November 1951, and in England (as *Robinson Crusoeland*) the following year. It went unreleased in the United States, however, until December 1954 — when a small Philadelphia-based distributor, Exploitation Productions, lived up to its name by trying to make a quick buck on the film.

The U.S. version, retitled *Utopia*, was cut from 98 to 82 minutes (as was the British issue); the editing actually improved the film, because most of the deleted footage was dreary stuff involving the romantic leads.

The film's American premiere was somewhat less than prestigious. It opened as the supporting feature for a documentary called *This is Your Army*, at the Globe Theater in New York. The *Times* reviewer called it "hectic silliness," and commented, "Mr. Laurel appears woefully haggard. No wonder. The boys never should have left home."

After a brief and limited release, the film virtually disappeared — much to the relief of Stan and Babe. Appropriately for this confused production, nobody remembered to copyright the film in the United States. As a result of its public domain status, *Utopia* is — ironically — now the most easily available Laurel and Hardy film. It has been released on Super 8 and 16mm film, on video discs, and is frequently sold in supermarkets on bargain-priced video cassettes (Hal Roach Studios has gone so far as to colorize the film). It continues to perplex unwary viewers who expect a typical L&H comedy.

You can get a few laughs out of *Atoll K*, but you have to make some allowances. First, try not to notice that Stan looks like death warmed over, and not warmed over very much. Next, overlook the fact that the other cast members' lips are flapping away in total asynchronization with the dialogue on the English-language soundtrack. Finally, concentrate solely on the occasional good L&H gags and ignore altogether the dreary "plot" footage. You can get a few laughs out of *Atoll K*, all right, if you just use your imagination.

Granted, there are those who can't sit through it. When Frederick Kohner was contacted in 1981, he mentioned that he had never seen the picture. A screening was arranged, but Kohner changed his mind. "I really don't want to see the film," he conceded. "It would be like self-flagellation."

Epilogue

The Fiddle and the Bow

Following *Atoll K*, Laurel and Hardy's future was clouded. Stan's health was still fragile in July 1951 — "There's a bug, but they don't know its name," he told a reporter — and he wasn't yet ready to resume work. Ironically, there had been an offer from Hollywood. Stan and Babe were considered for supporting roles in a Technicolor musical comedy called *Two Tickets to Broadway*, to be produced by Howard Hughes at RKO. Their roles were re-written first for Bert Lahr and Eddie Foy Jr., and then for Smith and Dale, who did appear in the finished film.

While there were no other offers from the big studios, Billy Wilder wanted to make a movie based on their lives. A Japanese studio then made the team a tentative offer, as did an Italian stage company. The most promising prospect came in May 1952, when the Scalera Film Company interested Stan and Babe in doing a musical comedy version of *Carmen*, to be produced in Rome. But this project, like so many others, fell through.

Early in 1952, Stan was sufficiently fit to work, and late in February he and Babe embarked on their second working tour of the United Kingdom, appearing in a new sketch entitled *A Spot of Trouble* (based on their 1930 two-reeler, *Night Owls*). The tour lasted through September, and again the boys played to packed houses and were mobbed by fans.

In October 1953, the team returned for a third British tour, in a sketch called *Birds of a Feather*. In mid-May 1954, Babe suffered a mild heart attack and also contracted pneumonia; the balance of the tour was cancelled, and the team returned to the States.

Laurel and Hardy's last appearance came about unexpectedly on December 1, 1954, when their career was celebrated on NBC TV's *This is Your Life*. "It was a staggering experience," Stan told a reporter some months later. "We've been planning to do something on TV. But we certainly never intended to start out on an unrehearsed network show!"

It was unrehearsed indeed: host Ralph Edwards had to ad-lib uncomfortably on live TV for several minutes before Stan and Babe arrived. Stan's criticism of the show in later years has prompted speculation that he had to be persuaded to go on. Lucille Hardy Price said the comedians were late because it simply took Babe longer than anticipated to walk from the Knickerbocker Hotel (where they were surprised by an NBC camera) to the El Capitan theater.

There were continual plans for a new L&H television series. In fact, al-

427

Arriving in Southampton, England, January 28, 1952.

though they weren't making new comedies, Stan and Babe were among the most popular personalities on TV in the early '50s. Roach had bought the rights to all of his MGM and United Artists releases in 1944; in the spring of 1951 they were leased to television distributor Regal Films.

The team received no residuals, since their Roach contracts had granted the studio all rights in perpetuity. But as Babe told a reporter, "It does our hearts good anyway. A year ago nobody knew us. When I went up to the corner grocery some kid would say, 'Get out of the way, fat.' Now they stop and say, 'You're Oliver Hardy, aren't you? Can I have your autograph?'"

Early in 1955, Stan and Babe agreed to make a new series of one-hour color "specials" (*Laurel and Hardy's Fabulous Fables*) for Hal Roach Jr. Stan had finished a story outline for the first special (*Babes in the Woods*) when he suffered a stroke on April 25 — 10 days before shooting was to begin. The project was shelved.

In the summer of 1956, the team was still optimistic about making new comedies for television. Late in July, Stan told reporter Bob Thomas, "I might be able to start a series now, but I want to wait... I wouldn't want to get started and then let people down."

Babe had been concerned about his own health in 1956, so much so that he went on a diet at the advice of his doctors and lost 150 pounds. He had been over 350 at the end of the last British tour; he now weighed 210, less than he had ever weighed in his adult life. Stan wanted to have some new publicity photos taken one day, and Babe complied. Babe doesn't look bad in these pictures — he simply doesn't look like Oliver Hardy. Stan's partner was now a man of medium build with sparse, silvery hair, and sagging skin where the double chin had been.

December 2, 1954: With Hal Roach junior and senior at the newly renamed
Lake Laurel and Hardy.

Early on the morning of September 14, 1956, Babe suffered a massive
stroke. His body was almost completely paralyzed; he was unable to speak, and
could barely eat. After a month at St. Joseph's Hospital in Burbank, Hardy was
brought back to his home on Woodland Avenue in Van Nuys.

Early in 1957, Lucille moved Babe into her mother's North Hollywood
home. There was no improvement in his condition; he wasted away to under
150 pounds. Hundreds of letters offering encouragement and get-well wishes
poured in, and these afforded Babe some comfort. But early in August he
suffered two more strokes which sent him into a coma. At 7:25 a.m. on August 7,
his heart stopped beating.

Tributes were printed around the world. The *New York Times* ran a touching editorial which noted, "There was a genuine craftsmen's lack of pretension
about Laurel and Hardy movies. They weren't masterpieces; you rarely recall
their names, and never the situations... You recall only skinny Laurel playing
against fat Hardy as a bow plays against a fiddle, and you think of the gay,
ingenious music."

The *London Times* offered an epitaph that would have probably pleased
Babe: "He was tall as well as fat, and he had a handicap of ten."

Stan spent most of his last eight years in a comfortable apartment on
Ocean Avenue in Santa Monica. He spent his days looking out at the ocean
and watching television. He hardly ever watched his own films. The fan mail
arrived in such abundance that he was always months behind, but he insisted
on answering all of it.

He wrote thousands of letters in his last years, answering questions about
the films and sending new gags to special friends. ("Here's one, hot off the
press," he wrote Alf Goulding. "A guy purchasing a brassiere for his wife. Girl:

Seven and a half inches? How did you measure that? Guy: In my derby hat. They were a tight fit!")

A steady procession of fans paraded into Stan's apartment. There had never been any sense of caste in Stan Laurel, so just plain folks were as welcome as celebrities. Dick Van Dyke, Peter Sellers, Jerry Lewis, Danny Kaye, Dick Cavett and Dick Martin were among those who came to pay tribute. Marcel Marceau came to visit several times. He owed Stan a debt of gratitude because Laurel had done a great deal to promote Marceau, after seeing the then-little known mime in Paris in 1950.

Jerry Lewis once offered Stan $100,000 a year to be a comedy consultant on his films, but Stan declined. He didn't need the money, either; he had invested in annuities during the '30s, and although his wealth had been greatly reduced by alimony and taxes, he was comfortable.

One of the few things that really rankled Stan was the widely believed rumor that he was living in poverty. An English writer started the falsehood when he published an article in November 1959 describing Laurel as "a forgotten man" with "few pleasures left for him in life."

While diabetes and a periodic hemorrhage in his left eye restricted some of his activities, Stan recovered almost completely from the mild stroke, and his health actually continued to improve until his last year. He found humor even in his ailments. "There was *nothing* that would make you feel sorry for Stan," asserted Lisa Mitchell, one of his frequent visitors. "You felt that he was like anyone else, had good and bad things happen to him, and now he was dealing one day at a time with not-so-terrific health."

After years of neglect from the film industry, Stan was finally recognized for his contributions toward the end. Late in 1961, with some urging from Dick Van Dyke, Jerry Lewis, Sheldon Leonard and others, the Academy of Motion Picture Arts and Sciences voted Stan an honorary Oscar. Accolades poured in; Stan was grateful for the attention, but often wished it would have come while Babe was still alive to share in the glory.

The greatest joy of Stan's later life was without a doubt his marriage to Ida. She was fiercely protective of him at times; she recognized that he still had a need to perform, though, and often withdrew quietly into another room while Stan entertained visitors.

He succumbed to a heart attack at 1:45 p.m. on February 23, 1965. The Hollywood community — which had so rejected him during the 1940s — eulogized him as a great artist.

A photographer named Gene Lester, who had visited Stan a few times, decided that the team's work should be commemorated with a TV special and enlisted the support of several celebrities. But CBS, concerned that Lester had little previous experience in television, took over the production. The well-intentioned *Salute to Stan Laurel* became a typical variety show, notable only for its lack of wit and occasional moments of bad taste. Once again, a committee of executives took the idea of a clever but unorthodox person, and packaged it into oblivion.

It was eerily similar to the way Stan and Babe had been treated by Fox and MGM during the 1940s. In their movies, L&H were the pure, simple souls exploited by an uncaring world; it's a pity that this was often the case in their careers as well. We're fortunate that, for a brief time, Laurel and Hardy were able to play their "gay, ingenious music" without someone else trying to conduct.

The last portrait session, 1956.

Stan at his Santa Monica, California, apartment, 1960.

During a two-week engagement in Brussels, December 1947.

Who's Who

By Randy Skretvedt and Jordan R. Young

The Supporting Players

AUBREY, JIMMY Born 1887, Bolton, England. Played the Terrible Turk opposite Chaplin on stage in Fred Karno's *A Night in the English Music Hall*. Starred in a series of Vitagraph comedies, supported by Babe. Played bits in three L&H films (notably a drunk in *That's My Wife*). Died 1984, Woodland Hills, Calif.

BERNARD, HARRY Born 1878, San Francisco. Started his career with Sennett in 1915. Appeared in 26 L&H films; first seen as truck driver in *Two Tars*, lastly as the harbor patrol captain in *Saps at Sea*. Also appeared in *The Milky Way*, *New Faces of 1937*, and several Charley Chase and Thelma Todd two-reelers. Died 1940, Hollywood, age 62; of cancer.

BLETCHER, BILLY Born Sept. 20, 1894, Lancaster, Pa. Worked with Babe at Vim Comedies and later played bits in several L&H comedies, notably the Chief of Police in *Babes in Toyland*. His best known roles were perhaps the voice of the Big Bad Wolf in *The Three Little Pigs*, and that of *The Lone Ranger* on radio. Died 1979, age 85.

BURNS, BOBBY (Robert Paul Burns) Born 1878, Philadelphia. Actor-writer Burns got his start in repertory companies, then went into vaudeville. In 1916 he co-starred with Walter Stull in Vim's *Pokes and Jabbs* comedies (in which he first worked with Babe Hardy) and appeared in Babe's *Plump and Runt* series. Essayed bit parts in 7 L&H comedies, notably as the blind man in *Below Zero*. Also appeared in a number of Three Stooges two-reelers, including *Pop Goes the Easel*. Died 1966.

BUSCH, MAE Born Jan. 20, 1897(?), Melbourne, Australia. Appeared in legitimate theatre and vaudeville before seeking a film career. Made her debut in *The Agitator* (1912), and subsequently became a Mack Sennett Bathing Beauty. Played major roles in a number of silent films, co-starring with Erich von Stroheim in *Foolish Husbands* and Lon Chaney in *The Unholy Three*. Mae appeared in 14 L&H films, most notably as Mrs. Hardy in *Sons of the Desert* and Charlie Hall's wife in *Them Thar Hills* and *Tit for Tat*. Died Apr. 19, 1946, Woodland Hills, Calif., age 49(?); after a long illness.

Victims Harry Bernard (left) in *Saps at Sea*, and Bobby Dunn (right) in a scene deleted from *The Bohemian Girl*.

COBURN, DOROTHY Born 1905, Great Falls, Mon. Appeared in 10 L&H comedies, beginning with *Sugar Daddies*. She was a flapper in *Putting Pants on Philip*, a nurse in *Leave 'em Laughing* and *The Finishing Touch*, and a cavewoman in *Flying Elephants*. Also a stand-in for Ginger Rogers and a stunt double for many western stars. Died 1978, Los Angeles, age 72; of emphysema.

COOKE, BALDY (Baldwin G. Cooke) Born 1888, New York. Cooke and his wife Alice toured in vaudeville with Stan (as members of the Stan Jefferson Trio), remaining close friends over the years. He appeared in 30 L&H films, beginning with *Two Tars*. Also worked with Our Gang and Charley Chase. Died 1953, Los Angeles, age 65.

CRAMER, RYCHARD EARL Born July 2, 1889, Bryan, Oh. Was a veteran stage actor when he entered films in 1928. Worked with L&H in four pictures; unforgettable as the judge in *Scram!* and the killer on the lam in *Saps at Sea*. Other films included *An American Tragedy*, *The Cat's Paw* with Harold Lloyd, *Hell's Island*, Lash LaRue westerns and Andy Clyde shorts. Died August 9, 1960, Los Angeles, age 71; of cirrhosis.

DUNN, BOBBY (Robert Dunn) Born 1891, Milwaukee. Appeared in several L&H comedies, beginning with *Duck Soup*, and notably as the shoplifter in *Tit for Tat*. Also worked with Charley Chase and had a bit in Harold Lloyd's *Speedy*. No relation to fellow supporting player Eddie Dunn. Died July 27, 1966, Hollywood.

FINLAYSON, JIMMY (James Henderson Finlayson) Born August 27, 1887, Falkirk, Scotland. After serving an apprenticeship in British music halls, Finlayson arrived in America as the star of the 1912 hit show, *Bunty Pulls the*

Charlie Hall and Mae Busch, ever-popular with L&H fans, as they appeared in *Tit for Tat.*

Strings. He made his earliest films for Ince and L-KO, before signing for a stint with Mack Sennett. In 1923 he joined Hal Roach Studios, where he finally made a name for himself. Jimmy appeared in 33 L&H comedies, beginning with *Love 'em and Weep; Big Business* and *Way Out West* provided his most memorable moments. Also co-starred frequently at Roach with Charley Chase. His other films included *The Dawn Patrol* (1931), *Hollywood Cavalcade, To Be or Not To Be* and *Royal Wedding.* Died Oct. 9, 1953, Hollywood, age 66; of a heart attack.

GARVIN, ANITA Born Feb. 11, 1907, New York. Began career as Mack Sennett Bathing Beauty at a precocious 12 years of age; became a Ziegfeld Girl at 13. Made film debut at Christie studios in 1924. Appeared in 11 L&H comedies, beginning with *Why Girls Love Sailors;* unforgettable as Mrs. Culpepper in *From Soup to Nuts* and the girl who slips on the pie in *The Battle of the Century.* Also did a dozen films with Charley Chase. Especially busy in in two-reel comedies; co-starred memorably with Edgar Kennedy in *A Pair of Tights.* Features include De Mille's *Dynamite* and *Trent's Last Case* with Raymond Griffith. Retired 1943.

GEMORA, CHARLES Born 1903, Philippines. Gemora (not Gamora) started his career as a sculptor at Universal; he later became an expert make-up man. Wearing his own gorilla costume, he went ape opposite L&H in *The Chimp* and *Swiss Miss.* His other films included *At the Circus* with the Marx Brothers; also created the Martian for *War of the Worlds,* and later became head of Paramount's makeup lab. Died Aug. 19, 1961, Hollywood, age 58; of a heart attack.

James Finlayson, as the villainous Captain Finn, in *The Bohemian Girl*.

GILBERT, BILLY (William Gilbert Baron) Born Sept. 12, 1893, Louisville, Ky. The son of professional opera singers, Gilbert began his career as a child. Made his Broadway debut in 1911, then went into burlesque and vaudeville; also active as a writer and director. Began film career in 1929. Appeared in many L&H comedies, most notably as Prof. Theodore von Schwarzenhoffen in *The Music Box*. Seen frequently in other Roach comedies; co-starred with Ben Blue in the *Taxi Boys* series. Other films included *A Night at the Opera, Snow White and the Seven Dwarfs* (as the voice of Sneezy), *His Girl Friday* and *The Great Dictator*. Died Sept. 23, 1971, Hollywood, age 78; of a stroke, after a long illness.

GRANGER, DOROTHY Born 1912, New London, Oh. Did stage and night club work before beginning in films. Seen with L&H in *Hog Wild*, The *Laurel-Hardy Murder Case* and *One Good Turn*. Also worked with Charley Chase, Clark & McCullough, Abbott & Costello and W.C. Fields (notably in *The Dentist*); featured as Leon Errol's wife in a long-running RKO series. Retired.

HALL, CHARLIE Born Aug. 19, 1899, Birmingham, England. Toured the British Isles with Albert Decourville and Fred Karno before emigrating to

Edgar Kennedy was more often infuriated than amused at the antics of Laurel and Hardy.

America in 1918. His close friendship with Stan lead to his appearance in 47 L&H films, beginning with *Love 'em and Weep* (1927). Played opposite Buster Keaton in *College* the same year. Hall's most memorable performances came with L&H in *Them Thar Hills* and its follow-up, *Tit for Tat*; his last appearance with the boys was in *Saps at Sea*. A frequent foil for Charley Chase, Thelma Todd and Leon Errol, he also worked with Wheeler & Woolsey and Abbott & Costello. Feature films included *The Gay Divorcee, The Hunchback of Notre Dame* and *Dressed to Kill*. Appeared twice as a contestant on TV's *You Bet Your Life*. Died Dec. 7, 1959, Hollywood, age 60.

HOUSMAN, ARTHUR Born Oct. 10, 1890, New York City. Made film debut around 1910 as a member of the Edison stock company. Worked with L&H five times, memorably as the drunk in *Scram!* and *Our Relations,* and lastly in a brief role in *The Flying Deuces.* Other films included *Sunrise, The Singing Fool, Movie Crazy, She Done Him Wrong, Show Boat, Go West* and several shorts — notably *Next-Door Neighbors* (1930), in which he co-starred with Edgar Kennedy. Died Apr. 7, 1942, Los Angeles, age 51; of pneumonia.

Billy Gilbert (left) was eternally flustered; Arthur Housman (right) was rarely sober, on or off camera.

KENNEDY, EDGAR (Edgar Livingston Kennedy) Born Apr. 26, 1890, Monterey, Ca. A vaudeville actor and professional boxer (he claimed to have gone 14 rounds with Jack Dempsey), Kennedy got his start in pictures with Mack Sennett. Appeared in a number of early Chaplin films, including *Tillie's Punctured Romance*. Co-starred in nine L&H films, notably as the gout-ridden uncle in *Perfect Day*; he also directed the boys in *From Soup to Nuts* and *You're Darn Tootin'*. Other films included *Duck Soup* with the Marx Brothers, *Tillie and Gus*, *A Star is Born*, *It Happened Tomorrow*, and Preston Sturges' *Mad Wednesday*. Also starred in RKO's long-running *Average Man* series. Died Nov. 9, 1948, Woodland Hills, Ca., age 58; of throat cancer.

LONG, WALTER Born Mar. 5, 1884 (?), Milford, N.H. Made his film debut in 1909, appearing in such classic silent films as *The Birth of a Nation*. A fixture of Ken Maynard and William Boyd westerns during the '30s; also appeared in a number of Broadway shows. The archetypal L&H villain, Long menaced the boys in *Pardon Us*, *The Live Ghost* and *Going Bye-Bye!* Other films included *Six of a Kind* and *Naughty Marietta*. Joined the Army during World War II and served with the Military Police in Washington, D.C. Died July 5, 1952, Los Angeles; of a heart attack.

LUCAS, WILFRED Born 1871, Ontario, Canada. Stage actor; began film career with Biograph in 1907. Remembered by L&H fans as the warden in *Pardon Us* and the dean in *A Chump at Oxford*. Other films included D.W. Griffith's *Intolerance*, Thelma Todd and Three Stooges two-reelers, *I Cover the Waterfront*, *Mary of Scotland*, *Modern Times*, and *Brother Orchid*. Died Dec. 13, 1940, Los Angeles, age 69.

Sam Lufkin served the boys well in 39 appearances with them, here in *Sons of the Desert*.

LUFKIN, SAM (Samuel William Lufkin) Born May 8, 1892, Utah. Appeared in 39 L&H films, beginning with *Sugar Daddies* and concluding with *Saps at Sea*. Often cast as a waiter or a cop, and sometimes played dual roles (as in *Two Tars*.) Also worked with Charley Chase, Harold Lloyd, Our Gang, The Three Stooges, and with W.C. Fields in *The Man On the Flying Trapeze*. Died Feb. 19, 1952, age 59; of uremia.

MIDDLETON, CHARLES B. Born Oct. 3, 1884 (?), Elizabethtown, Ky. Stage actor; entered films in 1927. Appeared in four L&H comedies, most notably as the commandant in *Beau Hunks* and *The Flying Deuces*. Other films included *I Am a Fugitive from a Chain Gang*, *Duck Soup* with the Marx Brothers, *Show Boat*, *Trail of the Lonesome Pine* and *The Grapes of Wrath*. Best remembered as Ming the Merciless in Buster Crabbe's *Flash Gordon* serials. Died Apr. 22, 1949, Los Angeles.

MORTON, JAMES C. Born 1884, Helena, Mon. Appeared in many L&H comedies, notably as the policeman in *Tit for Tat* and the bartender in *Way Out West*. Also worked with the boys on their 1940 and 1942 stage tours. Other features included *Rhythm in the Clouds* and *Topper Takes a Trip*. Busy in two-reelers with Charley Chase, Thelma Todd and the Three Stooges (notably *A Pain in the Pullman*). Died Oct. 24, 1942, Reseda, Calif., age 58.

OAKLAND, VIVIEN Born 1895. Worked in vaudeville. Remembered by L&H fans as Laurel's wife in *Love 'em and Weep*, Hardy's wife in *That's My Wife*, the judge's wife in *Scram!* and the sheriff's wife in *Way Out West*. Also appeared in the silent epic *Uncle Tom's Cabin* and *Oh Sailor Behave!* with Olsen & Johnson. Died 1958, Hollywood.

Neither Charles Middleton nor Ellinor Vanderveer had any respect
for Stan and Ollie.

POLLARD, DAPHNE Born 1890, Melbourne, Australia. Played Mrs. Hardy in
Thicker Than Water and *Our Relations*, and the maid in *Bonnie Scotland*.
Later did a vaudeville act based on her scenes in L&H comedies. Other
features included Monogram's *Kid Dynamite*. Died 1978, Los Angeles.

SANDFORD, TINY (Stanley J. Sandford) Born Feb. 26, 1894, Osage, Iowa.
Sandford (not Sanford) began his career with the Daniel Frawley stock
company; he broke into films in 1910. Appeared in a number of early Chaplin
shorts before his employment at Roach studios. Tiny did a total of 23 L&H
films, first seen as a conductor in *45 Minutes From Hollywood*, and lastly in *Our
Relations*. Other films included Chaplin's *The Circus* and *Modern Times*, and
The Iron Mask (as Porthos, one of the Three Musketeers). In *Show Boat*, he
shared several scenes with Stanley Fields, who replaced him as the sheriff in
Way Out West. Died Oct. 29, 1961, Los Angeles, age 67.

TODD, THELMA Born July 29, 1905, Lawrence, Mass. Became a teacher but
ended up in Hollywood after winning a beauty contest. Worked with Charley
Chase and Harry Langdon at Roach, where she also co-starred in her own
series of two-reelers with ZaSu Pitts and then Patsy Kelly. A marvelous foil for
L&H as Lady Plumtree in *Another Fine Mess* and Lady Rocburg in *The Devil's
Brother*. Also co-starred in *Monkey Business* and *Horse Feathers* with the
Marx Brothers. Died Dec. 16, 1935, Santa Monica, Calif., age 30; of carbon
monoxide poisoning.

VANDERVEER, ELLINOR Born Aug. 5, 1886. Vanderveer's film career
spanned three decades, beginning in the '20s. Did extra work for Sennett
before she became a regular on the Roach lot, where she played high society
ladies in seven L&H comedies. Worked regularly with Charley Chase, The
Three Stooges, Abbott & Costello and Our Gang (notably in *Washee Ironee*.)
Died May 27, 1976, Loma Linda, Calif., age 89.

Noah Young threatens to install air conditioning in *Sugar Daddies*.

YOUNG, NOAH Champion weight lifter. A frequent foil for L&H (notably in *Do Detectives Think?* and *Sugar Daddies*, lastly in *Bonnie Scotland*.) Often played opposite Charley Chase and Harold Lloyd (*Grandma's Boy, Safety Last*, etc.) Other films included *Ham and Eggs at the Front* and a number of Ken Maynard westerns. Died 1958.

The Technical Crew

BRUCKMAN, CLYDE A. Born 1894, San Bernardino, Calif. Collaborated on the scripts of several classic Buster Keaton comedies, and co-directed *The General*. Directed five L&H shorts in 1927; later directed Harold Lloyd in *Movie Crazy* and W.C. Fields in *The Man on the Flying Trapeze*. Spent the last 20 years of his career at Universal and Columbia reworking the brilliant gags he created during the first five. Died Jan. 4, 1955, Los Angeles, age 60; suicide, with a gun borrowed from Keaton.

BUTLER, FRANK Born 1890, Oxford, England. Butler, head of Hal Roach's scenario department in the mid-'30s, collaborated on the screenplays of *Babes in Toyland* and *Bonnie Scotland*, among many other films at Roach. Other screenwriting credits include *The Milky Way, Road to Singapore, My Favorite Blonde, Wake Island* and Leo McCarey's *Going My Way*, which won him an Oscar. Died June 10, 1967, Hollywood, age 77.

CURRIER, RICHARD Born Aug. 26, 1892, Denver, Colo. Began editing films in 1911 at the Selig studio in Edendale, Calif. Replaced Thomas J. Crizer as head of the Roach editing department in 1920; credited as editor of virtually every Roach release until December 1932. Worked at Paramount in the '30s, often on W.C. Fields and Burns and Allen films; returned briefly to the Roach lot in the early '40s and later worked for Monogram. Ran his own editorial service in Hollywood before retiring. Died Dec. 14, 1984, age 92; after a series of strokes.

DARLING, W. SCOTT Born Toronto, Canada. Wrote short fiction for magazines before joining Christie Studios as a writer in 1918; directed at both Universal and Christie. Wrote L&H's last four Fox features. Other writing credits include *The Ghost of Frankenstein* and *Sherlock Holmes and the Secret Weapon*.

FOSTER, LEWIS R. Born 1900, Brookfield, Mo. Directed two Charley Chase shorts, including the classic *Movie Night*, before directing L&H in *Double Whoopee* and other shorts. Won Academy Award for best original story for *Mr. Smith Goes To Washington*. Other writing credits include *The Last Outpost*, *The Farmer's Daughter* and *The More the Merrier*. Also directed many feature films. Died June 10, 1974, age 73.

FRENCH, LLOYD Born 1900, San Francisco. Began career with Roach in 1919, remaining there 14 years. Served as assistant director on most 1927-1933 L&H comedies. Left Roach to direct Shemp Howard and others at Vitaphone; later directed short subjects with Edgar Kennedy and Edgar Bergen. Writing credits include many Three Stooges and other Columbia shorts. Died May 24, 1950, age 50.

GUIOL, FRED L. Born 1898, San Francisco. Worked as a prop boy on D.W. Griffith's *Hearts of the World*. By 1919 he was at Roach, photographing Harold Lloyd comedies; began directing there in 1923. Became closely associated with George Stevens, collaborating on the screenplays of *Gunga Din* and *Giant*; produced *Talk of the Town* and served as associate director on *Shane*. Died May 23, 1964, age 66.

HARBAUGH, CARL Born 1886. As Roach's chief gag-writer in the late-1920s, he contributed to many L&H scripts. Other writing credits include Keaton's *College* and *Steamboat Bill Jr.* His appearance as a woodchopper in L&H's *The Devil's Brother* was deleted from the film. Died 1960, Hollywood.

HATLEY, THOMAS MARVIN Born Apr. 3, 1905, Reed, Okla. Pre-med student and part-time jazz pianist before becoming musical director for Hal Roach Studios, 1930-39. Composer of L&H's famed "Coo Coo" song and the popular "Honolulu Baby." Hatley's scores for *Way Out West*, *Block-Heads* and *There Goes My Heart* earned him three Oscar nominations. Also scored *Pick a Star*, *Topper Takes a Trip* and *Captain Fury*. Later played piano in cocktail lounges. Died Aug. 23, 1986, Hollywood, age 81; of cancer.

HORNE, JAMES WESLEY Born Dec. 14, 1881, San Francisco. Began career in 1911. Directed many L&H shorts and features from 1928-1937, beginning with *Liberty* (uncredited) and concluding with *Way Out West*. Other directorial credits include *College* with Buster Keaton and *Holt of the Secret Service*. Died June 29, 1942, Los Angeles, age 60; of a cerebral hemorrhage.

Composer T. Marvin Hatley never lost his modesty, or his smile.

JONES, F. RICHARD Born 1894. Served as production chief for Mack Sennett and occasional director, notably on the Mabel Normand feature, *Mickey* (1918). Became Roach's production supervisor in the mid-'20s and was responsible for training Laurel as a director. Jones left Roach in 1927 after supervising the earliest L&H comedies. Died Dec. 14, 1930, age 36.

JORDAN, BERT Born 1887, Cambridge, England. Began his career as a film actor in 1913, then became a film perforator and cameraman for Lions Head Film Company. Worked as standby cameraman on D.W. Griffith's *Intolerance* after moving the to U.S. in 1915. Worked as an editor at Vitagraph before joining Roach in 1921. L&H's official (but often uncredited) editor remained at the studio into the '50s, cutting Roach TV series; Jordan later moved to Desilu where he worked on *The Real McCoys*. His editing of *Of Mice and Men* won him an Oscar nomination. Died Sept. 10, 1983, age 96; of pneumonia.

LANGDON, HARRY Born June 15, 1884, Council Bluffs, Iowa. Joined the circus at 12 and later appeared in vaudeville. Began film career 1924 making two-reel comedies with Mack Sennett. Achieved legendary status with his first feature, *The Strong Man*, before a swift decline in popularity. Emerged as a screenwriter late in his career, collaborating on the scripts of four L&H comedies, beginning with *Block-Heads*. Also co-starred with Babe in *Zenobia*. Died Dec. 22, 1944, Hollywood, age 60; of a cerebral hemorrhage.

LLOYD, ART Born Oct. 1896, Los Angeles. Began his career circa 1909 as a 13-year-old assistant photographer; at 16, he was a full-fledged cameraman. Worked at Paramount before joining Roach in 1923; became and remained Laurel's favorite cameraman. During World War II Lloyd served in the Signal Corps, teaching cinematography to soldiers. Suffered a paralyzing stroke in the

Cameraman Art Lloyd (left) and director James Parrott (right) were among Laurel and Hardy's most valuable associates.

late '40s, possibly due to radiation exposure while photographing the Bikini Atoll explosion. Died Nov. 25, 1954, age 58.

MARSHALL, GEORGE E. Born Dec. 29, 1891, Chicago. Started out as a newspaper reporter; entered films as an extra circa 1912. Began long career as director by making Harry Carey westerns, then Ruth Roland serials. Directed L&H in *Their First Mistake, Towed in a Hole* and *Pack Up Your Troubles*. Other credits include *You Can't Cheat an Honest Man, Destry Rides Again, Murder He Says*, and many Bob Hope and Jerry Lewis comedies. He acted in a feature film and an episode of TV's *Police Woman* shortly before his death. Died Feb. 17, 1975, Los Angeles, age 83.

McCAREY, LEO Born Oct. 3, 1898, Los Angeles. Began his film career as Mack Sennett's script clerk in 1918. Was assistant director to Tod Browning at Universal before joining Hal Roach, where he started as a gagwriter and became Supervising Director for Charley Chase and Laurel and Hardy. Went on to direct the Marx Brothers in *Duck Soup*, W.C. Fields in *Six of a Kind* and Harold Lloyd in *The Milky Way*. McCarey twice won the Academy Award for Best Director, for *The Awful Truth* and *Going My Way*. Also dabbled in songwriting. Died July 5, 1969, Santa Monica, Calif., age 70; of emphysema.

PARROTT, JAMES GIBBONS Born 1897, Baltimore, Md. Younger brother of Charley Chase. Began career in 1921, appearing in Hal Roach comedies under the name of Paul Parrott. Laurel and Hardy's preeminent director from 1928–1933; also directed many Chase comedies, as well as Todd-Kelly and *Boy Friends* shorts. He was an uncredited writer on the Marx Brothers' *Duck Soup* and co-wrote several L&H features. Died May 10, 1939, Hollywood, age 42; of a reported heart attack.

Title writer "Beanie" Walker (left) and sound engineer Elmer Raguse (right) in a moment of relaxation.

RAGUSE, ELMER R. Born 1901, Springfield, Mass. Helped develop sound recording equipment at Bell Telephone in the '20s and was recording engineer for Victor Talking Machine Co. before he became supervisor of the Roach sound department. His work on *Topper*, *Of Mice and Men* and other films earned him five Oscar nominations for sound recording and two for special effects.

ROGERS, CHARLEY Born in England. Appeared on British and American stages in a comedy act called *The Iceman*, before beginning his association with L&H at Roach in 1928, as a gagman and bit actor. Began co-directed L&H films in 1933, and continued to write for the team until their association ended with Roach late in 1939; he later worked on the script for *Air Raid Wardens* and appeared in *The Dancing Masters*. Rogers also co-starred with Harry Langdon in two features, *Misbehaving Husbands* and *Double Trouble*, and worked on the script for *Abroad With Two Yanks*. Died circa 1960, Los Angeles; of injuries sustained in an auto accident.

ST. CLAIR, MALCOLM Born 1897, Los Angeles. Worked for Mack Sennett, then collaborated with Buster Keaton on two early shorts. Directed four of L&H's Fox films, beginning with *Jitterbugs*. Other directorial credits include *The Canary Murder Case*, *A Trip to Paris* and *Hollywood Cavalcade*. Died June 1, 1952, Pasadena, Calif., age 55.

SEAWRIGHT, ROY Born Nov. 19, 1905, Los Angeles. Began his film career as Hal Roach's office boy; worked in the prop department until he was given a job as animator in 1927. In addition to his imaginative (if low-budget) optical effects on L&H films, Seawright won three Oscar nominations for his work on *Topper Takes a Trip*, *One Million B.C.* and *Topper Returns*. In the late '40s, he became a pioneer in the television commercial field when he co-founded Cascade Pictures. Retired.

SHIELD, LEROY Born Oct. 2, 1893, Waseca, Minn. Began touring as a concert pianist at 15. Conductor-arranger for Victor Talking Machine Co., later supervisor of recording. Began scoring films for Roach in 1930; wrote stock themes used in most of Roach's early sound comedies. Musical director at NBC in Chicago for many years; conducted music for dozens of radio programs. Died Jan. 9, 1962, Ft. Lauderdale, Fla., age 68.

STEVENS, GEORGE Born Dec. 18, 1904, Oakland, Calif. Made stage debut at the age of five. Began film career at Hal Roach in 1924, as assistant cameraman on *The King of Wild Horses*. Principal cameraman for L&H from 1927-1931. Made directorial debut on Roach's *Boy Friends* series. Went on to direct such enduring classics as *Alice Adams, Gunga Din, Woman of the Year, A Place in the Sun, Shane* and *Giant*. Died Mar. 8, 1975, Lancaster, Calif., age 70; of a heart attack.

WALKER, HARLEY M. Born 1884 (?). Walker wrote a sports column, "The Wisdom of Blinky Ben," for the *Los Angeles Examiner* before joining Roach in 1916 as title writer and head of the editorial department. A brilliant title writer in the silent era, less skilled at dialogue. Wrote dialogue for Universal comedies after leaving Roach in 1932 and worked on several Paramount features. Died June 23, 1937, Chicago; of a heart attack.

Sources

With few exceptions, this book is based upon interviews conducted by the author, or upon material written or published when the Laurel and Hardy films were made.

Key interviews include those with HENRY BRANDON, January 21, 1981; LOU BRESLOW, November 3, 1980; RICHARD CURRIER, August 26, 1980; MARVIN HATLEY, October 12, 1979; July 30, 1980; September 14, 1980; October 23, 1981; BERT JORDAN, April 5, 1980; FREDRICK KOHNER, August 3, 1981; VENICE LLOYD, July 9, 1980; July 30, 1980; August 18, 1980; October 23, 1981; GLEN MacWILLIAMS, June 22, 1983; GEORGE MARSHALL, interviewed by Jordan R. Young, July 17, 1974; other material recorded September 21, 1974; LUCILLE HARDY PRICE, October 23, 1981; supplemented with other material from discussions with the author, 1974-1986; HAL ROACH, January 21, 1981; February 20, 1981; also interviewed by Vance Piper, April 20, 1980; additional material recorded during personal appearances, October 6, 1979; December 8, 1979; July 31, 1981; June 4, 1981; THOMAS BENTON ROBERTS, June 14, 1980; BETTY GOULDING SAUNDERS, July 15, 1981; ROY SEAWRIGHT, August 16, 1980; August 24, 1980; and ANITA GARVIN STANLEY, interviewed by Jordan R. Young, June 9, 1978; also by the author, January 28, 1981; November 14, 1981.

The Stan Laurel quotes derive from a number of sources, the major ones being interviews conducted by W.T. Rabe for a radio documentary in the early 1960s; by Boyd Verb for *Films in Review*, 1959; by Arthur Friedman for UCLA, August 14, 1957; and by Philip K. Scheuer for the *Los Angeles Times*, December 29, 1929 and July 8, 1951. The *Times* was also the primary source of information on Laurel's marital and legal affairs.

Production information, including the "Production histories," was compiled from Hal Roach studio general manager L.A. French's 1928 production log, courtesy of Venice Lloyd; from back issues of *Film Daily*, *The Hollywood Reporter*, *Daily Variety* and *Hollywood Filmograph*; and from Roach studio records housed at the USC Doheny Library.

The USC library also provided access to Roach payroll ledgers and board meeting minutes, containing information on studio finances, salaries and contracts; original publicity material; and a legal deposition dated December 21, 1938, wich detailed the conflicts during production of *Swiss Miss* and *Block-Heads*. Additional information on contracts was provided by Richard W. Bann.

Douglas Hart and John McLaughlin were the primary source of shooting scripts and press sheets. Several silent scripts were provided by California State University, Fullerton, library; scripts for *Babes in Toyland*, *Way Out West* and *Block-Heads* were located at the Academy of Motion Picture Arts and Sciences; the Fox scripts were furnished by the USC Doheny library.

Biographical information for the "Who's Who" appendix derives largely from *International Motion Picture Almanac*, *Film Daily Yearbook* and interviews with many of the subjects.

Index

THEIR NEW FULL- LENGTH FEATURE PICTURE!

Stan *LAUREL* Oliver *HARDY* in SONS OF THE DESERT

An M-G-M Picture

SONS OF THE DESERT is an international organization devoted to perpet-
uating the work and memory of Laurel and Hardy. More than 100 chapters, or
"tents," exist worldwide. For information about the Sons, write to 5151 White
Oak Avenue #127, Encino, California 91316.

ORDER FORM

Please send the following books:

Qty   Amount

____ *Laurel and Hardy* paperback @ $14.95 $_____

____ *Laurel and Hardy* hardcover @ $34.95   _____

____ *Spike Jones* paperback @ $14.95   _____

____ *Spike Jones* hardcover @ $29.95   _____

____ *Reel Characters* paperback @ $9.95   _____

____ *Reel Characters* hardcover @ $19.95   _____

                                    Total for books   _____

        Postage: add $1.50 first book, 50¢ each additional   _____

                    California residents please add 6% tax   _____

                            Amount enclosed (U.S. funds)   _____

Ship to:

_____

_____

_____

IF THIS IS A LIBRARY COPY, PLEASE PHOTOCOPY THIS PAGE.
SATISFACTION GUARANTEED OR PURCHASE PRICE REFUNDED.

(m)oonstone press

P.O. Box 142, Beverly Hills CA 90213